Rethinking the Carolingian reforms

Manchester University Press

Rethinking the Carolingian reforms

Edited by

Arthur Westwell, Ingrid Rembold and
Carine van Rhijn

MANCHESTER UNIVERSITY PRESS

Copyright © Manchester University Press 2023

While copyright in the volume as a whole is vested in Manchester University Press, copyright in individual chapters belongs to their respective authors, and no chapter may be reproduced wholly or in part without the express permission in writing of both author and publisher.

Published by Manchester University Press
Oxford Road, Manchester M13 9PL

www.manchesteruniversitypress.co.uk

British Library Cataloguing-in-Publication Data

A catalogue record for this book is available from the British Library

ISBN 978 1 5261 4955 8 hardback
ISBN 978 1 5261 7878 7 paperback

First published 2023

The publisher has no responsibility for the persistence or accuracy of URLs for any external or third-party internet websites referred to in this book, and does not guarantee that any content on such websites is, or will remain, accurate or appropriate.

Typeset
by Deanta Global Publishing Services, Chennai, India

Contents

List of illustrations	page vi
List of contributors	vii
Acknowledgements	ix
List of abbreviations	x

	Introduction: rethinking the Carolingian reforms – Carine van Rhijn	1
1	Gender and horizontal networks in Carolingian monasticisms (up to c. 840) – Ingrid Rembold	32
2	Analysing Attigny: contextualising Chrodegang of Metz's influence on the life of canons – Stephen Ling	65
3	A Carolingian 'reform of education'? The reception of Alcuin's pedagogy – Cinzia Grifoni and Giorgia Vocino	96
4	Correcting the liturgy and sacred language – Els Rose and Arthur Westwell	141
5	Error assessment: how to distinguish between true and false? – Irene van Renswoude	176
6	*Reformatio* and *correctio* in Carolingian theology and orthodoxy: reformation or *aggiornamento*? – Kristina Mitalaité	207

Bibliography	241
Index	277

Illustrations

Figures

4.1 Correction of a scribal error in St. Gall SB 40, p. 309 (detail) *page* 170
4.2 Correction of Latin orthography in St. Gall SB 40, p. 312 (detail) 171

Tables

2.1 A comparison of *Codex Carolinus*, no. 5, [G3], p. 480, and A. Boretius (ed.), *MGH Capit.* 1 (Hanover: Hahn, 1883), no. 14, c. 3, p. 33   *page* 71
4.1 Latin words and their etymological explanation   155
4.2 Latin words explained through synonyms   156
4.3 Explanation of Latin words through paraphrasis   158
4.4 *Nostra lingua* in *Dominus vobiscum*   166

Contributors

Cinzia Grifoni is a postdoctoral researcher at the Institute for Medieval Research of the Austrian Academy of Sciences in Vienna. Her work focuses on the study of Latin and the Bible in early medieval Europe. She currently runs a project called *Margins at the Centre: Book Production and Practices of Annotation in the East Frankish Realm (ca. 830–900)*.

Stephen Ling is an independent scholar working as a research development officer at the University of Salford. His research focuses on eighth- and ninth-century attempts to define and distinguish monks and canons.

Kristina Mitalaité is a senior researcher at the Department of Research of Ancient and Medieval Cultures, Lithuanian Culture Research Institute (Vilnius). Her research examines Carolingian controversies, theology and the history of iconoclasm.

Ingrid Rembold is a lecturer in medieval history at the University of Manchester. Her research examines themes relating to governance, monasticism and Christianisation in the early medieval ages.

Irene van Renswoude is a professor of medieval manuscripts and cultural history at the Department of Book History of Amsterdam University; she is also a senior researcher at the Department of Knowledge and Art Practices at the Research Institute Huygens ING.

Carine van Rhijn is a cultural historian of the early middle ages at the Department for History and Art History at Utrecht University (the Netherlands).

Els Rose holds the chair in medieval Latin at Utrecht University. She has published widely on early medieval Latin liturgy, particularly the liturgy of Frankish Gaul.

Giorgia Vocino is a postdoctoral researcher at the University of Orléans. She works on practices of learning in the early Middle Ages and is particularly interested in the study of early medieval textual communities and networks of knowledge.

Arthur Westwell is a wissenschaftlicher Mitarbeiter at the University of Regensburg. He is currently undertaking research on the Carolingian sacramentaries of Saint-Amand, which is funded by the Deutsche Forschungsgemeinschaft.

Acknowledgements

This book is the product of collaboration and would not have been possible without the input of those who participated in our *correctio* conferences. We would particularly like to thank Elina Screen, Rutger Kramer, Rosamond McKitterick, Sven Meeder, Ed Roberts and Julia Smith. We are also grateful to our anonymous peer reviewers and Meredith Carroll, Laura Swift and the rest of the editorial team at Manchester University Press, as well as Tim Hertogh and Jonathan Tickle for their help in compiling the bibliography and index, respectively.

Abbreviations

Capit.	*Capitularia regum Francorum*
Capit. episc.	*Capitula episcoporum*
CCCM	*Corpus Christianorum Continuatio Mediaevalis*
CCSL	*Corpus Christianorum Series Latina*
Conc.	*Concilia*
CSEL	*Corpus Scriptorum Ecclesiasticorum Latinorum*
DD Karol. 1	*Diplomata Karolinorum 1*
DD LdF	*Diplomata Ludovici Pii*
DD Lo I	*Diplomata Lotharii I*
Epp.	*Epistolae (in Quart): Epistolae Merowingici et Karolini aevi*
Fontes iuris	*Fontes iuris Germanici antiqui in usum scholarum separatim editi*
MGH	*Monumenta Germaniae Historica*
PG	*Patrologia Graeca*
PL	*Patrologia Latina*
SRG	*Scriptores rerum Germanicarum in usum scholarum separatim editi*
SS	*Scriptores*
SSRM	*Scriptores rerum Merovingicarum*

Introduction: rethinking the Carolingian reforms

Carine van Rhijn

This book sets out to challenge current interpretations of Carolingian culture, and especially its perceived *correctio* (correction), reform or renaissance. It is the product of discussions among a group of early medievalists interested in different aspects of the Carolingian period, ranging from monasticism to historiography, and from education to liturgical practice. What most have in common is a focus on manuscripts, which is exactly where new ideas about Carolingian culture originate. Received ideas about the Carolingian reforms lean heavily on kings and their prescriptive texts, as well as the products of a small intellectual elite at the court and at a handful of important intellectual centres. Especially in the past decade, which has witnessed the digitisation of impressive numbers of manuscripts, researchers have become able to study a much wider range of texts and entire codices than ever before, and hence move beyond editions. As a result, the traditional images centred on courts, kings and top-down mechanisms have started to be questioned. All authors of this volume, too, have tried to make space for a broader image of Carolingian culture.

Of course, the influence of Charlemagne and his dynasty on the change and improvement of society and culture can hardly be underestimated, but all the same, their role needs to be qualified. They were the movers and shakers who understood that Christian rulership meant an obligation to improve the lives and morals of the Franks, and they were the single most important patrons who poured enormous amounts of resources into all kinds of efforts to that effect. Without making these kings and emperors any less important, however, it is essential to realise that crowned heads did not operate in a vacuum. Many often understudied texts and manuscripts testify to a much wider circle of people involved in the ideals of moral improvement and change for the better, be it the anonymous schoolmaster who developed a better method of teaching Latin, the equally unnamed cleric who created new forms of liturgy or all the people in monastic libraries who copied, re-organised, commented on and studied each other's books. These mostly anonymous inhabitants of the Carolingian world were no mere passive recipients of royal prescriptions or other admonishments. They were active agents who helped shape and re-shape the ideas and ideals of their world, and their texts and manuscripts should be studied side by side with those composed by well-known authors at well-known centres of the time.

Once it is conceded that the continuous attempts to change and improve many aspects of the Carolingian world were initiated and carried out not only by a royal court and its powerful agents but also by a much wider group of literate people all over the kingdom, we need to rethink what exactly we mean by Carolingian reform or *correctio*. As this introduction will explain, the terms generally used to describe and analyse these phenomena are, at their core, fossils from earlier ages of scholarship, and therefore closely connected to the questions asked at that time. Up until far into the twentieth century, research was mostly interested in Charlemagne and the revival of classical culture. Even though research foci have shifted considerably, the traditional key concepts are still in use, often without much reflection. In order to re-evaluate these inherited frameworks and look for new perspectives, it is important first of all to take a good hard look at the concepts of reform, renaissance and *correctio* as they stand, for these are the lenses through which changes in Carolingian culture are usually analysed and described. How these terms are problematic through their explicit or implicit connotations and what exactly a new, wider approach might involve is the subject of the rest of this introduction.

Knowledge, education and the road to salvation

I beg your brotherhood also, that you read carefully these chapters which I have briefly laid down for the improvement [*ad emendationem*] of life, and commit them to memory, and that by reading them and the Holy Scriptures you may set right [*componatis*] the morals and improve [*emendetis*] life, and with the people put under you, the Lord being your helper, you may strive to reach the heavenly kingdom.¹

Here we have, in a nutshell, what was perhaps the single most important idea that inspired the flourishing of Carolingian culture from the later eighth century onwards: God's own people, no matter their position or place in the world, should strive to lead Christian lives and shine with virtue in the eyes of their stern God in order to reach the Kingdom of Heaven.² These were, in other words, not improvements for their own sake: the process of continuous betterment had a clear purpose, which was to keep everybody on the path to eternal life. The road to salvation, according to the author of this preface to a much longer text, was a never-ending, individual process of learning, improving one's morals and bettering one's life with God's help and that of his 'brotherhood', the pastoral experts. This introduction is followed by a text full of advice and instructions to priests, to be communicated by them to the laity. Soon after it was written in central France around the year 800, it found its way all over the Empire. Already in the first quarter of the ninth century, it was in Bavaria, anonymously, bound in as a previously separate *libellus* at the end of a manuscript with works by Alcuin of York.³ A bit later

---

1 P. Brommer (ed.), *MGH Capit. episc.* 1 (Hanover: Hahn, 1984), pp. 103–42, here p. 103: 'Obsecro etiam fraternitatem vestram, ut haec capitula, quae ad emendationem vitae breviter digessi, assidue legatis et memoriae commendetis et eorum sive sanctarum scripturarum lectione mores componatis, vitam emendetis et cum subditis plebibus opitulante domino ad regna caelestia pergere certetis.' Translation based on P. E. Dutton (ed.), *Carolingian Civilization: A Reader* (Peterborough, Ont.: Broadview Press, 1993), pp. 94–106, here p. 94.
2 See M. de Jong, 'Charlemagne's church', in J. Story (ed.), *Charlemagne: Empire and Society* (Manchester: Manchester University Press, 2005), pp. 103–35; on the centrality of salvation see J. R. Davis, *Charlemagne's Practice of Empire* (Cambridge: Cambridge University Press, 2015), pp. 396–9.
3 For descriptions of the contents of the manuscript Munich Bayerische Staatsbibliothek clm 14727, see H. Mordek, *Bibliotheca capitularium regum Francorum manuscripta: Überlieferung und Traditionszusammenhang der fränkischen Herrschererlasse* (Munich: Monumenta Germaniae Historica, 1995), pp. 345–8; P. Brommer (ed.), *MGH Capit. episc.* 1, pp. 85–6.

we find it in manuscripts in important monastic libraries including Lorsch, St. Gall and Fulda, and by the tenth century it had found its way to Northern Italy and England.[4] In all but a couple of the extant manuscripts, the text fails to mention its eminent author: Bishop Theodulf of Orléans, adviser of Charlemagne himself and one of the most important intellectuals of his day. The ideas expressed in his text travelled anonymously but were eagerly copied all the same, for these were important thoughts. Advice about reaching heaven by admonishing everybody to improve their lives and morals was clearly in high demand, and the salvation of the entire kingdom was pictured as the sum total of the efforts of all these many single individuals.

It is significant that an important and learned man like Theodulf, author of sophisticated poetry and theological treatises of the highest level, took the time to compose this text full of sensible, basic advice for the priests of his diocese. The salvation of the inhabitants of the ever-expanding Carolingian empire included *all* inhabitants, not just crowned, aristocratic or learned heads. This meant that bishops and priests should accept their responsibility to teach, preach and show by their living example of good morals and behaviour what was expected from the people in their pastoral care. Salvation for all was the ultimate goal, and to that end everyone should learn about all the small steps that they must take along that long and bumpy road. The text therefore offers admonishments and advice to priests and laity alike to navigate the obstacles that hindered the way to the Heavenly Kingdom. Knowledge about the right beliefs, the right behaviour and, simply, the right way of leading one's daily existence was crucial. The instructions range from practical to spiritual. At the same time, they show how one bishop thought about the instruction of the Franks on the ins and outs of their religion, which reached much further than what happened in church.

Theodulf's is just one in an entire choir of voices concerned with the enormous task of emending the lives and morals of the population of the Carolingian world in the late eighth and ninth centuries

---

4 For an overview of the extant manuscripts see *MGH Capit. episc.* 1, pp. 76–99; R. Pokorny (ed.), *MGH Capit. episc.* 4 (Hanover: Hahn, 2005), pp. 76–80.

with the purpose of showing them the way to heaven. It is generally accepted that even though the exact starting point of this operation cannot be pinpointed, the *Admonitio generalis* issued in 789 best expresses the ideals formulated by the court.[5] This long capitulary issued by Charlemagne in order to 'set right wrongs' and assure the kingdom of God's grace contains a blueprint for a future, better society.[6] Every segment of society, from bishops and counts to 'everyone' (*omnibus*) had a place in these plans. The preoccupation with change for the better for the ultimate salvation of all runs like a red thread through this and many other prescriptive and programmatic texts of the time: the royal court devoted more capitularies to the subject, ecclesiastical councils met and produced texts of instruction and admonishment and an increasing number of named and anonymous bishops followed Theodulf's example and composed guidelines for the diocesan clergy and their flocks.[7] But our sources are not confined to prescriptions: many texts and manuscripts bear witness to the efforts of people who tried to teach or learn, experiment or change for the better. We have a remarkable amount of such sources for the Carolingian era, much more than for the preceding and following periods, and the production of these texts and manuscripts went hand in hand with the flourishing of learning, teaching and intellectual life.

In the perception of Carolingian intellectuals, everyone's road to 'correctness' was paved with education and knowledge – judges needed to know what it meant to be just, churchmen ought to master rituals and have substantial religious knowledge and the laity

---

5 *Admonitio Generalis*, ed. and trans. H. Mordek et al., *Die Admonitio Generalis Karls des Grossen*, MGH Fontes iuris 16 (Hanover: Hahn, 2012).

6 For an interpretation of the programmatic royal capitularies as blueprints for the future see T. M. Buck, *Admonitio und Praedicatio. Zur religiös-pastoralen Dimension von Kapitularien und kapitulariennahen Texten (507–814)*, Freiburger Beiträge zur mittelalterlichen Geschichte 9 (Frankfurt: Peter Lang, 1997).

7 An overview of the relevant capitularies and conciliar proceedings can be found in G. Brown, 'Introduction: the Carolingian Renaissance', in R. McKitterick (ed.), *Carolingian Culture: Emulation and Innovation* (Cambridge: Cambridge University Press, 1994), pp. 1–52, here pp. 11–28. Episcopal instructions have been edited as three volumes in the series *MGH Capit. episc.* (Hanover: Hahn, 1984–1995).

needed to learn and understand the precepts of their religion and what these meant for their daily lives.[8] It is well known that, as a result of these ideas, unprecedented energy and resources were put into finding, copying and studying texts, gathering and distributing knowledge about more or less any subject, teaching and scholarship. It was this powerful cocktail of interest in change for the better, the centrality of education and learning and sustained generous patronage that set the scene for the remarkable cultural phenomena that are the subject of this volume.[9] Not all of this was entirely new, but it is beyond dispute that its sheer scale and the energy and resources poured into it were unprecedented. However, it is important to bear in mind that the shared goal of these efforts was not the process of improvement itself, but the open gates to the heavenly kingdom that would, God willing, await all.

What exactly this phenomenon should be called, and how it should be understood and interpreted, is a different matter entirely. In most scholarship, Carolingian culture is usually assessed, described and interpreted through the lenses of renaissance, reform or *correctio* respectively, each term laden with the connotations and scholarly theories of nearly two centuries of debate. None of the terms is neutral; all of them steer our focus and understanding and in their own ways limit the discussion. In each case, it is the processes of change that take centre stage in the scholarship, not so much the ultimate purpose of salvation for all. These terms have become such permanent fixtures in debates between historians that they are often used loosely and unreflectively – any change observed in the Carolingians' organisation of any aspect of society, for instance, is easily labelled as reform, whereas any manuscript in which correction of Latin can be observed is often more or less automatically viewed as a result of *correctio*. It makes one wonder:

---

8 As set out in for instance the *Admonitio generalis*: c. 62 (on judges), cc. 80 and 81 (on clerical knowledge), c. 79 (on lay religious knowledge).
9 The term 'culture' is used in the widest sense of the word here, and is not confined to high-level artistic products or intellectual endeavours, following R. E. Sullivan, 'The context of cultural activity in the Carolingian age', in R. E. Sullivan (ed.), *'The Gentle Voices of Teachers': Aspects of Learning in the Carolingian Age* (Columbus, OH: Ohio State University Press, 1995), pp. 51–105.

what exactly is the difference between reform and change, and what distinguishes *correctio* from correction? Even though it is now generally accepted that political and cultural aspects such as these are part of the same bigger story, no single commonly used term seems to be fitting to describe the full (political, religious, cultural, etc.) range of observable attempts at change and improvement in the Carolingian period: accordingly, historians tend towards renaissance or *correctio* if the subject of their research is cultural, while reform is often reserved for the world of institutional religion and politics. It is therefore important to understand how and why these terms came into being in the first place, what their connotations were and are, and what exactly we see and do not see through the perspectives on the Carolingian world that each of them provides.

Labels and claims about Carolingian culture

The question of what exactly we should call, and how we should interpret, the upsurge in activities intended to change and improve society that started to unfold in the second half of the eighth century has been one of the longest-standing debates among scholars interested in the history and culture of the Carolingian period. This debate is an especially complex one, since none of the terms used to describe these phenomena – most commonly renaissance, reform and *correctio* – are uncontroversial. Moreover, the discussion has now gone on so long and has branched off in so many different directions that no two scholars mean exactly the same thing when they use the same words. At the same time, however, each term carries connotations that inevitably steer our thinking. The idea of a Carolingian reform, for instance, automatically leads to ideas of politics and top-down directives, while the term renaissance evokes ideas of flawless Latin and intellectual debates.

While each label is used as an umbrella term, describing (or claiming to describe) what was happening in Carolingian culture and society as a whole, they at the same time highlight certain aspects (flawless Latin, royal admonishments) at the expense of many others. Inevitably, large parts of the Carolingian world are left out of sight. To mention just one example, the term renaissance generally leads to a focus on a small group of named intellectuals who often operated close to the court. Thanks to historians interested in this 'renaissance', we know a lot about the works and thoughts of scholars such as Alcuin of York, Theodulf of Orléans or Amalarius of Metz, whose voluminous writings have generally been edited at least once. However, little attention has gone out to hundreds of anonymous authors who wrote a very substantial number of the texts still extant from this period. Many of these texts do not exist in a modern edition, if they have been edited at all, and as a result, have been largely overlooked in assessments of Carolingian culture.[10] Approaching the Carolingian world through the concept of renaissance, then, often results in a focus on just a small part of the evidence for the intensification of written culture, study and learning.

An even more significant issue with this terminology is the fact that Carolingian authors themselves did not have a convenient and consistent term to describe their efforts as we tend to understand them. The main reason for this, I think, is that scholars of the past two centuries or so have focused mostly on the improvements, changes or cultural products themselves, while all these things were, in the eyes of early medieval authors, just steps towards the greater purpose of salvation. That our sources use plenty of expressions to convey this purpose is telling in itself. To be sure, in some very specific and rare cases kings used terms like *corrigere* and *emendare* to highlight in an appropriately rhetorical fashion the perceived importance and religious correctness of the changes and improvements they prescribed for their Christian subjects. In most cases, however, changes simply happened and did not get named or labelled at all.[11] This has two implications for any study of these subjects. In the first place, we should always bear in mind that the terms reform, *correctio* or renaissance do not correspond to clearly distinguishable concepts in early medieval minds; their minds were focused elsewhere. To modern scholars, the use of these terms is

---

10 See, for instance, the expositions of the creed, gathered by S. Keefe, *A Catalogue of Works Pertaining to the Explanation of the Creed in Carolingian Manuscripts*, Instrumenta Patristica et Mediaevalia (Turnhout: Brepols, 2012), in which she has collected nearly 400 texts. Many of these are anonymous and/or unedited.

11 See p. 17.

Introduction 9

perhaps unavoidable for lack of better alternatives, but they can never be self-explanatory. Secondly, any label used to describe such phenomena is never a neutral descriptor but always shorthand for a set of modern scholarly claims that colour its connotations and thereby influence our interpretations.[12] How this works and how this impacts scholarship is best shown by briefly retracing the origins and histories of the terms renaissance, reform and *correctio*.

Carolingian renaissance

When in 1839 Jean Jacques Ampère first proposed to use the label 'renaissance' for Charlemagne's reign, he did so just six years after Jules Michelet had invented the term for what we still call the Italian Renaissance of the fifteenth and sixteenth centuries.[13] Ampère, writing a history of literature, defined renaissance as a period of revival of interest in the writings of classical antiquity after a period of cultural decline. He therefore not only viewed Charlemagne's reign as a renaissance, but also saw an Ottonian renaissance, which he interpreted, both in their own unique ways, as precursors to the Italian Renaissance. His use of the term was very specific: the Carolingian renaissance concerned a revival of interest in the literature of classical – hence pre-Christian – Rome, which Charlemagne made happen more or less single-handedly (though Ampère does mention Alcuin) and seemingly out of nowhere.[14] This example

---

12 An important recent contribution to the discussion is C. Leyser, 'Review article: church reform – full of sound and fury, signifying nothing', *Early Medieval Europe*, 24 (2016), 478–99.
13 J. Michelet, *Histoire de la France* (6 vols, Paris: Hachette, 1833–44); for an analysis of his understanding of 'renaissance' see E. Patzelt, *Die Karolingische Renaissance: Beiträge zur Geschichte der Kultur des frühen Mittelalters* (Vienna: Österreichischer Schulbücherverlag, 1923, reprinted Graz: Akademische Druck- und Verlagsanstalt, 1965), pp. 10–12. For important reflections on the historiographical context in which the historical concept of 'Carolingian renaissance' first saw the light, see R. E. Sullivan, 'Introduction: factors shaping Carolingian studies', in Sullivan (ed.), *'The Gentle Voices of Teachers'*.
14 J. J. Ampère, *Histoire littéraire de la France avant le douzième siècle* (3 vols, Paris: Hachette, 1839), III, p. 33.

shows well how this newly invented label was used as a claim: a rebirth supposed cultural 'death' in the preceding period, the relevant revival was that of the pre-Christian classics, and the only efforts that mattered were those of the king and his close entourage of a handful of intellectuals at the court.[15] The purpose of the operation was self-evident: the rebirth of Roman culture at its highest point. This element of 'rebirth of the classics' became central in the definition of renaissances after 1860, when Jacob Burckhardt's *Die Cultur der Renaissance in Italien* was first published and received widely with great enthusiasm.[16] From its very onset, the idea of a Carolingian renaissance was therefore a derivative of that of the Italian Renaissance, whereby its definition rested on a few characteristics seemingly shared with an altogether totally different phenomenon that unfolded three-quarters of a millennium later.

The first critical sounds started to be heard in the early twentieth century, notably with the publication in 1923 of Erna Patzelt's *Die Karolingische Renaissance*, in which she categorically rejected the idea that the period from the fifth to the eighth centuries was 'a period of spiritual darkness and cultureless barbarism'. She instead favoured an interpretation of cultural continuity: there was no fall of the Roman empire in a Gibbonian sense and no extreme cultural rupture in what we would now call the Merovingian era. Instead, she considered these centuries as the 'organic and lively connection' between the late Roman and Carolingian periods. Without the decline and death of Roman culture, she argued, the idea of a re-birth or *re-naissance* made no sense at all.[17] Patzelt was not alone

---

15 See here especially Brown, 'Introduction', pp. 2–6 where he highlights the conceptual connection between Dark Ages and renaissance.

16 J. Burckhardt, *Die Cultur der Renaissance in Italien: ein Versuch* (Basel: Schweighauser, 1860).

17 Patzelt, *Die Karolingische Renaissance*, preface to the edition of 1923: 'Die Zeit des frühen Mittelalters galt daher weiten Kreisen als eine Epoche geistiger Finsternis und kulturloser Barbarei, das Wirken Karls des Grossen erschien nur durch die Annahme verständlich, es hätte damals die Absicht bestanden, den Aufbau der Kultur durch Wiedererneuerung der Antike vorzunehmen.' Jack Goody has recently reiterated this point by stating that something needs to die first before it can be reborn; see J. Goody, *Renaissances: The One or the Many?* (Cambridge: Cambridge University Press, 2010), p. 11. For an important recent contribution to the discussion,

in this: many other scholars have since brought forth arguments to qualify or reject the idea of a Carolingian renaissance.[18]

With scholarly consensus shifting against the 'decline and fall' model, the paradigm of 'transformation of the Roman world' became dominant in the late twentieth century.[19] This has, perhaps surprisingly, not led to the complete abandonment of the term Carolingian renaissance. John Contreni, for instance, consistently uses it for his research on small court-based groups of intellectuals and their highly sophisticated writings, but readily concedes that 'what the Carolingians really wanted to achieve was reform and correction of their society'.[20] In Contreni's view of this renaissance, notions of decline, fall and cultural collapse do not play any role to speak of. The original connotations of revival of classical (albeit not only pre-Christian) culture and learning most certainly do, but as part of a wider 'reform'. Janet Nelson, in turn, also uses the concept

---

in which the author points out how vibrant and alive the Merovigian church was, see I. Wood, 'Reform and the Merovingian church', in R. Meens et al. (eds), *Religious Franks: Religion and Power in the Frankish Kingdoms: Studies in Honour of Mayke de Jong* (Manchester: Manchester University Press, 2016), pp. 95–111.

18 The literature on the subject is substantial. Particularly significant contributions include L. Thorndike, 'Renaissance or Prenaissance?', *Journal of the History of Ideas*, 4 (1943), 65–74; W. Treadgold (ed.), *Renaissances before the Renaissance: Cultural Revivals of Late Antiquity and the Middle Ages* (Stanford, CA: Stanford University Press, 1984); J. Contreni, 'The Carolingian Renaissance: education and literary culture', in R. McKitterick (ed.), *The New Cambridge Medieval History* II, *ca. 700–ca. 900* (Cambridge: Cambridge University Press, 1995), pp. 721–55; Sullivan (ed.), *'The Gentle Voices of Teachers'*. Note how every author defines the phenomenon differently, while the idea of 'revival of the classics' and 'correct Latin' stay firmly in place.

19 The 1990s witnessed an enormous scholarly effort to explore and substantiate the transformation paradigm in the shape of the European Science Foundation project 'The transformation of the Roman world', which has resulted in twelve collections of articles. See http://archives.esf.org/coordinating-research/research-networking-programmes/humanities-hum/completed-rnp-programmes-in-humanities/the-transformation-of-the-roman-world.html (accessed 21 February 2022). The twelve volumes came out as a Brill series; see https://brill.com/view/serial/TRW (accessed 21 February 2022).

20 Contreni, 'The Carolingian Renaissance', p. 712.

of renaissance, but in a recent article she appears to use the term in a manner more or less equivalent to what others would label reform. Nelson discusses the practice of law ('legal renaissance'), stressing its connection to the Carolingian 'religious renaissance' and the way in which legal practices built on Roman traditions.[21] These two examples (there are many more) illustrate well how the meaning and connotations of the term have changed over time, and how the notion of a Carolingian renaissance has become blurred at the edges to such an extent that it now seems to overlap with, or even to fit into, the larger container term of reform. At the same time, it is clear that specific connotations of rebirth and Roman culture continue to colour the term.

Carolingian reform

The case of the term reform is a bit more complex, since the history of its use in the context of the Carolingian world brings together two distinct ways in which it has become anchored in scholarly thought. The first one concerns the Latin term. Unlike renaissance, the verb *reformare* and its corresponding noun form, *reformatio*, did exist in the early middle ages as clearly distinguishable elements of inherited late Roman, Christian lines of thinking. Gerhart Ladner, in his influential work *The idea of reform* (1959), explored the way in which ideas of reform developed in the age of the Church Fathers, starting with their very beginnings in the Epistles of Paul.[22] This meaning of *reformatio*, inherited by Carolingian intellectuals through their study of the Fathers, comes down to the process of perpetual, individual self-improvement in the image of Christ that was expected from every Christian in order to deserve the Kingdom of Heaven. At the same time, such reform is not linear or progressive. It has as its benchmark the pristine state of the soul, which was

---

21 J. L. Nelson, 'Revisiting the Carolingian Renaissance', in J. Kreiner and H. Reimitz (eds), *Motions of Late Antiquity: Essays on Religion, Politics, and Society in Honour of Peter Brown*, Cultural Encounters in Late Antiquity and the Middle Ages 20 (Turnhout: Brepols, 2016), pp. 331–46, here especially p. 341.

22 See also Kristina Mitalaitė's contribution in Chapter 6 of this volume.

by definition in the past.[23] It cannot be emphasised enough, as Julia Barrow rightly states, that until the eleventh and twelfth centuries the Latin verb *reformare* in the sense of changing for the better was only used for individuals and not as a term describing institutional change; monastic or conciliar documents using the word in the ninth century generally use it in the related but different sense of rebuilding or restoring. Moreover, the term quite simply does not appear very often at all in either the patristic age or in the time of the Carolingians.[24] After the eleventh century, the meaning of the term was stretched ever further so that it came to include, for instance, the planned change of entire monastic communities and later, at the Fourth Lateran Council of 1215, the institutional improvement of the church as a whole. This means that *reformatio* in any collective meaning of the word, or as a way to indicate the purposeful improvement of groups or institutions, post-dates the Carolingian period by several centuries. Projecting the Latin term as it was used in the high and late middle ages back onto the Carolingian world is therefore anachronistic and does not do justice to its contemporary meanings in the eighth and ninth centuries.

The second way in which the term reform has entered the writings of historians is, as in the case of renaissance, through scholarly borrowings in the nineteenth century. Historians have, until recently, taken hardly any notice of the terminological problems just sketched, so that the term reform could, as it were, slip in via the scholarly literature. Barrow outlines how, from the early nineteenth century onwards, the term was used by scholars to describe processes of purposeful change for the better in the western Church, for instance

---

23 G. B. Ladner, *The Idea of Reform: Its Impact on Christian Thought and Action in the Age of the Fathers* (Cambridge, MA: Harvard University Press, 1959). An important precursor to Ladner's work is K. Burdach, 'Sinn und Ursprung der Worte Renaissance und Reformation', *Sitzungsberichte der Königliche Preussischen Akademie der Wissenschaften*, 13 (1910), 594–646.

24 J. Barrow, 'Ideas and applications of reform', in T. F. X. Noble and J. M. H. Smith (eds), *The Cambridge History of Christianity. Early Medieval Christianities, c.600–c.1100* (Cambridge: Cambridge University Press, 2008), pp. 345–62, here pp. 347–8; J. Barrow, 'Developing definitions of reform in the church in the ninth and tenth centuries', in R. Balzaretti et al. (eds), *Italy and Early Medieval Europe: Papers for Chris Wickham* (Oxford: Oxford University Press, 2018), pp. 501–11, here especially p. 511.

the 'reforms' that took shape under Pope Gregory VII, or those promulgated at the Fourth Lateran Council of 1215. By the 1800s, however, the word reform had become laden with rather optimistic, forward-looking associations of progress and a better world in the future, both of which were completely alien to an early medieval context. In the slipstream of the Reformation, Gregory VII could be viewed (at least by Protestant historians) as a kind of Luther, just as the eleventh century could be seen as a period of church reform not unlike the Reformation.[25] Small wonder, perhaps, that in the early twentieth century both Boniface and Charlemagne came to be described as reformers of the church, liturgy and education.[26] The Carolingian reforms as a term invented by church historians, therefore, borrowed from nineteenth-century scholarship on the high middle ages through the lens of the Reformation.[27] This notion of reform was focused on the church and underlined progress into the future, improvement of wrongs in a top-down fashion and – in an interesting parallel with the idea of renaissance – a way forward from a preceding age of decline or 'decadence'. In the course of the twentieth century, reform became the term preferred by most scholars to label change and improvement in the church, but increasingly also for other aspects of the Carolingian world.

A very important step towards a more integrated view of Carolingian politics, culture and religion was proposed by Walter Ullmann in his Birkbeck lectures of the academic year 1968–69, when he suggested that what was then still called the Carolingian renaissance could, in fact, not be seen as separate from Charlemagne's wider political aspirations – the 'literary renaissance' (which, inspired

---

25 Barrow, 'Ideas and applications', pp. 349–50.
26 See, for example, E. Bishop, 'The liturgical reforms of Charlemagne: their meanings and value', *The Downside Review*, 38 (1919), 1–16; T. Reuter, '"Kirchenreform" und "Kirchenpolitik" im Zeitalter Karl Martells: Begriffe und Wirklichkeit', in J. Jarnut et al. (eds), *Karl Martell in seiner Zeit* (Sigmaringen: Thorbecke, 1994), pp. 35–59. Boniface is still going strong as a reformer, however: see, for example, L. E. von Padberg, *Bonifatius: Missionar und Reformer* (Munich: Beck, 2003).
27 Note that use of the term reform for the time of the Investiture Controversy and Lateran IV also has its critics, for instance G. Tellenbach, *Die westliche Kirche vom 10. bis zum frühen 12. Jahrhundert* (Göttingen: Vandenhoeck & Ruprecht, 1988); see also Leyser, 'Church reform', here especially 482–5.

by the work of Josef Fleckenstein, he also calls *Bildungsreform*[28]) was 'an epiphenomenon, a byproduct'.[29] According to Ullmann, Charlemagne's intentions to transform society as a whole rested on battling ignorance through the improvement of education, for which texts, intellectual reflection and knowledge were needed.[30] This idea of a cultural renaissance as part of a broader political-religious reform has found wide acceptance; reform (or sometimes *correctio*) is often employed as a shorthand for the entire package.[31]

In current usage, the term reform has become very elastic indeed and can cover more or less any observable type of change proposed or introduced in the time of the Carolingians, including those of coinage, methods of land management, weights and measures, the organisation of the army or the calculation of the Easter date.[32] The emphasis in all these cases is solidly on the process of change itself, not its desired outcome. Its usual connotations and claims are that, in essence, reform consisted of top-down processes of (mostly institutional) change presented as improvements, which were part of court-driven political agendas. What remains a fundamental

---

28 J. Fleckenstein, *Die Bildungsreform Karls des Grossen als Verwirklichung der Norma Rectitudinis* (Bigge-Ruhr: Josefs, 1953). Right at the start of his book, at p. 1, Fleckenstein explains how renaissance is not the same as reform.
29 W. Ullmann, *The Carolingian Renaissance and the Idea of Kingship: The Birkbeck Lectures 1968–9* (London: Methuen, 1969), pp. 4–6.
30 *Ibid.*, pp. 6–7.
31 Chris Wickham carefully stays away from both 'renaissance' and 'reform' and has instead coined the term 'Carolingian experiment'. This may turn into a new shoot on the old tree: his 'experiment' is very much like this idea of reform, but his emphasis is solidly political. See C. Wickham, *Medieval Europe* (New Haven, CT: Yale University Press, 2016): chapter 4, pp. 61–79, entitled 'The Carolingian experiment, 750–1000'. Wickham is notably more optimistic about the effects of this 'experiment' than in his earlier work, C. Wickham, *The Inheritance of Rome: A History of Europe from 400 to 1000* (London: Penguin, 2009), pp. 382–4, where he calls it 'the Carolingian project'.
32 A. Miskimin, 'Two reforms of Charlemagne? Weights and measures in the middle ages', *The Economic History Review*, 20 (1967), 35–52; R. McKitterick, *The Frankish Church and the Carolingian Reforms, 789–895* (London: Royal Historical Society, 1977); A. Borst, *Die karolingische Kalenderreform*, MGH Schriften 46 (Hanover: Hahn, 1998).

problem with the term, quite apart from its anachronistic connotations when applied to groups of people or entire institutions, is that all this elasticity has led to vagueness: reform can no longer be distinguished from intentional change, and the term implies that such intentional changes are part of a larger programme. Should all recorded attempts to change any aspect of the Carolingian world really be read as part of one big master plan ('the Carolingian reforms') thought out at the court? Or, alternatively, were certain changes part of this 'reform', while others were not? What exactly *was* this reform, and where do its conceptual boundaries run? These questions are, of course, unanswerable since the Franks were themselves not aware of any such definition of reform, and they certainly did not consciously initiate a reform movement. Such a watered-down notion of reform as change that focuses on the court and top-down regulations, moreover, does not do justice to the many anonymous people not directly connected to the court who did their best to improve their corners of the Carolingian world for the greater purpose of salvation, for instance by writing new didactic texts, composing novel liturgies or gathering texts in new manuscripts. While the perspective that reform provides is definitely wider in scope than that of renaissance, it still does not account for the idea that Carolingian culture involved the whole of society and these changes were undertaken for the shared purpose of reaching heaven.

Carolingian correctio

In an article published in 1964, Percy Ernst Schramm voiced his objections against the term Carolingian renaissance, which he believed led to misunderstandings about Charlemagne and his time. Jacob Burckhardt's concept of Renaissance fitted well for the fifteenth century, but analysing Carolingian culture through this concept would inevitably lead to distortion: 'Should we borrow the name "renaissance" …? *Wir sagen: Nein!* [We say: No!]'[33] Instead,

---

33 P. E. Schramm, 'Karl der Grosse: Denkart und Grundauffassungen – Die von ihm bewirkte "correctio" ("Renaissance")', *Historische Zeitschrift*, 198 (1964), 306–45, here 339: 'Sollen wir für sie weiter den Namen

Schramm proposed to use a term from the early middle ages itself which better described what the Carolingians thought they were doing. The best candidate in his opinion was *correctio* (correction), which he used to refer to Charlemagne's (and later Louis the Pious's and Charles the Bald's) *Bildungsreform* ('educational reform'): a top-down, cultural phenomenon.[34]

As was the case with the previous terms, *correctio* entered the historian's vocabulary with a precise meaning which soon became watered down; the term is now generally used as a near-synonym for the equally fuzzy reform in the elastic sense just sketched.[35] To mention just one important recent example, Julia Smith defines *correctio* as 'the adjustment of Christians' behaviour to bring it into line with the teaching of Scripture and the church fathers', which is an interesting amalgam of reform in its widest sense (the improvement of society) and the cultural and educational connotations of Schramm's *correctio* (as well as the older idea of renaissance).[36] Such a definition corresponds rather well to Theodulf of Orléans's admonishments to his priests with which we started, even though the bishop himself does not use any term to label his ideas.[37] Unlike Schramm, however, Smith points out how reform is the problematic term, and how *correctio* should replace it – again a clear indication of how the meanings of all three terms have changed, grown together and/or moved apart over time.

"Renaissance" ausleihen, der ja seit Jacob Burckhardt einen festen, auch zeitlich eingegrenzten Begriffsinhalt hat? Wir sagen: Nein!'

34 Schramm, 'Karl der Grosse', 342. He did not propose to bin the term renaissance altogether, but to reserve it for 'politisch ausgerichtete, bewusst an der Antike (einschliesslich der christlichen Antike) orientierte Bestrebungen'.

35 See, for instance, the index to Story (ed.), *Charlemagne*, p. 326: 'reform: see *correctio*', while 'renaissance' is a separate lemma.

36 J. M. H. Smith, '"Emending evil ways and praising God's omnipotence": Einhard and the uses of Roman martyrs', in K. Mills and A. Grafton (eds), *Conversion in Late Antiquity and the Early Middle Ages: Seeing and Believing* (Rochester, NY: University of Rochester Press, 2003), pp. 189–223, here p. 189.

37 Smith, 'Emending evil ways', p. 190. Here, Schramm took his cue from Fleckenstein, who in *Die Bildungsreform*, p. 11 pointed out that the Carolingians used a series of terms to describe this efforts, such as *reformare, emendare, restaurare, corrigere*.

What remains rather stable throughout such fluctuations, as we have seen for the other two terms, are the implicit or explicit general connotations of each term. For *correctio*, the most important one is that, unlike renaissance and (for the most part) reform, this word was actually part of the Carolingian vocabulary of change and improvement. By using this term, scholars claim to be authentic, and stay as close as possible to what Carolingians themselves thought. While this is a valid reason for using it, and *corrigere* (the corresponding verb form to *correctio*) is indeed a word that turns up in sources from the Carolingian period, the idea that it reflects notions of reform or improvement in this way cannot be sustained.

The Carolingian vocabulary of change for the better

When Schramm proposed *correctio* as a substitute for renaissance, he considered a series of other terms also used in Carolingian texts, for instance, *emendare* (to emend), *restituere* (to restore), *renovare* (to renew) and even *reformare* (to reform).[38] His supposition that these words were generally used by Carolingian authors to describe attempts to improve society has been widely received and accepted by many without further interrogation. This is how the use of the term *correctio* has gained currency, even though his choice of *correctio* was not based on a thorough study of primary sources but rather reflected Schramm's own interpretation of Charlemagne's efforts. Here it is important to note that Charlemagne was long considered to be the larger-than-life architect and engine of a whole, top-down, operation – the nineteenth century saw him causing a renaissance more or less by himself, and he kept this lead role when *correctio* and reform became the preferred frames. Understandably, such ideas of Charlemagne's centrality led – and still lead – scholars to focus on prescriptive texts produced at his court or under his aegis, and accordingly, much research zoomed in, and still zooms in, on royal capitularies, conciliar proceedings, a few letters and not much more. As a result, the way in which Carolingian *correctio* was, and often is, understood is through one corpus of very specific texts.

---

38 Schramm, 'Karl der Grosse', 341.

Although there is much to be said for using terminology that was used in the period itself by those at the helm of Carolingian society, there are three problems with Schramm's ideas that merit some detailed attention here. The first problem is that *correctio* (and *emendare*, *corrigere*, *reformare*) are, in fact, extremely rare in prescriptive (and any other) texts from Charlemagne's time. The second problem is that when the term *correctio* appears, in the majority of the cases by far it does *not* carry the meaning intended by Schramm but refers to the punishment, penance or improvement of individual Christians. Even within this small corpus, words such as *correctio* and *emendatio* are generally not used when some change or improvement of practices is described or proclaimed.

A few facts and figures will illustrate the infrequency with which these terms appear and show how the use of *correctio* as a better and typically Carolingian alternative to renaissance or reform distorts our image – even though that was exactly what Schramm tried to prevent by proposing the term.[39] In the capitularies issued under Charlemagne, the noun *correctio* occurs exactly once (counting all declensions), namely in the Bavarian capitulary of 810, where the term describes the way in which robbers, murderers and adulterers should be punished – so not in a meaning equivalent to our modern understanding of reform.[40] Neither the *Admonitio generalis*, usually understood as the key programmatic text for both Charlemagne's reform and *correctio*, nor the *Epistola de litteris colendis*, his letter admonishing monastic communities to improve study and education, contains the term a single time.[41] In the proceedings of councils that convened during Charlemagne's lifetime, we find three instances of *correctio*. The Council of Rheims (813) contains the only instance of the term in the way Smith defines it, where it

---

39 I have relied on the search function of the dMGH for the numbers in this section.
40 See A. Boretius (ed.), *MGH Capit.* 1 (Hanover: Hahn, 1883), no. 69, c. 5, p. 159: 'Ut latrones vel homicidae seu adulteri vel incestuosi sub magna districtione et correctione sint correpti secundum eoa Baiuvariorum vel lege'.
41 The *Epistola de litteris colendis* can be found in *MGH Capit.* 1, no. 29, pp. 78–9.

mentions the *correctio* of the whole Christian empire.[42] A search in several digital repositories did not turn up any other instances of the term in the meaning we are looking for in other texts dating from Charlemagne's lifetime.[43] All in all, there is very little evidence indeed, and Schramm's use of *correctio* does not appear to reflect a Carolingian understanding of the term.

The other words listed by Schramm (*corrigere, emendare, renovare, reformare, revocare*[44]) seem to have been used only rarely in the sense of his *Bildungsreform* or that of more recent readings of 'reform'. The *Admonitio generalis*, to mention just one important example, does contain the verbs *corrigere* and *emendare*, but not *reformare, renovare* or *revocare*. In the preface, Charlemagne famously expresses the wish to 'correct (moral) errors' (*errata corrigere*) after the example of king Josiah who travelled in his kingdom 'while correcting' (*corrigendo*).[45] This can, indeed, be read as a programmatic statement in line with Schramm's and Smith's ideas, but after this evocative preface, the words return rarely in the actual chapters: after the introduction, *corrigere* in all its forms appears twice, *emendare* three times, across 80 chapters and 30 pages of the modern edition. In these instances, the objects of correction are mostly individuals behaving the wrong way. Chapter 65, for instance, deals with wizards and storm-makers whose evil ways should be 'emended or condemned' (*emendentur vel damnentur*), while clerics who falsely pretended to be monks (c. 75) should be 'corrected and emended' (*corrigendos atque emendandos*); the one exception is 'un-emended books' (*inemendatos libros*), which should, of course, be improved or avoided.[46]

---

42 See A. Werminghoff (ed.), *MGH Conc.* 2.1 (Hanover: Hahn, 1906), no. 35, p. 254: 'et ad mercedem praefati gloriosissimi principis nostri seu correctionem totius Christiani imperii'.

43 For this section, I have looked for all grammatical forms of 'correctio' in texts dating from the late eighth and early ninth century in the digital *MGH*, the Library of Latin Texts and the digital Patrologia Latina.

44 Schramm, 'Karl der Grosse', 341. For the specific uses of *reformare* see Barrow, 'Developing definitions', pp. 502–4.

45 *Admonitio generalis*, p. 182.

46 *Admonitio generalis*, cc. 64, 70, 75, pp. 216, 224, 228.

To come back to the second point, what did *correctio* mean in the time of Charlemagne? *Correctio* as a royal, rhetorical term to claim the intention to improve society or institutions is clearly the exception rather than the rule, even in the prescriptive corpus. Usually, the term is used in the context of individual moral improvement, penance or punishment. We find this usage in a much wider range of texts, and many instances of this term are connected in some way to pastoral care and the individual's road to heaven. This *correctio* turns up (albeit still infrequently), for instance, in episcopal statutes, texts concerning penance and sermons.[47] What is noteworthy here is how *correctio* in its most general usage is never about situations or practices or circumstances that needed 'correction', but always about people and their sinful or mistaken behaviour which would exclude them from eternal life. There is clearly a connection between the uses of *correctio* in these individual contexts and its rare collective meaning that seems to hinge on the duties of kings and pastors to look after the well-being of their subjects and flocks – in the end, all efforts at individual *correctio* should ideally lead to the salvation of society as a whole.[48] Strikingly, whenever Charlemagne's capitularies or the conciliar proceedings of his day prescribe the improvement of practices, situations or circumstances, *none* of the keywords signalled by Schramm is used. These prescriptions are generally formulated as prohibitions, or briefly describe how things should be. To mention just a couple of examples from the *Admonitio generalis*: dubious saints should not be celebrated (c. 42); virgins should not be veiled before they are twenty-five years old (c. 46); clerics and monks should live up to what they promise to God in their vows (c. 26); and clerics who have a disagreement

---

47 The indices in *MGH Capit. episc.* 4 are instructive: see the lemmata 'correctio' (occurs five times in three volumes of texts); 'corrigere' (always in the sense of punishment, five times); 'emendatio' (thirteen times). This shows the terms are very rare in these texts; compare, for instance, 'fornicatio' and 'ebrietas'.
48 How exactly this worked, and via which texts or authorities, is an interesting and important question, but it is beyond the scope of this chapter. For important reflections on Charlemagne as a 'super-bishop' see De Jong, 'Charlemagne's church', pp. 103–35.

should be judged by their bishop and not by a lay person (c. 28).[49] The envisaged changes for the better, in other words, are described in a straightforward fashion and did not need any of the terms flagged by Schramm to underline their importance. Throughout the entire Carolingian period, this image does not seem to change: compared to the other meanings of the term, the use of *correctio* to indicate the improvement of Christian society is very rare indeed, and its use in Schramm's sense is confined to sporadic instances in prescriptive texts issued with royal authority.[50]

As a final point: Charlemagne did not invent the wheel in those rare cases that he used *correctio* or *corrigere* in a collective sense. These terms had been part of the vocabulary of rulership and of legal language since the Roman period, and occur in other early medieval contexts (Lombard, Visigothic). Closer to home, Charlemagne's Merovingian predecessors used these terms too, albeit equally infrequently. In the early sixth century, for instance, the Merovingian king Childebert proclaimed that 'the people' (*plebs*) should be 'corrected' (*corrigatur*, presumably one individual at the time), while King Guntramn considered it to be the bishops' task to 'correct' the people through their preaching (*praedicatione corrigite*) and to lead errant sheep back to the right path through their pastoral *correctio* (*et excedentes ad viam recti itineris correctio pastoralis adducat*).[51] These terms formed part of the royal rhetoric of improvement and

---

49 *Admonitio generalis*, c. 42, p. 202: 'ut falsa nomina martyrum et incertae sanctorum memoriae non venerentur'; c. 46, p. 202: 'ut uirgines non uelentur ante xxv annos nisi rationabili necessitate cogente'; c. 26, p. 196: 'ut clerici et monachi in suo proposito et uoto, quod deo promiserunt, permaneant'; c. 28, p. 196: 'ut, si clerici inter se negotium aliquod habuerint, a suo episcopo diiudicentur, non a secularibus'.
50 To mention just one example: *Admonitio ad omnes regni ordines* (823–825), *MGH Capit.* 1, no. 150, c. 15: 'Et si talis causa in qualibet provincia aut in aliquo comitatu orta fuerit, quae aut ad inhonorationem regni aut ad commune damnum pertineat, quae etiam sine nostra potestate corrigi non possit, nos diu latere non permittatis, qui omnia Deo auxiliante corrigere debemus; quia, quicquid hactenus in his, quae ad pacem et iustitiam totius populi pertinent et ad honorem regni et communem utilitatem, aut a nobis aut a vobis neglectum est, debemus Deo auxiliante certare, qualiter abhinc nostro et vestro studio emendatum fiat.'
51 *MGH Capit.* 1, nos 2 and 5, pp. 2, 11.

rulership, leading to God's approval and salvation for all, and their usage in this context endured beyond the Carolingians as well: witness, for instance, the German Emperor Heinrich II who in 1023 decreed that 'all injustice ... should be corrected' (*omnia iniustitia ... pleniter corrigeretur*).⁵² There was, in other words, a tradition of kings sporadically using these terms in their official prescriptive texts; Charlemagne and his dynasty constitute but one chapter in its much longer story.

The dominant use of *correctio* in the Carolingian period pertained overwhelmingly to pastoral contexts and concerned individual people as opposed to situations or abuses. Even though all individual processes of *correctio* would ideally add up to the *correctio* and salvation of society as a whole, the term was never self-evident shorthand for 'the improvement of society' in the Carolingian period.

This short overview has shown how the terminology to describe Carolingian culture and its development has, through its connotations, claims and colourings, encouraged researchers to look at the same texts and contexts over and over again. Even when the preferred term changed, undertones of royal agency, top-down processes, classical culture and other ideas that were attached to the previous term of preference were integrated into the new term. This is how we have ended up with a particular set of ideas about Carolingian culture and the improvement of society that reflects the interests of previous generations of scholars more than it does the full range of extant written sources that can shed light on the Carolingian world.

Small wonder, perhaps, that those assessing the success of 'the Carolingian reforms' have not been overly optimistic. Philippe Depreux, for instance, in an article discussing the 'ambitions and limits of the cultural reforms in the Carolingian period', concludes that the ideals were surely lofty, but any cultural revival in the sense of a renaissance is unlikely ever to have reached an audience more

---

52 L. Weiland (ed.), *MGH Constitutiones et acta publica imperatorum et regum* 1 (Hanover: Hahn, 1893), no. 35, c. 3, p. 79.

substantial than learned circles at the court.[53] In instances like these, it is eminently clear how connotations of the terminology used can be misleading: if we look for a renaissance in the Carolingian period that is even remotely like the Renaissance of the late Middle Ages (in the sense of a deliberate revival of classical culture for its own sake), we are not going to find it. Similarly, if we look for reform as cultural revival with Renaissance-esque criteria in mind (such as flawless Latin, imitation of the Classics and high-level artistic and intellectual products), it is primarily at the royal court that we will find texts that meet these standards. The assumptions that these terms carry here lead to a kind of short-sightedness that overlooks the wider context, and this is exactly why it is important to de-focus these terms and the ideas that underlie them. A similar argument can be made to the disappointment of those who assume that uniformity was one of the outcomes desired by those involved in improving the Carolingian world.[54] Uniformity in our modern sense is a concept completely alien to the early middle ages – 'correct' was measured by a number of criteria and allowed for wide variety. Susan Keefe's research into baptismal expositions is an excellent case in point: when Charlemagne asked bishops to write down how baptisms were performed in their diocese, dozens of different answers reached the court. They all had a few things in common, for instance a catechumenate preceding the ritual, and triple immersion during the ritual, but varied in all but such 'set' elements. Yet, these procedures were all received (and in many cases copied and distributed) as correct ritual that would make the candidate into a real Christian, and there was never any attempt to create one

---

53 P. Depreux, 'Ambitions et limites des réformes culturelles à l'époque Carolingienne', *Revue Historique*, 623 (2002/3), 721–53, here 750: 'on ne peut se partir de l'idée que le renouveau culturel des temps carolingiens, ce qui relève vraiment de la "renaissance", ne concerna que peu de monde: essentiellement l'entourage du souverain et les élites, certains clercs et moines'.

54 See, for example, R. McKitterick, 'The Carolingian renaissance of culture and learning', in Story (ed.), *Charlemagne*, here p. 155: 'Despite these efforts to promote a standard religious observance, harmony rather than uniformity was achieved; a great diversity of practice prevailed and many local communities persisted in the use of versions of texts to which they had become accustomed.'

standard rite.⁵⁵ This was not due to any failure to live up to an ideal of standardisation, but reflects a different, more flexible attitude towards correct ritual.

Such perceptions of failure are, in other words, directly dependent on modern horizons of expectation which are, in turn, informed by assumptions inherent in the terminology. The question then becomes a different one: how do we approach a period of intense cultural activity, study, creativity and experimentation through the full width of texts and manuscripts of the time? When we keep in mind that the hope of salvation was what ties all efforts at change and improvement together, and that people from all walks of life could participate in their own ways, wider perspectives open up.

Carolingian culture: the road to salvation

If the discussion of the terms renaissance, reform and *correctio* has shown one thing, it is that all three of them have led to a rather limited idea of where one should look for Carolingian culture and the inextricably connected attempts to improve Christian life and morals to gain eternal life for all. The notion of Charlemagne's central agency, inherited from a long tradition of scholarship, has led to a steady focus on the court and its directives, on texts and manuscripts of the highest quality, on the reception and imitation of the classics and on the most sophisticated early medieval intellectuals. Thus far, as we have seen, Carolingian culture has often been treated as an elite affair with little bearing on the wider world. To do justice to the extant texts and manuscripts, our traditional focal points need to be recontextualised. Court, kings and capitularies are important, but they are all part of a larger story and new starting points for research are needed to take into account the full range of evidence. For the purpose of this book, two main questions have

---

55 S. Keefe (ed.), *Water and the Word, Volume II. Baptism and the Education of the Clergy in the Carolingian Empire: Editions of Texts* (Notre Dame, IN: University of Notre Dame Press, 2002) contains the editions of sixty-one different texts about baptism related to Charlemagne's inquiry. Between them, they explain or describe many different rituals.

been used to open up a wider approach to the subject: first, that of agency, and secondly, that of networks of knowledge.

While there is no dispute that the Carolingian royal family and its court circles brought forward ideas to effect change and moral improvement, or about the undoubtedly vast resources they poured into patronage, the culture of the Carolingian world was shaped and carried by a group of people much larger than the king and his loyal and wealthy *potentes*. Surely Charlemagne and his powerful counts and bishops took initiatives with far-reaching consequences throughout the realm, but this does not mean that the only agency relevant for explaining the extant texts and manuscripts was located in their hands. When we are prepared to bring (anonymous) authors into the story who operated outside the direct sphere of influence of the court, but all the same took their own initiatives to gather knowledge, undertake didactical experimentation or work with texts inherited from antiquity in new ways, a much more dynamic image of Carolingian culture comes into view.

In such a world, the royal court with its remarkable residents still remains unique, but it is no longer an oasis in a cultural desert or a hub of activity in a landscape of passive reception. Instead, we are confronted by new vistas: the Carolingian world becomes more densely populated with people who were not just the obedient recipients of top-down directives, but authors and compilers who took their own initiatives to find the best responses possible to local challenges. An anonymous school-master in a monastic establishment at the edge of the Carolingian world probably did not need the prompting of his or her king to try and devise a better schoolbook, for instance, in the same way that bishops or priests did not need the lists of subjects for proper preaching in the *Admonitio Generalis* to think up good themes for their sermons. All of these different people may have been inspired by different local circumstances and agendas, but they shared mentalities and ideals that had been around for a long time. What all those in positions of responsibility had in common was not only their local priorities, but also an awareness of their duty to look after the moral well-being of the people in their care and lead them to heaven. Knowledge, study and teaching were central to this. The texts and manuscripts that are the subjects of the majority of the chapters in this book all bear witness to this awareness.

Connected to the issue of agency, it is important to realise that the initiatives, patronage or commissions of all these people and institutions (court included) during the best part of two centuries cannot be viewed as one consistent, well-thought-out programme that explains every development or change that we see happening across this period. One does not need anachronistic concepts of reform to understand what moved authors to write, preachers to preach or, for that matter, kings to rule: trying to improve, to change for the better, was part and parcel of the kind of responsibility just outlined. Whether running a school, managing a diocese or ruling over a kingdom, 'making things better' was – and is! – part of the responsibilities that come with the office. What clearly fluctuated between the Merovingian and the Carolingian periods were the resources available to do so, the enthusiasm with which initiatives were developed, as well as a prolonged period of peace and safety for those involved. The relatively long period of internal peace during Charlemagne's reign was surely conducive to scholarship and preoccupations with moral standards; it was also a particularly wealthy period in which many felt inclined to participate in patronage. That the Carolingians were more fortunate in these matters does not mean that the dynasties before and after them felt radically differently about their responsibilities or wanted the same things any less. In that sense, the Carolingian period is a particularly intense, well-funded and creative chapter in the much longer history of the culture of change and moral improvement for the sake of collective salvation. How exactly it was different (or not) ought to be the subject of future research, for which the widest range of sources possible should be used. Instead of burdening the Carolingian period with renaissances or reforms, it becomes possible to study Carolingian culture as part of a longer story, and thereby recognise what makes this period special.

The second central building block is networks of knowledge as a way to approach the exchange and multiplication of texts, books and knowledge in this period. Again, vertical corridors of the distribution of texts and ideas should not be discounted, but understood side by side with the many horizontal processes of debate and exchange that can be observed in the manuscript record. Likewise, prescriptions are certainly important to understand ideals and the way in which they travelled. However, understanding how people sought to cultivate the moral health of the Franks and to improve their knowledge needs to build on a much wider range of material than simply ideals and instructions from above. We need to be aware that many authors and students were perhaps primarily occupied with local needs and drew on the resources and knowledge at hand to meet such challenges. That court intellectuals formed networks, sent each other books, wrote to and for each other and sometimes corresponded extensively is well known, but this is just the tip of yet another iceberg: networks of knowledge spanned the entire Carolingian world and by no means involved important intellectuals alone.[56]

Recent research has already started to show the importance of horizontal networks of exchange, for instance, those between larger and smaller monasteries and episcopal centres that facilitated the mobility of books, people and thereby knowledge.[57] Such networks, moreover, show dynamics of their own. Some monasteries, for instance, seem to have collaborated intensively with other hubs throughout the realm; others operated on a more modest, local scale, while some abbeys seem to have been purposefully excluded from such networks.[58] Understanding connections between people and institutions helps to understand how people came by their texts and books, how texts and ideas travelled and how discussions developed – or failed to do so. It also allows us to compare what people with access to manuscripts actually did and did not do with such knowledge. Studying liturgical texts, grammatical handbooks or treatises based on the insights of classical rhetoric, to mention just a few examples, allows us to appreciate the wealth of Carolingian cultural production. Importantly, at the same time it

---

56 See Chapter 3 for Cinzia Grifoni and Giorgia Vocino's contribution to this volume.
57 S. Meeder, *The Irish Scholarly Presence at St Gall: Networks of Knowledge in the Early Middle Ages* (London: Bloomsbury, 2018); interest in such research is also witnessed by the Leverhulme Project 'Insular Manuscripts AD 650–850: networks of knowledge' in which the British Library and the Universities of Galway, Dublin and Vienna participate. For a description see http://blogs.bl.uk/digitisedmanuscripts/2017/03/insular-manuscripts-ad-650-850-networks-of-knowledge.html (accessed 21 February 2022).
58 See Chapter 1 for Ingrid Rembold's contribution to this volume.

makes it possible to analyse the bandwidth within which new ideas, improvements and experiments were considered useful and acceptable. Many roads could lead to heaven; the interesting question is why people chose the ones they did.

This book

This series of studies addresses varied aspects of the traditional discourse about Carolingian 'reform', re-framing and re-interpreting them from diverse perspectives. In this sense it resembles a 'taster menu' more than that it offers an overarching new narrative about Carolingian culture; most of all, it hopes to inspire scholars to test these ideas in their own fields of research.

Chapter 1, written by Ingrid Rembold, takes us to Carolingian monasteries and monasticisms (plural). It is about female communities that were *not* part of the attempts to regulate institutionalised religious life, and it specifically avoids integrating all forms of Carolingian monastic life into one theoretical male (or unisex) default. After all, female communities *were* different: not only were they dependent on men with priestly ordinations and legal know-how, but they were also often smaller and/or dependent on elite families and were cloistered much more strictly than male communities. Female monasteries were like islands, excluded from consensus-making assemblies, barred from travel and participation in horizontal networks, in other words, all those ways of communication that stimulated and facilitated the spread of ideas traditionally labelled monastic reform. So what was 'Carolingian monastic reform' if it did not include female institutions?

Stephen Ling, in Chapter 2, discusses another important aspect of the traditional 'reform' narrative: the organisation of canonical clergy. Chrodegang of Metz wrote a Rule for Canons that has been generally accepted as the lens through which the success or failure of reform could be measured. However, should we interpret persistent diversity in the organisation of cathedral communities, long after Chrodegang wrote his Rule, as 'failure to reform'? Non-monastic communities existed in a wide variety, each with its own longstanding traditions and each receptive or resistant to outside attempts at regulation. Some bishops even ignored Chrodegang and his Rule completely. On the ground, and no matter the existence of the Rules of Benedict and Chrodegang, the distinction between communities of monks and canons was and remained ambiguous and adaptable to local preferences and circumstances. What mattered was adherence to authoritative and canonical texts respecting local traditions, not the creation of uniformity. Local agency, not top-down regulation, set the tone.

In Chapter 3, Cinzia Grifoni and Giorgia Vocino challenge the idea that a top-down, universal 'reform' of education took place in the Carolingian period: schools had their own traditions, school masters developed their own methods and new texts were not necessarily received with equal enthusiasm everywhere. The case studies in this chapter show that the model of an all-powerful court issuing calls to reform to mostly passive recipients does not do justice to a wide variety of local initiatives and 'ways of doing things'. Even though new knowledge could spread like a virus, some less well-connected places were left 'uncontaminated', while others were altogether 'immune'. More important than the availability of Alcuin's works on grammar, for instance, were the networks of horizontal exchange of knowledge and a school's pre-existing traditions, as well as the interests and decisions of individual masters. These determined how centres of education worked to improve their teaching, and the shape that pedagogy would take was thus a principally local affair.

In Chapter 4, Els Rose and Arthur Westwell offer new perspectives on the so-called 'liturgical reforms', an umbrella term under which a plethora of texts and initiatives hides. Carolingian rulers and intellectual elites emphasised the importance of correct – 'Roman' – religious ritual (to be performed, of course, in flawless Latin), but did this ever amount to anything like a top-down, uniformising reform of liturgical practices? Expositions of the liturgy created all over the Carolingian world, both anonymous and not, show a high degree of variety in form and content; nevertheless, they were all expressions of the same set of general ideals regarding correct ritual. Such correctness, then, could take many different shapes and forms. In the eyes of Carolingian authors, 'correct' and 'uniform' were not the same thing. Trying to reduce the lively culture of liturgical explanation and change to a simple model of reform towards uniformity does no justice at all to this phenomenon. The key to understanding the very rich corpus is probably a variety of local attempts at teaching (future) clerics, in order that they understand the rituals and their texts well and could communicate this knowledge to their lay flocks. In terms of the use of Latin, too, similar patterns can be observed: correct Latin as it was perceived at the time had space for variety in spelling and grammar.

The wider significance of *correctio* in the sense of righting what is wrong is the subject of Irene van Renswoude's Chapter 5. In the context of heated theological debates of the Carolingian period, it was essential to determine what was true and reliable in order to recognise the false knowledge that would lead to eternal damnation, especially since this period witnessed the rediscovery and composition of new texts and the development of new modes of interpretation. How did the Carolingian intellectual elite deal with differences of interpretation that were potentially dangerous? How did they 'correct' authors who admitted they had erred in their writings?

Kristina Mitalaitė, in the final chapter, explores the meaning of the terms *correctio*, *renovatio* and *reformatio* in their theological sense: were Carolingian scholars thinking of 'change for the better' with an eye to the early church, as has been often maintained by modern scholars, or did they mean the continual process of moral betterment that would bring every believer closer to God and salvation? Various exegetical commentaries on the book of Genesis and the Epistles of Paul shed light on this question: *renovatio* and *reformatio* were always envisaged as individual processes in which every person strives to be spiritually 'reformed' and 'remade' in God's image. Though wise pastors could point others in the right direction, a person could only correct him- or herself. In accordance with St Paul's letters and largely with the same patristic sources, these authors saw personal reform not as backwards-looking in the sense that it returned man to an earlier, pristine state, but as something that looked to the future of the Last Judgement. They might frame the details of the process differently, but they all agreed that the key to individual reform was to lead a virtuous life in accordance with God's will. Shared ideas about *correctio* and *reformatio* crystallised through controversies and debates with, for instance, the Spanish adoptionists and Greek opponents of the *filioque* clause. At the same time, it is clear that in the field of theology, too, ideas of orthodoxy and correctness were not uniform, but rather a chorus of different voices interpreting similar themes.

1

Gender and horizontal networks in Carolingian monasticisms (up to c. 840)

Ingrid Rembold

In *The Ladder of Divine Ascent*, a twelfth-century icon based on the earlier treatise of John of Climacus, Eastern orthodox monks climb a wide, sloping ladder, their hands raised in prayer despite their precipitous ascent; at the top Jesus himself awaits, his arm outstretched. Along the way, demons lurk with bows and ropes, ready to ensnare unwitting monks and pull them to their demise, to the flames of hell and the bestial mouth of Satan himself. While such ladder imagery was largely absent in the Carolingian world, the 'narrow path' to salvation (Matthew 7:13–14) which it represented was well known. Over the course of the Carolingian period, with each repeated attempt to regulate Christian observances according to one's gender, religious vocation and secular office, each group's path to salvation was more tightly defined, and hence made narrower still. We see ladders erected not only for male monks and the ever more sharply delineated category of male canons, but for all the other groups which made up society as well: female monastics, bishops, counts, laymen and laywomen, etc., each set off along their own trajectory, each serving their defined role. The resulting scene lacks the icon's simplicity; rather, it reminds one of the fire escapes of a crowded Greenwich Village block, each rowhouse with its own designated ladder to salvation.

The Carolingian world took comfort in labels. Society was to be divided into clearly demarcated categories; if everyone knew their

---

* I would like to thank the participants in the *correctio* workshops for their extremely useful feedback; I have also benefited enormously from conversations with and feedback from Eliza Hartrich, Kate Sykes and Graeme Ward.

role, they could act accordingly.¹ Contemporary memoranda, now designated by the modern term 'capitularies' due to their chapter (*capitula*) structure, were very clear on this point. 'To bishops', 'to counts', 'to all': each chapter was directly addressed to its intended audience, to the precise group to whom its ensuing regulations applied. This definitional project went into overdrive, in particular, in relation to contemporary monasticisms, as church councils and rulers alike accepted the Benedictine Rule – or rather, to adopt Albrecht Diem's important correction, Carolingian *interpretations* of the Benedictine Rule – as synonymous with monastic observances.² Those who lived within monastic communities but did not live according to this Rule were henceforth to live 'canonically' (according to the decisions, or canons, of church councils). In 816, in order to reduce the ambiguity of this newly formalised category, two florilegia (or collections) of canonical regulations were compiled and supplemented with various new chapters: these were to form the rule-texts for (male) canons and 'nuns who lived canonically'.³

To demarcate, delimit and define a uniform Benedictine 'monasticism', wholly separate from its canonical counterpart, has long been the goal scholars attributed to the so-called 'Carolingian monastic reform'.⁴ Such an ambitious definitional project was,

---

1 R. Kramer et al. (eds), *Monastic Communities and Canonical Clergy in the Carolingian World (780–840): Categorizing the Church* (Turnhout: Brepols, 2022); A. Diem, 'The Carolingians and the *Regula Benedicti*', in Dorine van Espelo et al. (eds), *Religious Franks: Religion and power in the Frankish Kingdoms: Studies in Honour of Mayke de Jong* (Manchester: Manchester University Press, 2016), pp. 243–61, here p. 244.
2 Diem, 'The Carolingians', pp. 243–61.
3 *Institutio canonicorum* and *Institutio sanctimonialium*, in A. Werminghoff (ed.), *MGH Conc.* 2.1 (Hanover: Hahn, 1906), no. 39, pp. 308–456.
4 See here especially the foundational work of Josef Semmler, whose contributions include J. Semmler, 'Traditio und Königsschutz', *Zeitschrift der Savigny-Stiftung für Rechtsgeschichte: Kanonistische Abteilung*, 45 (1959), 1–33; J. Semmler, 'Reichsidee und kirchliche Gesetzgebung bei Ludwig dem Frommen', *Zeitschrift für Kirchengeschichte*, 71 (1960), 37–65; J. Semmler, 'Mönche und Kanoniker im Frankenreich Pippins III. und Karls des Großen', in Max-Planck-Institut für Geschichte (ed.), *Untersuchungen zu Kloster und Stift* (Göttingen: Vandenhoeck & Ruprecht, 1980), pp. 78–111; J. Semmler, 'Iussit…princeps renovare…praecepta: Zur verfassungsrechtlichen Einordnung der Hochstifte und Abteien in der karolingischen Reichskirche',

of course, never fully realised in practice. For this reason, I will continue to use the terms 'monasticism' and 'monks' to encompass the full spectrum of communal religious life in what follows, thereby rejecting the narrower identification of 'monastic' with 'Benedictine'.[5] Indeed, Carolingian attempts to delimit categories necessarily existed in dynamic tension with messier external realities; to define and regulate *the* monastic life presupposed substantial differences in both monastic ideals and monastic praxis on the ground. Carolingian projects, insofar as they ever pursued uniformity as their goal, were predicated upon the lived experience of diversity.[6] After all, the first person to put the Benedictine Rule on the Carolingian agenda, Boniface, was himself an outsider: as a transplant to the late Merovingian/early Carolingian East, Boniface was confronted by church structures unfamiliar to his own Anglo-Saxon monastic formation.[7] The church councils convened under his aegis were the first to promote the Benedictine Rule as the standard for monastic observance on the continent, and one could argue that they did so precisely as a result of Boniface's outside perspective.[8] While Boniface's admonishments to observe the Benedictine Rule recur in later Carolingian church canons, we see a crescendo in such injunctions in the last quarter of the eighth century, at precisely the moment when the Carolingian world expanded beyond all recog-

---

in J. F. Angerer and J. Lenzenweger (eds), *Consuetudines monasticae: eine Festgabe für Kassius Hallinger aus Anlass seines 70. Geburtstages*, Studia Anselmiana 85 (Rome: Pontificio Ateneos S. Anselmo, 1982), pp. 97–124; J. Semmler, 'Benedictus II: una regula – una consuetudo', in W. Lourdaux and D. Verhelst (eds), *Benedictine Culture, 750–1050* (Leuven: Leuven University Press, 1983), pp. 1–49.

5 See here also the comments of Felten, *Vita religiosa*, p. 11.
6 See here R. Kramer, *Rethinking Authority in the Carolingian Empire: Ideals and Expectations during the Reign of Louis the Pious* (Amsterdam: Amsterdam University Press, 2019); see also Carine van Rhijn's introduction to this volume.
7 For the association of eighth-century Anglo-Saxons on the continent with the promotion of the Benedictine Rule more generally, see J. Palmer, *Anglo-Saxons in a Frankish World, 690–900* (Turnhout: Brepols, 2009), pp. 177–92; do note, however, Palmer's point that Boniface's Anglo-Saxon formation was not necessarily exclusively Benedictine, here pp. 185–7.
8 *MGH Conc.* 2.1, no. 1, c. 7, p. 4; no. 2, c. 1, pp. 6–7.

nition. Previously separate regional monasticisms, each with their own traditions, came together for the first time in the same polity, all bound together by loyalty to the same king. Practices were compared, and questions arose. 'Were there monks in Gaul, before the tradition of the rule of Saint Benedict came into these dioceses?' asked Charlemagne, evidently with some concern, in 811.[9] The question would never have occurred to his Neustrian (West Frankish) forebears, for the simple reason that they were not confronted with alternative regional monasticisms. Following the death of his son Louis the Pious in 840, and the division of the Carolingian empire into three kingdoms, such questions again receded.

In its early-medieval European context, the Carolingian world was exceptional for one simple reason: its scale. From the late eighth century, as the Carolingian polity grew, the horizons of western European monasticisms were correspondingly broadened. The diverse array of early medieval monasticisms were brought into conversation with each other for the first time. People, manuscripts and ideas were on the move; structures promoting such interchange, such as assemblies, councils and the court itself, especially in the period up to 840 – the period of this chapter's focus – formalised and gave institutional shape to these emerging networks. These horizontal networks of monasticisms, along with the rulers and bishops responsible for regulating them, were the moving force behind monastic regulations and the business of monastic definition: they were the main agents, in short, for what has been traditionally labelled 'Carolingian monastic reform'. These networks not only set the agenda but built consensus behind these new initiatives; in short, they were an integral part of the process by which these ideals were embedded, to greater or lesser degrees, within individual communities' praxis. These newly expanded horizontal monastic networks were not all-encompassing, however: they

---

9 A. Boretius (ed.), *MGH Capit.* 1 (Hanover: Hahn, 1883), no. 71, c. 12, p. 162: 'Inquirendum etiam, si in Gallia monachi fuissent, priusquam traditio regulae sancti Benedicti in has paroechias pervenisset'. See also *ibid.*, no. 72, c. 12, p. 164; see further R. Kramer, 'Monasticism, reform and authority in the Carolingian era', in A. I. Beach and I. Cochelin (eds), *The Cambridge History of Medieval Monasticism in the Latin West* (Cambridge: Cambridge University Press, 2020), pp. 432–49, here pp. 437–8.

were, by design, overwhelmingly male. And so too those changes identified by modern historians as 'Carolingian monastic reform' were applied overwhelmingly to male communities, while female communities were addressed with their own, explicitly gendered, set of prescriptions. There was no singular 'Carolingian monastic reform' for the simple reason (among many others) that there was no singular ideal of 'Carolingian monasticism': rather, like all other parts of Carolingian society, monasticisms were fundamentally and insurmountably gendered.

Gendered monastic identities

As Stuart Airlie wrote, 'office could de-gender'. He was writing of queenship, but the same point could be applied to monks.[10] At many points in the early medieval history of monasticisms, we see monastic models and practitioners transcending societal gender norms: we have 'virile' women (not to mention the *virago*, or 'female man'), transvestite and transgender (here particularly female to male) monks, 'double' monasteries and what Diem has described in terms of the creation of 'unisex' monastic models – rule-texts designed for one gender and then adapted or applied wholesale to the other.[11] Others have discussed monasticism in terms of a 'third gender', and indeed monastic expectations for both masculinity and femininity diverged, at times substantially, from their lay equivalents.[12] Gender

---

10 S. Airlie, 'Private bodies and the body politic in the divorce case of Lothar II', *Past & Present*, 161 (1998), 3–38, here 33.
11 A. Diem, 'The gender of the religious: wo/men and the invention of monasticism', in J. Bennet and R. Karras (eds), *The Oxford Handbook of Women and Gender in Medieval Europe* (Oxford: Oxford University Press, 2013), pp. 432–46.
12 For historiography on a monastic third gender, see J. A. McNamara, *Sisters in Arms: Catholic Nuns through Two Millennia* (Cambridge, MA: Harvard University Press, 1998), pp. 144–7; I. Réal, 'Nuns and monks at work: equality or distinction between the sexes? A study of Frankish monasteries from the sixth to the tenth century', in Beach and Cochelin (eds), *The Cambridge History of Medieval Monasticism*, pp. 258–77, here p. 259, note 3. While Réal herself argues that the lived experience of monasticism in this period largely reflected the expectations of 'binary gender categories',

historians have, quite rightly, mined early medieval monasticisms for examples of gender fluidity and flexibility. But here the Carolingian world comes up short: while 'virile' women still appear in hagiographical narratives, and while female monastic models were still adapted for male use and vice versa, the female and male religious were increasingly strictly demarcated in contemporary normative texts (separate ladders, separate trajectories).[13] In the Carolingian world, the practice of monasticism was becoming explicitly and pointedly gendered.

Historians have differed in their approaches to this issue. Some scholars, notably Jo Ann McNamara, Jane Schulenburg and more recently Steven Vanderputten, have addressed female monasticism as a largely discrete subject of analysis, while others have argued against such 'sequestering', instead arguing for a more integrated approach.[14] Yet analysing female and male monasticism as an integrated historical phenomenon likewise has its downfalls: disparities in evidence can lead to male voices being amplified, and one can inadvertently end up analysing a 'male-as-default' monasticism, in which extrapolations from male experiences are made to stand in as the interpretative scaffolding for lone female voices.

---

she raises the interesting point that female and male experiences converged most for monastic scholars: here p. 273.

13 For 'virile' women in Carolingian hagiography, see especially J. Smith, 'The problem of female sanctity in Carolingian Europe, c. 780–920', *Past & Present*, 146 (1995), 3–37, here 18–20. For the application of female monastic models for male use, and vice versa, in the Carolingian world, see F. Lifshitz, *Religious Women in Early Carolingian Francia: A Study of Manuscript Transmission and Monastic Culture* (New York: Fordham University Press, 2014), here especially pp. 177–8; A. Diem, 'Choreography and confession: the *Memoriale qualiter* and Carolingian monasticism', in Kramer et al. (eds), *Monastic Communities and Canonical Clergy*.

14 McNamara, *Sisters*; J. T. Schulenburg, *Forgetful of Their Sex: Female Sanctity and Society, ca. 500–1100* (Chicago, IL: University of Chicago Press, 1998); S. Vanderputten, *Dark Age Nunneries: The Ambiguous Identity of Female Monasticism, 850–1050* (Ithaca, NY: Cornell University Press, 2018). Contrast to the comments of R. Choy, *Intercessory Prayer and the Monastic Ideal in the Time of the Carolingian Reforms* (Oxford: Oxford University Press, 2016), pp. 22–3; Diem, 'The gender'; please note, however, that both of these excellent scholars avoid falling into the 'male-as-default' trap.

In the Carolingian world, by contrast, male-as-default thinking appears relatively rare; rather, gender was such a fundamental social category as to be embedded in all communication. 'To priests', 'to bishops', 'to monks and the entire clergy': the chapters of both capitularies and church councils not only made their intended audience very clear, but also very clearly gendered. Here, Latin, with its inflected (gendered) forms, undoubtedly lent a hand: grammatical gender was not merely an inherited artefact, but rather a structuring principle that both reflected and reinforced broader gendered attitudes (and one turns here to Antony Corbeill's aptly titled work on classical Latin, *Sexing the World*).[15] But such gendered designated audiences went well beyond sheer grammatical necessity. Take, for example, the following Latin terms for the female and male religious: *monacha, monachus*, and *canonica, canonicus* – morphological stems with gendered suffixes. *Monachus*, the male form, occurs frequently in Carolingian normative texts, to be identified with Benedictine monasticism and clearly differentiated from the newly emerged and frequently employed category of *canonicus* (canon, or cleric); other, more general categories which could (at various points) embrace either category, such as brothers (*fratres*), 'servants of God' (*servi Dei*) or 'monasteries of men' (*monasterii virorum*), appear less frequently. By contrast, *monacha*, the female corollary to the Benedictine *monachus*, surfaces only rarely. This term is employed more frequently in mid-eighth-century texts, before its correlation to Benedictine monasticism had been firmly established.[16] The term *canonica*, or 'canoness', is itself entirely absent – appearing only once, misspelt, as a scribal error (*canicarum*) to be corrected back to its male form (*canonicorum*); indeed, the morpheme *canonic-* is only ever applied to female communities in its ungendered, adverbial form (canonically, *canonice*) as part of an

---

15 A. Corbeill, *Sexing the World: Grammatical Gender and Biological Sex in Ancient Rome* (Princeton, NJ: Princeton University Press, 2015).
16 This discussion of terminology can be confirmed by a quick survey of the MGH edition of Carolingian capitularies (up to 840). For *monacha* (which should in any case be taken as non-specific before the late eighth century), see *MGH Capit.* 1 no. 14, c. 20, p. 36; no. 21, p. 52; no. 89, c. 3, p. 189; no. 175, c. 1, p. 358; A. Boretius and V. Krause (eds), *MGH Capit.* 2 (Hanover: Hahn, 1897), no. 196, c. 53, p. 42; *MGH Conc.* 2.1, no. 24, c. 29, p. 211.

Gender and horizontal networks 39

additional clause to describe women's way of life.[17] Instead, the preferred term for female religious, whether Benedictine ('monastic') or canonical, was the unspecific *sanctimonialis* (translated hereafter as 'nun'), employed alongside the equally non-descriptive *nonna* (nun) or *puella* (generally *monasterium puellarum*, or 'monastery of girls'), *ancilla* (generally *ancilla Dei*, or 'maidservant of God') or *virgo* (*virgo Deo sacrata* or 'virgin consecrated to God'), among other terms.[18]

Here, we encounter what Vanderputten has identified as the ambiguity of female religious identities: contemporary usage highlighted their gender and religious vocation, but not the form that that religious vocation took.[19] While men were largely discussed in

---

17 For this, see Erfurt, Forschungsbibliothek Gotha, Memb. I 84, 402 v, available online at https://nbn-resolving.org/urn:nbn:de:urmel-f72988ea-e48d-4855-b3f4-12e08774fc810 (accessed 31 March 2022); *MGH Capit.* 2, no. 196, c. 53, pp. 42–3. I am grateful to the anonymous reviewer for this excellent point, among many others. Interestingly, there are references to the *regula canonicorum et canonicarum*, e.g. *MGH Capit.* 1, no. 138, c. 3, p. 276, but even this chapter refers to *sanctimoniales* when discussing actual women (as opposed to a designation for the rule for canonesses).

18 For *sanctimonialis*, see *MGH Capit.* 1, no. 33, cc. 18, 20, 33, 40, pp. 95, 97–8; no. 35, cc. 34–5, p. 103; no. 72, c. 13, p. 164; no. 105, c. 1, p. 215; no. 138, c. 3, p. 276; no. 149, c. 1, p. 302; no. 150, c. 10, p. 305; no. 158, c. 6, p. 319; no. 169, pp. 341–2; no. 179, c. 13, p. 369; *MGH Capit.* 2, no. 196, cc. 16, 30, 50, 53, pp. 34, 38, 42–3; no. 203, c. 6, p. 66; no. 205, c. 5, p. 73; no. 206, c. 8, p. 76; *MGH Conc.* 2.1, no. 24, cc. 2, 22, 27–8, pp. 207, 210–11; for *nonna*, see *MGH Capit.* 1, no. 10, c. 6, pp. 25–6; no. 11, c. 1, pp. 27–8; no. 23, c. 19, p. 63; no. 55, c. 1, p. 142; no. 127, p. 249; *Admonitio Generalis*, ed. and trans. H. Mordek et al., *Die Admonitio Generalis Karls des Grossen*, MGH Fontes iuris 16 (Hanover: Hahn, 2012), c. 17, p. 192; for *puella* (=*monasterium puellarum*), see *MGH Capit.* 1, no. 33, c. 18, p. 95; no. 154, c. 10, p. 313; no. 169, p. 341; *MGH Capit.* 2, no. 196, c. 53, p. 43; for *ancilla* (=*ancilla Dei*), see *MGH Capit.* 1, no. 10, cc. 6–7, pp. 25–6; no. 12, c. 3, p. 29; no. 14, c. 11, p. 35; no. 72, c. 13, p. 164; for *virgo* (=*virgo Deo sacrata*), see *MGH Capit.* 1, no. 35, c. 20, p. 103; no. 138, c. 25, p. 279; *Admonitio generalis*, cc. 40, 52, pp. 200, 206. For this point, see also Felten, *Vita religiosa*, pp. 33, 60–4; T. Schilp, *Norm und Wirklichkeit religiöser Frauengemeinschaften im Frühmittelalter* (Göttingen: Vandenhoeck & Ruprecht, 1998), pp. 17, 54, 64–6; Vanderputten, *Dark Age Nunneries*, p. 21.

19 Vanderputten, *Dark Age Nunneries*, here especially pp. 18–22; see here also McNamara, *Sisters*, pp. 178–9.

capitularies and conciliar chapters as monks or canons, women were discussed as unspecified nuns first, and as monastic or canonical thereafter, if at all; their way of life (*conversatio*) was denoted by an adverb or an additional clause ('quae regulariter vivant', 'quae canonice vivant') as opposed to being expressed through the original identifying noun. Often, though, women's 'Benedictine' or 'canonical' status was not mentioned at all. One can point to chapter 20 of the 813 Council of Mainz which refers to 'canons or monks and nuns'; here, the vocation of men was specified while that of women remained ambiguous.[20] This disparity in the conceptualisation of the female and male religious was made even more clear in a chapter discussing the physical arrangement of cloisters in the conciliar acts of the Council of Aachen in 836:

> Therefore the manner [in which this is enforced] ought to be according to the discipline of their congregations, that is so that [male] canons may live religiously according to what is contained in that book, in which their way of life is collected; [male] monks should live according to the rule given by the blessed Benedict unanimously, insofar as it is possible, and they should follow the regular life of their religion in all things. Nuns [*sanctimoniales*] should live according to that, which is appropriate to the fragility of their sex, and they should be given over to their religion with all diligence.[21]

---

20 *MGH Conc.* 2.1, no. 36, c. 20, pp. 266–7: 'canonici vel monachi atque nonnanes'.
21 A. Werminghoff (ed.), *MGH Conc.* 2.2 (Hanover: Hahn, 1908), no. 56, c. 39, pp. 713–14: 'Modus autem erga ipsarum congregationum disciplinam hic esse debet, id est ut canonici secundum id, quod continetur in libro, qui de eorum vita collectus est, religiose conversentur; monachi vero secundum traditam a beato Benedicto regulam unanimiter, quantumcumque posse est, cuiusque religionis regularem vitam in omnibus sectentur. Sanctimoniales denique secundum id, quod earundem sexus fragilitati congruit, religioni cum omni diligentia subdantur.' See here also Vanderputten, *Dark Age Nunneries*, p. 26. For further evidence of the 'blurring' of these female categories, one could point to the incorporation of a female version of the *Memoriale qualiter* (a text associated with the promotion of male Benedictine observance) into the text of the *Institutio sanctimonialium* in one manuscript copy, as described in Diem, 'Choreography'; cf. A. Werminghoff, 'Die Beschlüsse des Aachener Concils im Jahre 816', *Neues Archiv der Gesellschaft für ältere Deutsche Geschichtskunde zur Beförderung einer Gesamtausgabe der Quellenschriften deutscher Geschichten des Mittelalters*, 27:3 (1901),

Here, the frequently invoked 'fragility' of the female sex transcended the boundary of monastic and canonical observance, as applied to male communities. The distinction between 'monastic' and 'canonical', so integral to the identities of the male religious, was deemed to be less salient for women.[22]

This gendered conceptualisation of monasticism was not merely a feature of the terminology; rather, it was further reflected in the organisation of contemporary capitularies and conciliar chapters. To be sure, these could be, and sometimes were, addressed to mixed-sex religious and their leaders (e.g. female and male monks or canons, abbots and abbesses).[23] More often, however, male monks, canons and the ambiguous category of *sanctimoniales*, or nuns, were dealt with in their own chapters, even in cases when the prescriptions applied were largely identical.[24] Even more interestingly, the internal organisation of these capitulary and conciliar texts can at times reveal a distinct conceptual space for the female religious. Take, for example, the chapters associated with the 794 assembly at Frankfurt, where male (Benedictine) monasticism largely forms

---

605–76, here 636–7. Diem, however, puts forward the appealing hypothesis that an earlier (now lost) version of the *Memoriale qualiter* may have been intended for female communities, including those which followed the *Regula cuiusdam ad virgines*, and that this text was later adapted to be applied to male Benedictine communities. In this case, this manuscript may instead represent a local attempt at harmonising the newly codified *Institutio sanctimonialium* with this existing model for female monastic observances, the latter of which was also adapted for application within male Benedictine communities.

22 This argument has been capably put forward in Vanderputten, *Dark Age Nunneries*, here especially pp. 27–8; see also Schilp, *Norm und Wirklichkeit*, pp. 24, 213–14.

23 For the treatment of abbesses, contrast to J. Nelson, 'Alcuin's letters sent from Francia to Anglo-Saxon and Frankish women religious', in A. J. Langlands and R. Lavelle (eds), *The Land of the English Kin: Studies in Wessex and Anglo-Saxon England in Honour of Professor Barbara Yorke*, Brill's Series on the Early Middle Ages, 26 (Leiden: Brill, 2020), pp. 355–72, here pp. 356–9; here, Nelson argues that abbesses were approached in broadly similar terms to their male counterparts in Carolingian capitularies.

24 For example, see *MGH Capit.* 1, no. 33, cc. 17–18, pp. 94–5.

the focus of chapters 11–19.[25] Female monasticism and abbesses, meanwhile, are only dealt with in chapters 46–7, with a variety of different concerns addressed in the intervening chapters.[26] In the 813 Council of Chalon-sur-Saône, issues surrounding male monasticism were largely subsumed into wider discussions (for example in chapters 6, 7, 12 and 24).[27] Only one chapter, chapter 22, addressed male monasticism directly, declaring the issue to be largely a moot point insofar as the tenets of male monasticism had already been definitively established by the Rule of Saint Benedict:

> Concerning abbots and monks, we will write only briefly, because almost all the regular monasteries established in these regions profess themselves to live according to the Rule of Saint Benedict; the teachings of Saint Benedict reveal in all ways how they ought to live.[28]

Female Benedictine monasticism, by contrast, is not only passed over in this chapter, but is entirely absent from the conciliar acts, save perhaps for a generic injunction regarding female monasteries of unspecified observance in chapter 52 (abbesses ought to be created who will guard their flock with great religion and sanctity, women as 'sacred vessels in the ministry of the Lord', etc.).[29] A separate booklet of admonition (*admonitiunculas*) addressed to canonical nuns, meanwhile, is appended in chapters 53–66, clearly demarcated from the rest of the text through explicit signposting in chapters 53 and 66 (before a short general conclusion in

---

25 For these chapters, see the important recent article of Takurô Tsuda: T. Tsuda, 'On the so called Capitulary of Frankfurt and communication between Charlemagne and Bavaria at the end of the eighth century', *Spicilegium*, 3 (2019), available online at www.spicilegium.net/03_tsuda.html (accessed 21 February 2022).
26 *MGH Conc.* 2.1, no. 19G, cc. 11–19, 24, 46–7, pp. 168–71.
27 *MGH Conc.* 2.1, no. 37, cc. 6–7, 12, 24, pp. 275–6, 278. For the 813 councils, see Kramer, *Rethinking Authority*, pp. 70–91.
28 *MGH Conc.* 2.1, no. 37, c. 22, p. 278: 'De abbatibus vero et monachis idcirco hic pauca scribimus, quia paene omnia monasteria regularia in his regionibus constituta secundum regulam sancti Benedicti se vivere fatentur; quae beati Benedicti documenta per omnia demonstrant, qualiter eis vivendum sit.' See here also Kramer, *Rethinking Authority*, pp. 85–6.
29 *MGH Conc.* 2.1, no. 37, c. 52, p. 284: 'vasa sancta in ministerio Domini'.

Gender and horizontal networks 43

chapter 67); this forms the last, and only discrete, section of the conciliar acts.[30]

This separate treatment of female and male monasticism is taken to its logical conclusion in the Aachen councils of 816–17, which have typically been read as the culmination of the 'Carolingian monastic reform' and hence been interpreted as decisive for the 'bifurcation' of early medieval monasticisms into two set paths: one Benedictine ('religious'), the other canonical ('secular').[31] More recently, Rutger Kramer has offered an important reappraisal to this interpretation, arguing that these councils, far from being a definitive beginning or end point, instead should be viewed as contributing to an ongoing process of systematisation, building upon a pre-existing conceptual division between canonical and Benedictine monasticism (as opposed to imposing it *ex novo*).[32] Yet, looking closer, this twofold division, was in fact threefold, insofar as these councils continued to subscribe to specifically gendered conceptions of monasticism, and went so far as to compile separate rule-texts for both canons and 'nuns who live canonically' (the *Institutio canonicorum* and the *Institutio sanctimonialium* respectively).[33] The documents concerned with Benedictine observance, meanwhile, were exclusively addressed to *male* Benedictine monks; female Benedictine nuns simply do not feature.[34] I would argue that this was not a case of accidental 'male-as-default' phrasing – which is, in any case, far less prevalent in medieval Latin than in modern English. Rather, the absence of chapters discussing Benedictine women suggests one

---

30 *Ibid.*, cc. 53–66, pp. 284–5. See here also Schilp, *Norm und Wirklichkeit*, pp. 52–8; Vanderputten, *Dark Age Nunneries*, pp. 16–17.
31 *MGH Conc.* 2.1, nos 39–40, pp. 308–466; J. Semmler (ed.), *Legislatio Aquisgranensis*, in *Corpus consuetudinem monasticarum I: Initia consuetudinis Benedictinae, consuetudines saeculi octavi et noni* (Sieburg: Schmitt, 1963), pp. 423–582.
32 Kramer, *Rethinking Authority*, pp. 59–121; see here also Schilp, *Norm und Wirklichkeit*, especially pp. 24–5, 46–7, 57–8.
33 *MGH Conc.* 2.1, no. 39, pp. 308–456.
34 *Legislatio Aquisgranensis*, nos 18, 20–1, pp. 433–6, 451–81. Do note, however, that the text of the *Memoriale qualiter*, which is closely associated with these reforms, does appear to have been applied to female communities, albeit in combination with the *Institutio sanctimonialium*; see note 21, pp. 40–1; Diem, 'Choreography'.

of two possibilities: first, that the council was unconcerned with regulating female Benedictine life; or, second, that they viewed the gender of female nuns as far more determinative than their mode of profession, to the extent that they viewed the *Institutio sanctimonialium*, a text which has generally regarded as having been compiled specifically for canonical nuns, as applicable to both female canonical and Benedictine communities – both of which were, for all intents and purposes, simply subsumed within the broader (and more salient) category of female communities.[35] If the latter, these councils may be seen to anticipate the 836 pronouncement of the Council of Aachen: male canons are to follow the *Institutio canonicorum*, male Benedictines are to follow the Benedictine Rule and (unspecified) nuns are to follow a way of life appropriate to the fragility of their sex.[36]

These examples of gendered monastic identities are in no way exhaustive. One can further turn to Benedict of Aniane's compendia of rule-texts, in which rules for nuns are assigned to their own discrete section.[37] Despite the continued application of the Benedictine Rule (a rule written for men) to both female and male communities, alongside other scattered instances, any sense of a 'unisex' monastic model, which Diem so persuasively argues for in the pre-Carolingian period, appears to be extremely limited in this later context.[38] By and large, Carolingian authors did not think in terms of a degendered 'monastic identity' which could be applied interchangeably to men or women.

---

[35] For the unsuitability of these categories to describe female communal life in this early period, see Schilp, *Norm und Wirklichkeit*, pp. 195–7, 214.

[36] See pp. 40–1. Here, it is worth further noting that a later feminised version of the Old English Benedictine Rule borrowed directly from the *Institutio sanctimonialium* (or excerpts thereof), suggesting, once again, that parts of this model were viewed as applicable to female nuns more broadly (irrespective of specifically 'canonical' status): see R. Jayatilaka, 'The Old English Benedictine Rule: writing for women and men', *Anglo-Saxon England*, 32 (2003), 147–87, here 164–6. For the similarities between the *Institutio sanctimonialium* and the Benedictine Rule, see further Schilp, *Norm und Wirklichkeit*, pp. 118–21.

[37] Diem, 'The gender', p. 442; McNamara, *Sisters*, pp. 155–6.

[38] Diem, 'The gender', pp. 432–46, here especially p. 444.

Widening the gender gap

Carolingian authors conceptualised female and male monasticism as discrete and separate entities and addressed them as such. And, in practice, female and male monasteries *were* different, and many of these differences preceded the Carolingians' rise to power. Nuns were not consecrated, and hence were barred from officiating mass and other sacraments; this made them reliant on small communities of dependent male clerics, whose very presence could threaten to mar their reputation for virginity and chastity (a more central concern for nuns than for their male counterparts).[39] Nuns' ability to manage and defend their propertied interests was restricted by societal norms and restrictions to their legal agency, thereby necessitating still further reliance on male advocates and managers; further compounding this, female communities were often smaller in scale and more explicitly 'familial' in their focus, and hence more directly reliant upon elite family fortunes.[40] Such differences were significant and would only become more so in the course of the Carolingian period, as more male monks took on sacramental grades and as the importance of monastic intercessory masses grew.[41] Yet the widening gap between female and male monasticism in the Carolingian period was not simply the result of accident; it was in many ways the intended outcome of purposefully gendered injunctions.

Take, for example, the Aachen councils of 816–17, which produced 'canonical' rule-texts for female and male communities as well as additional chapters on the interpretation of the Benedictine Rule

---

39 For the emphasis on *female* virginity and chastity, see M. Eber, 'Loose canonesses? (Non-)gendered aspects of the Aachen *Institutiones*', in Kramer et al. (eds), *Monastic Communities and Canonical Clergy*, pp. 217–39; Réal, 'Nuns and monks', pp. 268–9; Schulenburg, *Forgetful of Their Sex*, pp. 127–75.
40 For the familial focus of Carolingian female monasticism, see especially Smith, 'Female sanctity', 25–8.
41 Choy, *Intercessory Prayer*; G. Constable, 'Carolingian monasticism as seen in the Plan of St Gall', in W. Fałkowski and Y. Sassier (eds), *Le monde carolingien: bilan, perspectives, champs de recherches: actes du colloque international de Poitiers, Centre d'études supérieures de civilization médiévale, 18–20 novembre 2004* (Turnhout: Brepols, 2009), pp. 199–217, here pp. 208–10.

for male communities. I will largely pass over the canonical texts here, as these works have already been approached from a gendered perspective in excellent scholarship, namely Thomas Schilp's path-breaking 1998 monograph and a forthcoming article by Michael Eber; while Eber identifies some common 'non-gendered' ground between these two texts, there are still many areas in which these two rule compilations, both of which sought to delineate the bounds of a 'canonical' life, diverged dramatically in practice.[42] Indeed, as Schilp persuasively argues, the *Institutio sanctimonialium*, far from simply being a 'translation [of the *Institutio canonicorum*] into the feminine' (a conclusion reached by its early-twentieth-century editor), draws on a long line of attempts to regulate specifically *female* monastic practice, and as such is emphatically gender-specific.[43] Yet, for all these divergences, at least a rule-text of sorts was produced for nuns who lived canonically; the same cannot be said for female Benedictine nuns, who were simply not addressed or even acknowledged by the councils.[44]

The chapters produced by these councils for male Benedictines were explicitly male gendered, and not just in the terminology employed. Conciliar acts from 816 discuss shaving, tonsuring and the provision of garments including a *rochum* (a specifically male-gendered garment that nuns were expressly forbidden from wearing); they further discuss monks' travel, the placement of monks at monastic dependencies (or 'cells') and the reception of guests within the refectory, all of which were expressly and repeatedly forbidden to female communities.[45] Similar concerns recur in the

---

42 Schilp, *Norm und Wirklichkeit*; Eber, 'Loose canonesses?'.
43 Schilp, *Norm und Wirklichkeit*, here especially pp. 36 and 59 (for the quotation), also pp. 48–58, 128–44; for the original comment of the editor (as cited by Schilp), see Werminghoff, 'Die Beschlüsse', 634: 'Uebersetzung ins Weibliche'. See also Eber, 'Loose canonesses?'.
44 For this point, see also Diem, 'Choreography'; Felten, *Vita religiosa*, footnote 147, p. 33; S. F. Wemple, *Women in Frankish Society: Marriage and the Cloister, 500 to 900* (Philadelphia, PA: University of Pennsylvania Press, 1981), p. 169.
45 *Legislatio Aquisgranensis*, no. 18, cc. 12, 14, 19, 24, pp. 435–6; no. 20, cc. 8, 13, 20, 24–5, 32, pp. 459–60, 462–6. See here also K. Bodarwé, 'Eine Männerregel für Frauen. Die Adaption der Benediktsregel im 9. und 10. Jahrhundert', in G. Melville and A. Müller (eds), *Female* vita religiosa

817 conciliar acts, which address such issues as shaving, monks' travel, the reception of guests, monastic cells and the residence of non-monks in the cloister.[46] Such issues were not relevant to either female bodies or female communities, the latter due to frequently expressed contemporary expectations of – if not the reality of – strict claustration. One could, of course, quite reasonably question the importance of these councils to Carolingian interpretations of the Benedictine Rule. The conciliar chapters agreed upon were, by and large, fiddling around the margins, sometimes simply updating this Mediterranean monastic rule for a largely North European audience, for example substituting measures of beer for wine, or allowing for some additional winter garments.[47] Larger Carolingian divergences from the Rule were, by contrast, deemphasised: rulers' routine appointment of abbots, including lay abbots, for example, was passed over without comment.[48] Yet the importance of these councils – or, at the very least the significance that they have been allotted in modern scholarship – can be traced back much more to the sense that these councils cemented a binary vision of communal life, in which one could only be Benedictine (as per the councils' interpretation of the Rule) or canonical (as per the councils' newly established canonical rules). Less attention has been paid to the fact that these councils only addressed male Benedictines, and hence only applied this binary classification of monastic and canonical – widely regarded as *the* linchpin of 'Carolingian monastic reform' – to men.[49]

The Aachen councils of 816–17 occupy a central place in scholarship, and for good reason: they represent the most comprehensive

---

between Late Antiquity and the High Middle Ages: Structures, Developments and Spatial Contexts, Vita regularis 47 (Zürich: Lit Verlag, 2011), pp. 235–72, here pp. 235–7. For the prohibition on nuns wearing *rocho*, see *MGH Conc.* 2.1, no. 24, c. 28, p. 211; see also Schulenburg, *Forgetful of Their Sex*, p. 163; Vanderputten, *Dark Age Nunneries*, pp. 23–4.

46 *Legislatio Aquisgranensis*, no. 21, cc. 2, 4, 11, 25, 29, pp. 473–5, 478–9.
47 See, for example, *Legislatio Aquisgranensis*, no. 18, cc. 19, 28, p. 436; no. 20, c. 20, pp. 462–3.
48 See here also Diem, 'The Carolingians', pp. 252–3.
49 The same could also be said of these councils' implementation: take, for example, the following Italian capitulary of Lothar: *MGH Capit.* 1, no. 160, pp. 321–2.

treatment of monasticism in both its Benedictine and canonical forms, as well as the closest engagement with written rule-texts, in the Carolingian period. Yet, as Kramer's work makes clear, they fit into a much longer series of empire-wide conversations on both the differentiation of Benedictine and canonical observances and on regulations surrounding monasticism more generally – and, more specifically into a much longer series of gendered conversations, the basic contours of which can be reconstructed from capitularies and conciliar chapters.[50] These of course include various 'unisex' prescriptions which applied to both female and male communities, but the majority of chapters addressed to monastic communities diverged along gender lines.

Take, for example, regulations surrounding entry into monastic life. Carolingian regulations address various situations surrounding the tonsuring of men; occasionally, chapters addressed female and male entry into monastic life (denoted by tonsuring and veiling) side by side.[51] Yet such scattered treatment of this issue for men stands in stark contrast to the vast quantity of ink spilt on restrictions on female veiling. According to a wide swathe of capitulary and conciliar chapters, women were not to be veiled under the age of twenty-five; without the permission of their husband, parent or (male) guardian; involuntarily; or soon after becoming a widow; they were likewise not to be veiled by abbesses or to veil themselves.[52] Here, the veiling of widows, in particular, provoked strong language; one council addressing the veiling of noble widows went so far as to invoke 'imperial terror and power'(!).[53] The emphasis on

---

50 Kramer, *Rethinking Authority*, pp. 59–121.
51 For specifically male restrictions on tonsuring, see, for example, *MGH Conc.* 2.1, no. 24, c. 44, p. 212. For examples which treat male and female entry into monastic life side by side, see, for example, *MGH Capit.* 1, no. 14, c. 11, p. 35; no. 138, c. 20, p. 278; no. 136, c. 21, p. 285; *MGH Conc.* 2.1, Appendix ad Concilia a. 813 B, c. 12, pp. 298–9.
52 *MGH Capit.* 1, no. 15, cc. 5, 14, 16, p. 38; no. 16, c. 4, p. 40; no. 35, c. 19, p. 103; no. 42, c. 6, p. 119; no. 43, c. 14, p. 122; no. 138, cc. 21, 26, p. 278–9; *Admonitio generalis*, cc. 46, 59, 74, pp. 202, 208, 228; *MGH Capit.* 2, no. 186, c. 2, p. 7; no. 196, cc. 47–50, p. 42; *MGH Conc.* 2.1, no. 38, cc. 27–8, p. 290; *MGH Conc.* 2.2, no. 50, cc. 40–44, 74, pp. 637–9, 672–3. See also McNamara, *Sisters*, p. 152; Wemple, *Women*, pp. 166–7.
53 *MGH Conc.* 2.2, no. 50, c, 74, pp. 673: 'terror imperialis atque potestas'.

abbesses not veiling women is mirrored by further restrictions on women assuming quasi-sacerdotal functions at the same time that even more male monks were assuming priestly office: women were not to go to the altar, even to assist or to prepare the space, and abbesses were not to give blessings.[54]

The starkest difference in regulations on female and male monasticism, however, concerned claustration – the extent to which female and male communities were confined within the 'cloister' and their contact with the outside 'lay' or secular world restricted.[55] Here, gendered differences can, in part, be viewed as the result of male canons' active involvement in pastoral ministry – a role which was not extended to women who lived canonically. Yet such differences also apply to Benedictine monks, who were not (in theory) meant to serve such functions; once again, gender was the main determinant. Regulations addressed to female communities lay great emphasis upon strict enclosure. Abbesses were not to leave their monasteries, or only with certain restrictions, such as when requested by the king or emperor himself; the enclosure of nuns was by contrast largely assumed rather than expressly stated.[56] The rest of the world was also locked out: lay contact with cloistered women was forbidden, and extensive regulations were imposed on male priests

---

54 See here, for example, *MGH Capit.* 1, no. 35, c. 6, p. 102; *Admonitio generalis*, cc. 17, 74, pp. 192, 228; *MGH Capit.* 2, no. 196, c. 52, p. 42; *MGH Conc.* 2.2, no. 50, cc. 41, 45, pp. 637–40. See also Lifshitz, *Religious Women*, pp. 7–8, 185–92; McNamara, *Sisters*, p. 153; Vanderputten, *Dark Age Nunneries*, pp. 23–4; Wemple, *Women*, pp. 143, 169.

55 This has received ample attention in scholarship: see, for example, Lifshitz, *Religious Women*, pp. 11–13; McNamara, *Sisters*, pp. 155–9; Réal, 'Nuns and monks', pp. 266–8; Schilp, *Norm und Wirklichkeit*, pp. 68–9, 85–90, 98–9; J. T. Schulenburg, 'Strict active enclosure and its effects on the female monastic experience (500–1100)', in J. A. Nichols and L. T. Shank (eds), *Medieval Religious Women I: Distant Echoes* (Kalamazoo, MI: Cistercian Publications, 1984), pp. 51–86, here especially pp. 56–9; Smith, 'Female sanctity', 31–2; Vanderputten, *Dark Age Nunneries*, pp. 5–7, 23; Wemple, *Women*, pp. 168–9.

56 *MGH Capit.* 1, no. 14, c. 6, p. 34; no. 20, c. 3, p. 47; no. 23, c. 19, p. 63; *MGH Conc.* 2.1, no. 24, c. 27, p. 210; no. 36, c. 13, p. 264; no. 37, c. 57, p. 284; no. 38, c. 30, p. 290; see also Schilp, *Norm und Wirklichkeit*, pp. 68–9.

who entered female communities to perform priestly offices.⁵⁷ By contrast, the regulations addressed to male communities, whether Benedictine or canonical, assume extensive engagement with the world beyond the cloister. In contrast to the engrained expectation of female enclosure, male monks had to be enjoined not to bring their issues directly to the palace (as indeed groups of monks from Fulda, Moyenmoutier and Saint-Denis are attested as doing); at one point, Frankish monks staying in various Italian monasteries had to be instructed to return to their own monasteries where they had made their profession.⁵⁸ Monks were repeatedly instructed not to engage in secular affairs, not to attend public courts, not to go to the palace, not to enter taverns, not to attend the gatherings of laymen and not to 'wander' without permission; they were only to be sent out on business once they had grown accustomed to monastic life.⁵⁹

---

57 *MGH Capit.* 1, no. 33, c. 18, p. 95; no. 42, c. 5, p. 119; no. 78, c. 5, p. 173; no. 79, c. 4, p. 175; *MGH Capit.* 2, no. 196, c. 53, pp. 42–3; *MGH Conc.* 2.1, no. 21, c. 12, pp. 193–4; no. 24, c. 21, p. 210; no. 34, c. 7, p. 251; no. 36, c. 26, p. 268; no. 37, cc. 60, 63, p. 285; no. 38, c. 29, p. 290; *MGH Conc.* 2.2, no. 50, c. 46, pp. 640–1; see also Schilp, *Norm und Wirklichkeit*, pp. 85–90.

58 For the monks of Fulda, see J. Raaijmakers, *The Making of the Monastic Community of Fulda, c. 744–c. 900* (Cambridge: Cambridge University Press, 2012), pp. 119–22; for Moyenmoutier, see Kramer, 'Monasticism', p. 432; for the petition of the community of Saint-Denis, see I. Rembold, 'The "apostates" of Saint-Denis: reforms, dissent, and Carolingian monasticism', in Kramer et al. (eds), *Monastic Communities and Canonical Clergy*, pp. 301–22; for the continued entanglement of male monasteries with secular matters more generally, see R. Kramer, 'Teaching emperors: transcending the boundaries of Carolingian monastic communities', in E. Hovden et al. (eds), *Meaning of Community across Medieval Eurasia* (Leiden: Brill, 2016), pp. 309–37. For prohibitions on monks appealing directly to the palace, see *MGH Capit.* 2, no. 196, c. 26, pp. 37–8; *MGH Conc.* 2.2, no. 50, c. 81, p. 675; for Frankish monks in Italian monasteries, see *MGH Capit.* 1, no. 94, c. 2, p. 198. One can further point to the extent of interchange between monks and their wider social world envisaged in the Plan of St. Gall: see Constable, 'Carolingian monasticism', pp. 215–17.

59 For prohibitions on monks engaging in secular affairs, attending public courts or going to the palace, see *MGH Capit.* 1, no. 14, c. 18, p. 36; no. 23, c. 30, p. 64; no. 33, c. 17, pp. 94–5; no. 35, c. 9, p. 102; no. 38, c. 17, p. 111; *Admonitio generalis*, cc. 23, 71, pp. 194, 224–6; *MGH Conc.* 2.1, no. 19G, c. 11, p. 168; no. 24, c. 25, p. 210; no. 35, cc. 29–30, p. 256; no. 36,

The fact that these regulations are all framed as negative statements should not distract us from the much wider orbit that the male religious inhabited: male monks, whether canonical or Benedictine, were not expected to be entirely enclosed within the bounds of the cloister. While female monasteries existed largely isolated from wider monastic communities, abbots and male monks could travel between monasteries and attend councils and synods – they were, in short, afforded access to wider, horizontal, male monastic networks, with all the attendant implications for their own monastic praxis.

Old boys' clubs

While Carolingian abbesses remained at a remove from all assemblies, councils and synods, their presence expressly forbidden, abbots and male monks were crucial participants in these discussions.[60] Take, for example, the account of the 802 council at Aachen given in the *Annals of Lorsch*:

> In the same synod he likewise gathered together all the abbots and monks who were there present, and they formed an assembly of their own; and the rule of the holy father Benedict was read out and learned men expounded it before the abbots and monks. And then he issued a command of general application to all the bishops, abbots, priests, deacons and the entire clergy that as clerics they were to live in accordance with the canons, each in his own station, whether in

---

cc. 12, 14, pp. 264–5; no. 37, c. 11, p. 276; *MGH Conc.* 2.2, no. 56, c. 26, p. 711. For prohibitions on entering taverns and/or drinking without permission, see *Admonitio generalis*, c. 14, p. 190; *MGH Conc.* 2.1, no. 19G, c. 19, p. 168; no. 35, c. 26, p. 256; no. 36, c. 12, p. 264. For the prohibition on attending the gatherings of laymen, see *MGH Conc.* 2.1, no. 24, c. 24, p. 210. For restrictions on monks wandering or going out on monastic business, see *MGH Capit.* 1, no. 14, c. 10, p. 35; no. 33, c. 17, pp. 94–5; *Admonitio generalis*, c. 71, pp. 224–6; *MGH Conc.* 2.1, no. 35, c. 25, p. 256; no. 36, c. 12, p. 264. See here also Schulenburg, 'Strict active enclosure', pp. 58–9. It should also be noted that *MGH Capit.* 1, no, 38, cited earlier, has been variously categorised as a conciliar text, a capitulary, an episcopal capitulary, or a formulary text: see here the helpful summary of R. Pokorny, *MGH Capit. episc.* 3 (Hanover: Hahn, 1995), p. 206.

60 Cf. Schilp, *Norm und Wirklichkeit*, p. 169.

cathedral or in a monastery or in any of the holy churches, as the holy fathers laid down; and that they were to correct in accordance with the precepts of the canons whatever faults or shortcomings might appear in the clergy or the people; and that they were to have corrected in accordance with the rule of St Benedict whatever might be done in monasteries or among monks in contravention of that same rule of St Benedict.[61]

Abbots and male monks are routinely attested as attending both councils and assemblies, sometimes forming their own *turma*, or column, to discuss matters among themselves.[62] Moreover, many of the archbishops and bishops in attendance at such bodies would have themselves been trained within a monastic setting and taken Benedictine vows; accordingly, their perspectives would also have been shaped by their monastic identities. By contrast, I have only been able to identify one instance in which representatives of female monastic communities are enjoined to attend such empire-wide discussions: the *Legislationis capitulum*, issued c. 826 by Louis the

---

61 For the translation, see P. D. King (trans.), *Charlemagne: Translated Sources* (Kendal: 1987), p. 145. For the original text, see *Annales Laureshamenses*, ed. G. H. Pertz, *MGH SS* 1 (Hanover: Hahn, 1826), 802, p. 39: 'Similiter in ipso synodo congregavit universos abbates et monachos qui ibi aderant, et ipsi inter se conventum faciebant, et legerunt regulam sancti patris Benedicti, et eum tradiderunt sapientes in conspectu abbatum et monachorum; et tunc iussio eius generaliter super omnes episcopos, abbates, presbyteros, diacones seu universo clero facta est, ut unusquisque in loco suo iuxta constitutionem sanctorum patrum, sive in episcopatibus seu in monasteriis aut per universas sanctas ecclesias, ut canonici iuxta canones viverunt, et quicquid in clero aut in populo de culpis aut de negligentiis apparuerit, iuxta canonum auctoritate emendassent; et quicquid in monasteriis seu in monachis contra regula Benedicti factum fuisset, hoc ipsud iuxta ipsam regulam sancti Benedicti emendare fecissent.'
62 Take, for example, *MGH Conc.* 2.1, no. 22, p. 196, no. 36, pp. 259–60; there are many further attestations of abbots and male monks at such bodies, such as in Ardo, *Vita Benedicti Anianensis*, ed. W. Kettemann, 'Subsidia Anianensia: Überlieferungs- und textgeschichtliche Untersuchungen zur Geschichte Witiza-Benedikts, seines Klosters Aniane und zur sogenannten "anianischen Reform"' (unpublished PhD dissertation, Gerhard-Mercator-Universität – Gesamthochschule Duisburg, 2000), pp. 139–223, here c. 36, p. 199; a translation is available in A. Cabaniss (trans.), *The Emperor's Monk: Contemporary Life of Benedict of Aniane by Ardo* (Ilfracombe: Arthur H. Stockwell, 1979), here c. 36.1, pp. 86–7.

Pious, instructs a wide swathe of officials including the vidames (*vicidomini*) of abbesses to attend an annual assembly in May.[63] These officials were presumably responsible for managing female communities' landed properties, and as such would not have had any authority over, or particular expertise in, the internal organisation and life of the community – in short, they represented female communities' interests as landowners as opposed to as their priorities as practising nuns. I will leave to one side the question of how far these councils and assemblies actively constructed, or merely simulated, empire-wide consensus: even if individual abbots and male monks were not accorded substantial agency in setting agendas at these meetings, their participation in these discussions nevertheless encouraged buy-in to the initiatives undertaken.[64] Correspondingly, the absence of abbesses and nuns had consequences: enclosed in their communities, they were not only unable to shape and influence regulations on female monasticism, but were moreover excluded from these consensus-building processes. They were shut out of the empire-wide monastic networks that these councils both built upon and in turn facilitated.

Of course, these monastic horizontal connections did not begin and end with councils. Take, for example, prayer confraternities. These could be single-sex, the direct product of all-male conciliar proceedings, as indeed Steve Ling explores in the next chapter.[65] Yet they sometimes provided women with the opportunity to be involved in local, diocesan networks. This was mandated, for example, by a council in 800.[66] Occasionally they provide evidence for female involvement in larger-scale networks, such as that revealed

---

63 *MGH Capit.* 1, no. 152, pp. 309–10.
64 On the absolute importance of the 'discourse community' to which both councils and assemblies contributed, see Diem, 'The Carolingians', pp. 246–7; Kramer, *Rethinking Authority*, pp. 43–9; on councils and consensus, see *ibid.*, pp. 61–9; R. Kramer, 'Order in the church: understanding councils and performing *ordines* in the Carolingian world', *Early Medieval Europe*, 25.1 (2017), 54–69.
65 See here Steve Ling's contribution in Chapter 2 of this volume. *MGH Conc.* 2.1, no. 15B, pp. 96–7; no. 31, p. 233; see here also McNamara, *Sisters*, p. 153.
66 *MGH Conc.* 2.1, no. 24, c. 47, p. 213.

in the *libri memoriales* of the female communities of Remiremont and San Salvatore in Brescia (and it is likely not coincidental that the former of these, Remiremont, is the only female monastery which we know took up Benedictine observance in this period).[67] More often, however, the evidence points more squarely towards predominantly male networks. While abbesses were forbidden from travelling to royal courts, these same courts served as fora for male churchmen, whether bishops or abbots, to form networks between themselves and (sometimes) with prominent lay courtiers. While nuns were expressly prohibited from sending out *winileodas* – which can be roughly translated as 'songs for a friend' and understood as a female equivalent to male protestations of friendship – male monks stayed in touch, for example through the exchange of letters averring *amicitia* (friendship), which appears to have served, in the Carolingian world at least, as a particularly male form of association often infused with homoerotic language.[68] While women were enclosed and barred from travel, the movement of monks between different communities created and maintained connections on a more individual level. All of this led to the creation of male monastic networks and the generalised diffusion of male monastic, and here especially male Benedictine, 'best practice'. Indeed, the 'exemplary' male monastery of Inden/Kornelimünster was founded by Louis the Pious and Benedict of Aniane close to the court at Aachen (itself a node in these horizontal networks) precisely in order to

---

67 For the *libri memoriales* of Remiremont and San Salvatore in Brescia, see V. Garver, *Women and Aristocratic Culture in the Carolingian World* (Ithaca, NY: Cornell University Press, 2009), pp. 77–102. For Remiremont's Benedictine observance, see Bodarwé, 'Eine Männerregel', pp. 243–6; Vanderputten, *Dark Age Nunneries*, pp. 18, 38–44, 56–9. On gender and Carolingian intellectual networks more generally, cf. Lifshitz, *Religious Women*, pp. 193–6, 200–2.

68 For the prohibition on sending *winileodas*, see *MGH Capit.* 1, no. 23, c. 19, p. 63; see also Schulenburg, *Forgetful of Their Sex*, pp. 354–5. For male *amicitia*, and here particularly the circle around Alcuin, see J. Boswell, *Christianity, Social Tolerance, and Homosexuality: Gay People in Western Europe from the Beginning of the Christian Era to the Fourteenth Century* (Chicago, IL: University of Chicago Press, 1981), pp. 188–93. Do note that these networks were not, however, exclusively male: e.g. for Alcuin's female correspondents, see Nelson, 'Alcuin's letters', pp. 360–71.

serve as a model of male monastic life, and to that end, it hosted a rotating cast of male monks sent from the foremost monasteries in the region.[69] Inden/Kornelimünster may have been unique in its prominence and *Königsnähe* (or 'closeness to the king'): nevertheless, throughout the empire, and in a less programmatic fashion, there are many other such examples of horizontal-ish interchange, in which one community served as a model and a source of advice to another. The Frankish male monastery of Corbie served as a 'mother house' to its Saxon offshoot, Corvey (also known as 'New Corbie'); the well-connected male monastery of Reichenau kept its close neighbour, St. Gall, abreast with the most recent monastic developments; and the male monastery of Aniane claimed for itself an exemplary role both among male Benedictine monasteries of Aquitaine and throughout the Carolingian world more broadly.[70] Here, and as we shall see in Cinzia Grifoni and Giorgia Vocino's chapter below, geography was no bar: many of the best-connected male monasteries were located near the frontiers of the Carolingian world, thus problematising modern conceptions of centre and periphery. In the Carolingian world, even the most geographically remote male monasteries could act as 'insiders'.

All of this attests to the structural and legislative barriers to female inclusion in horizontal monastic networks. There is one further body of evidence on which to draw: royal charters to monasteries. Traditionally, these have been interpreted as indicative of top-down governance; however, as more recent work of Mark Mersiowsky and Eliza Hartrich makes clear, this could not be further from the case. Mersiowsky's 2015 work allots greater agency to charters' recipients (or rather, as he termed them, petitioners), who actively appealed to rulers for specific privileges; the ruler, by contrast, played a more strictly reactive (passive) role.[71] Hartrich's groundbreaking 2017 article, meanwhile, uses late medieval English

---

69 Ardo, *Vita Benedicti abbatis Anianensis*, c. 35, p. 197; trans. in Cabaniss, *The Emperor's Monk*, c. 35.2, p. 85 – for the lack of such a 'model' monastery for women, see McNamara, *Sisters*, p. 161; Wemple, *Women*, p. 169.
70 Ardo, *Vita Benedicti abbatis Anianensis*, c. 18, p. 172; trans. in Cabaniss, *The Emperor's Monk*, c. 18.1, pp. 64–5.
71 M. Mersiowsky, *Die Urkunde in der Karolingerzeit: Originale, Urkundenpraxis und politische Kommunikation*, Schriften der Monumenta

urban charters as evidence for inter-urban networks, giving preference to these horizontal ties above the vertical connections between individual towns and rulers. Hartrich interprets urban charters, and particularly the granting of 'new' rights, not only as legal guarantees of rights and privileges, but also, and more importantly, as statements of corporate identity, intended to reinforce towns' status and position to other members of their urban networks.[72] These strands of her analysis may likewise be applied to the Carolingian period, and more specifically, to royal grants of free election and royal immunity, which allowed monks to elect their own abbot or abbess, and to exist free of various types of outside interference, respectively.

The reasons behind my focus on these types of grants are threefold. Firstly, while grants of immunity and free election had long been a feature of the Frankish ecclesiastical landscape – and thus do not constitute new forms of grants, such as those analysed by Hartrich – these grants nevertheless took on more standardised, 'copy and paste' formats, here especially under Louis the Pious.[73] Accordingly, the diffusion of these grants, which primarily followed such new, 'innovative' formats, can be analysed, in a manner akin to Hartrich's 'new' rights, as revealing connections and networks between different monastic houses.[74] Secondly, the granting of both

---

Germaniae Historica, 60 (2 vols, Wiesbaden: Harrasowitz, 2015), vol. II, pp. 546–604.

72 E. Hartrich, 'Charters and inter-urban networks: England, 1439–1449', *English Historical Review*, 132:555 (2017), 219–49.

73 While charters appear to have been largely standardised in Louis the Pious's chancery, there was still the potential for recipients to draft charters themselves for the emperor's approval (generally referred to by the German term *Empfängerausfertigung*); nevertheless, this has only been demonstrated at select centres with close ties to the Carolingian chancery, such as Saint-Denis: see Mersiowsky, *Die Urkunde*, pp. 113–15. In other contexts – such as under Louis the Pious's sons in their roles as sub-kings and, in Lothar's case, as co-emperor – the potential for this type of 'collaborative' production may have been higher, although it is difficult to tell given the more varied language of their charters. In this regard, it is worth pointing to Mersiowsky's assessment of the production of charters under Charles the Bald (following Louis the Pious's death): see *ibid.*, pp. 144–5.

74 See here especially Hartrich, 'Charters', 228.

immunity and free election increased dramatically in frequency under Charlemagne and Louis the Pious; the sheer multiplicity of these types of grants allows us to build a more representative picture of monastic networks in this period. Indeed, if actively petitioning for immunity and/or free election is accepted as a sign of inclusion in a horizontal network, then evidence for horizontal networks – and here, specifically, *male* horizontal networks – abounds. Thirdly, and lastly, is the connection between these types of grants and the promotion of Benedictine monasticism, a point which will require more thorough elucidation.

Let us turn first to grants of free election to monasteries. This was often linked to the recipient institutions' observance of the Benedictine Rule, whether in terms of their selection of an abbot who would 'prevail to rule that congregation according to the rule of the blessed Benedict', or in terms of the grant and conduct of the election itself (as the principle of free abbatial election was laid out within the Rule itself).[75] An unusually programmatic statement of this connection may be found in Louis the Pious's 821/822 grant to Aniane, in which Louis the Pious confirms Tructesind's election as the community's abbot, advising him to admonish and correct the monks at Aniane according to their 'age and bodily strength'. He gives the community at large directions for the procedure that they should follow lest 'it happens – which we in no way desire – that he [Tructesind] deviates from the rule given to you by the aforementioned blessed Benedict'.[76] After a long discussion, replete with admonitions, Louis makes one final grant:

> that whenever by divine calling the aforementioned abbot or his successor pass from this light, as long as you can find one, who may prevail to rule that congregation according to the rule of the blessed

---

75 For the former, see e.g. T. Kölzer (ed.), *MGH DD LdF* (3 vols, Wiesbaden: Harrassowitz, 2016), I, no. 212, p. 525: 'ipsam congregationem secundum regulam sancti Benedicti regere valeant'; for the latter, see e.g. *MGH DD LdF* II, no. 243, p. 610: 'licentiam habeant secundum regularis vite inst[itutionem] elegendi sibi abbatem'.

76 *MGH DD LdF* I, no. 200, pp. 493–7, here p. 496: 'secundum etatem vel valitudinem corporis vel infirmitatis cuiuslibet molestiam'; 'Quod si forte evenerit, quod nos non obtamus, ut ille extra regulam vobis a memorato Benedicto obtime traditam in aliquo deviaverit.'

Benedict, you may have that licence to always elect an abbot through this written and strengthened authority.⁷⁷

Likewise, the connection to Benedictine comes to the fore in Pippin II of Aquitaine's 838–9 grant of free election to the male monastery of Solignac, which contains a provision explicitly forbidding the election or appointment of lay or canonical abbots.⁷⁸ Such considerations did not just come into play on the rulers' side. The importance of such privileges to monasteries' self-definition (and self-identification as 'Benedictine') may be judged by the preservation and copying of royal charters, as well as their incorporation into hagiographical and historiographical narratives. The prose version of Candidus's *Vita Eigili* may have passed over Louis's 816 grant of free election to Fulda (presumably due to the fact that it was obtained during the unhappy tenure of an unpopular and soon-to-be deposed abbot).⁷⁹ Nevertheless, the election of Abbot Eigil according to the model laid out in chapter 64 of the Benedictine Rule and its confirmation by Louis the Pious formed the work's central drama.⁸⁰

For immunity, and its connection to the promotion of Benedictine observance, we may turn to the work of Josef Semmler, who in his 1959 article portrayed a close correlation between royal protection (*Königsschutz*), by this point a constituent part of grants of immunity, and what he termed 'monastic reform' under Louis the Pious:

---

77 Ibid., p. 497: 'ut quandocumque divina vocatione predictus abba vel successores eius de hac luce migraverint, quamdiu inter vos tales invenire potueritis, qui ipsam congregationem secundum regulam sancti Benedicti regere valeant, per sepescriptam et roboratam nostram auctoritatem licentiam habeatis semper eligendi abbates'.
78 M. L. Levillain (ed.), *Recueil des actes de Pépin Ier et de Pépin II, rois d'Aquitaine (814–48)*, Chartes et diplômes relatifs à l'histoire de France 8 (Paris: Imprimerie nationale, 1926), no. 69, pp. 185–98, here p. 196. Note that this was a reissue of a grant previously made by his father.
79 *MGH DD LdF* I, no. 93, pp. 225–8.
80 Candidus, *Vita Aegil*, ed. G. Becht-Jördens, *Vita Aegil Abbatis Fuldensis a Candido ad Modestum edita prosa et versibus: Ein Opus geminum des IX. Jahrhundert*s (Marburg: Selbstverlag G. Becht-Jördens, 1994); see also Raaijmakers, *Fulda*, pp. 237–64.

A few examples may suffice to demonstrate the close connection between internal monastic reform according to the example of Benedict of Aniane and the placement of the reformed monastery under the protection of the king: St.-Hilaire-de-Carcassone (reformed by Abbot Nampius – royal protection in 814/5), St. Peter in Gent (reformed by Einhard – royal protection in 815), St. Wandrille (reformed by Ansegis – royal protection in 815), Montolieu (reformed by Abbot Olemund – royal protection 815), St.-Maur-des-Fossés (reformed by Count Bego – royal protection in 816), Inden (model monastery with 'anianische' observance – royal protection in 817), Belle Celle (reformed by Benedict of Aniane – royal protection in 819), Conques (founded by Louis the Pious – royal protection in 819), Montièrender (reformed by an imperial commission – royal protection in 827), St. Colombe in Sens (reformed by Benedict of Aniane – royal protection in 833), St. Gall (reformed by Grimald, royal protection and restoration to the status of royal monastery in 854).[81]

Various quibbles may be raised with Semmler's formulation: his male-as-default analysis; his implicit conception of 'monastic reform' as a discrete process with an achievable end goal; his designation of a distinctive 'anianische' observance, which may simply be the creation of an ambitious hagiographer; and his employment of the anachronistic category of 'royal monastery' (*Königskloster*).[82]

---

81 Semmler, 'Traditio und Königsschutz', 12–13: 'Wenige Beispiele mögen genügen, den engen Zusammenhang zwischen innerklösterlicher Reform nach dem Muster Benedikts v. Aniane und der Unterstellung des reformierten Klosters unter den Schutz des Königs aufzuzeigen: St.-Hilaire-de-Carcassone (Reform durch Abt Nampius) – Königsschutz 814/5, St. Peter in Gent (Reform durch Einhard) – Königsschutz 815, St. Wandrille (Reform durch Ansegis) – Königsschutz 815, Montolieu (Reform durch Abt Olemund) – Königsschutz 815, St.-Maur-des-Fossés (Reform durch Graf Bego) – Königsschutz 816, Cornelimünster (Musterabtei anianischer Observanz) – Königsschutz 817, Belle Celle (Reform durch Benedikt v. Aniane) – Königsschutz 819, Conques (Gründung durch Ludwig d. Fr.) – Königsschutz 819, Montièrender (Reform durch eine kaiserliche Kommission) – Königsschutz 827, St. Colombe in Sens (Reform durch Benedikt v. Aniane – Königsschutz 833, St. Gallen (Reform durch Grimald) – Königsschutz bzw. Rückführung in den Status Königsklosters 854'.
82 For a thorough reevaluation of Benedict of Aniane's role in Carolingian monasticism, see Kramer, *Rethinking Authority*, pp. 169–213.

The correlation he observed between monastic immunity/protection and the assertion of Benedictine monastic identity, however, is difficult to dispute. I would argue that grants of immunity and/or free election are, in and of themselves, indicative of a degree of engagement with wider Carolingian currents, but they also point towards the incorporation of monasteries into local, regional or empire-wide networks. Entry into these networks, and the sense of corporate and largely Benedictine identity they helped to engender, could be instrumental in individual communities' implementation of Benedictine observance. What is striking here, once again, is the almost complete absence of female institutions from these networks: a gendered analysis of these grants cannot fail to observe the overwhelming preponderance of male recipient institutions.

Two hundred and seven grants of immunity and/or free election (sometimes alongside other privileges) were made to institutions in the period 751 to 840 – that is, from Pippin's assumption of kingship to the death of Louis the Pious (and including grants made by Louis the Pious's sons in his lifetime).[83] These grants were issued to a total of 127 unique recipients (including monasteries, bishoprics, patriarchates and the papacy), of which only six, or 4.7 per cent, were female institutions (Argenteuil, Bonmoutier, Hohenburg, Saint-Julien in Auxerre, Santa Maria Theodata in Pavia and San Salvatore in Brescia).[84] These female institutions received only eight grants in total (3.9 per cent). If Louis the Pious's *deperdita* (lost charters) are included as per Kölzer's 2017 edition, the total rises to 275 grants of immunity and/or free election to 174 unique recipients. Eight (4.6 per cent) of these unique recipients were female institutions, which received a total of ten grants (3.6 per cent).[85] Of

---

83 E. Mühlbacher (ed.), *MGH DD Karol. 1* (Hanover: Hahn, 1906); *MGH DD LdF*; T. Schieffer (ed.), *MGH DD Lo I* (Berlin: Wiedemann, 1966); *Recueil des actes de Pépin*. I have not listed these individually due to sheer volume of grants made.

84 The grants made to female institutions are as follows: *MGH DD Karol. 1*, no. 49, pp. 68–9; no. 135, pp. 185–6; *MGH DD LdF* I, no. 84, pp. 206–7, no. 203, pp. 501–2; vol. II, no. 246, pp. 615–16; no. 372, pp. 929–31; *MGH DD Lo I*, no. 12, pp. 76–8; no. 35, pp. 112–15.

85 The additional *deperdita* for female institutions are as follows: *MGH DD LdF* II, no. 5, p. 1037; no. 158, p. 1138.

course, charters have been lost or destroyed over time, and female-dependent institutions may well have been included in immunities granted to bishoprics or male communities. Likewise, there were presumably more male religious institutions, although it is of course impossible to quantify Carolingian monasticism. Nevertheless, these figures reveal a sharply gendered diplomatic practice.

Part of this discrepancy may be explained by the necessity of petition. As Mersiowsky has demonstrated, the impetus for such grants came from the recipient institutions and was put forward in the form of a petition, which required the petitioner to come to court, or, less frequently to find someone else to act on their behalf. In the case of male institutions, the petitioner was almost invariably the abbot or bishop, with only very occasional exceptions for founders or other officials.[86] By contrast, prohibitions on travel largely prevented abbesses from such recourse. Only four abbesses travelled in person to seek grants: Abbess Ailina of Argenteuil in 769, Abbess Radoara of San Salvatore in Brescia in an undated grant made during Charlemagne's reign, presumably in the early 780s, Abbess Asia of Santa Maria Theodata in Pavia in 833, and the so-called *monacha* Amalberga of San Salvatore in Brescia in 837.[87] The first two of these occur relatively early, before Carolingian prohibitions had gained full force. The latter two petitions were lodged with Lothar during his father's lifetime – the 833 grant in the context of the ongoing rebellion against Louis's authority – and were unusual grants in other regards. The grant to Amalberga of San Salvatore in 837 saw Lothar acting together with his wife, the Empress Hirmingard, one of a handful of occasions in which female imperial authority is invoked by his chancery.[88] The grant to Santa Maria Theodata, meanwhile, mentions that Lothar has 'established the venerable Abbot Gisleramnus in that place as inspector, that throughout his life the rule of the blessed Benedict may be followed there in all ways due to his zeal': the nuns were to

---

86 Mersiowsky, *Die Urkunde* II, pp. 546–604, here especially pp. 562–3, 573–6, 580–1, 587–90, 593–4.
87 *MGH DD Karol. 1*, no. 49, pp. 68–9; no. 135, pp. 185–6; *MGH DD Lo I*, no. 12, pp. 76–8; no. 35, pp. 112–15.
88 *MGH DD Lo I*, no. 35, pp. 113; see also Mersiowsky, *Die Urkunde* II, pp. 589–80.

be allowed immunity and free election, but were to live under the strict supervision of a male authority.[89] In this regard, one could also point to the 825 grant of Pippin I of Aquitaine to the female monastery of Sainte-Croix, in which Pippin granted many of the same provisions as immunity, but reserved to himself the privilege of hearing all disputes pertaining to the monastery.[90] Even in the cases when abbesses were granted special dispensation to come to court, they were still to be supervised in other ways.

For the remainder of the grants to female institutions, petitions were put forward by an abbot, by a count (who held the female institution in benefice), twice by Empress Judith, and once, in the absence of a petition altogether, Louis the Pious acted of his own accord (when granting the institution in benefice to his daughter).[91] This frequency of imperial agency is highly unusual and reflects the more top-down impulses involved in the rule of female communities. Of course, the top was often engaged in other matters, and so rarely took the initiative.

In short, the charter evidence serves to underscore the extent of female exclusion from the horizontal networks that played such a key role in the building consensus around Carolingian monastic regulations, and here, in particular, the promotion of male Benedictine monasticism. As far as female communities were concerned, Carolingian regulations were perhaps most successful at severing institutional networks through prohibitions on travel and a renewed focus on the male supervision of female communities.[92] It is thus hardly surprising that we are so relatively lacking in female examples of what historians have identified as the key tenets of Carolingian male-as-default 'monastic reform'.[93] Women were held to substantially different and explicitly gendered standards; moreo-

---

89 *MGH DD Lo I*, no. 12, pp. 76–8: 'Gisleramnum quoque venerabilem abbatem in eodem loco constituimus inspectorem, quatenus diebus vitae suae studio in omnibus regula ibi exequatur sancti Benedicti'; see also Mersiowsky, *Die Urkunde*, II, p. 590.
90 *Recueil des actes de Pépin*, no. 3, pp. 9–12.
91 *MGH DD LdF* I, no. 84, pp. 206–7, no. 203, pp. 501–2; vol. II, no. 246, pp. 615–16; no. 372, pp. 929–31; see also Mersiowsky, *Die Urkunde* II, p. 582.
92 See here also the remarks of McNamara, *Sisters*, pp. 150–1, 161–2.
93 See here further Bodarwé, 'Eine Männerregel', pp. 235–58.

Gender and horizontal networks 63

ver, without horizontal networks, there was quite simply insufficient buy-in to wider institutional changes. Carolingian abbesses and their subordinates were not so much deprived of the agency to effect changes within their communities as they were excluded from the contexts and networks which might persuade them to do so.

Conclusions: revisiting 'reform'

Where does all of this leave us in terms of 'Carolingian monastic reform'? Certainly, our use of 'reform' does not reflect contemporary usage. The verb 'reform' appears in a few scattered contexts, for example in a couple of charters discussing the adoption of a new monastic order at individual male monasteries.[94] Only once does it appear to have been used more programmatically, in an exhortation to bishops to ensure the *Institutio sanctimonialium* was applied within female communities, 'just as the teaching of ecclesiastical offices, which was very much neglected, is reformed with effort'.[95] The verbs *emendare* (to emend) and *corrigere* (to correct) occur somewhat more frequently, but are still generally not used in a programmatic manner – though interestingly, one can point here again to the somewhat programmatic use of *emendare* and its noun form, *emendatio*, in relation to female communities in two conciliar texts.[96] The noun forms of these verbs (*reformatio, emendatio, cor-*

---

94 E.g. *MGH DD LdF* II, no. 309, p. 763; no. 315, p. 776. See here also the important work of Julia Barrow: J. Barrow, 'Developing definitions of reform in the church in the ninth and tenth centuries', in R. Balzaretti et al. (eds), *Italy and Early Medieval Europe: Papers for Chris Wickham* (Oxford: Oxford University Press, 2018), pp. 501–11, here pp. 501–6; J. Barrow, 'Ideas and applications of reform', in T. F. X. Noble and J. Smith (eds), *The Cambridge History of Christianity* (Cambridge: Cambridge University Press, 2008), pp. 345–62, here pp. 350, 356–8.
95 *MGH Conc.* 2.2, no. 48, c. 14, p. 592: 'quomodo disciplina officii ecclesiastici nimium neglecta per studium reformetur'. The same chapter appears in *MGH Capit.* 1, no. 179, c. 13, p. 369.
96 For the more programmatic use of *emendare* and its noun form *emendatio* in relation to female communities, see *MGH Conc.* 2.1, no. 38, c. 26, p. 290; *MGH Conc.* 2.2, no. 56, c. 36, p. 713; for other uses of *emendare* in relation to monasteries, see *MGH Capit.* 1, no. 14, cc. 5–6, 10, pp. 34–5; no. 33, cc.

rectio) are only rarely employed; contemporaries did not often reify these concepts into abstract nouns. This is not, in itself, an ironclad argument against the term 'reform': in the absence of contemporary usage, the concept of 'monastic reform' could still be justified if it provided a useful category of analysis. Yet historians' category of 'monastic reform' contains problematic male-as-default assumptions: the legislative priorities applied to male communities have been taken as representative, and those applied to female communities neglected. So too the processes by which these priorities were defined and community buy-in generated have been approached through a male-as-default lens. 'Carolingian monastic reform', as described by historians, was predominately experienced by men.

Joan Kelly-Gadol's pathbreaking 1977 article, 'Did women have a Renaissance?', opens with the following reminder: 'One of the main tasks of women's history is to call into question accepted schemes of periodisation.'[97] Here, Kelly-Gadol is not simply identifying the non-inclusion of women in the Renaissance: she is pointing out the inadequacy of conceptual models which rely upon male-as-default thinking. We chose our conceptual frameworks, and we can reject the terms – and the wider reified frameworks they invoke – handed down to us by previous generations of historians. Historians of both 'monastic reform' and of the Carolingian 'reforms' in all their different guises – *correctio*, *emendatio*, renaissance, what have you – should take note.

13, 15, pp. 93–4; no. 102, c. 3, p. 209; no. 160, c. 2, pp. 321–2; no. 170, c. 80, p. 348; *MGH Capit.* 2, no. 203, c. 4, p. 66. For the use of *corrigere* in relation to monasteries, see *MGH Capit.* 1, no. 160, c. 2, pp. 321–2; no. 179, c. 11, p. 369; *MGH Capit.* 2, no. 259, c. 1, p. 267; *MGH Conc.* 2.1, no. 11, p. 62; *MGH Conc.* 2.2, no. 48, c. 12, p. 592.

97 J. Kelly-Gadol, 'Did women have a Renaissance?', in R. Bridenthai and C. Koonz (eds), *Becoming Visible: Women in European History* (Boston, MA: Houghton Mifflin, 1977), pp. 139–64, here p. 139; see here also J. Smith, 'Did women have a transformation of the Roman world?', *Gender & History*, 12:3 (2000), 552–71.

2

Analysing Attigny: contextualising Chrodegang of Metz's influence on the life of canons

Stephen Ling

The successive attempts of Carolingian kings and their bishops to regulate the life of the canonical clergy and distinguish them from their monastic brethren are often cited as a key component of the Carolingian 'church reform'. Central to this narrative is Chrodegang of Metz, whose *Regula canonicorum* (*Rule for canons*, written c. 755) has been seen as the first concrete attempt to enforce the distinction between monks and the canonical clergy and to regulate the latter's lives in a systematic manner. Chrodegang's success has been touted by scholars, and the longstanding historiographical focus on 'reform' has meant that references to communities of clerics or even lapsed monastic houses are often seen through the prism of Chrodegang's rule.[1] It has been assumed that this rule was influential within Chrodegang's lifetime, yet for all its apparent influence only four manuscripts of the rule survive.[2] Other

---

1 J. Semmler, 'Chrodegang, Bischof von Metz', in F. Knöpp (ed.), *Die Reichsabtei Lorsch: Festschrift zum Gedenken an ihre Stiftung 764* (Darmstadt: Hess. Histor. Komm, 1973), pp. 229–45; E. Ewig, 'Saint Chrodegang et la réforme de l'église franque', in *Saint Chrodegang. Communications présentées au colloque tenu à l'occasion du douzième centenaire de sa mort* (Metz: Editions le Lorrain, 1967), pp. 25–53; E. Morhain, 'Origine et histoire de la *Regula canonicorum* de Saint Chrodegang', in *Miscellanea Pio Paschini, Studi di Storia Eccelesiastica*, vol. 1 *Lateranum*, N.S. XIV (1948), 173–85; M. A. Claussen, *Reform of the Frankish Church: Chrodegang of Metz and the Regula Canonicorum in the Eighth Century* (Cambridge, Cambridge University Press, 2005), particularly pp. 61–2.
2 Bern, Burgerbibliothek 289 (Metz, s. viii/ixin); Leiden, Bibliotheek der Rijksuniversiteit, Voss. Lat. F. 94 (Western France, possibly the vicinity of Tours, s. ix2/3); Vatican, Biblioteca Apostolica Vaticana, pal. lat. 555

evidence suggests a plurality of approaches continued to exist long after the creation of Chrodegang's rule. In 811, Charlemagne wrote to his bishops asking: 'About the life of those who are called canons, what sort ought it to be?'[3] Likewise, the prologue to the *Institutio canonicorum* of 816 stated that Louis the Pious desired its creation 'because the definition of the life of canons was dispersed among the sacred canons and the sayings of the holy fathers'.[4] Through a close analysis of the *Regula canonicorum*, and the concurrent efforts of Chrodegang's episcopal brethren to regulate the lives of their communities, this chapter will reframe Chrodegang's rule as one of many attempts to regulate episcopal communities in the mid-eighth century. Particular attention will be paid to motivations which led Chrodegang to compose his rule and to how his text was received by other key ecclesiastical players, both during and soon after his lifetime.

The *Totenbund* of Attigny (762): establishing a spiritual network

In 762, the royal villa at Attigny hosted a large church council including five archbishops, twenty-two bishops and seventeen

---

(Franco-German border area, s. ix1, possibly at Lorsch during s. xvi); Leiden, Bibliotheek der Rijksuniversiteit, BPL 81 (Orval/Luxembourg, s. xi/xii). For a discussion of the manuscripts of Chrodegang's Rule, see B. Langefeld, *The Old English Version of the Enlarged Rule of Chrodegang* (Frankfurt: Lang, 2003), pp. 31–55.

3 A. Boretius (ed.),*Capitula tractanda cum comitibus, episcopis et abbatibus*, *MGH Capit.* 1 (Hanover: Hahn, 1883), no. 71, p. 161: 'De vita eorum qui dicuntur canonici, qualis esse debeat?'; trans. J. L. Nelson, 'The voice of Charlemagne', in R. Gameson and H. Leyser (eds), *Belief and Culture in the Middle Ages: Studies Presented to Henry Mayr-Harting* (Oxford: Oxford University Press, 2001), p. 86. While published translations are used in what follows, they may be lightly adapted.

4 A. Werminghoff (ed.), *MGH Conc.* 2.1 (Hanover: Hahn, 1906), no. 39a, p. 312: 'ut, quia canonicorum vita sparsim in sacris canonibus et in sanctorum patrum dictis erat indita'; trans. J. Bertram, *The Chrodegang Rules: The Rules for the Common Life of the Secular Clergy from the Eighth and Ninth Centuries: Critical Texts with Translations and Commentary* (Aldershot: Ashgate, 2005), p. 132.

abbots from across Francia. Those who attended the council formed a memorial confraternity (*Totenbund*), which contractually bound its members to perform mutual intercessory prayer.[5] This mutual prayer, in turn, created spiritual bonds between the disparate monasteries and basilicas of the kingdom and acted as a statement of religious and political brotherhood.[6] Chrodegang, who had served as primate of the Frankish church since 754, played a leading role in the proceedings, and his name heads the list of episcopal signatories of the *Totenbund*.[7] Chrodegang likely refers to this confraternity within the prologue to the *Regula canonicorum*, stating, 'I rely therefore on the help of my spiritual brethren, who have urged me to this work of recovery [*recuperationem*], in deciding to outline a brief decretal [*parvum decretulum*]'.[8] Accordingly, the *Totenbund* provides a useful window into Chrodegang's network at the peak of his career. The discussion below will focus on the following prominent signatories at Attigny: Chrodegang of Metz (d. 766), Lull of Mainz (d. 786), Heddo (d. 776) and Remi (d. 783) of Strasbourg, Willibald of Eichstätt (d. c. 787), Wilicar of Saint-Maurice d'Agaune (later Archbishop of Sens) (d. c. 785) and Fulrad of Saint-Denis (d. 784). It will examine the way of life practised within Francia's premier foundations, while also sampling from a wide geographical

---

5 R. Choy, *Intercessory Prayer and the Monastic Ideal in the Time of the Carolingian Reforms* (Oxford: Oxford University Press, 2016), pp. 122–3; Claussen, *Reform*, pp. 56–7.
6 For discussions of confraternities in early middle ages see G. G. Meersseman and G. P. Pacini, *Ordo Fraternitatis: confraternite e pietà dei laici nel Medioevo* (Rome: Herder, 1977), I, pp. 3–35; O. G. Oexle, 'Conjuratio et ghilde dans l'Antiquité et dans le Haut Moyen Âge: Remarques sur la continuité des formes de la vie sociale', *Francia*, 10 (1982), 1–19; M. McLaughlin, *Consorting with Saints: Prayer for the Dead in Early Medieval France* (Ithaca, NY: Cornell University Press, 2018), pp. 67–101.
7 Claussen, *Reform*, pp. 55–7; J. M. Wallace-Hadrill, *The Frankish Church* (Oxford: Clarendon, 1983), pp. 172–80; E. Ewig, 'Saint Chrodegang', pp. 28–53.
8 Bertram (ed.), *Chrodegang Rules, Regula sancti Chrodegangi*, prologue, Latin p. 27, trans. p. 52: 'fratrumque spiritualium consolatione adiutus, atque ad recuperationem provocatus volui, necessitate compulsus, parvum drecretulum facere'; Claussen, *Reform*, p. 207.

area, including both the newest (Eichstätt, founded c. 742) and oldest (Saint-Maurice d'Agaune and Saint-Denis) communities attested at Attigny.

Chrodegang of Metz, Pope Zacharias and the impetus behind the creation of the *Regula canonicorum*

In the late 740s, Chrodegang was a rising star at the Frankish court. His family was closely tied to the Carolingian dynasty, and Chrodegang was himself a strong supporter of Charles Martel and Pippin III, to whom he owed his successive appointments as palace referendary, then bishop of Metz (c. 747).[9] It was in this period that Pippin III and his clerical advisors sought papal guidance on a number of key ecclesiastical questions, and it seems likely Chrodegang was involved in this effort, whether in his role as referendary or as bishop. Although the court's letter to the papacy does not survive, Pope Zacharias's response is preserved in the *Codex Carolinus*, a collection of 99 papal letters sent to the Frankish court between 739 and 791.[10] Zacharias also wrote to Boniface providing instructions that its contents were to 'read in the assembly of priests' and

---

9 The referendary was one of the principal legal officers of the Merovingian court; he was tasked with the creation and archiving of royal charters and letters and the processing of petitions to the court. By the late eighth century, this role was superceded by that of chancellor. For an overview of Chrodegang's career and family see Claussen, *Reform*, pp. 20–9; 'Liber de Episcopis Mettensibus', ed. and trans. D. Kempf, in *Paul the Deacon, Liber de Episcopis Mettensibus: Edition, Translation, and Introduction* (Leuven: Peeters, 2013), pp. 86–7. It is unclear precisely when Chrodegang became bishop of Metz; tradition dates his elevation to 742, but he is first recorded as bishop in 748: A. d'Herbomez (ed.), *Cartulaire de l'abbaye de Gorze*, Mettensia 2 (Paris: C. Klincksleck, 1902), no. 1, pp. 1–4; Claussen, *Reform*, p. 26.
10 *Codex Carolinus*, ed. W. Gundlach, *MGH Epp.* 3 (Berlin: Weidmann, 1892), no. 3, pp. 479–87; trans. R. McKitterick and D. van Espelo, *Codex Epistolaris Carolinus: Letters from the Popes to the Frankish Rulers, 739–791* (Liverpool: Liverpool University Press, 2021), no. 5, pp. 165–80. For discussion of the letter, see also A. T. Hack, *Codex Carolinus: Päpstliche Epistolographie im 8. Jahrhundert* (Stuttgart: A. Hiersemann, 2006), I, pp. 226–8, 306–9.

that Boniface was to be present at the synod.[11] The pope therefore intended his response to be disseminated to the Frankish clergy and to be given the authority associated with wider conciliar approval.[12] Accordingly, his letter likely formed the basis for a council held at some point between 745 and 747.[13]

Although often overlooked, this papal letter is a seminal text in the history of the regulation of the canonical clergy. For the most part, Zacharias answered the court's questions by referring back to the councils of the early church and to previous papal decretals.[14] However, at the end of the first chapter, which addressed '[h]ow the metropolitan bishop ought to be honoured', the pope felt the need to add the following instruction by his own 'apostolic authority', permitting a bishop to live with their communities 'holding to the rule of monastic discipline':

> And so we likewise enjoin by dint of apostolic authority that a bishop should use his vestments according to his stature [rank], similarly also the cardinal priests. And if they have the desire to live a monastic life, they should still be dressed in their more elegant garments as they discharge their prescribed preaching to the people [*plebi*] under them, and keep their profession quietly in their hearts, so that God who sees in secret may repay them openly. Indeed it is written: 'Be sorry for the things you say in your hearts, and in your beds'. For the honour of the garment does not commend us, rather the splendour of

---

11 Boniface, *Epistolae*, ed. E. Dümmler, *MGH Epp.* 3 (Berlin: Weidmann, 1892), no. 77, p. 349; trans. E. Emerton, *Letters of Saint Boniface* (New York, NY: Columbia University Press, 1940), p. 135.

12 For the importance of conciliar procedure and the relationship between conciliar decrees and canon law, see G. I. Halfond, *The Archaeology of Frankish Church Councils, AD 511–768* (Leiden: Brill, 2010), pp. 174–9.

13 There has been much debate over the significance and size of these councils. While Jarnut argued that no councils were held in Francia between 745 and 747, Hartmann draws on the evidence of Boniface's letters to suggest councils met in both 745 and 747. See J. Jarnut, 'Bonifatius und die fränkischen Reformkonzilien (743–748)', *Zeitschrift der Savigny-Stiftung für Rechtsgeschichte, Kanonistische Abteilung*, 66 (1979), 26; W. Hartmann, *Die Synoden der Karolingerzeit im Frankenreich und Italien* (Paderborn: Schöningh, 1989). For a summary of their views, see Halfond, *Church Councils*, p. 259.

14 McKitterick and Van Espelo (trans.), *Codex Epistolarius Carolinus*, p. 165.

our souls. Monks, furthermore, are not to lapse in their use of woollen clothing, following the norms and rules of monastic discipline, as well as the tradition of the holy, proven fathers. For if in renouncing worldly things they have behaved themselves wholly as God intended, they ought to abstain from anything illicit, so that, insofar as they suffered bodily, they may be worthy to receive a comparable prize from God. Indeed, the apostles were given a divine mandate not to have two tunics, meaning, of course two woolen tunics, not linen. He therefore who has obeyed the Lord's precept, sticking to good deeds, will have eternal life.[15]

Zacharias's advice permitted the monasticisation of the cathedral close and this may well have provided the impetus to Chrodegang and the other Frankish bishops to enforce a more monastic interpretation of life within their communities. This can be seen in the conciliar chapters issuing from the Synod of Ver (755), which quoted directly from chapter nine of the Council of Antioch (341), re-emphasising the authority of bishops within their dioceses.[16] In his letter, Zacharias had signposted the Frankish court to this precise section of the text stating: 'Likewise the canons of the council

---

15 *Codex Carolinus*, no. 3, pp. 480–1: 'Nam et nos ab apostolica auctoritate subiungimus, ut episcopus iuxta dignitatem suam indumentis utatur; simili modo et presbiteri cardinales. Et si monachica vita velle habeant vivendi, plebi quidem sibi subiectae preclariori vestae induti debitum praedicationis persolvant et in secreto propositum sui servent cordis, ut, qui videt in abscondito, Deus reddat illis in palam; scriptum quippe est: "Quae dicitis in cordibus vestris, et in cubilibus vestris conpungimini". Non enim nos honor commendat vestium, sed splendor animarum. Monachi vero lanea indumenta iuxta normam et regulam monachicae disciplinae atque traditionem sanctorum probabilium patrum sine intermissione utantur. Si enim, abrenuntiantes ea quae sęculi sunt, tota se Deo intentione contulerunt, de omnibus inlicitis debent abstinere, ut, quantum corpori suo sustinuerint laborem, tantum remunerationis praemium a Deo percipere mereantur. Apostolis quippe divinum datum est mandatum, duas tunicas non habendi – tunicas dixit utique laneas, non lineas. Qui ergo oboedierit dominico praecepto, bonis actibus inhaerens, habebit vitam aeternam'; trans. McKitterick and Van Espelo, *Codex Epistolarius Carolinus*, pp. 169–70.
16 *Concilium Antiochensum: Canones*, ed. C. H. Turner, *Ecclesiae Occidentalis: Monumenta Iuris Antiquissima* (Oxford: Clarendon, 1913), II:2, pp. 232–311, here c. 9/87 [Dionysius recensions], p. 259.

Table 2.1 A comparison of *Codex Carolinus*, no. 5, [G3], p. 480, and A. Boretius (ed.), *MGH Capit.* 1 (Hanover: Hahn, 1883), no. 14, c. 3, p. 33

Pope Zacharias's Letter (747), Ch. 1 *The Honour due to Metropolitan Bishops, Chorepiscopis and parish priests*	The Synod of Ver (755), Ch. 3
Unusquisque enim episcopus habeat suae parrochiae potestatem, ut regat iuxta reverenciam singulis competentem. [That is to say, each and every bishop should have power within his diocese, so they might be at hand, reverently and appropriately guiding all things.]	*Ut unusquisque episcoporum potestatem habeat in sua parrochia tam de clero quam de regularibus vel saecularibus, ad corrigendum et emendandum secundum ordinem canonicam spiritale ut sic vivant, qualiter Deo placere possint.* [Let each and every bishop have power within his diocese so all clerics, regular and secular, will be corrected and emended to live according to the spirit of the canonical order, in a manner which might be pleasing to God.]

of Antioch, chapter 9, contain the following [...] For each and every bishop should hold sway over his own diocese.'

This demonstrates the active afterlife of Zacharias's letter, as does the very fact of its preservation within the *Codex Carolinus*. This letter had meaning and utility to those bishops concerned with maintaining their authority and working out how to regulate their episcopal communities, and the link between these two strands is explicit.

The Synod of Ver is often closely linked with Chrodegang and the similarities between its prologue and that of the *Regula canonicorum* illustrate that these two documents are related.[17] However, there was no wider effort to promulgate the *Regula canonicorum* at Ver; instead, the episcopate drew inspiration from Zacharias's advice empowering each bishop to 'correct and emend' clerics

---

17 On the relationship between the Synod of Ver and the prologue to the rule, see Claussen, *Reform*, pp. 62–3.

within his diocese to ensure they lived according to the *ordinem canonicam*. These terms were left deliberately ambiguous and it is notable that the phrase 'canonical clergy' favoured by Chrodegang is not included; rather, it emphasises the vague notion that 'regulars' and 'seculars' formed part of the canonical order. Likewise, the specific texts associated with the *ordinem canonicam* are not mentioned and are left to local discretion.

It is notable that five of the 27 bishops who signed the confraternity document chose to highlight the monastic nature of their episcopal residencies.[18] Such episcopal communities, while living a monastic life, were manned in part by a clerical retinue who assisted the bishop in his pastoral duties. The use of the term 'regulars' may reflect the input of bishops who led 'monasticised' communities. Thus, while the Synod of Ver is an expression of Chrodegang's interests, it also reflected the concerns, interests and traditions of the wider episcopacy.

Alongside the use of Zacharias's letter at the Synod of Ver, Chrodegang closely mirrored Zacharias's advice in his *Regula canonicorum*, combining this papal letter with the Benedictine rule and with the precepts of other esteemed authors.[19] Following Zacharias, the *Regula canonicorum* maintains a consistent focus on episcopal authority, clerical rank and the clothing of the congregation. This is particularly clear in chapter 2 of the text, which specifically addresses 'the order of the congregation of canons'. Here, Chrodegang adapts chapter 63 of the Benedictine rule, replacing its hierarchy based on the date of monastic 'conversion' with a hierarchy based on one's clerical grade:

> The canons shall keep their order in which they were ordained in their rank according to the legitimate and holy institute of the Roman

---

18 *MGH Conc.* 2.1, no. 13, p. 73: 'Uuilliharius episcopus de monasterio sancti Maurici; [...] Theodulfus episcopus de monasterio Laubicis; [...] Yppolitus episcopus de monasterio Eogendi; Iacob episcopus de monasterio Gamundias; [...] Uuillibaldus episcopus de monasterio Achistadi'.
19 Although he does not discuss Zacharias's letter, for an excellent analysis of the sources Chrodegang used to construct his rule see Claussen, *Reform*, pp. 114–206.

church, on every occasion whatever, that is to say, in the church, or wherever they meet together.[20]

The emphasis here on the 'holy insitute of the Roman church' may well allude to Zacharias's letter.[21] Similarly, in chapter 8, the clergy are expected to present themselves daily to the bishop or his representative, 'vested properly', and on Sundays and feast days this was extended to all the clerics of the city who were expected to attend vigils and lauds, remaining 'vested in their proper rank, and [...] stand[ing] according to rank until mass has been celebrated'.[22] Chapter 21 continues this focus on hierarchy, commanding that within the refectory 'each [should] go to his table according to his degree'.[23] Chapter 29 deals directly with the clothing of the community and mirrors Zacharias's letter, specifying that once a year priests and deacons were to be presented with tunics, 'or should be given the wool to make themselves two tunics a year'.[24] Finally, chapter 34 commands that the *matricularii* (almsfolk) of the city were to present themselves to the bishop twice a year; here, the people (*plebi*) in the fullest sense were subjected to episcopal authority.[25]

In dealing with these *matricularii* the author of the *Regula canonicorum* combines Zacharias's focus on dress with other advice found within his letter, notably from chapter 10, which states that '[c]lerics who oversee poorhouses or are ordained in monasteries and martyrs' basilicas are to remain under the power of the bishop of that

---

20 Bertram (ed.), *Chrodegang Rules, Regula sancti Chrodegangi*, c. 2, Latin, p. 30, trans. p. 55: 'Ordine(m) suos canonici ita conservent, ut ordinati sunt in gradibus suis secundum legitimam vel sanctam institutionem romani eccclesia, in omnibus omnino locis'.
21 Chrodegang consistently makes use of the word *insitutio* when refering to his own work and to other 'canonical' texts, a theme picked up in the later *Institutio canonicorum* issued in 816.
22 Bertram (ed.), *Chrodegang Rules, Regula sancti Chrodegangi*, c. 8, Latin pp. 33–4, trans. pp. 60–1. This inclusion of the extra-claustral clergy is also discussed in c. 33 of the rule, Latin p. 49, trans. pp. 79–80.
23 *Ibid.*, c. 21, Latin p. 40, trans. p. 68: 'et ut dispositus ordo est, unusquisque ad suam mensam accedat'.
24 *Ibid.*, c. 29, Latin p. 45, trans. p. 74.
25 As Claussen points out, Chrodegang sought to expand the purity of the cloister to the wider city of Metz throughout his rule: Claussen, *Reform*, pp. 248–89, here particularly pp. 257–8.

particular diocese, according to the traditions of the holy fathers'.[26] This section of Zacharias's letter is all the more compelling given its focus on episcopal authority within martyrs' basilicas, as this would have chimed with those bishops who resided within such basilica communities, such as Wilicar of Saint-Maurice d'Agaune.

The use of Zacharias's advice at both a conciliar level and within the *Regula canonicorum* reframes Chrodegang's efforts to regulate the life of his canonical clergy. His efforts should not be seen in isolation; rather, he was one of many 'spiritual brethren' grappling with the thorny issue of defining the way of life practised by their episcopal communities. The rest of this chapter will carefully examine how Chrodegang's contemporaries sought to establish their authority over their episcopal communities and how these attempts compare to Chrodegang's own efforts at Metz.

Chrodegang and his neighbours: Lull of Mainz (d. 786) and Heddo of Strasbourg (d. 765)

In 754, Chrodegang was given the pallium and raised to the rank of archbishop by Pope Stephen II.[27] This act not only made him primate of the Frankish church but confirmed Chrodegang's local authority over other bishops. In this role, he chaired the councils convened at Ver (755), Verberie (756), Compiègne (757) and Attigny (762).[28] The strong congruence between the prologues of Chrodegang's rule and the Synod of Ver, alongside the public confirmation of his

---

26 *Codex Carolinus*, no. 5, p. 747, trans. McKitterick and Van Espelo, p. 173: 'Clerici, qui praeficiuntur ptochiis vel ordinantur in monasteriis et basilicis martyrum, sub episcoporum, qui unaquaque civitates sunt, secundum sanctorum patrum traditiones potestate permaneant nec per contumatiam ab episcopo suo desiliant'. It is possible that this section of the text was composed by Angilramn, Chrodegang's successor as bishop of Metz. See S. Ling, '"Superior to canons, and remaining inferior to monks": monks, canons and Alcuin's third order', in R. Kramer et al. (eds), *Monastic Communities and Canonical Clergy*.
27 *Liber pontificalis*, I pp. 334–447; trans. Raymond Davis, *The Lives of the Eighth-Century Popes: Liber Pontificalis, 715–817 AD* (Liverpool: Liverpool University Press, 1992), pp. 60–4.
28 Halfond, *Church Councils*, pp. 192–200, 243–4; Claussen, *Reform*, p. 47.

privilege for the monastery of Gorze at the Council of Compiègne, attest to a close association between Chrodegang's conciliar activity and his local efforts to define the way of life practised by his monks and canons.[29] More significantly, an undated letter from Bishop Lull of Mainz to Chrodegang reveals that he attempted to spread the use of his *Regula canonicorum* more widely. Lull reports that he had used 'your newest canonical institute' to excommunicate the priest Willefrith, who had ordained another priest without episcopal approval and who 'despised' both Chrodegang's 'institutional decrees' and Lull's power within the diocese of Mainz.[30] The use of language in this letter is telling: Lull refers to Chrodegang's rule in precisely the same manner as Chrodegang, calling it a canonical institute (*canonica institutio*). More importantly, the manner of his excommunication corresponds directly to the prescriptions of chapter 17 of Chrodegang's rule, which outlines how wayward clerics who 'in any way despis[e] and contraven[e] this little institute (*instituciuncule*)' should 'suffer excommunication'.[31]

Lull was not a natural ally of Chrodegang; the two were rivals seeking to present themselves as natural successors to Boniface's political and religious authority.[32] Lull had even sought to escape Chrodegang's jurisdiction by forging a papal privilege claiming that Pope Zacharias had raised Boniface's successors at Mainz to

---

29 Claussen, *Reform*, pp. 47–53, 60–6.
30 Boniface, *Epistolae*, *MGH Epp.* 3, no. 110, pp. 396–7: 'quod in parrochiam nostram contra ius canoncum a Willefritho presbitero quidam adductus est presbiter in alia ordinatus parrochia [...]Qui, et institutionis vestrae decreta contemnens et in parrochia nostra constitutus, nostrum sprevit magisterium [...] Sed cum nec ita emendatus penitere de praeteritis voluit, novissime secundum canonicam insitutionem vestram excommunicatus est a me'; trans. J. Palmer, 'The "vigorous rule" of Bishop Lull: between the Bonifatian mission and Carolingian church control', *Early Medieval Europe*, 13:3 (2005), 263–4.
31 In chapter 8, Chrodegang calls it *instituciunculam nostram* ('our little institute'), while in chapter 17, he calls it an *instituciuncule* ('little institute'): see Bertram (ed.), *Chrodegang Rules, Regula sancti Chrodegangi*, c. 8, pp. 33, 38.
32 For an overview of Lull's career: Palmer, 'Vigorous rule', 249–76.

archepiscopal status.³³ Despite this rivalry, Lull did not oppose the introduction of Chrodegang's 'new institute' (*novissime secundum canonicam institutionem*); instead, he drew on it in his attempts to expand his authority over both the town and diocese of Mainz. This pragmatism must have played a key part in Lull's adoption of Chrodegang's Rule, helping him to establish and maintain his authority over his diocese and govern his clerics.

Heddo, bishop of Strasbourg, was another one of Chrodegang's suffragans who worked closely with the archbishop.³⁴ One of the earliest attestations of Chrodegang as bishop comes from the witness list of Heddo's privilege for the monastery of Arnulfsau-Schwarzach (749).³⁵ In turn, Heddo witnessed Chrodegang's own privilege to Gorze issued in 757.³⁶ This document offers an interesting counterpoint to Chrodegang's episcopally focused rule. The privilege commanded the monks to follow the Benedictine rule, to hold no property and to let nothing come before the 'work of God' (*opus dei*). The separation of the monastic community at Gorze from the episcopal community of Metz was also emphasised within the document:

> It is fitting that we preserve the monks' quiet and order and tranquillity for them so that they may not be disturbed or plundered or despoiled against the order of reason – not by us nor our archdeacon or any other delegate of St Stephen [of Metz].³⁷

The monastic community were given the right to freely elect their own abbot, albeit with the consent of the bishop, and while everyone was clearly subjected to the bishop's authority and 'protection', monks and canons were to be kept firmly apart and given

---

33 E. Knibbs, *Ansgar, Rimbert and the Forged Foundations of Hamburg-Bremen* (Farnham: Ashgate, 2011), p. 31.
34 Claussen, *Reform*, p. 54; Ewig, 'Saint Chrodegang', p. 52.
35 *Regesta Alsatiae aevi merovingi et karolini, 490–918*, ed. A. Bruckner (Strasbourg: P. H. Heitz, 1949), no. 166, pp. 97–100.
36 *Ibid.*, no. 177; *Cartulaire de l'abbaye Gorze*, no. 4, pp. 9–13.
37 *Ibid.*; B. Rosenwein, *Negotiating Space: Power, Restraint and Privileges of Immunity in Early Medieval Europe* (Ithaca, NY: Cornell University Press, 1999), p. 104.

different roles.[38] Heddo of Strasbourg drew directly on the privilege for Gorze when issuing his own privilege for the monastery of Ettenheim in 762, adopting Chrodegang's 'protective' model which emphasised monastic freedom alongside episcopal authority.[39]

Heddo was clearly receptive to Chrodegang's ideas and innovations, and Josef Semmler and Charles Munier have argued that Heddo and his successor Remi (d. 783) introduced Chrodegang's rule as a means to regulate the canonical clergy at Strasbourg.[40] Heddo was active within his diocesan city and began the process of rebuilding and enlarging the cathedral church of Strasbourg, work that continued during Remi's episcopacy. This physical renewal was likely accompanied by new attempts to regulate the life of the cathedral community, and Remi's testament of 778 provided for 'those clerics, our canons', here using the nomenclature found within Chrodegang's rule.[41] Given the other similarities in approaches taken by Heddo and Chrodegang, at the very least it seems likely that the bishops of Strasbourg looked to Metz as a model for the way of life practised by their own canons in Strasbourg.

Yet a close examination of Remi's testament illustrates a key difference between the way of life practised at Metz and Strasbourg. In his bequest, Remi gave precise details of an endowment for the cathedral community, donating the monastery of Schönenwerd, St Leodegar to the community, but ensuring his family's precarial control of Schönenwerd for at least three generations:

> That I myself and my successors, my niece Scholastica, and my great-nephew Raderamn, as long as we live, [...] shall hold usufruct [over the monastery of Schönenwerd, St. Leodegar] and each year at the festival of St Mary [...] we shall give 20 *solidi* of silver. And we wish

---

38 K. R. Rennie, *Freedom and Protection: Monastic Exemption in France, c. 590–c.1100* (Manchester: Manchester University Press, 2018), p. 48; Rosenwein, *Negotiating*, pp. 101–6.
39 Rosenwein, *Negotiating*, pp. 105–6, especially footnote 22.
40 Semmler, 'Chrodegang', p. 237, footnote 108; C. Munier, 'Le premier millénaire', in F. Rapp (ed.) *Le diocèse de Strasbourg* (Paris: Beauchesne, 1982), p. 21.
41 *Urkunden und Akten der Stadt Strassburg*, ed. W. Wiegand (Strasbourg: K. J. Trübner, 1879), no. 15, p. 13: 'illic clerici nostri canonici'; Semmler, 'Chrodegang', p. 237, footnote 108.

that those clerics our canons receive the *soldi* as our alms so that they [the canons] rightly please God and St. Mary day and night, giving service and entreating the Lord on our behalf. And let our names be written in the Book of Life [*liber vitae*], and also let my little body rest in that crypt, which I built as a new construction.[42]

This precept runs counter to chapter 31 of Chrodegang's rule, which contains a detailed account of how to join the order of canons.[43] Here, the rule invoked the image of the apostolic community, in which all things were held in common, and made it clear that while a canon may own property and receive a stipend from it, he had to ensure that 'any property' would descend 'not to [his] earthly heirs and relations, but to the church'.[44] Remi circumvented this requirement, securing his family's private control of the monastery of St Leodegar while also ensuring that the cathedral community was well endowed.

Chapters 30–4 of the *Regula canonicorum* are different in tone from the main body of the rule and form something of an addendum to the rest of the text. This section moves away from the exposition of normative texts to address some of the practical challenges faced by canons, including how to handle property.[45] This change

---

42 *Urkunden und Akten der Stadt Strassburg*, no. 15, p. 13: 'Quod ego ipse et Scolastica nepta mea et Raderamnus abnepos meus, dum adviximus, per tuum beneficium domna mea et successores mei, qui tunc temporis esse videntur, habere debeamus sub usufructuario, et censum annis singulis ad festivitatem sanctae Marie in dedicatione ipsius altarius, quod modo dedicavimus, solidos 20 argento dare debeamus. Et hoc volumus, ut ipsos solidos illic clerici nostri canonici in nostra elymosina recipiant, ut ipsos melius delectent die noctuque deo et sanctae Marie deservire et pro nobis dominum exorare, et ut nomina scripta sint in libro vite, et ut corpusculum meum in illa cripta, quam novo opere feci, requiescat'.
43 Bertram (ed.), *Chrodegang Rules, Regula sancti Chrodegangi*, c. 31, Latin pp. 46–8, trans. pp. 76–9.
44 *Ibid.*, c. 31, Latin p. 47, trans. p. 77. For the importance of this apolostolic model see M. A. Claussen, 'Practical exegesis: the Acts of the Apostles, Chrodegang's *Regula canonicorum* and early Carolingian reform', in D. Blanks et al. (eds), *Medieval Monks and their World: Ideas and Realities* (Leiden: Brill, 2006), pp. 119–47.
45 For a discussion of the final section of the Rule see Claussen, *Reform*, pp. 92–113; Claussen, 'Practical exegesis', pp. 119–46; for chapter 31 particularly see Ling, 'Superior to canons'.

in tone suggests that these chapters may have been composed at a later point than the main body of the text, perhaps by Chrodegang's successor as bishop of Metz, Angilramn.[46] The focus on property is reflective of the concerns of the 780s and 790s; take, for example, chapter 41 of the Council of Frankfurt (794), which condemned the familial inheritance of episcopal property.[47] Given the disparity between Chrodegang's rule and Remi's behaviour, it is perhaps unsurprising that Angilramn of Metz was missing from the witness list of Remi's bequest.[48]

The case of Strasbourg demonstrates some of the complexities involved in delineating the canonical way of life in the mid-eighth century. Chrodegang's renewal of Metz may have offered a model for others to follow, but individual bishops and the longstanding traditions of their foundations continued to shape the precise nature of their communities. It may be anachronistic to imagine the wholesale adoption of the *Regula canonicorum*, and the limited manuscript evidence does point to the text being used partially. In fact, the oldest extant copy of the rule, Bern, Burgerbibliothek 289 (Metz, s. viii/ix^{in}), perhaps in use in Metz as a chapter book at the time of Angilramn and Remi, is arranged out of order and is missing the first eight and last three chapters.[49] Such chapter books illustrate how elements of the *Regula canonicorum* could have been adapted and used without the requirement for the wholesale adoption of the rule. In Bern 289, elements of Chrodegang's rule are placed in a codex with other practical and advisory texts including the *Ordo romanus*, the sermons of Gregory the Great and the epistles of Jerome.[50] These canonical texts would have complemented Chrodegang's rule, offering practical tools to ensure episcopal communities were living correctly according to the 'canonical order'.

---

46 For Angilramn's role see Ling, 'Superior to canons'.
47 *MGH Conc.* 2.1, no. 19, p. 170; trans. H. R. Loyn and J. Percival, *The Reign of Charlemagne* (London: Edward Arnold, 1975), pp. 61–2.
48 *Urkunden und Akten der Stadt Strassburg*, no. 15, pp. 13–14.
49 Bertram (ed.), *Chrodegang Rules, Regula sancti Chrodegangi*, pp. 24–5; Langefeld, *Enlarged Rule*, pp. 32–3.
50 The contents of Bern 289 are summarised as part of the Early Medieval Monasticism Project: www.earlymedievalmonasticism.org/manuscripts/Bern-289.html (accessed 21 February 2022).

Certainly, the bishops and canons of Strasbourg did not keep abreast of the developments of the canonical life as practised in neighbouring Metz. If, like their episcopal superiors, the canons at Strasbourg passed their private property to their families, then there was a clear and substantive difference in the ways of life practised by the two communities, even if they shared a similar 'canonical' model. Heddo and Remi may have adapted elements of Chrodegang's rule to suit the needs of their own community, but it seems unlikely they imposed his rule in full. This may be indicative of a wider practice amongst the episcopate of picking and choosing which models and texts they thought best for their communities. The *Regula canonicorum* is itself the product of such actions, with Chrodegang combining elements of the Benedictine rule, Julian Pomerius (Pseudo-Prosper) and of course the advice of Pope Zacharias, in order to compose a new interpretation of the canonical way of life.[51]

Willibald of Eichstätt (d. c. 786)

Moving beyond the more receptive figures of Heddo and Lull, Bishop Willibald of Eichstätt seems to have ignored both Chrodegang's rule and his wider efforts to physically separate monks and canons. Willibald was well connected with the Frankish and Bavarian courts, the Bonifatian mission and Chrodegang of Metz.[52] In 740, Willibald was sent by Pope Zacharias to assist Boniface in his mission, and in 742 he was consecrated bishop of Erfurt. As this site was unsuitable, Willibald soon withdrew to Eichstätt, founding a new monastery there.[53] In the 740s and 750s Eichstätt therefore represented the newest diocese and episcopal foundation within Francia. Although as a Bavarian bishop, his diocese lay within a

---

51 For the sources of Chrodegang's Rule see Claussen, *Reform*, pp. 114–206.
52 For an overview of Willibald's career see D. Parsons, 'Some churches of the Anglo-Saxon missionaries in southern Germany: a review of the evidence', *Early Medieval Europe*, 8:1 (1999), 31–40; I. Wood, *The Missionary Life: Saints and the Evangelisation of Europe, 400–1050* (London: Routledge, 2001), pp. 64–6.
53 Parsons, 'Churches', pp. 36–40.

somewhat contested zone of Carolingian authority, Willibald continued to maintain his links with the wider Frankish episcopate, and he was present at the German Council (742/743); took part in the *Totenbund* of Attigny, where he signed himself 'Bishop of the Monastery of Eichstätt'; and witnessed Remi's testament.[54] With these links, he must have been aware of Chrodegang's activities and his rule.

Willibald was also a well-travelled figure: the details of his exciting adventures across the Mediterranean and the Holy Land are recorded in Huneberc of Heidenheim's *Hodoeporicon*.[55] This travelogue/hagiography was composed during its subject's lifetime, and the author claims to relate the tales told to her by Willibald, 'in dictation from his own mouth'.[56] As such it provides excellent details of Willibald's career and presents insights into the nature of his community at Eichstätt. After returning from his travels in the Holy Land, Huneberc reports that Willibald joined the community of Monte Cassino (732), holding many offices within the cloister; there, he observed 'in every detail the monastic observance as laid down by the Benedictine rule'.[57] According to the *Hodoeporicon*, Willibald continued to favour a monastic form of life when establishing his episcopal community at Eichstätt, combining what he

---

54 *MGH Conc.* 2.1, no. 13, pp. 72–3; *Urkunden und Akten der Stadt Strassburg*, no. 15, pp. 13–14.
55 *Vitae Willibaldi et Wynnebaldi auctore sanctimoniali Heidenheimensi*, ed. O. Holder-Egger, *MGH SS* 15:1 (Hanover: Hahn, 1887), pp. 80–117; trans. C. H. Talbot, in T. F. X. Noble and T. Head (eds), *Soldiers of Christ: Saints and Saints' Lives from Late Antiquity and the Early Middle Ages* (Pennsylvania, PA: Penn State University Press, 1995), pp. 141–65; Huneberc was identified as the author of the *Hodoeporicon* by Bischoff; see B. Bischoff, 'Wer ist die Nonne von Heidenheim?', *Studien und Mitteilungen zur Geschichte des Benediktinerordens und seiner Zweige*, 49 (1931), 387–97; for a discussion of the relationship between Huneberc and her subject see O. Limor, 'Pilgrims and authors: Adomnàn's *De Locis Sanctis* and Hugeburc's *Hodoeporicon Sancti Willibaldi*', *Revue Bénédictine*, 114:2 (2004), 253–75.
56 *Vita Willibaldi*, p. 87, trans. p. 144: 'Ista non apocriforum venia erratica dissertione relata esse cognoscamus, sed sicut illo ipso vidente et nobis referente de ori sui dictatione audire et nihilominus scribere destinavimus, duobus diaconibus testibus mecumque audientibus'.
57 *Ibid.*, c. 5, p. 102, trans. p. 161.

had witnessed at Monte Cassino with other practices he had seen during his travels:

> Afterwards he began to build a monastery in the place called Eichstätt, and he shortly afterwards practised the monastic life there according to the observance which he had seen at St. Benedict's [Monte Cassino], and not merely there, but also in many other monastic houses which he had examined with his experienced eye as he travelled through various lands.[58]

Yet alongside this preference for monasticism, Huneberc highlights the episcopal and clerical nature of the community at Eichstätt, stating that the veracity of her account could be corroborated by Willibald's 'deacons and other subordinates'.[59] She demonstrates a clear understanding of the difference between clerics, monks and the laity, addressing each in turn:

> Here begins the life of the brothers Willibald and Wynnebald, addressed to all priests, deacons and princes of the ecclesiastical order. To all those most beloved in Christ, clerics known under the honorable title of priest, and deacons of the excellent nature, and abbots, as well as princes of the secular order: our pious bishop [Willibald] by virtue of his pastoral care appointed you, some as priests in the holy order, others as deacons chosen for sobriety and chasteness, others as monks in the cenobitical army, still others – choosen for their skilful study of text – into the garb of scholars in order to study, to teach, and thus to inculcate a better standard of government in the realm.[60]

More tellingly the *Hodoeporicon* concluded with a hyperbolic summary of Willibald's achievements as bishop with a distinct focus on the clergy:

---

58 *Ibid.*, c. 6, p. 105, trans. p. 163: 'Postquam ille de Roma in istam venibat provinciam cum tribus contribulis suis, et tunc 40 et unis annorum aetate, iam gnarus et grandevus, sacri episcopatus gradum accepit, et in loco que dicitur Eihstat monasterium construere incipiebat atque oceo ibidem sacram monasterialis vitae disciplinam in usum prioris vitae, quod videndo ad Sanctum Benedictum, et non solum ibi, sed in aliis multis monachorum mansionibus'.
59 *Ibid.*, c. 6, p. 105, trans. p. 163: 'ex illius ore dictata perscripsimus in monasterio Heidanheim, testibus mihi diaconis eius et aliis nonnullis iunioris eius'.
60 *Ibid.*, p. 86, trans. p. 143.

All throughout the land of Bavaria, now dotted about with churches, priests' houses and the relics of the saints, he [Willibald] amassed treasures worthy of our Lord. From these places antiphons now resound, sacred lessons are chanted, a noble throng of believers shout aloud the miracles of Christ and with joyful hearts echo from mouth to mouth triumphant praises of their Creator.[61]

It is notable that the 'antiphons' and 'sacred lessons' come not from monasteries, but 'priests' houses' and 'churches'. Ultimately, Eichstätt is portrayed not as a site of idealised monastic tranquillity, but as pastoral in nature, a site of training from which the purity of the cloister could be spread to the *plebi* and the wider diocese.[62]

Chrodegang and Willibald were active at the same time and drew on similar Benedictine exemplars to regulate the life of their episcopal communities. Given Willibald's association with Boniface and other key members of the Frankish episcopate, it seems highly likely that Willibald, like Chrodegang, would have been aware of Zacharias's 747 ruling, which permitted bishops to live with their communities, 'holding to the rule of monastic discipline', and this chimes closely with Huneberc's description of the way of life practised at Eichstätt. Willibald and Chrodegang were therefore following a similar path when they established the way of life of their own communities, albeit applying a slightly different interpretation of key texts and rulings. More than one approach was clearly acceptable here; what mattered was to ensure that authoritative and canonical texts were used to ensure clerical discipline, and likewise to ensure that episcopal authority was maintained.

The way of life at Saint-Maurice d'Agaune and Saint-Denis

Two of the most significant figures who signed the *Totenbund* in 762 were Fulrad of Saint-Denis (d. 784) and Archbishop Wilicar

---

61 *Ibid.*, c. 6, p. 106, trans. p. 164.
62 I explore this idea further in S. Ling, 'Interactions between the clerical enclosure and the extra-claustral clergy: a sacred space with porous walls', in C. Bielmann and B. Thomas (eds), *Debating Religious Space and Place in the Early Medieval World* (Leiden: Sidestone Press, 2018), pp. 127–39.

of Sens (d. c. 785), the latter of whom also presided as the abbot of Saint-Maurice d'Agaune. Fulrad and Wilicar were both close associates of Chrodegang, and in 753–4 all three men were given the honour of escorting Pope Stephen to the meeting with Pippin III at Saint-Denis.[63] Fulrad was referred to as the 'archpriest' of Francia, while Wilicar eventually succeeded Chrodegang as primate of the Frankish church.[64] Saint-Denis and Saint-Maurice were both ancient and prominent abbeys: they counted among the six ancient basilicas granted immunity from episcopal control by Queen Balthild (d. 680) and commanded to live under a regular order.[65] However, from the mid-eighth century and into the early ninth century, questions were emerging about the particular form of religious profession practised within these basilicas. Were these communities monastic or canonical, and what role did the bishops play in regulating the lives of clerics living in monasteries? These concerns can certainly be detected as early as Zacharias's letter to the Frankish court. Chapter 10 reaffirmed bishops' authority over clerics who were 'ordained in monasteries and martyrs' basilicas', while chapter 13 discussed monks who became clerics, emphasising that they 'should not deviate from their own profession', and that even if they lived beyond the cloister should be 'as they were in the monastery'.[66] Such issues came to a head in the reign of Charlemagne with the controversy over the nature of Alcuin's community at Saint-Martin of Tours, and Charlemagne himself raised this point in the *Capitula tractanda cum comitibus, episcopis et abbatibus*: [67]

---

63 *Liber pontificalis*, I, pp. 334–447, trans. Davis, pp. 60–4.
64 For a brief summary of Wilicar's importance, see J. L. Nelson, *King and Emperor: A New Life of Charlemagne* (London: Allen Lane, 2019), p. 124; D. Bullough, 'The dating of the Codex Carolinus nos. 95, 96, 97, Wilchar, and the beginnings of the Archbishopric of Sens', *Deutsches Archiv für Erforschung des Mittelalters*, 18 (1962), 223–30.
65 *Vita sanctae Balthildis*, ed. B. Krusch, *MGH SSRM* 2 (Hanover: Hahn, 1888), c. 9, p. 488; for a brief overview of this immunity, see Rennie, *Freedom and Protection*, pp. 35–6.
66 *Codex Carolinus*, no. 5, c. 10, p. 747, trans. McKitterick and Van Espelo, p. 173: 'ordinatur in monasteriis et basilicis martyrum'; c. 13, p. 747, trans. p. 174: 'non debet eos a proprio proposito deviare ... sicut in monasterio fuit'.
67 I discuss the community at Tours in Ling, 'Superior to canons'.

About the *conversatio* of monks, and whether any can be monks except those who observe the Rule of Benedict. It must be asked if there were monks in Gaul before the tradition of the Rule of St Benedict reached these diocese?[68]

Following the compilation of the *Institutio canonicorum* in 816, Saint-Maurice d'Agaune became a house of canons, while the brethren of Saint-Denis were later accused of having 'ceased holding to the monastic way of life'.[69] Given this trajectory, the prominence of Fulrad and Wilicar, and their association with Chrodegang, understanding how these communities and their leaders understood their way of life in the mid-eighth century is key to understanding both the impact of Chrodegang's rule and wider attitudes to the regulation of monks and the canonical clergy.

Wilicar of Sens (d. c. 785) and the monastery of Saint-Maurice d'Agaune

Wilicar of Sens is an understudied figure often overshadowed by his contemporaries. Tracing his career is difficult, as figures bearing that name served as archbishop of Vienne, bishop of Sion, abbot of Saint-Maurice and archbishop of Sens.[70] Although there has been

---

68 *Capitula tractanda cum comitibus, episcopis et abbatibus*, pp. 161–2, trans. Nelson, p. 86: 'De conversatione monachorum, et utrum aliqui monachi esse possint praeter eos qui regulam sancti Benedicti observant. Inquirendum etiam, si in Gallia monachi fuissent, priusquam traditio regulae sancti Benedicti in has parroechias pervenisset'. Nelson argues within this text we may detect the voice of Charlemagne: Nelson, 'Voice of Charlemagne', pp. 76–88.

69 J. Tardif (ed.), *Monuments Historiques* (Paris: J. Claye, 1866), no. 124, pp. 87–8. See also R. F. Beckonhofer, *Day of Reckoning: Power and Accountability in Medieval France* (Philadelphia, PA: University of Pennsylvania Press, 2004), pp. 13–14; S. Ling, 'The cloister and beyond: regulating the life of the canonical clergy in Francia, from Pippin III to Louis the Pious' (unpublished PhD dissertation, Leicester, 2015), pp. 96–8; I. Rembold, 'The "apostates" of Saint-Denis: reform, dissent, and Carolingian monasticism', in Kramer et al. (eds), *Monastic Communities and Canonical Clergy*, pp. 301–22.

70 Sion is also called Sitten. For discussions on the identification of Wilicar, see J. Theurillat, *L'abbaye de Saint-Maurice: des origines à la réforme canoniale*

some debate over whether these offices were held by separate figures, there is significant evidence to suggest that they were all in fact held by one man. Writing in the mid-ninth century, Ado of Vienne claimed Wilicar was driven from Vienne to Saint-Maurice by Charles Martel's military campaigns.[71] Although an imperfect source, this no doubt draws on a local tradition associating the Bishop of Vienne with the monastery of Saint-Maurice. The link between the bishopric of Sion and Saint-Maurice d'Agaune is more clear-cut as the monastery lies within Sion's diocese.[72] Archaeological excavations at Saint-Maurice have unearthed a large hall which included a podium located against its western wall. This podium has been interpreted as the likely site of Wilicar's *cathedra* (bishop's chair) when he served as bishop-abbot.[73] Radiocarbon dating of organic material found in the hall suggests that it was in use between the second half of the seventh century and the first half of the eighth century.[74]

Wilicar was first recorded as Archbishop of Sens when he headed a delegation of Frankish bishops sent to the Council of Rome in 769.[75] Two years later, in 771, he is attested alongside Fulrad of

(Sitten: Extrait de Vallesia, 1954), pp. 112–21; Bullough, 'The dating', 227–30; A. Helvétius, 'L'abbaye d'Agaune de la fondation de Sigismond au règne de Charlemagne (515–814)', in B. Andenmatten and Laurent Ripart (eds), *L'abbaye de Saint-Maurice d'Agaune, Vol. 1: Histoire et Archéologie* (Gollion: Infolio éditions, 2015), pp. 126–30. Bullough also argues strongly in favour of Wilicars of Sens's association with the bishop of Mentena (a member of the papal curia), as he is addressed as co-*episcopus* within *Codex Carolinus* nos 7, 11, 14, 22 and 30. In *Codex Carolinus* no. 25 Wilicar received papal instruction to ordain 'nos vice' as bishop, a right received for members of the *curia*: D. Bullough, 'The dating of the Codex Carolinus nos. 95, 96, 97, Wilichar, and the beginnings of the archbishopric of Sens', *Deutsches Archiv für Erforschung des Mittelalters*, 18 (1962), 227–30, here 229, nos 40 and 41.

71 Ado, *Chronicon*, ed. G. Pertz, *MGH SS* 2 (Hanover: Hahn, 1829), p. 319.
72 *MGH Conc.* 2.1, no. 13, pp. 72–3.
73 A. Antonini, 'The monastery of Saint Maurice of Agaune (Switzerland) in the First Millenium', in Bielmann and Thomas (eds), *Debating Religious Space*, pp. 143–58, here p. 155.
74 *Ibid.*, p. 156.
75 *Liber pontificalis*, I, c. 17, p. 473; trans. Davis, pp. 96–7.

Saint-Denis chairing the Council of Corbény.[76] On this occasion, the revised version of the *Annales regni Francorum* lists Wilicar not as archbishop of Sens, but as bishop of Sion.[77] A second strand of evidence supports the hypothesis that Wilicar of Sens also served as bishop of Sion/Saint-Maurice. In the late eighth century, the relics of St Victor, the Theban martyr and the companion of Saint-Maurice, were brought to Sens; this relic translation is usually attributed to Wilicar.[78]

By the mid-eighth century, the monastery of Saint-Maurice d'Agaune was already a site with long, prestigious and sacred history.[79] Its liturgical practice of perpetual psalmody (*laus perrenis*) was hugely influential, serving as the model for several key foundations including Saint-Denis.[80] The community had long enjoyed immunity from episcopal control; the formulary of Marculf preserves a grant which not only prohibits the local bishop from extending his power over the abbey, but also permits the brethren to appoint their own abbot.[81] Yet this independence was eroded during Wilicar's tenure as Bishop of Sion, during which time he oversaw a physical remodelling of the monastery and asserted direct episcopal control over the monastery; the latter is most clearly to be seen in the creation of a forged foundation charter, which reinterpreted the history of Saint-Maurice d'Agaune as a strictly episcopal foundation.[82]

---

76 *Annales regni Francorum*, ed. F. Kurze, *MGH SRG* 6 (Hanover: Hahn, 1895), 771, p. 32; trans. B. Scholz, *Carolingian Chronicles* (Ann Arbor, MI: University of Michigan Press, 1970), pp. 35–127, here p. 48.
77 Bullough believed that the author of the Revised Annals was mistaken in this designation, however, given Wilicar's prominent position as primate of the Frankish church, it seems unlikely that the reviser would make such an error. Bullough, 'The dating', 227–30.
78 Helvétius, 'L'abbaye d'Agaune', p. 128.
79 B. Rosenwein, 'One site, many meanings: Saint-Maurice d'Agaune as a place of power in the early middle ages', in M. de Jong et al. (eds), *Topographies of Power in the Early Middle Ages* (Leiden: Brill, 2001), pp. 283–4.
80 B. Rosenwein, 'Perennial prayer at Agaune', in S. Farmer and B. Rosenwein (eds), *Monks and Nuns, Saints and Outcasts: Religion in Medieval Society* (Ithaca, NY: Cornell University Press, 2000), pp. 37–57.
81 Rosenwein, 'One site', pp. 283–4.
82 This remodelling has much in common with Fulrad's work at Saint-Denis, itself aimed at emulating St. Peter's in Rome. For the archaeological developments at Saint-Maurice, see A. Antonini, 'Archéologie du site abbatial (des

This document, preserved in a twelfth-century manuscript, purports to be a charter of King Sigismund (515) but drew inspiration from two texts associated with Fulrad of Saint-Denis.[83] The first was the 757 privilege granted on Fulrad's petition by Pope Stephen II, permitting the community of Saint-Denis the right of direct appeal to the papal see, a claim now made for Saint-Maurice d'Agaune.[84] The second was Charlemagne's 774 foundation charter for the priory of St Hippolyte which he then granted to Fulrad of Saint-Denis; this charter was quoted more or less verbatim within the forgery.[85] As Rosenwein argues, these correlations strongly suggest the text was composed during Fulrad's tenure as abbot and thus can be attributed to his contemporary, Wilicar of Sens.[86] The charter gives an account of a synod attended by King Sigismund and four prominent local bishops: Maximus of Geneva, Victorius of Grenoble, Viventiolus of Lyon and Theodore of Martigny. Although they lived in different periods, all four of these figures are linked to the community of Saint-Maurice d'Agaune.[87] The fourth-century Theodore of Martigny is remembered as the original founder of the monastery, while the sixth-century figures of Maximus of Geneva, Victorius of Grenoble and Viventiolus of Lyon have all been associated with King Sigismund's re-foundation of the monastery.[88] The structure of the forged charter, which takes the form of a dialogue between the four bishops, is intriguing and, as François Masai highlighted, echoes

---

origines au Xe siècle', in Andenmatten and Ripart (eds), *L'abbaye de Saint-Maurice d'Agaune, Vol. 1*, pp. 59–109.

83 For the text and manuscript history see Theurillat, *Saint-Maurice*, pp. 57–85; M. Reymond, 'La charte de Sigismond pour Saint-Maurice d'Agaune 515', *Zeitschrift für Schhweizerische Geschichte*, 6 (1926), 1–60; Rosenwein, 'One site', pp. 285–7.
84 Rosenwein, 'One site', pp. 286–7. For the 757 privilege see A. J. Stoclet, 'Fulrad de Saint-Denis (v. 710–784), abbé et archprêtre de monastères "exempts"', *Le Moyen Âge*, 88 (1982), 210–35, for the text of the privilege see 234–5.
85 Theurillat, *Saint-Maurice*, p. 67.
86 Rosenwein, 'One site', p. 287.
87 I. Wood, 'A prelude to Columbanus: the monastic achievement in the Burgundian territories', in H. B. Clarke and M. Brennan (eds), *Columbanus and Merovingian Monasticism* (Oxford: B. A. R., 1981), pp. 15–19.
88 Antonini, 'Saint Maurice', p. 143.

the structure and organisational principles of the *Regula sanctorum patrum* (*Rule of the four fathers*), which depicts a council in which four eminent churchmen decide on the form of life to be practised by the community.[89] This may suggest that the *Regula sanctorum patrum* was used as the basis for life at Saint-Maurice. It is perhaps significant that this rule omits the title of abbot and instead uses the phrase 'the one who presides' (*qui praeest*); this may well have identified it as a suitable text for use within an episcopal community.[90]

Throughout the charter, while the rights and duties of the abbot are outlined, no founding abbot is named; instead, the text creates a memory of Saint-Maurice d'Agaune as an episcopal foundation closely tied to the diocesan structures of Burgundy.[91] Viventiolus of Lyon – the possible author of the *Vita patrum Iurensium*, which was composed for the community of Saint-Maurice d'Agaune in the sixth century – was given a particularly prominent role within the description of this council.[92] In response to a question posed by King

---

89 F. Masai, 'La *Vita patrum Iurensium* et les debuts du monachisme à Saint-Maurice d'Agaune', in J. Autenrieth and F. Brunhölzl (eds), *Festschrift Bernhard Bischoff* (Stuttgart: A. Hiersemann, 1971), pp. 52–3; For the rule of the four fathers see J. Neufville (ed.), 'Règle des IV pères et seconde règle des pères: texte critique', *Revue Bénédictine*, 77 (1967), 47–106; trans. T. G. Kardong, 'The rule of the four fathers: a new English translation and commentary', *American Benedictine Review*, 54:2 (2003), 142–80.

90 On the titles used in the *Regula sanctorum patrum*, see C. Stewart, 'The literature of early western monasticism', in B. M. Kaczynski (ed.), *The Oxford Handbook of Christian Monasticism* (Oxford: Oxford University Press, 2020), pp. 85–100. The *Regula sanctorum patrum* was also adapted for use by the clerical confraternity in Bern, Burgerbibliothek AA.90.11, suggesting that this text may have been viewed more widely as a suitable text for governing the life of the canonical clergy. For an analysis of Bern, Burgerbibliothek AA.90.11, see Ling, 'The cloister and beyond', Appendix.

91 For an exploration of institutional memory and identities, albeit in an Anglo-Saxon context, see S. Foot, 'Reading Anglo-Saxon charters: memory, record, or story?', in E. M. Tyler and R. Balzaretti (eds), *Narrative and History in the Early Medieval West* (Turnhout: Brepols, 2006), pp. 39–67.

92 G. Moyse, 'Les origines du monachisme dans le diocèse de Besançon (Ve-Xe siècles)', *Bibliothèque de l'Ecole des Chartes*, 131:1 (1973), 21–104, here 44–5. This attribution has been recently questioned in A. Dubreucq, 'Les relations entre Condat et Agaune', in N. Brocard et al. (eds), *Autour de Saint Maurice* (Besançon: Fondation des archives historiques de l'Abbaye de Saint-Maurice, 2012), pp. 133–46, here pp. 144–5.

Sigismund (d. 542), he set forth the fundamentals of the way of life practised within the community, emphasising the authority of the abbot and his deans as well as the abbot's right of direct appeal to the papal see. The abbot was also to set the clothing and diet of the community, and all were to share a common dormitory, refectory and warming room.[93] Viventiolus's prominence in the text might indicate that the *Vita patrum Iurensium*, composed for Saint-Maurice d'Agaune in the sixth century, still influenced the community's way of life.[94] This description of the community further draws on elements of the Benedictine rule, particularly in chapters 21 and 55, though within the text Victorius of Grenoble rejects the Benedictine principle of monastic silence.[95] As Laurent Ripart has suggested, this may have been a way of emphasising the importance of the *laus perrenis* which was different to the liturgical practices of the Benedictine rule.[96] Here, we see a marked difference in the ways of life practised at Metz and Saint-Maurice d'Agaune, as Chrodegang was a proponent of monastic silence within the cathedral close.[97]

From this close analysis of Wilicar's actions at Saint-Maurice d'Agaune, we can discern some parallels with Chrodegang's efforts at Metz: both bishops sought to assert episcopal authority and worked to ensure their episcopal communities lived in accordance with authoritative and canonical texts. Crucially, however, the traditions and models they implemented were significantly different. At Saint-Maurice, there was no clear distinction between clerics and monks, and the 765 donation of Ayroenus specifically highlights that columns (*turmae*) of monks and clerics lived side by side performing the office.[98] Similarly, Wilicar's actions at Saint-Maurice go further than Chrodegang's 'protection' of Gorze. Rather than pre-

---

93 Theurillat, *Saint-Maurice*, pp. 78–9; see also Masai, 'La *Vita*', pp. 52–3.
94 M. Dunn, *The Emergence of Monasticism: From the Desert Fathers to the Early Middle Ages* (Oxford: Blackwell, 2000), p. 88.
95 Theurillat, *Saint-Maurice*, p. 78; Masai, 'La *Vita*', pp. 52–3.
96 L. Ripart, 'Les temps séculiers (IXe-Xe siècle)', in Andenmatten and Ripart (eds), *L'abbaye de Saint-Maurice d'Agaune, Vol. 1*, pp. 134–49, here pp. 138–9.
97 RC, cc. 4, 21 and 27.
98 Theurillat, *Saint-Maurice*, no. 35, pp. 119–20: 'Ut, quitquit exinde ipsi clerici vel ipsi monachi de ipsa turma Valdensis'.

serving monastic independence under episcopal guidance, Wilicar imposed his direct authority over the monastery, creating a fictitious history of the abbey as a longstanding episcopal foundation.[99]

Most significantly, Chrodegang and Wilicar drew on different local traditions and texts to regulate the life of their episcopal communities. For Chrodegang, Benedictine precepts were paramount, while Wilicar's forged charter was more ambivalent towards this rule, placing it alongside other pre-established local texts such as the *Regula sanctorum patrum* and the *Vita patrum Iurensium*. Rather than following Chrodegang's models from Gorze and Metz, Wilicar appears to have modelled his own grant of immunity on that of Saint-Denis, and this not only attests to the longstanding connection between these two communities, but also emphasises the close ties between Saint-Maurice and St. Peter's, Rome. His actions also corresponded to Zacharias's advice regarding both episcopal communities living 'according to the rule of monastic discipline' and the authority of bishops over clerics living within monastic communities.

Fulrad (d. 784) and Saint-Denis

Much like Saint-Maurice d'Agaune, Saint-Denis was one of the premier religious houses of the Frankish realm. As a royal burial site of both Merovingian kings and their Carolingian successors, the prayers of the community had a particularly important cultic and symbolic function.[100] Here, as at Saint-Maurice, the community practised the *laus perennis* and had received immunity from episcopal control under Queen Balthild (680).[101] Unlike Saint-Maurice,

---

99 A. Helvétius, 'L'abbaye d'Agaune de la foundation de Sigismond au règne de Charlemagne (515–814)', in Andenmatten and Ripart (eds), *L'abbaye de Saint-Maurice d'Agaune*, Vol. 1, pp. 111–33, here pp. 126–30.
100 J. J. Emerick, 'Building *more romano* in Francia during the third quarter of the eighth century: the abbey church of Saint-Denis and its model', in C. Bolgia et al. (eds), *Rome Across Time and Space: Cultural Transmission and the Exchange of Ideas, c.500–1400* (Cambridge: Cambridge University Press, 2011), pp. 127–50, here pp. 142–50.
101 *Vita Balthildis*, c. 9, p. 488.

the abbots of Saint-Denis were able to retain this independence from episcopal control throughout the eighth century. In part, this success was due to Abbot Fulrad's political and religious prominence. He served as palace chaplain and in 750 was appointed abbot of Saint-Denis; he was further sent to Rome to seek papal approval for Pippin's usurpation.[102] In these various roles, he worked closely with both Chrodegang and Wilicar. Fulrad's close association with Chrodegang has led to the inference that Saint-Denis was influenced by his rule and had 'lapsed' into a canonical form of life.[103] Yet defining the exact form of life practised by Fulrad and his community at Saint-Denis is difficult. Fulrad held both the offices of palace chaplain and abbot of Saint-Denis, and he was often referred to by both titles; for instance, the *Liber pontificalis* called him 'the venerable abbot and priest'.[104] As an abbot, his function was clearly monastic, yet as chaplain his role was clerical. Obeying the dietary requirements of monastic custom while partaking in court life would have been difficult. Fulrad was granted great authority by both the Carolingian kings and the papacy; notably, in 757 he received papal approval to build monasteries throughout the kingdom without recourse to local bishops. This privilege also placed Saint-Denis under papal protection – and it is this document which, as discussed earlier, inspired Wilicar's own forged privilege for Saint-Maurice d'Agaune.[105] These supra-diocesan powers elevated Fulrad above the Frankish episcopate, leading Pope Hadrian to refer to him as 'Fulrad, the abbot [and] archpriest of Francia'.[106]

Fulrad's testament gives some clue as to how he viewed himself and his community. Fulrad describes himself in priestly rather

---

102 *Annales regni Francorum*, 749, p. 8, trans. Scholz, p. 39. For Fulrad's political role see J. Story, 'Cathwulf, kingship, and the royal abbey of Saint-Denis', *Speculum*, 74:1 (1999), 1–21.
103 R. McKitterick, *The Frankish Kingdoms under the Carolingians, 751–987* (London: Routledge, 1983), pp. 58–9.
104 *Liber pontificalis*, pp. 454–5, trans. Davis, pp. 72, 75.
105 Stoclet, 'Fulrad de Saint-Denis', 210–35.
106 P. Jaffé (ed.), *Regesta Pontificum Romanorum* (Leipzig: Veit, 1885), no. 2410, p. 293: 'Fulradum, abbatem, Franciae archipresbyterum'. See also Emerick, 'Building *more romano*', p. 137; Stoclet, 'Fulrad de Saint-Denis', 210.

than abbatial terms, stating that he was 'unworthy to be associated with the title *sacerdos*'; he likewise refers to Saint-Denis as a church rather than a monastery, calling its members the 'servants of God', an umbrella term which likely referred to both clerics and monks. The testament also highlighted Saint-Denis's role as both a place of prayer, where the office was performed 'day and night', and of pastoral care – notably, with regard to the latter, it was through the prayers and intercessions of the 'pilgrim paupers' that Fulrad hoped to secure his redemption. This interest in the paupers that visited the church suggests a more pastoral focus than that contained within the Benedictine rule, emphasising the openness of the church at Saint-Denis. The rebuilding of Saint-Denis during this period was closely modelled on the T-shaped plan of St. Peter's in Rome, and, as Judson Emerick has suggested, these links were more than architectural: Fulrad sought to imitate St. Peter's role as the 'pastoral church par excellence', creating a cult site for both royal rituals and pilgrims.[107] Given that the monastery was the burial place of Charles Martel and Pippin III, it well suited the political and spiritual needs of Carloman and Charlemagne to maintain the abbey as a public place of worship.

Despite these pastoral and clerical concerns, in other places, Fulrad maintained a monastic focus. At the council of Attigny (762), the delegates who signed the confraternity document were divided into two groups, bishops and abbots. Chrodegang led the bishops, while Fulrad led the abbots. Chrodegang and Fulrad appear to lead their respective orders in prayer; here, unlike in his testament, Fulrad overtly characterises Saint-Denis as a monastery.[108] Likewise, the 777 immunity granting Saint-Denis control over the Alsatian monastery of Salonnes uses explicitly monastic language to describe both Saint-Denis and Salonnes:

> The king found that the privilege contained the provision that neither bishop Angilramn, nor his successors nor any archdeacons or *missi* from his church at Metz could exercise the bishop's right to do

---

107 R. Krautheimer, 'The Carolingian revival of early Christian architecture', *The Art Bulletin*, 24 (1942), 1–38; Emerick, 'Building *more romano*', pp. 142–50.

108 *MGH Conc.* 2.1, no. 13, pp. 72–3.

> ordinations or bless the chrism and altars at Salonnes unless asked to do so by the abbot of Saint-Denis ... henceforth no bishop at all, neither Angilramn nor his successors, may touch the monastery of Salonnes. Rather it is to be under the immunity and privilege of Saint-Denis, in accordance with the Rule, like the other churches that belong to the house of Saint-Denis.[109]

Here we may also see a Gorze in reverse, as Metz's episcopal power was eroded in the face of the monastic rights of Saint-Denis. From this, it seems Saint-Denis remained monastic at least in name, but its practices and public nature had much in common with episcopal sites such as Saint-Maurice d'Agaune.

Both Saint-Denis and Saint-Maurice drew on their own established traditions to govern the life of their communities, and both Fulrad and Wilicar emphasised the closeness of their communities to Rome. It is worth noting that St. Peter's basilica would also have been manned by a mixed clerical and monastic retinue performing the divine office and caring for pilgrims, a model easily adapted for the prominent cult sites of Saint-Denis and Saint-Maurice d'Agaune.[110]

Conclusion

The period between c. 750 and c. 785 saw widespread episcopal concern about the nature of life practised within episcopal communities, as shown by the query sent to Pope Zacharias and his response. This letter acted as a spur to Chrodegang's composition of the *Regula canonicorum*, and while this text was promoted within Chrodegang's immediate circle and was received by some, others drew on other texts and traditions to enforce discipline within their communities. Lull certainly viewed the *Regula canonicorum* as a useful tool in his bid to enforce episcopal discipline; however, Remi of Strasbourg's testament shows how uses of Chrodegang's

---

109 E. Mühlbacher (ed.), *MGH DD Karol. 1* (Hanover: Hahn, 1906), no. 118, pp. 164–8, trans. Rosenwein, *Negotiating*, p. 116.
110 A. Thacker, 'Popes, emperors and clergy at Old St. Peter's from the 4th to the 8th century', in R. McKitterick et al. (eds), *Old St. Peter's, Rome* (Cambridge: Cambridge University Press, 2013), pp. 137–57.

Rule were tempered by the needs and inclinations of local bishops who deftly selected which texts, traditions and practices should be used to regulate the life of their communities. The regulation of the canonical clergy and episcopal communities was not achieved via the straightforward implementation of one standard 'reform' text; instead, bishops drew on the established traditions of their communities and the best practices they had witnessed to set the way of life within their foundations. Thus, Wilicar could draw the *Regula sanctorum patrum* and the *Vita patrum Iurensium* at Saint-Maurice d'Agaune, while Willibald could look to Monte Cassino and the Benedictine rule at Eichstätt.

At the heart of all of these renewals lay common and long-standing attempts to improve the church through endowments and physical reconstruction, and to do so with the aid and help of the network of 'spiritual brethren' which made up the church as a whole.[111] The different approaches taken by these bishops were not mutually exclusive; rather, they were collaborative and reinforced a wider effort to enforce episcopal discipline while ensuring that all lived 'canonically'. Together, they contributed to an ongoing conversation about which texts and traditions represented the best way to govern the clergy. Given this variety of traditions and texts used to regulate the canonical clergy, it is no wonder that Charlemagne should ask, 'About the life of those who are called canons, what sort ought it to be?'[112]

---

111 Bertram (ed.), *Chrodegang Rules, Regula sancti Chrodegangi*, Latin p. 27, trans. p. 52.
112 *Capitula tractanda cum comitibus. episcopis et abbatibus*, p. 161, trans. Nelson, p. 86.

3

A Carolingian 'reform of education'? The reception of Alcuin's pedagogy

Cinzia Grifoni and Giorgia Vocino

If one were asked to name one guiding spirit behind the phenomenon that has been called a Carolingian renaissance, *renovatio* or *correctio*, Alcuin of York would immediately come to mind. His role and influence in shaping Carolingian ideology have been repeatedly explored and highlighted: more specifically, Alcuin's ideas and vocabulary have been identified in both the *Admonitio generalis* and the *Epistola de litteris colendis*, namely the two main pillars which have been made to support the entire historiographical framework of 'the Carolingian Renaissance'.[1] Alcuin worked for a new, corrected, edition of the Bible; he advised the king on the ways

---

* Cinzia Grifoni's research has received funding from the Austrian Science Fund (FWF) under the Elise Richter Programme (Project No. V-811 G).

1 The bibliography on Alcuin's works is too extensive to be fully cited here, but for his role in spearheading Charlemagne's reform movement and for further references, see D. A. Bullough, *Alcuin: Achievement and Reputation* (Leiden: Brill, 2004). On Alcuin's authorship of the two manifestos of the Carolingian renaissance, see W. Hartmann, 'Alkuin und die Gesetzgebung Karls des Grossen', in K. Schmuki and E. Tremp (eds), *Alkuin von York und die geistige Grundlegung Europas* (St. Gallen: Verlag am Klosterhof, 2010), pp. 33–48; F.-C. Scheibe, 'Alcuin und die *Admonitio generalis*', *Deutsches Archiv für Erforschung des Mittelalters*, 14 (1958), 221–9; L. Wallach, 'Charlemagne's *De litteris colendis* and Alcuin. A diplomatic-historical study', *Speculum*, 26:2 (1951), 288–305. For a recent discussion of the *Admonitio generalis*, see J. J. Contreni, 'Let schools be established ... for what? The meaning of *Admonitio generalis*, chapter 70 (*olim* 72)', in G. Boone (ed.), *Music in the Carolingian World: Witnesses to a Metadiscipline* (Columbus, OH: Ohio State University Press, in press).

in which new peoples should embrace Christianity; he intervened in doctrinal disputes and fought heresy; he commented on the Holy Scriptures; and he actively tried to restore the correct pronunciation and spelling of classical Latin.[2] All of these aspects of Alcuin's work have been approached in historiography as constituent parts of the Carolingian reforms and more particularly the reform of education, the reform of the Latin language, the reform of the Bible and, at a more general level, the 'reform of the Church'.

This chapter explores the work of Alcuin the teacher, the *magister Albinus* who wrote schoolbooks focusing on the arts of speech conceived to guide students on the path to wisdom and towards salvation.[3] What was the impact of Alcuin's pedagogy? Did it

---

2 Alcuin's Bible, produced at Tours around 800, circulated widely in the ninth century, which has for a long time been considered proof that his edition had been promoted as an official text and thus became highly influential, an assumption that is today questioned; see G. Lobrichon, 'Le texte des bibles alcuiniennes', *Annales de Bretagne et des Pays de l'Ouest*, 111:3 (2004), 209–19. On Alcuin's famous letters on the conversion and baptism of the Saxons and the Avars see O. M. Phelan, *The Formation of Christian Europe: The Carolingians, Baptism and the* Imperium Christianum (Oxford: Oxford University Press, 2014), esp. chapter 3, pp. 94–146. On Alcuin's doctrinal disputes, namely his intervention at the council of Frankfurt in 794, his debate against Felix of Urgell in 799 and his treatises against adoptionism, see J. Marenbon, 'Alcuin, the Council of Frankfurt and the beginnings of medieval philosophy', in R. Berndt (ed.), *Das Frankfurter Konzil von 794* (2 vols, Mainz: Selbstverl. der Ges. für Mittelrheinische Kirchengeschichte, 1997), II, pp. 603–15; also I. van Renswoude, 'The art of disputation: dialogue, dialectic and debate around 800', *Early Medieval Europe*, 25:1 (2017), 38–53. Regarding Alcuin's exegetical work, several commentaries are mentioned in the *Vita Alcuini*, but not all of them have survived: see *Vita beati Alcuini*, c. 21, ed. C. Veyrard-Cosme, *La Vita beati Alcuini (IXe s.). Les inflexions d'un discours de sainteté. Introduction, edition et traduction annotée du texte d'après Reims, BM 1395 (K 784)* (Paris: Institut d'études augustiniennes, 2017), pp. 296–301. Finally, for Alcuin's interventions in Latin spelling and pronunciation, see R. Wright, 'How Latin came to be a foreign language for all', in R. Wright (ed.), *A Sociophilological Study of Late Latin* (Turnhout: Brepols, 2002), pp. 3–17, esp. pp. 14–17, as well as, in the same volume, R. Wright, 'Viva Voce', pp. 49–68 and R. Wright, 'Alcuin's De Orthographia and the Council of Tours (A.D. 813)', pp. 127–46.
3 L. Holtz, 'Alcuin et la renaissance des arts libéraux', in P. L. Butzer, M. Kerner and W. Oberschelp (eds), *Karl der Grosse und sein Nachwirken. 1200*

indeed change or influence the ways in which these disciplines were taught in the classroom? Can we observe how, where and by whom Alcuin's didactic texts and instructions were received and implemented? And when looking at patterns of transmission, school practices and networks of knowledge, should the historiographic concept of Carolingian reform (or *correctio*) still be considered the most fitting conceptual framework to make sense of our sources? In order to answer these questions, the following pages will first explore the transmission and the reception of Alcuin's *Opera didascalica*.[4] The analysis will then focus on the evidence provided by the kingdom of Italy, a region where Alcuin's treatises and teaching instructions met centuries-long school traditions: the study of a particular manuscript and the contextualisation of the late reception of Alcuin's didactic works south of the Alps will shed light on the ways and channels through which texts circulated in the early Middle Ages. The reception of Alcuin's educational programme will then be assessed in a centre of learning connected to the Anglo-Saxon master through his most influential pupil, Hrabanus Maurus (d. 856). The study of the texts and manuscripts produced at Wissembourg, where Hrabanus's pupil Otfrid taught, allows us to measure to what extent an Alcuinian pedagogy produced the desired results when implemented in an actual school of the Carolingian empire.

Jahre Kultur und Wissenschaft in Europa (2 vols, Turnhout: Brepols, 1997), I, pp. 45–60. For a more comprehensive understanding of the importance of Alcuin's pedagogy in the Carolingian cultural landscape, see also J. J. Contreni, 'Learning for God: education in the Carolingian age', *The Journal of Medieval Latin*, 24 (2014), 89–129 and J. J. Contreni, 'The pursuit of knowledge in Carolingian Europe', in R. E. Sullivan (ed.), *The Gentle Voices of Teachers. Aspects of Learning in the Carolingian Age* (Columbus, OH: Ohio State University Press, 1995), pp. 106–41.

4 This is the title under which Alcuin's didactic treatises were grouped in the edition published in the Patrologia Latina collection, see J.-P. Migne (ed.), *PL* 101 (Paris: Migne, 1851), cols 847–1002.

Alcuin's *Opera didascalica*: transmission and reception

Alcuin wrote five didactic treatises dedicated to the learning of the Latin language and the arts of the *trivium* (i.e. grammar, rhetoric and dialectic): the *Ars grammatica* introduced by a short work known as the *Disputatio de vera philosophia*, *De rhetorica*, *De dialectica* and *De orthographia*, the first four of which were written in dialogue format.[5] If what survives of Alcuin's *Opera didascalica* does indeed focus on the arts of speech, we know that Alcuin was also interested in the *quadrivium* (i.e. arithmetic, geometry, music and astronomy) and particularly in astronomy (e.g. *De ratio lunae*

---

5 For the *Ars grammatica* and the *Disputatio de vera philosophia*, see L. Holtz, 'L'œuvre grammaticale d'Alcuin dans le contexte de son temps', in Schmuki and Tremp (eds), *Alkuin von York*, pp. 129–49. For some translated excerpts from both the *Disputatio de vera philosophia* and the *Ars grammatica* see R. Copeland and I. Sluiter, *Medieval Grammar and Rhetoric. Language Arts and Literary Theory, AD 300–1475* (Oxford: Oxford University Press, 2012), pp. 272–87. The critical edition of Alcuin's *Ars grammatica*, a text transmitted by over twenty manuscripts, is currently in preparation for a publication in the *CCCM*; in the meantime, see Alcuin, *Opera didascalica*, cols 849–901. For an assessment of the wide circulation of the text see now I. Grigoras, '*Breuiarium Artis grammaticae Alcuini*: edition and study', *The Journal of Medieval Latin*, 30 (2020), 183–226. *De rhetorica* has recently been edited and studied in A. Costrino, 'Alcuin's *Disputatio de rhetorica*. A critical edition with studies of aspects of the text, the stemma codicum, the didactic diagrams and a reinterpretation of sources for the problem of the duality of the dialogue' (unpublished PhD dissertation, University of York, 2016); for this text, see also M. S. Kempshall, 'The virtues of rhetoric: Alcuin's *Disputatio de rhetorica et de virtutibus*', *Anglo-Saxon England*, 37 (2008), 7–30 as well as S. Ramsey, 'A reevaluation of Alcuin's *Disputatio de rhetorica et de virtutibus* as consular persuasion: the context of the late eighth century revisited', *Advances in the History of Rhetoric*, 19:3 (2016), 324–43; for some translated excerpts see Copeland and Sluiter, *Medieval Grammar*, pp. 287–98. For a recent reassessment of the *De dialectica*, see E. M. E. Rädler-Bohn, 'Re-dating Alcuin's *De dialectica*: or, did Alcuin teach at Lorsch?', *Anglo-Saxon England*, 45 (2016), 71–104; the Latin text of the treatise can be read in Alcuin, *Opera didascalica*, cols 949–76. Finally, *De orthographia*, which survives in two versions, is studied and edited (redaction *a*) in Alcuin, *De orthographia*, ed. S. Bruni (Florence: Sismel, 1997); redaction *b* can be read in Alcuin, *Opera didascalica*, cols 901–20.

and his *computus*).⁶ Alcuin's approach to teaching is illustrated more explicitly in his *Disputatio de vera philosophia* where he explains that an education in the seven liberal arts is essential to achieve wisdom, which he understood as the ability to correctly understand and expound scripture.⁷ The liberal arts are thus conceived as instruments of Christian knowledge, as they had traditionally been defined in Augustine's *De doctrina christiana* as well as in Cassiodorus's *Expositio psalmorum* and *Institutiones*.⁸ To put it in Alcuin's own words, an education in the liberal arts was meant to turn students into 'invincible defenders of the true faith and upholders of the truth'.⁹

It is tempting to think of Alcuin's *Opera didascalica* as a coherent educational programme, but manuscript evidence suggests otherwise: none of the many manuscripts transmitting his treatises brings together the five texts to form a didactic *summa*. Alcuin's writings on the liberal arts were not conceived as part of a unified school programme, neither in the author's design nor in the understanding of those who continued to copy and use his works. Alcuin's didactic texts were not written to be adopted in every school of Charlemagne's realm, and there is no 'Alcuinian programme' that the Frankish ruler tried to implement in the territories under his

---

6 B. Englisch, 'Alkuin und das Quadrivium in der Karolingerzeit', *Annales de Bretagne et des Pays de l'Ouest*, 111:3 (2004), 163–74; K. Springsfeld, *Alkuins Einfluß auf die Komputistik zur Zeit Karls des Großen* (Stuttgart: Franz Steiner, 2002).
7 Copeland and Sluiter (trans.), *Medieval Grammar*, pp. 275–6, for the Latin text, see Alcuin, *Opera didascalica*, cols 853–4.
8 M. Alberi, '"The better paths of wisdom": Alcuin's monastic "true philosophy" and the worldly court', *Speculum*, 74:4 (2001), 896–910, on Augustine's influence at 901; M. Irvine, *The Making of Textual Culture. 'Grammatica' and Literary Theory, 350–1100* (Cambridge: Cambridge University Press, 1994), on Alcuin's *Ars grammatica* at pp. 313–33 and more specifically on his philosophical understanding of the liberal arts at pp. 318–20.
9 Alcuin, *Opera didascalica*, col. 854: 'Quatenus hinc inde armati verae fidei defensores et veritatis assertores omnimodis invincibiles efficiamini'. The crucial relation between knowledge and the interpretation of Holy Scriptures is explored in this volume by Irene van Renswoude (Chapter 5) with regards to doctrinal controversies and by Kristina Mitalaitė (Chapter 6), who, looking at Carolingian exegesis, highlights the didactic quality of some biblical commentaries – namely those by Haimo of Auxerre.

rule. Alcuin's treatises were not written in a single time span, and they were not conceived as a step-by-step or 'beginner-to-advanced' learning programme. The *De orthographia* appears to be the last one to have been composed and it seems likely, particularly in the light of the most recent studies, that the *De rhetorica* and the *De dialectica* were written before the *Ars grammatica*.[10] However, if Alcuin did not design a coherent didactic programme to be received and used in Carolingian schools, his texts nevertheless travelled far and wide and did so with surprising speed. The swift circulation of his *Opera didascalica* is a striking feature of its transmission: Alcuin was still alive when some of the manuscripts that have come down to us were copied.[11] If circulation and dissemination are to be considered as criteria to measure the impact of a medieval author's work, Alcuin's didactic treatises were indeed tremendously influential, particularly in Carolingian times.[12] The numbers of ninth-century manuscripts transmitting his works are exceptional: over twenty manuscripts each (including fragments) for the *Ars grammatica*, *De rhetorica* and *De dialectica* and some twenty manuscripts for the *De orthographia*.[13] These are impressive numbers, but what is even more impressive is that ninth-century manuscripts represent the largest share in the overall transmission of these works across the whole Middle Ages. Alcuin's treatises continued to be copied sporadically, but numbers tell us that an active interest in them declined as time passed.[14]

10 Rädler-Bohn, 'Re-dating Alcuin's *De dialectica*'.
11 The list of the manuscripts transmitting Alcuin's works dating to the ninth century has been published by D. Ganz, 'Handschriften der Werke Alkuins aus dem 9. Jahrhundert', in Schmuki and Tremp (eds), *Alkuin von York*, pp. 185–94.
12 Ganz, 'Handschriften', p. 185.
13 The *Ars grammatica* manuscripts are mostly accompanied by the *De vera philosophia*; for a provisional list of the surviving manuscripts, see M.-H. Jullien and F. Perelman (eds), *Clavis scriptorum latinorum medii aevi. Auctores Galliae 735–987* (Turnhout: Brepols, 1999), II, pp. 21–2. David Ganz's list does not include the manuscripts of the *De orthographia*, but they can be found, together with the presentation of a *stemma codicum*, in Bruni (ed.), *Alcuino. De orthographia*, pp. xxxii–xxxvi, lvi.
14 For a quick overview of the *Opera didascalica*'s manuscript transmission, see Jullien and Perelman (eds), *Clavis scriptorum*, II, pp. 21–2 (*Ars*

The obsolescence of these texts is particularly striking for the *De orthographia*, whose last surviving continental copy dates from the tenth century.[15] This is surprising since the *De orthographia* is a work at the core of Alcuin's ambition to restore a more correct, more classical spelling and pronunciation of the Latin language: it was written when he was in Tours (ca. 796–800) at a time when he was working on his edition of the Bible.[16] The short treatise circulated quickly and widely, but Alcuin's teaching did not eradicate 'bad Latin' and 'bad spelling': 'regional' and 'local' spelling, clearly influenced by the spoken language, were not 'corrected', as manuscript evidence patently demonstrates.[17] Therefore, while his treatise circulated widely, and while other orthographies (such as those written by Cassiodorus and Bede) likewise enjoyed increased circulation in this period, the results did not appear to have matched Alcuin's ambitions. How and why did things go sideways?

Examining the patterns of circulation allows us to better understand the transmission and the influence of Alcuin's didactic works. Early copies of his *Opera didascalica* survive from centres that were either connected to Alcuin through his personal acquaintances (pupils and friends) or closely connected to the Carolingian court. The earliest surviving copy of the *Ars grammatica* was produced at Saint-Martin of Tours (introduced by the *De vera philosophia* in

---

grammatica), pp. 131–2 (*De dialectica*), p. 143 (*De orthographia*) and pp. 160–1 (*De rhetorica*).

15 Redaction *b* continued to be copied in England: see V. Law and J. P. Carley, 'Grammar and arithmetic in two thirteenth-century English monastic collections: Cambridge, Sidney Sussex College, MS 75 and Oxford, Bodleian Library, MS Bodley 186 (S. C. 2088)', *The Journal of Mediaeval Latin*, 1 (1991), 140–67.

16 See the introduction to the edition of the redaction *a*, Bruni, *Alcuino. De orthographia*, pp. i–lxxix.

17 See for instance the 'creative Latin' of the manuscripts studied by C. van Rhijn, '"Et hoc considerat episcopus, ut ipsi presbyteri non sint idiothae": Carolingian local *correctio* and an unknown priests' exam from the early ninth century', in R. Meens et al. (eds), *Religious Franks: Religion and Power in the Frankish Kingdoms: Studies in Honour of Mayke de Jong* (Manchester: Manchester University Press, 2016), pp. 162–80. Also, see later in this chapter the nine poems composed at Wissembourg in the late ninth century as well as the contribution focusing on liturgical manuscripts by Els Rose and Arthur Westwell in Chapter 4 of this volume.

Sankt Gallen, SB 268, early ninth century), but was readily available also at Luxeuil (introduced by the *De vera philosophia* in Naples, Biblioteca Nazionale IV.A.34, early ninth century) and Corbie (Paris, BNF lat. 13377, early ninth century); the treatises *De rhetorica* and *De dialectica* were copied together at Verona (Munich BSB Clm 6407, ca. 800), Freising (Munich BSB Clm 13984, early ninth century), Echternach (Vatican Library, Reg. lat. 1209, early ninth century) and in south-western Germany (later in the Murbach library, Oxford, BL, Junius 25, early ninth century), but they also circulated separately and early copies could be found at Lyon (*De dialectica* in BAV, Pagès 1, before 814), Saint-Amand (*De rhetorica* in Valenciennes BM 404, early ninth century) and Lorsch (*De rhetorica* is listed in the library catalogue A dated to ca. 830); the *De orthographia* was copied during Alcuin's lifetime both in Salzburg (redaction *b* showing contaminations with the redaction *a*, Vienna, ÖNB Cod. 795, ca. 799) and in the monastic *scriptorium* of St. Gall (redaction *a*, Sankt Gallen, SB 249, ca. 800).[18] The swift

---

18 Sankt Gallen, SB 268 can be consulted online at www.e-codices.unifr.ch/en/list/one/csg/0268 (accessed 21 February 2022). For Naples, Biblioteca Nazionale IV.A.34, see L. Munzi, *Multiplex Latinitas. Testi grammaticali latini dell'Alto Medioevo* (Naples: Istituto universitario orientale, 2004), pp. 69–70. Paris, BNF lat. 13377, is copied in the so-called Maurdramnus script and can be viewed online at https://gallica.bnf.fr/ark:/12148/btv1b90667074 (accessed 21 February 2022). A black and white reproduction from microfilm of Munich BSB Clm 6407 can be viewed at https://daten.digitale-sammlungen.de/~db/0003/bsb00036088/images/ (accessed 21 February 2022). The manuscript Munich BSB Clm 13984 can be consulted online at https://daten.digitale-sammlungen.de/~db/0004/bsb00042784/images/ (accessed 21 February 2022); the codicological unit (fos 1–47) gathering the *De rhetorica* and the *De dialectica* was copied from Munich BSB Clm 6407. Vatican Library, Reg. lat. 1209 is written in a very pointed Insular script and is available online at https://digi.vatlib.it/view/MSS_Reg.lat.1209 (accessed 21 February 2022). Oxford, BL, Junius 25 is available online at https://digital.bodleian.ox.ac.uk/objects/4df4cdd2-14d8-4256-ae07-a09917b3408e/(accessed 21 February 2022). BAV, Pagès 1, also known as the 'Codex Leidradi', previously belonged to the collection of the Casa dei Padri Maristi at Rome and is digitised at https://digi.vatlib.it/view/MSS_Pages.1 (accessed 21 February 2022). Valenciennes BM 404 is available at https://gallica.bnf.fr/ark:/12148/btv1b8452582n (accessed 21 February 2022). For the entry in the

transmission of Alcuin's didactic works can be best explained by thinking in terms of networks of knowledge, that is, networks in which proximity was not determined by geographical distance or by belonging to the same institution, but by the personal connections between masters, pupils and centres of learning.[19] Take, for example, Arn of Salzburg, who was one of Alcuin's dearest friends and correspondents: his copy of the *De orthographia* (Vienna, ÖNB Cod. 795) shows signs of a personally tailored text, which was possibly designed by Alcuin himself for his friend.[20] Alcuin's works were also quickly available in Echternach (Vatican Library, Reg. lat. 1209), where Alcuin had a close personal link to Abbot Beornred, to whom he both dedicated the *Vita Willibrordi* and sent along copies of late antique grammatical writings.[21] Similarly, Bishop Leidrad of Lyon, one of Alcuin's pupils and Arn of Salzburg's friend, donated a manuscript (Vatican Library, Pagès 1) containing a collection of dialectical texts to the church of Lyon. Among these texts can be found a paraphrased Latin commentary on Aristotle's *Categories* known as *Categoriae decem*, a text rediscovered by Alcuin, who sent a copy to Charlemagne and then used it extensively for the

---

Lorsch library catalogue, see A. Häse, *Mittelalterliche Bücherverzeichnisse aus Kloster Lorsch. Einleitung, Edition und Kommentar* (Wiesbaden: Harrassowitz, 2002), p. 97. Vienna, ÖNB Cod. 795 contains a miscellany of texts copied by different scribes, some from Saint-Amand, others from Salzburg; for a description see Bullough, *Alcuin: Achievement*, pp. 44–51; this manuscript is also available online at https://digital.onb.ac.at/RepViewer/viewer.faces?doc=DTL_3112149&order=1&view=SINGLE (accessed 21 February 2022). Finally, Sankt Gallen, SB 249 is available online at www.e-codices.unifr.ch/en/list/one/csg/0249 (accessed 21 February 2022).

19 The importance of these networks for the circulation of Carolingian texts and books has recently been highlighted by S. Meeder, *The Irish Scholarly Presence at St. Gall: Networks of Knowledge in the Early Middle Ages* (London: Bloomsbury, 2018). To appreciate the width of Alcuin's reach, see also M. Garrison, 'Les reseaux d'Alcuin et la formation d'une culture européenne', *Annales de Bretagne et des Pays de l'Ouest*, 111:3 (2004), 319–31.

20 M. Diesenberger and H. Wolfram, 'Arn und Alkuin 790 bis 804: zwei Freunde und ihre Schriften', in M. Niederkorn-Bruck and A. Scharer (eds), *Erzbischof Arn von Salzburg* (Vienna: Oldenbourg, 2004), pp. 81–106.

21 Bullough, *Alcuin: Achievement*, pp. 224 and 317.

composition of his *De dialectica*.²² Leidrad's manuscript shows a particularly strong connection to Alcuin's teaching material, which he may have personally consulted and where he could read excerpts from his master's *De dialectica*.²³ Finally, Alcuin's *De vera philosophia*, this time transmitted without the *Ars grammatica*, can also be found in Walahfrid Strabo's *Vademecum* (Sankt Gallen, SB 878, copied between 825 and 849).²⁴ Walahfrid, a student at Fulda under Hrabanus Maurus, included Alcuin's material in his own didactic handbook, and the principles illustrated in the *De vera philosophia* seem to have influenced his approach to and understanding of the arts of speech.²⁵ If Alcuin's social network played an essential role in the dissemination of his works, the hubs of such a network are not so easily identified: there are no doubts that Saint-Martin of Tours was one of the main centres for the production and transmission of his texts, but the role of the Carolingian court, for instance, is difficult to assess. Alcuin and many of his pupils and friends (Arn of Salzburg, Richbod of Lorsch, Leidrad of Lyon and Angilbert of Saint-Riquier, among others) gravitated around it and, if there was no proactive promotion of the Anglo-Saxon master's works on the

---

22 Rädler-Bohn, 'Re-dating Alcuin's *De dialectica*'. For a detailed analysis of the content of the manuscript and the project behind the miscellany of texts, see P. Radiciotti, '*Romania* e *Germania* a confronto: un codice di Leidrat e le origini medievali della minuscola carolina', *Scripta*, 1 (2008), 121–44.
23 Palaeographical evidence has recently been brought forward to support the hypothesis that Alcuin personally annotated the manuscript, see F. Troncarelli, 'Il diavolo nello specchio. I disegni di Alcuino nel *codex pagesianus*', *Litterae Caelestes*, 8 (2017), 75–112, on the annotations attributed to Alcuin himself at 79. More prudently Louis Holtz considers Leidrad's manuscript to be a copy of Alcuin's exemplar, see Holtz, 'L'œuvre grammaticale', p. 144, footnote 47. The hypothesis that the manuscript was made of different parts gathered together by Leidrad only at a later stage, see F. Troncarelli, 'Il diavolo nello specchio', 78–9.
24 The manuscript can be viewed online at www.e-codices.unifr.ch/fr/list/one/csg/0878 (accessed 21 February 2022). Its complex structure and content are analysed in R. Corradini, 'ZeitNetzWerk. Karolingische Gelehrsamkeit und Zeitforschung im Kompendium des Walahfrid Strabo' (unpublished Habilitation, University of Vienna, 2014).
25 On the scholarly connections shown by the texts gathered in this miscellany, see also W. M. Stevens, *Rhetoric and Reckoning in the Ninth Century. The 'Vademecum' of Walahfrid Strabo* (Turnhout: Brepols, 2018).

part of Charlemagne, the social encounters that took place in the hallways of the court as well as the likely local availability of new texts written by members of the royal entourage in the Frankish ruler's library certainly created the opportunities for their further dissemination.[26]

Travelling in the bags of Alcuin's pupils: the case of Munich, BSB Clm 6407

The swift transmission of Alcuin's didactic works is best explained by looking at networks of knowledge that surviving ninth-century books bring to light. This process can be illustrated by the example of a manuscript produced in Verona, a city far from the Frankish heartland. However, despite geographical distance, Verona was not a city on the periphery of Charlemagne's realm: the connections enjoyed by its foreign bishops, appointed by the Frankish ruler himself, drew Verona close to Carolingian courts, more specifically the court gathered around Charlemagne as well as the Italian court surrounding the king's son Pippin, who had been appointed as king of the former kingdom of the Lombards in 781.[27] Pippin, only a child at the time of his ascension to the throne, ruled with the help of some of Charlemagne's most trusted advisors, among them two of Alcuin's closest friends: Angilbert of Saint-Riquier, *primicerius* (i.e. chief administrator) at the Italian court and most likely a former pupil of Alcuin, and Adalhard of Corbie, who acted as regent and whom the Anglo-Saxon scholar considered a spiritual brother.[28]

---

26 On the court library of Charlemagne see B. Bischoff, *Manuscripts and Libraries in the Age of Charlemagne* (Cambridge: Cambridge University Press, 1994), pp. 56–75, esp. at p. 56: 'We can confidently assume that the court library served as the archive for works which originated at the court or at the order of Charlemagne as well as for works written by former members of his circle'.

27 On Italy under King Pippin, see M. Stoffella, 'Staying Lombard while becoming Carolingian? Italy under King Pippin', in C. Gantner and W. Pohl (eds), *After Charlemagne: Carolingian Italy and Its Rulers* (Cambridge: Cambridge University Press, 2020), pp. 135–47.

28 Alcuin, *Epistolae*, ed. E. Dümmler, *MGH Epp.* 4 (Berlin: Weidmann, 1895), nos 9 and 11, pp. 34–5 and 37. On Adalhard's regency in Italy, see B. Kasten,

Moreover, Alcuin portrayed himself as a teacher (*magister*) to the young king in his short pedagogical dialogue known as *Disputatio Pippini cum Albino*, which provides definitions of some elementary words and abstract concepts.[29] Consequently, a personal teacher–pupil connection between Alcuin and the king of Italy cannot be ruled out, and this bond may also explain why Verona was among the earliest centres where Alcuin's *Opera didascalica* was copied.

Verona was one of the Italian royal cities (*sedes regiae*) where Pippin's court resided, as recorded in a poem celebrating the glories of the ancient town.[30] The manuscript containing Alcuin's *De rhetorica* and *De dialectica* produced in Verona around 800 (Munich, BSB Clm 6407) is the earliest surviving copy for both works and reveals a direct link to the environment in which these texts were first produced and used, namely Alcuin's classroom.[31] Both works may have first travelled to Italy with his Anglo-Saxon pupil Wizo, better known under the Latin nickname Candidus.[32] He was one of Alcuin's closest collaborators and often acted as his messenger: he travelled to Salzburg to work for Arn in 798 and accompanied the Bavarian archbishop to Rome between 799 and 801. The analysis of the texts copied in Clm 6407 further unveils a strong connection to Alcuin's teaching and interests. Alongside his *De rhetorica* and

---

Adalhard von Corbie. Die Biographie eines karolingischen Politikers und Klostervorstehers (Düsseldorf: Droste, 1986), esp. pp. 42–7.

29 On this text, see C. Grifoni, 'Un giovane promettente: la rappresentazione alcuiniana di Pipino d'Italia nella *Disputatio Pippini cum Albino* (con traduzione italiana del testo)', in G. Albertoni and F. Borri (eds), *Il regno di Pipino, i Carolingi e l'Italia (781–810)* (Turnhout: Brepols, forthcoming).

30 The rhythmic composition is edited under the title *Laudes Veronensis civitatis*, ed. E. Dümmler, *MGH Poetae*, I (Berlin: Weidmann, 1881), pp. 118–22. For an English translation, see P. Godman, *Poetry of the Carolingian Renaissance* (London: Duckworth, 1985), pp. 180–6.

31 Bullough believes Clm 6407 was copied directly from a Tours exemplar, but no evidence is provided for this assumption, see Bullough, *Alcuin: Achievement*, p. 105, footnote 262.

32 Candidus's biography is reconstructed in J. Marenbon, 'Candidus [Hwita, Wizo]', *Oxford Dictionary of National Biography* (Oxford: Oxford University Press, 2004), IX, pp. 888–9 as well as C. A. Jones, 'The sermons attributed to Candidus Wizo', in K. O'Brien et al. (eds), *Latin Learning and English Lore: Studies in Anglo-Saxon Literature for Michael Lapidge* (2 vols, Toronto: University of Toronto Press, 2005), I, pp. 260–83, esp. 260–3.

De dialectica, the Verona manuscript includes a dialectical *florilegium* (a collection of excerpts from various authorities), including two chapters explicitly attributed to Alcuin (*dicta Albini diaconi de imagine Dei*) and Candidus (*dicta Candidi presbyteri de imagine Dei*).[33] Clm 6407 is the only manuscript which transmits this *florilegium* in its entirety (fifteen chapters), although the text circulated more widely and at least some of its chapters were available in early ninth-century Lyon and Lorsch.[34] Other Carolingian scholars personally acquainted with Alcuin, such as Paulinus of Aquileia, Hrabanus Maurus and Theodulf of Orléans, knew the *florilegium* and used it in their own writings.[35] The connection between the study of the arts of speech and the understanding of scripture and Christian doctrine – the cornerstone of Alcuin's pedagogy – is made clear in Clm 6407 by bringing together rhetorical, dialectical and theological works. The compiler included a text explaining the ways in which scripture should be interpreted (fos 82–9), two expositions of the faith (fos 104v–5 and 106v–8v), a letter on the baptismal *ordo* traditionally attributed to Alcuin (fos 105r–6v), a short exposition on the seven seals of the Apocalypse (fos 108v–9v) and excerpts from various church councils on Christ's human and divine nature (fos 110–14v).[36] This selection of texts is not only largely shaped by Alcuin's teaching, but also reflects his personal engagement in the doctrinal disputes of his time: the exposition on baptism and the *Symbolum* written down on fos 105r–8v specifically address Adoptionist beliefs and were copied in the ninth

---

33 For the study of the *florilegium*, see J. Marenbon, *From the Circle of Alcuin to the School of Auxerre. Logic, Theology and Philosophy in the Early Middle Ages* (Cambridge: Cambridge University Press, 1981), pp. 32–56 and for its edition pp. 144–66. The attribution of the whole collection to Candidus has been refuted by F. Dolbeau, 'Le *Liber XXI sententiarum* (CPL 373): Édition d'un texte de travail', *Recherches Augustiniennes et Patristiques*, 30 (1997), 113–65, on the *Dicta Candidi* esp. 162–5.
34 For the list of the earliest surviving manuscripts, see Marenbon, *From the Circle of Alcuin*, p. 149.
35 Marenbon, *From the Circle of Alcuin*, p. 42.
36 For a detailed description of the full content of the manuscript, see G. Glauche, *Katalog der lateinischen Handschriften der Bayerischen Staatsbibliothek München. Die Pergamenthandschriften aus dem Domkapitel Freising*, II (Wiesbaden: Harrassowitz, 2011), pp. 206–11.

century in other centres staffed by Alcuin's fellow courtiers, friends and pupils (notably Salzburg, Cologne, Corbie, Fulda, Orléans and Wissembourg).[37] The didactic purpose of the collection gathered in Clm 6407 is underlined by Susan Keefe, who defines the manuscript as a 'schoolbook concerned for the instruction of the clergy'.[38] Surprisingly, the book was not used in Verona's cathedral school: it left the Italian city soon after having been produced and ended up in Freising where it was used as an exemplar to make a new copy of Alcuin's *De rhetorica* and *De dialectica* (Munich, BSB Clm 13084) under either Bishop Atto (783–811) or his successor Hitto (811–36).[39] It is thus plausible to picture Clm 6407 travelling in the bags of yet another scholar moving through the same hubs of the wide-reaching Carolingian network of knowledge that had allowed Alcuin's teaching material to reach Verona only a few years earlier.

Manuscript transmission thus shows that Alcuin's *Opera didascalica* circulated intensively and widely in ninth-century Europe. Does this however mean that his texts formed the standard programme locally implemented in schools under Carolingian rule? The case of Clm 6407 calls for caution as the manuscript soon left Verona and no copies seem to have been made locally. Moreover, and more significantly, Italy provides evidence challenging the idea of a 'reform of education' deliberately and widely implemented in the territories under Carolingian rule.

---

37 S. Keefe, *A Catalogue of Works Pertaining to the Explanation of the Creed in Carolingian Manuscripts* (Turnhout: Brepols, 2012), p. 93, no. 90. The baptismal *ordo*, certainly used if not written by Alcuin himself, was a bestseller in Carolingian times (seventeen ninth-century manuscripts); see S. Keefe, *Water and the Word: Baptism and the Education of the Clergy in the Carolingian Empire* (2 vols, Notre Dame, IN: University of Notre Dame Press, 2002), I, pp. 80–4, with edition of the text in II, pp. 238–45.
38 Keefe, *A Catalogue of Works*, pp. 279–80. Keefe more precisely calls it a 'monastic schoolbook', but the manuscript was most likely copied in the scriptorium of Verona cathedral.
39 Glauche, *Katalog der lateinischen Handschriften*, p. 315. The manuscript can be viewed online at https://daten.digitale-sammlungen.de/~db/0004/bsb00042784/images/ (accessed 21 February 2022).

A delayed reception: Alcuin's *Opera didascalica* in post-Carolingian Italy

The circulation of Alcuin's didactic works was limited in Italy. *De rhetorica* and *De dialectica* can only be found in two surviving ninth-century manuscripts: Clm 6407 and Vat. lat. 3850.[40] As we have seen, the former soon left Italy, and the latter does not easily unveil its history. The late ninth-century Caroline minuscule used in Vat. lat. 3850 shows signs of insular influence (Irish abbreviations for *est* and *et*) and scribes continued to use uncial forms for some letters (namely *a*, *d*, *n*), which suggests production in late ninth-century northern Italy.[41] The book content brings together school texts and liturgical pieces.[42] A late ninth-century dating for the manuscript is confirmed by its inclusion of an excerpt from the liturgical compilation known as the Pseudo-Alcuin's *De divinis officiis*, a text including borrowings from Amalarius of Metz's and Remigius of Auxerre's liturgical works.[43] The poems *Qui rogo*, *O uos aetas* and *Me lege* that are often transmitted with Alcuin's *De dialectica* and *De rhetorica* were copied in the Vatican manuscript, but the

---

40 The manuscript, a small-sized book dated to the late ninth century, can be consulted at https://digi.vatlib.it/view/MSS_Vat.lat.3850 (accessed on 21 February 2022).
41 See S. Gavinelli, 'Early Carolingian Italy', in F. T. Coulson and R. G. Babcock (eds), *The Oxford Handbook of Latin Palaeography* (Oxford: Oxford University Press, 2020), pp. 262–77.
42 While Alcuin's *De dialectica* and *De rhetorica* fill most of the manuscript (fos 1r–21v and 21v–43r respectively), the following works were copied in the last pages (fos 43v–6v): an alphabetical hymn in honour of Christ and the apostles; an excerpt (ch. 51) from the late ninth-century treatise known as the Pseudo-Alcuin's *Liber de divinis officiis*; a grammatical text entitled *Glosa Prisciani minoris*; and a short collection of liturgical instructions for Easter celebrations grouped under the title *De cena dominica*.
43 On this text see M. Andrieu, 'L'*Ordo romanus antiquus* et le *Liber de divinis officiis* du Pseudo-Alcuin', *Revue des sciences religieuses*, 5 (1925), 642–50. Given the heterogeneous nature of liturgical compilations and the lack of a critical edition, it is impossible to know for certain if chapter 51 – the one copied down in Vat. lat. 3850 – existed before its inclusion in Pseudo-Alcuin's *De divinis officiis* or circulated independently from it.

diagrams illustrating the key concepts of both arts were omitted.[44] While Clm 6407 presents marginal annotations and glosses suggesting the manuscript's use in the schoolroom, the empty margins of Vat. lat. 3850 provide no hints as to the context in which the manuscript might have been read. However, the evidence provided by medieval library catalogues shows that books containing Alcuin's *De rhetorica* could be owned by priests: the books which the monastery of Bobbio acquired from the priest Theodorus included a copy of *De rhetorica Karoli et Albini magistri*, and another book belonging to the priest Peter contained the *Micrologia Fulgentii, rhetorica Caroli et Albini et periermeniarum Apulei et alia quaedam*.[45] Later, in 984, Bishop Oldericus of Cremona bequeathed his cathedral library some of his personal books including a collection of dialectical works containing Porphyry (most probably the *Isagoge* accompanied by Boethius's commentary) and Alcuin's *De dialectica*.[46] It is therefore tempting to postulate that Vat. lat. 3850 may have also belonged to the personal book collection of a cleric or a priest who added useful liturgical texts for the exercise of his duties into the last folios of the manuscript.

While *De rhetorica* and *De dialectica* circulated in Carolingian Italy, no witnesses of the *Ars grammatica* and the *De orthographia* have been preserved from the ninth century. Alcuin's grammatical works do not seem to have been used in the schools of the peninsula. Surviving library catalogues confirm this absence: the detailed tenth-century catalogue produced in the monastery of Bobbio shows that grammatical teaching remained firmly rooted in late-antique teaching practices.[47] Italy relied on centuries-long school traditions, which appear to have been resilient to a Carolingian

---

44 On the three poems see P. Lendinara, 'A poem for all seasons: Alcuin's "O vos, est aetas"', in G. Dinkova-Bruun and T. Major (eds), *Teaching and Learning in Medieval Europe. Essays in Honour of Gernot R. Wieland* (Turnhout: Brepols, 2017), pp. 123–46.
45 G. Becker, *Catalogi Bibliothecarum Antiqui* (Bonn: M. Cohen, 1885), pp. 72–3, items 32.587 and 32.610.
46 *Ibid.*, p. 81, item 36.81: 'Porphirii librum et eius maius comentum cum argumentis dialecticae artis Alcuini in uno volumine'.
47 See the group of books belonging to the monastic library and containing works dedicated to the *trivium* in *Ibid.*, pp. 68–70, items 32.356–479.

'reform' of education. Priscian and Donatus were the authorities for the study of grammar, while the treatises on orthography by Pseudo-Caper, Agroecius and Bede – that is, Alcuin's sources for his *De orthographia* – continued to be preferred.[48] Italy was also the region where Latin was still closer to the spoken language, therefore an active command of Latin did not need to be reintroduced and promoted as was the case north of the Alps.[49] Alcuin's grammatical books had been designed for students who learned Latin as a second language, which did not fit the profile of Italian students.[50] Furthermore, the connections which Alcuin drew so prominently

---

48 Priscian's *Institutiones grammaticae* and Donatus's *Ars maior* and *Ars minor* continued to be copied, excerpted and commented, but it would be too long to provide a full list of the surviving manuscripts from Carolingian and post-Carolingian Italy: it suffices to mention the annotated copy of the sixteen books of Priscian's *Institutiones* copied at Verona around 800 (Sankt Gallen, SB 903) and the contemporary grammatical miscellany building upon Donatus's *Ars grammatica* (Berlin, SBPK Diez B Santen 66) that was assembled by a well-connected scholar working in close association with the Carolingian court in Italy. On this manuscript see G. Vocino, 'Between the palace, the school and the forum: rhetoric and court culture in late Lombard and Carolingian Italy', in Gantner and Pohl (eds), *After Charlemagne*, pp. 250–74, at pp. 266–8. For the use of Bede, one can point to the schoolbook produced in late eighth-century Montecassino under the supervision of Paul the Deacon (Paris, BNF lat. 7530) which contained Bede's *De orthographia*, a treatise also owned by the monastic libraries of San Salvatore at Monte Amiata and Cava de' Tirreni in the eleventh century; see M. Lapidge, 'Beda Venerabilis', in P. Chiesa and L. Castaldi (eds), *La trasmissione dei testi latini del Medioevo* (Florence: Sismel, 2008), III, pp. 44–140, esp. pp. 44–50. For the use of Agroecius and Pseudo-Caper, the monastic library of Bobbio owned in the tenth-century two copies of the *De orthographia* by Agroecius and Pseudo-Caper; see Becker, *Catalogi Bibliothecarum*, p. 69, items 21.410–11. More generally on the early medieval transmission of orthographic treatises see P. De Paolis, 'L'insegnamento dell'ortografia latina fra Tardoantico e alto Medioevo: teorie e manuali', in L. Del Corso and O. Pecere (eds), *Libri di scuola e pratiche didattiche. Dall'Antichità al Rinascimento* (Cassino: Università di Cassino, 2010), I, pp. 229–91.
49 See note 75. Holtz, 'L'œuvre grammaticale', pp. 132–43; V. Law, 'Grammars and language change: an eighth-century case', in V. Law, *Grammars and Grammarians in the Early Middle Ages* (London: Longman, 1997), pp. 188–99.
50 It is only in the tenth century that the awareness of the existence of an Italian vernacular is made evident in the sources, see A. Zamboni, *Alle*

in his didactic treatises between rhetoric and Christian ethics, and between dialectic and the defence of the Christian faith, do not appear to have featured in ninth-century Italy.[51]

This does not mean that Italy rejected novelties or that Italian school practices never changed or were never 'reformed': a Carolingian reframing of education can be detected in Italy, but only in late and post-Carolingian times. Alcuin's grammar eventually found interested readers in Italy and had some measurable impact, but this notably occurred over a century after the date of its writing: a manuscript produced in ninth-century Francia and containing Alcuin's *Ars grammatica* travelled to Italy in the tenth century (Milan, Biblioteca Ambrosiana O 95 sup.), where a poem dedicated to Otto I and his wife Adelheid, possibly composed for their imperial coronation, was added in the last pages.[52] Additional evidence is provided by the recent discovery in the Capitular Library of Vercelli revealing a tenth-century booklist written on a leaf that was trimmed and damaged in the course of its later reuse as a pastedown (Vercelli, Bibl. Cap., Fragment 50, olim MS CXXXVIII, fol. 147v).[53] This inventory lists thirty-seven books once belonging to a local chapter library.[54] Among these, two manuscripts contained

---

origini dell'italiano. Dinamiche e tipologie della transizione dal latino (Rome: Carocci, 2000).

51 In a recent article François Bougard stated that 'the genres considered as "typically" Carolingian – the exegetical commentaries ... the mirrors of princes, the theological and doctrinal treatises – are decidedly not the work of Italy, or of Italians'; see F. Bougard, 'Was there a Carolingian Italy? Politics, institutions and book culture', in Gantner and Pohl (eds), *After Charlemagne*, pp. 54–81, quote at p. 66.

52 Alcuin's *Ars grammatica* (fos 1v–31v) is followed by his *De vera philosophia* (fos 32v–34r). The verse compositions in honour of Otto I and Adelheid as well as one of Peter of Pisa's *carmina* (*Hic sunt prata meis*) and a poem for the feast of the Virgin Mary were added by a tenth-century hand. See B. Bischoff, *Katalog der festländischen Handschriften des neunten Jahrhunderts (mit Ausnahme der wisigotischen)* (3 vols, Wiesbaden: Harrassowitz, 1998–2017), II, no. 2650, p. 164.

53 W. Rudolf, 'A tenth-century booklist in the Biblioteca Capitolare of Vercelli', *Manuscripta*, 62:2 (2018), 249–77.

54 At the bottom of the booklist one can read: 'Et iste cum supradictis sunt capituli Vercellensis'. The chapter alluded to in the booklist might be the old chapter of Santa Maria Maggiore, although also Vercelli Cathedral

Alcuin's works: the first is identified as a *Liber domni Alcuini volumen I*, the second as *Quaterni de Franco et Saxo volumen I*, which undoubtedly refers to the *Ars grammatica*, a dialogue between two students, Franco and Saxo. This booklist was produced within the circle of Atto of Vercelli's collaborators in the mid-tenth century. The dating is confirmed by recent research on Atto's works revealing that the Italian bishop knew and used Alcuin's *De dialectica* in the glosses of his most enigmatic text, the *Perpendiculum*.[55] This treatise may therefore have been included in one of the two books mentioned in the list.

One might wonder why Alcuin's grammatical works suddenly found an interested audience in the tenth-century kingdom of Italy. The late Carolingian transmission and reception of Alcuin's *Opera didascalica* appear to have been mediated by another influential Carolingian centre of learning: the school of Auxerre.[56] The texts produced and read by the Auxerre masters – and particularly the teaching of Remigius and his commentaries on the *auctores* – swiftly found their way into Italy.[57] These works had a profound impact on school practices and the features of the texts produced locally. The 'glossematic style' of the *Gesta Berengarii* (910s) and Atto of Vercelli's *Perpendiculum* (950s) is close to the style of Heiric of Auxerre's *Vita sancti Germani*, Abbo of Saint-Germain's *Bella Parisiacae urbis* and Odo of Cluny's *Occupatio*.[58] These similarities

---

(Sant'Eusebio) had its own library; see Rudolf, 'A tenth-century booklist', 271–7.

55 G. Vignodelli, 'The making of a tenth-century self-commentary: the glosses to Atto of Vercelli's *Perpendiculum* and their sources', in M. Teeuwen and I. van Renswoude (eds), *The Annotated Book in the Early Middle Ages. Practices of Reading and Writing* (Turnhout: Brepols, 2017), pp. 157–96, at p. 185.

56 D. Iogna-Prat (ed.), *L'école carolingienne d'Auxerre, de Muretach à Remi, 830–908* (Paris: Beauchesne, 1991) and again Marenbon, *From the Circle of Alcuin*.

57 Haimo of Auxerre's *Commentarium in Isaiam* survives in a tenth-century manuscript still in Vercelli (Biblioteca Capitolare MS LXXXII) and was annotated by Leo, bishop of Vercelli (998–1026).

58 See the introduction to G. Vignodelli (ed.), *Attone di Vercelli, Polipticum quod appellatur Perpendiculum. Edizione critica, traduzione e commento* (Florence: Sismel, 2019), pp. 1–117, on the dating and the context of

A Carolingian 'reform of education'? 115

are best explained by the authors' familiarity with the teachings of the Auxerre school.[59] Moreover, in his works, Atto of Vercelli made a clear Alcuinian connection between the *trivium* and a Christian education geared towards the correct understanding of the scripture and the virtuous exercise of the priestly office.[60] The moral dimension of the arts of speech, which Alcuin had so strongly promoted, thus comes out clearly in Atto's writings. The Anglo-Saxon master's teachings had been integrated into the school programmes at Vercelli, but this happened much later than it might have been expected, and the change was brought about by the mediation of a different network of knowledge based around the hub of Auxerre.

One is left to wonder why the school of Auxerre had a measurable impact in the kingdom of Italy and Alcuin did not, despite the swift and wide circulation of his works and his royal backing. The answer might be found in the networks connecting Alcuin to his learned friends and his most talented pupils. It was through the hubs of these networks that Alcuin's pedagogy was disseminated, and through its pupils it came to be used in the classroom. After all, in medieval times, knowledge worked like a virus: it circulated quickly through personal connections, and where no contact could be established, knowledge could not travel and replicate. This virus metaphor also invites us to consider immunity and resilience. Institutions and communities with no connection to Alcuinian networks of knowledge could not be touched by a 'reform' inspired by Alcuin's teaching. It might be obvious, but it is worth stating that being schooled at Corbie in Francia, at Redon in Brittany, at Ripoll in Carolingian Catalonia or at Novalesa in northwestern Italy did not

---

writing especially pp. 19–28. Michael Lapidge defined as 'hermeneutic' or 'glossematic' a literary style featuring the 'ostentatious parade of unusual, often very arcane and apparently learned vocabulary'; see M. Lapidge, 'The hermeneutic style in tenth-century Anglo-Latin literature', *Anglo-Saxon England*, 4 (1975), 67–111, quote at 67.

59 On the links between the kingdom of Italy and the Auxerre school see F. Duplessis, 'Les sources des gloses des *Gesta Berengarii* et la culture du poète anonyme', *Aevum*, 89:2 (2015), 205–63.

60 The principles underpinning Atto's school programme emerge more clearly in his treatise *De pressuris ecclesiasticis*, ed. J. Bauer, 'Die Schrift "De pressuris ecclesiasticis" des Bischofs Atto von Vercelli. Untersuchung und Edition' (unpublished PhD dissertation, Tübingen, 1975).

116   *Rethinking the Carolingian reforms*

give access to the same networks and resources. Furthermore, even those centres that were exposed to Alcuinian knowledge, such as Verona, may have developed antibodies that made them more resilient to it: well-stocked libraries, centuries-long school practices and local authoritative literary traditions rendered the demand for new acquisitions considerably less urgent.[61] However, these variables and the configuration of networks could change over time, and in the late ninth and early tenth centuries, the connections between scholars from the kingdom of Italy and the Auxerre masters triggered an actual change in school programmes and practices. Through a new network of knowledge, and without any pronounced royal patronage, the works of the Auxerre school influenced the ways in which Italian scholars conceived the use of the arts of speech.

The reception of Alcuin's pedagogy in monastic schools: the case of Wissembourg and Otfrid's school

The holdings of the medieval library of Wissembourg provide another valuable case study to measure the impact of Alcuin's pedagogy. Unlike what we have seen in ninth-century Italy, the approach and methods developed by Alcuin for the study of Latin and the Bible exerted a considerable influence on the local school practices within a few decades after his death.[62] Significant evidence is provided by the extant manuscripts, both those produced in the local scriptorium and those acquired for the Wissembourg library around

---

61 The low share of manuscripts produced in ninth-century Italy (9 per cent of the total) has been stressed by Bougard, 'Was there a Carolingian Italy?', at pp. 64–5.
62 H. Butzmann, *Die Weissenburger Handschriften*, Kataloge der Herzog-August-Bibliothek Wolfenbüttel. Die neue Reihe 10 (Frankfurt: Vittorio Klostermann, 1964), pp. 50–9 and 42–50 describes the activity of the Wissembourg scriptorium around the year 800 and in the first half of the ninth century, respectively. The earliest significant attempts to enrich the local library holdings were made under Abbot Gerhoh (819–26).

the middle of the ninth century, a period which is often regarded as the 'golden age' in the history of the monastic community.[63]

The content and the purposes of these books reveal that Alcuin's concerns and methods were known at Wissembourg, even if his own work is scarcely represented among the extant manuscripts.[64] What we have seen earlier with regard to Salzburg and Echternach applies to Wissembourg, too: the local impact of Alcuin's pedagogy cannot be explained as the automatic dissemination and mechanical reproduction of works sponsored by the court. Instead, it was the scholarly and personal connections binding Alcuin to his pupils and friends, and these in turn to a further circle of acquaintances, which provided occasions and paths for the spread of his concerns and priorities, if not of his own work, at Wissembourg around the mid-ninth century.[65] Here, local teachers took care to adapt the master's approach to the needs of their particular audiences and implemented their own pedagogical tools.[66] In some cases, contem-

---

63 Butzmann, *Weissenburger Handschriften*, pp. 59–65; W. Kleiber, *Otfrid von Weißenburg. Untersuchungen zur handschriftlichen Überlieferung und Studien zum Aufbau des Evangelienbuches* (Bern: Niemeyer, 1971), pp. 131–60; E. Hellgardt, *Die exegetischen Quellen von Otfrids Evangelienbuch* (Tübingen: Niemeyer, 1981), pp. 65–97; S. Krämer, *Handschriftenerbe des deutschen Mittelalters. Teil 2: Köln-Zyfflich*, Mittelalterliche Bibliothekskataloge Deutschlands und der Schweiz. Ergänzungsband 1 (Munich: Beck, 1989), pp. 822–4. A corpus of around 150 medieval manuscripts and fragments of Wissembourg origin or provenance is still available today.
64 Butzmann, *Weissenburger Handschriften*, p. 305, s.v. *Alcuinus*, shows that exegetical and metric works by Alcuin occur in only four manuscripts from Wissembourg, of which two are the commented editions of the Gospels and of the Prophet Jeremiah ascribed to Otfrid of Wissembourg. For Otfrid's use of Alcuin's commentary on John, see C. Grifoni, 'Reading the Catholic epistles: glossing practices in early medieval Wissembourg', in Teeuwen and van Renswoude (eds), *The Annotated Book*, pp. 705–42, at p. 722.
65 For the bond of *amicitia* connecting Alcuin to his pupils, see S. Steckel, *Kulturen des Lehrens im Früh- und Hochmittelalter. Autorität, Wissenskonzepte und Netzwerke von Gelehrten* (Cologne: Böhlau, 2011), pp. 148–95.
66 S. Cantelli Berarducci, 'L'esegesi della Rinascita Carolingia', in G. Cremascoli and C. Leonardi (eds), *La Bibbia nel Medio Evo* (Bologna: Edizioni Dehoniane Bologna, 1996), pp. 167–98, at 185–9 and 198. R. Guglielmetti, 'Un'esegesi incontentabile', in I. Pagani and F. Santi (eds), *Il*

porary manuscripts provide evidence of the actual results of these teachers' efforts, since they contain works and exercises by their pupils. Perhaps these results would not have made Alcuin proud. Certainly, they demonstrate that the effects of his pedagogy varied significantly from place to place and were not always as uniform and brilliant as most historiography on the so-called Carolingian 'renaissance' has concluded. Nevertheless, they represent creative local attempts to reach a higher degree of knowledge in order both to attain wisdom and to change for the better.[67]

In the turmoil preceding and following Louis the Pious's death, the monastery of Wissembourg, located as it was at the border with Lotharingia, became increasingly relevant to the East Frankish realm from a strategic perspective.[68] Consequently, it enjoyed the patronage of King Louis the German and reached the peak of its economic wealth. Having more economic resources at their disposal, Wissembourg scholars enriched the local library holdings remarkably, by both importing and producing new books.[69] Modern scholarship has shown that the leading mind behind this considerable intellectual effort was the priest-monk Otfrid, who served at Wissembourg as both a teacher and an exegete roughly from 840 onwards, most notably completing an exhaustive Gospel harmony in vernacular rhymes called the *Liber Evangeliorum*, which is regarded as one of the earliest works of German literature and which still assures him a certain renown in German-speaking regions.[70] Otfrid's outstanding role in the cultural flourishing of his community is best explained if we consider his scholarly networks.

---

    secolo di Carlo Magno. Istituzioni, letterature e cultura del tempo carolingio (Florence: Sismel, 2016), pp. 177–200, especially from p. 195.
67 See note 9.
68 M. Innes, *State and Society in the Early Middle Ages: The Middle Rhine Valley, 400–1000* (Cambridge: Cambridge University Press, 2000), pp. 198–222; E. J. Goldberg, *Struggle for Empire. Kingship and Conflict under Louis the German, 817–876* (Ithaca, NY: Cornell University Press, 2006), pp. 156–8.
69 Kleiber, *Otfrid*, pp. 133–46; Hellgardt, *Die exegetischen Quellen*, pp. 65–81.
70 Otfrid von Weißenburg, *Evangelienbuch*, ed. W. Kleiber and E. Hellgardt (2 vols, Tübingen: Max Niemayer, 2004–7). On Otfrid's life and work see W. Haubrichs, 'Eine prosopographische Skizze zu Otfrid von Weißenburg', in W. Kleiber (ed.), *Otfrid von Weißenburg* (Darmstadt: Wissenschaftliche

A Carolingian 'reform of education'?   119

In the 830s Otfrid spent some years at Fulda, where he perfected his theological skills under Hrabanus Maurus, the most prolific among Alcuin's pupils and one of the main actors in the further development of his master's methods.[71] Around this time, Otfrid also possibly visited Hilduin of Saint-Denis, another pupil of Alcuin's, as some necrologic entries and three short poems appear to demonstrate.[72] The scholarly formation Otfrid received at Fulda, and potentially Saint-Denis, proved relevant for his ensuing activity. Upon his return to Wissembourg, he promoted the study of Latin and the Bible through his own teaching and by supervising both the acquisition and the production of new manuscripts.[73] Otfrid's approach shared several features with that of Alcuin and Hrabanus: like them, for example, he used Priscian's grammar to teach Latin at a proficient level; he regarded the liberal arts as a preparatory step to the study of the Bible; he paid special attention to the teaching of Latin poetry; and he made exhaustive efforts to produce 'new' explanations of several biblical books.[74] Nevertheless, in all of these areas, Otfrid developed his own particular pedagogical tools in order to better meet the specific needs of his community.

Nine, or perhaps ten manuscripts contain evidence of Otfrid's own teaching endeavours. He supervised the production of five

---

Buchgesellschaft, 1978), pp. 397–413; W. Schröder and H. Hartmann, 'Otfrid von Weißenburg', in R. Bergmann (ed.), *Althochdeutsche und altsächsische Literatur* (Berlin: de Gruyter, 2013), pp. 322–45.

71 S. Cantelli Berarducci, *Hrabani Mauri Opera Exegetica: Repertorium Fontium*, Instrumenta Patristica et Mediaevalia 38 (3 vols, Turnhout: Brepols, 2006), I, pp. 18–45.

72 W. Haubrichs, 'Nekrologische Notizen zu Otfrid von Weißenburg', in H. Wenzel (ed.), *Adelsherrschaft und Literatur* (Bern: Lang, 1980), pp. 7–113, at 33–44. See also Lapidge's introduction to Hilduin of Saint-Denis, *The Passio S. Dionysii in Prose and Verse*, ed. M. Lapidge (Leiden: Brill, 2017), pp. 18–20.

73 Kleiber, *Otfrid*, pp. 147–60; Hellgardt, *Die exegetischen Quellen*, pp. 88–94.

74 On the Carolingian reception of Priscian's *Ars grammatica*, see F. Cinato, *Priscien glosé. L'Ars grammatica de Priscien vue à travers les gloses carolingiennes*, Studia Artistarum 41 (Turnhout: Brepols, 2015), who builds upon the pivotal work by Louis Holtz on the topic. On the study and production of Latin poetry at Wissembourg, see T. Hennings, *Ostfränkische Sammlungen von Dichtung im 9. Jahrhundert*, Nova Mediaevalia 19 (Göttingen: Vandenhoeck & Ruprecht, 2021), pp. 180–97.

commented editions of the Bible, a format in which the biblical text and its explanation feature side by side on the manuscript leaves. In these, he wrote the vast majority of the *scholia* in his own hand.[75] As for the study of Latin, on which we shall concentrate hereafter, Otfrid did his best to match the expectations of a better command of Latin, which Charlemagne and Alcuin had expressed for instance in the *Epistola de litteris colendis* – probably the most famous witness to the court's cultural vision – and his teacher Hrabanus had so actively supported.[76] In so doing, Otfrid joined the flock of those inspired scholars, who, building on their talents, their networks and favourable economic conjunctures, worked to improve both their own and their audiences' knowledge.

The study of Latin was a sizeable challenge in ninth-century Wissembourg, where the Frankish dialect from the southern Rhine area was spoken – that is, one of those languages which modern scholars subsume under the umbrella concept of Old High German. Three extant manuscripts enable us to appreciate the efforts made by Otfrid, his colleagues, as well as his pupils to this end. The first of these is a copy of Priscian's *Ars grammatica*, whose production Otfrid oversaw and which he provided with a substantial number of autographic glosses in Latin and in the vernacular. This same book also contains annotations by a fellow teacher, whose explanations of the text follow on from those of Otfrid. Secondly, there is a manuscript containing Priscian's metric *Description of the World* (*Periegesis*), produced and annotated by one of Otfrid's local colleagues. This book is a further witness to the vivid interest

---

75 Kleiber, *Otfrid*, pp. 102–12, detected Otfrid's hand in ten manuscripts of the collection Weissenburges of the Herzog August Bibliothek. See also Grifoni, 'Reading'.

76 See note 1. *Epistola de litteris colendis*, ed. E. E. Stengel, *Urkundenbuch des Klosters Fulda, Band 1.2: Die Zeit des Abtes Baugulf*, Veröffentlichungen der Historischen Kommission für Hessen und Waldeck X 1.2 (Marburg: N. G. Elwer, 1956), pp. 246–54, no. 166. What Charlemagne and Alcuin wished by issuing this text was a change of focus in the study of Latin from a passive to an active command, so that pupils, and in particular the most talented among them, might learn to speak Latin correctly, at least when reading it aloud, and to write it flawlessly.

A Carolingian 'reform of education'? 121

in Priscian's output at Wissembourg.[77] Here, the glosses are particularly relevant, since they show us which tools local teachers employed in order to understand the Latin text and the metric rules of the poem. Finally, a third manuscript provides evidence of the local study of Latin and in particular of Latin poetry: an anthology of Prudentius's poetic work with marginal explanations in Otfrid's own hand. This book is particularly remarkable since its final leaves accommodate a selection of anonymous poems which were added by a local pupil after Otfrid's death. These enable us to appreciate the actual results of Latin teaching at Wissembourg and to measure tangibly the impact of Alcuin's pedagogy within this particular community around the end of the ninth century. Let us examine the three manuscripts in more detail.

The MS Wolfenbüttel, Herzog August Bibliothek, 50 Weissenburg contains an elegant edition of the first sixteen books of Priscian's *Ars grammatica*, namely his substantial explanation of the eight parts of speech. The two final books of Priscian's grammar concerning syntax were not included, although they are recorded in the *Capitulatio* ('table of chapters') on f. 1v.[78] The manuscript was ruled to contain an impressive amount of text: 38 lines written in a neat, small-sized Caroline minuscule occupy almost the entirety of the available space on each page.

This copy of the *Ars grammatica* was read in detail, right after the manuscript had been completed, as the ca. 2,000 glosses in Latin, and ca. 150 in Old High German reveal. Of these, only the latter have been studied thoroughly thus far.[79] The contents and

---

77 Traces of the study of Priscian at ninth-century Wissembourg are also preserved in the MS Vatican, BAV, Reg. lat. 423, fos 65r–68v containing short excerpts from book IX and X of Priscian's *Ars grammatica* with glosses (Hellgardt, *Die exegetischen Quellen*, pp. 74, 80; Cinato, *Priscien glosé*, p. 577). Manuscript evidence of the local study of Latin at a more elementary level has not survived.
78 Butzmann, *Weissenburger Handschriften*, p. 187. The manuscript can be consulted online: http://diglib.hab.de/?db=mss&list=ms&id=50-weiss (accessed 21 February 2022). Cinato, *Priscien glosé*, discusses the independent transmission of the first sixteen books of Priscian's grammar on pp. 68–73 and records this codex on pp. 581–2.
79 W. Kleiber, 'Otfrid von Weißenburg als Priscian-Glossator. Eine sprachhistorische Skizze', in R. Bergmann and S. Stricker (eds), *Die althochdeutsche*

functions of the Latin glosses, as well as their interplay with those in the vernacular, are the subject of an ongoing research project.[80] Wolfgang Kleiber, who engaged with the palaeographic analysis of these annotations, recognised the hand of two distinct glossators, one of which has been identified as Otfrid himself. According to Kleiber, Otfrid wrote the majority of the Latin glosses and more than 130 annotations in the vernacular. The second teacher added his explanations soon after Otfrid's and complemented, or in some cases simply repeated, their contents.[81]

If we consider, for instance, the words *dyonima vel trionyma* ('either two or three elements of one's proper name'), which Priscian analysed when discussing the Roman onomastic system, both words received a double explanation: Otfrid added the example of the Apostle Peter's name (*ut Simon Petrus*) above *dyonima*, and the other glossator added the name of the Roman poet Ovid (*Ovidius Naso*).[82] Similarly, Otfrid added the name of a further apostle above *trionyma* (*ut Iudas Taddeus Lippeus*), while the second glossator added the name of a further Roman poet (*ut Publius Virgilius Maro*). Otfrid's example, which derives ultimately from Jerome's *Commentary on the Gospel of Matthew*, testifies to his attempt to Christianise grammar and to substantiate Priscian's theory with

---

und altsächsische Glossographie. Ein Handbuch (Berlin: de Gruyter, 2009), II, pp. 1601–10.

80 Cinzia Grifoni's project 'Margins at the Centre' will produce a digital edition and a commentary of the annotations contained in this manuscript: see www.oeaw.ac.at/en/imafo/research/historical-identity-research/projects/margins-at-the-centre (accessed 21 February 2022).

81 Kleiber, *Otfrid*, pp. 107–9. See also W. Kleiber, 'Zur Sprache der althochdeutschen Glossen Otfrids in Cod. Guelf, 50 Weiss.', in R. Bergmann et al. (eds), *Althochdeutsch, Band 1: Grammatik. Glossen und Texte* (Heidelberg: Carl Winter Universitätsverlag, 1987), pp. 532–44, at 535. In contrast, M. Gibson, 'Milestones in the study of Priscian, circa 800 – circa 1200', *Viator*, 23 (1992), 17–33, at 20–21, ascribed the writing of the glosses to 'some half dozen different hands'. The project 'Margins at the Centre' will analyse in detail how the teachers involved in the glossing of this copy of Priscian's *Ars* worked and interacted (see note 79).

82 See Priscian, *Institutiones grammaticae*, ed. M. Hertz, in H. Keil (ed.), *Grammatici Latini* II (Leipzig: Teubner, 1855), II, 29, p. 61 and MS Wolfenbüttel. HAB, 50 Weiss., f. 10v, l. 25.

A Carolingian 'reform of education'?

names taken from the Bible.[83] The second glossator instead reproduced a more traditional set of examples, which recur, for instance, in a tenth-century annotated copy of Priscian's *Ars grammatica* held at Cologne.[84] It remains to be established whether Otfrid too drew from a pre-existing corpus of annotations for this passage or rather created new explanations.

In the following line, the two teachers complemented each other again when explaining the word 'homeland' (*patria*). Otfrid wrote: 'homeland is the territory belonging to a single town/district' (*patria est territorium unius civitatis*). The second glossator added a very similar, and yet more thorough, explanation, which partly recurs in the *Liber Glossarum*.[85] He wrote: 'homeland is both the territory of one's own town and the territory adjoining to the town, i.e. the country' (*patria est proprie civitatis et adiacens territorium civitati id est pagus*). Annotations with a more basic explanatory function are also well represented throughout the book, as are suggestions for further readings. On f. 10v, line 28, for instance, the second glossator reminded himself and his pupils to read what the grammarian Donatus had written about the intonation of interrogative pronouns (*lege Donatum de accentibus*).

All in all, these glosses mirror the efforts of two local teachers who were concerned not only with explaining the rules of Latin grammar to their pupils, but also with enriching and diversifying the information contained in Priscian's text with material from the Bible and from other available sources. Moreover, their choice to engage with Priscian's rather than, say, Donatus's grammar can be regarded as a result of Otfrid's education and training under Alcuin's former pupil Hrabanus. Indeed, following on from Alcuin's extensive engagement with Priscian's work, Otfrid's teacher Hrabanus thoroughly studied Priscian's grammatical output paying special

---

83 See Jerome, *Commentariorum in evangelium Matthaei libri IV*, ed. D. Hurst and M. Adriaen, *CCSL* 77 (Turnhout: Brepols, 1969), I, 1520–6, p. 64.
84 Köln, Erzbischöfliche Diözesan- und Dombibliothek, Cod. 200, f. 15v, first marginal gloss: 'ut ovidius naso et publius virgilius'; see https://digital.dombibliothek-koeln.de/hs/content/zoom/290998 (accessed 21 February 2022).
85 See the entry PA802 (*Patria – proprie civitatis pagus in quo quis nascitur*) in the digital edition of the *Liber Glossarum*: http://liber-glossarum.huma-num.fr/index.html (accessed 21 February 2022).

attention to prosody and metrical issues.[86] Otfrid and his entourage shared this special interest in poetry, as indeed both of the following manuscripts illustrate.

The manuscript Vatican City, Biblioteca Apostolica Vaticana, Vat. lat. 11506 contains Cicero's *De inventione*, an annotated version of Priscian's *Periegesis* and several medical recipes which were added on the recto of the first leaf. A single scribe wrote all these texts at Wissembourg in the third quarter of the ninth century.[87] Priscian's text follows Cicero's work without interruption and runs from the last page of the eighth quire (f. 62v) until the end of the codex. The *Periegesis* constitutes an adaptation and Latin translation of the geographical treatise by the second-century Greek geographer Dionysius of Alexandria; it takes the form of a poem and consists of more than 1,000 hexameters.[88]

Vat. lat. 11506 was annotated immediately following its production. According to José Ruysschaert, who catalogued the manuscript, the copyist of the main texts was also responsible for the writing of all the glosses.[89] Their distribution suggests that he had more interest in Priscian's geographical poem than in Cicero's rhetorical treatise. Indeed, while the quires containing Cicero's text feature only a few marginal remarks, a substantial quantity of multi-layered explanations are included with Priscian's poem.

---

86 See Alcuin, *Excerptiones super Priscianum*, ed. L. Holtz and A. Grondeux, CCCM 304 (Turnhout: Brepols, 2020); Hrabanus Maurus, *Excerptio de arte grammatica Prisciani*, ed. J.-P. Migne, PL 111 (Paris: Migne, 1852), cols 613–78, with L. Holtz, 'Raban Maur et l' *Excerptio de arte grammatica Prisciani*', in P. Depreux et al. (eds), *Raban Maur et son temps*, Collection Haut Moyen Âge 9 (Turnhout: Brepols, 2010), pp. 203–18.

87 Hellgardt, *Die exegetischen Quellen*, pp. 73–4 and 80 was the first to identify Wissembourg as the scriptorium of production of this book. For the description of the manuscript, see J. Ruysschaert, *Bibliothecae Apostolicae Vaticanae codices manu scripti recensiti. Codices vaticani latini. Codices 11414–11709* (Vatican City: Biblioteca Apostolica Vaticana, 1959), pp. 155–6; Bischoff, *Katalog*, III, p. 457, no. 6949. For the digital reproduction, see https://digi.vatlib.it/view/bav_vat_lat_11506 (accessed 21 February 2022).

88 P. van de Woestijne (ed.), *La Périégèse de Priscien* (Brugge: De Tempel, 1953), esp. pp. 14–15 on the Vatican manuscript.

89 Ruysschaert, *Codices vaticani latini*, p. 156.

A Carolingian 'reform of education'? 125

These annotations have not been studied thus far. The modern editor of the *Periegesis* only remarks on a few similarities between them and the glosses contained in two other near-contemporary manuscripts.[90] One could therefore speculate that, at least in some cases, Priscian's poem circulated together with a specific apparatus of explanations which the Wissembourg copyist transcribed along the main text. However, only a detailed comparison of the manuscripts involved will shed light on this aspect.

As for now, a preliminary investigation of the annotations of Vat. lat. 11506 shows that they explain the text in two different ways. On the one hand, they highlight the narrative structure of the poem and paraphrase its wording with an approach revealing a rather elementary didactic function.[91] On the other hand, however, they enrich the information conveyed by Priscian through expansions and intertextual references.[92] This second category of explanations addressed more proficient pupils, showing that the same text could be used to serve different pedagogical tasks. Priscian's *Periegesis* is full of geographical references, astronomic material, marvellous anecdotes and ethnographic descriptions, all of which served to fuel the curiosity of readers. The annotator (or his exemplar) often searched for further information in Isidore's *Etymologies* and in the glossographical tradition.[93] In around forty cases, he preferred to

---

90 *La Périégèse de Priscien*, ed. Woestijne, pp. 15–17 and 25–7 for the manuscripts dubbed *F* and *R*.
91 For instance, red additions in the margins of f. 62v mark the narrative structure of the poem's opening (*invocatio*, *praefatio*, *de tribus terrae partibus*). Literal explanations, synonyms and paraphrases of single terms occur mostly in the interlinear.
92 See S. O'Sullivan, 'Text, gloss, and tradition in the early medieval West: expanding into a world of learning', in Dinkova-Bruun and Major (eds), *Teaching and Learning in Medieval Europe*, pp. 3–24.
93 On the bottom left margin on f. 62v we read, for instance: 'Libia dicta quod hinc Libs ventus flat' (Libya derives its name from the wind Libs blowing from here), an entry contained in the *Liber Glossarum* (entry LI105 of the digital edition) and stemming from Isidore's *Etymologies* XIV.5.1. On f. 73r a marginal scholion referring to *heroum* of the text explains the difference between *erus* and *heros*: 'erus sine aspiratione dominus. heros cum aspiratione productaque penultima vir fortis intelligitur' ('The word "erus" without aspiration means "lord". The word "heros" with aspiration and a long penult means "a strong man"'). The *Liber Glossarum* (entries ER314 and

copy long excerpts from Solinus's *Collectanea rerum memorabilium*. For instance, at f. 66v a reference sign links the word 'Nilum' (the river Nile) of the *Periegesis* to an extensive passage describing the most remarkable features of one of its inhabitants, the crocodile.[94] The use of specific extracts from Solinus in order to expand on the content of the *Periegesis* provides us with the first evidence of the reception of the *Collectanea* at Wissembourg in the third quarter of the ninth century, a fact that has not been recorded thus far.[95] It remains to be investigated whether the Wissembourg glossator found Solinus's excerpts already attached to Priscian's poem in his exemplar or whether its inclusion in this compilation was the result of his own work.

A palaeographical comparison reveals that the traits of the glossator's hand differ substantially from those ascribed to Otfrid.[96] Since this scholar worked in the Wissembourg scriptorium in the third quarter of the ninth century, he was probably either one of Otfrid's fellow teachers or one of his pupils. At any rate, Otfrid was not alone in his engagement with Priscian's work. As such engagement is not detectable at Wissembourg before Otfrid's time, we may conclude that the increased local interest in Priscian was the result of Otfrid's own intellectual effort. In so doing, he spread the knowledge and teaching methods that he had learned through his own formation under scholars who had themselves been part of Alcuin's network.

The MS Wolfenbüttel, Herzog August Bibliothek, 77 Weissenburg is the third manuscript which provides evidence of the study of Latin and in particular of Latin poetry at Wissembourg. Produced in the

---

HE168) records this difference but does not pay attention to the quantity of the penultimate syllable of 'heros'. This information might reflect the interests of the Wissembourg glossator in some prosodic details of the poem.

94 The scholion reproduces C. I. Solinus, *Collectanea rerum memorabilium* 32, 22–4, ed. T. Mommsen (Berlin: Weidmann, 1895), p. 143.

95 On Solinus's reception in the ninth century see V. von Büren, 'Une édition critique de Solin au IXe siècle', *Scriptorium*, 50:1 (1996), 22–87, at 25–6, and D. Ganz, 'Does the Copenhagen Solinus contain the autograph of Walahfrid Strabo?', in N. Golob (ed.), *Medieval Autograph Manuscripts* (Turnhout: Brepols, 2013), pp. 79–86.

96 Against Hennings, *Ostfränkische Sammlungen*, p. 190.

local scriptorium in the second half of the ninth century, it contains the *Liber Apotheosis* and the *Hamartigenia* by the late antique poet Prudentius as well as a short extract from his *Contra Symmachum*, which was copied before the last section of the *Apotheosis*, most likely by mistake (fos 22v–5v). Several contemporary annotations, both in Latin and in Old High German, were added to Prudentius's poems.[97] An anonymous metric riddle originally marked the conclusion of this poetic anthology. Around the end of the ninth century, however, a further nine short poems, which modern scholarship regards as school exercises, were added onto the final leaves of the manuscript.

According to Wolfgang Kleiber, Otfrid oversaw the production of this book. Moreover, he himself wrote part of the texts and the overwhelming majority of the glosses.[98] In particular, he decided to conclude the collection of poetry with the metric riddle mentioned

---

97 Kleiber, *Otfrid*, pp. 109–10; S. Stricker, 'Die Prudentiusglossierung', in R. Bergmann and S. Stricker (eds), *Glossenstudien. Ergebnisse der neuen Forschung* (Heidelberg: Universitätsverlag Winter, 2020), pp. 313–22. Kleiber is convinced of the Wissembourg origin of this book. Butzmann, *Weissenburger Handschriften*, p. 231, located its production in 'Südwestdeutschland', while Bischoff, *Katalog*, III, p. 511, no. 7420, regarded a Wissembourg origin as merely possible. For the digital reproduction of the manuscript, see http://diglib.hab.de/?db=mss&list=ms&id=77-weiss (accessed 21 February 2022).

98 For Prudentius's place within the early medieval grammatical teaching and his relevance to Otfrid's output see S. O'Sullivan, *Early Medieval Glosses on Prudentius' Psychomachia: The Weitz tradition* (Leiden: Brill, 2004), pp. 3–21. Otfrid's glosses on Prudentius are multi-layered. Some of them emend spelling mistakes of the main text and insert punctuation. Others give information of morphological (e.g. on f. 38r: 'idololatria. adiectio sillabae') or etymological nature (e.g. on f. 14v: 'egregius. id est qui gregem antecellit id est multitudinem'). Others provide Latin synonyms and, in fourteen cases, a translation of Prudentius's words into Old High German. Finally, others enrich the text with information of either historical, encyclopaedic or exegetical nature. A long entry concerning several lemmata of Prudentius's poems, which Otfrid added on f. 49v after the explicit of the *Hamartigenia*, demonstrates that he drew his annotations from an already circulating thematic glossary. Indeed, Otfrid copied again the single segments of this entry into the body of the manuscript attaching them to the concerned lemma. A modest amount of the annotations contained in this codex cannot be ascribed to Otfrid's hand.

above, which he penned in his own hand right after Prudentius's *Hamartigenia* (fos 50r–v). The riddle, called *Quadam nocte* from its opening words, is regarded as an Irish work and has been attributed to Clemens Scottus. It is attested at Fulda, and this is probably the centre from which Otfrid imported it to Wissembourg.[99]

In the English translation by David Howlett, *Quadam nocte* reads as follows:[100]

> On a certain night black Dub and a second man, Whitey by name,
> by chance entered together under single roofs.
> Whitey brought out with himself three times five shining men,
> and the black man in [his] fashion equal men black in colour.
> 'Whitey, which of us first', the second man had said,
> 'is going to foresee the watches, for I shall follow your sayings'.
> In reply to these things Whitey responds with a calm voice:
> 'By my judgement I do not wish to oppress anyone,
> lest a new contention through me inspire fellows to arms,
> but for you I shall not remove my counsel.
> I shall dispose all the fellows to lie down in order,
> whom the ninth lot may choose for the watches.
> But the white throng should sit mixed together with the black men,
> so that no man may think me to wish to deceive men'.
> Four men of excellent whiteness, five little black men,
> two little white men, and one black man,
> three resplendent men, one little black man with darkened skin,
> thereafter one white man, and two coallike men,
> two gleaming men, three men with darkened covering,
> thereafter one snowy man, and two horrible men,[101]

---

99 K. Strecker (ed.), *Versus Scottorum I. Problemata Arithmetica*, MGH Poetae IV 2.3 (Berlin: Weidmann, 1923), pp. 1117–20; D. Howlett, 'Two mathematical poets', *Peritia*, 21 (2010), 151–7 provides a new edition, an English translation and a brilliant analysis of the riddle; Hennings, *Ostfränkische Sammlungen*, p. 191 discusses the probable Fulda origin of Otfrid's model. H. Hoffmann, *Schreibschulen des 10. und des 11. Jahrhunderts im Südwesten des Deutschen Reichs*, 2 vols (Hannover: Hahn, 2004), vol. 1, p. 316 states that the final four verses of the riddle on f. 50v were not written by Otfrid but by two further scribes around the end of the ninth century.
100 Howlett, 'Two mathematical poets', 152–3.
101 Howlett translates here the Latin text: *hinc niveus unus horribilesque duo*. Otfrid copied a slightly different and more polite version of this verse,

> two little white men resplendent with beautiful skin,
> all of whom a single and black man follows.
> By this ingenious device the ninth lot fell thus on all little black men,
> on the crowd, the white one lacks a lot.
> The black leader alone with the dark soldiery
> thoroughly vigilant, not pleased, led the watches until day.
> But the white man, especially gifted with ingenuity, and his own men
> took calm sleep in the entire night.

It is not easy to understand why Otfrid chose to round off his Prudentian anthology with a text of a completely different nature. Perhaps the reason lies in a formal detail. Since it is composed in elegiac couplets, the riddle provided Otfrid's pupils with a metric scheme that Prudentius's mostly hexametric poems did not feature, thus enriching the set of poetic models included in the collection. *Quadam nocte* is described as a play (*ludus*) in other early medieval manuscripts, which suggests that it was primarily viewed as an entertaining text in the school context (though its ideas of colourism notably do not accord with our modern sense of humour).[102] It could well have served as a model for young pupils keen to try their own experiments with poetry and, at the same time, have some fun solving the riddle.

Indeed, both the amusing tone and the metre of *Quadam nocte* recur in the ensuing nine short poems, which were copied by a single scribe in several writing stages onto the final leaves of the manuscript (fos 50v–2r) around the end of the ninth century. Except for two of them, the fourth and the ninth, all of these texts were composed in elegiac couplets, here presumably following the example of *Quadam nocte*. The complete translation of the poems contained in the appendix to this chapter shows that they also shared its cheerful

---

which reads: *candidus hic unus carboneique duo* (MS Wolfenbüttel, Herzog August Bibliothek, 77 Weissenburg, f. 50r, l. 20).
102 Howlett, 'Two mathematical poets', 151.

tone and were meant to entertain the reader, as stated explicitly in poem 6.[103]

The scribe who penned the poems engaged with the anthology contained in the manuscript 77 Weiss. and felt free to enrich its contents. For instance, at two different points, he restored some missing verses, copying them from another exemplar of Prudentius's poetry, which remains unidentified. Furthermore, he wrote a Mass chant with neumes on f. 1r.[104]

The first two poems feature a title which names the deacon Ercanbert and the subdeacon Ferdingus as their respective authors. A further four poems (nos 5, 6, 8 and 9) are flanked by a small 'e' in the margin. This led Karl Strecker to regard the deacon Ercanbert as the author of these texts as well. We know from other occurrences of the names that Ferdingus and Ercanbert were members of the monastic community of Wissembourg.[105] Further hints contained here and there, for instance the mention of the Lauter, the river

---

103 These poems were published first by E. Dümmler (ed.), 'Weissenburger Gedichte', *Zeitschrift für deutsches Altertum und deutsche Literatur*, 19 (1876), 115–17, then by K. Strecker (ed.), *Weissenburg, MGH Poetae 5*, 1.2 (Leipzig: Hiersemann, 1937), pp. 504–7: we have used the latter for the Latin text. K. Helm, 'Otfrid-Nennungen?', *Beiträge zur Geschichte der deutschen Sprache und Literatur*, 66 (1942), 134–45, and Hennings, *Ostfränkische Sammlungen*, pp. 191–4, provide an interpretation of their content.

104 The additions to Prudentius's text occur on fos 25v and 47v of MS 77 Weiss. Hoffmann, *Schreibschulen*, p. 316 remarked that this very writer copied also the letter occurring on f. 99v of MS Wolfenbüttel, HAB, 62 Weiss., which curiously features some neumes in the margin. According to Hartmann, however, the Mass chant with neumes occurring on MS 77 Weiss., f. 1r was not written by this copyist: it is the trope *Ecclesiae sponsus illuminator gentium*, on which see: http://cantusindex.org/id/g00596.Tp1 (accessed 21 February 2022). We cautiously suggest that a further two poems contained on f. 134v of MS Wolfenbüttel, HAB, 60 Weiss. stemmed from the same writer, too: they feature very similar palaeographical traits and a vocabulary reminiscent of the nine poems we are dealing with.

105 Strecker (ed.), *Weissenburg*, p. 504 remarks that Ferdingus and Ercanbert were clerical monks belonging to the Wissembourg community, since their names recur in the local list of loans which was written into the final leaves of MS Wolfenbüttel, HAB, 35 Weiss. See also Butzmann, *Weissenburger Handschriften*, pp. 39–41.

flowing through Wissembourg, suggest that these texts originated locally.

Their very content and named addressees raise the impression that they were written by local students. Teachers, young pupils and poets of various ability occur repeatedly in the texts, as well as the request of forgiving the modest command of prosodic and metric rules. In the first poem, Ercanbert praises a new teacher, who would put an end to the pupils' idleness and ignorance. The new teacher is presented as a good cultivator, while the monks are an uncultivated land. In poem 2, Ferdingus's little verses (*versiculi*) praise Ercanbert as a learned young man and a friend, who is proficient enough to sail, at least metaphorically, on the vessel of his wisdom and to achieve great results. In the third poem, a young pupil begs his teacher to accept his little verses (*versiculi*) and his small sentences (*parvula dicta*) for the first time, and to have mercy on his modest skills, since he cannot concentrate on the study of grammar. Nevertheless, he proudly addresses the teacher in transliterated ancient Greek as a *calós héros* ('a beautiful hero'), in the final verse.[106] Wisiricus is the teacher's name: he is probably the good cultivator occurring in poem 1 as well as the *didasculus* addressed, again with a Graecism, in poem 6.[107] His name recurs a second time in poem 8. Since poem 1 and probably also poems 6 and 8 were written by Ercanbert, perhaps also this third stems from his pen.

Poems 4 and 5 contain an *ad hominem* attack in good old Horatian style. Poem 4 is an invective against Hartwig, a man of noble birth but heretical belief, who died in the village of Brumath, near Wissembourg. He is blamed for being a tramp (*vagabundus*, like the despised *monachi gyrovagi* of the Benedictine Rule) and for

---

[106] See the footnotes attached to the translation for the occurrences of other Graecisms throughout the poems. See also M. C. Ferrari, 'Pangite celi, reboemus odas', *Zeitschrift für schweizerische Kirchengeschichte*, 83 (1989), 155–76, at 168.

[107] Dümmler (ed.), 'Weissenburger Gedichte', 118 stresses that a Wisiricus is remembered in the Wissembourg Martyrologium (MS Wolfenbüttel, HAB, 45 Weiss., f. 59v) as having fallen under pagan attacks, perhaps in the year 926. The research project 'Margins at the Centre' will investigate whether the teacher Wisiricus contributed to the glossing of the Wissembourg manuscripts described in this chapter (see note 79).

preferring the delights of the world to the love of God: was he perhaps a former monk of the Wissembourg community? Interestingly, this poem is written in hexameters, in evident contrast with the other texts we are dealing with. Perhaps the author used hexameters on purpose, in order to conform to the metre typical of the satirical genre and, in particular, of Horace's *Satires*, which were read at Wissembourg at this time.[108]

Poem 5 was probably written by Ercanbert and is also a satire, at least as for its content. The target is the fastidious Thiodolt and his presumptuous conviction of being a good poet. Modern scholarship has capitulated in front of the lack of coherence and the obscure allusions contained in this text.[109] We think that the poem was meant to be a parody of Thiodolt's own verses. As it seems, Thiodolt is accused to be only able to reproduce slavishly the words of his teacher, i.e. the words he would learn during Latin classes. Probably, he is mocked for his lack of creativity, since he would put into verses only the terms he had learnt at school, perhaps in order to better memorise them. In fact, the Latin words used in the poem (*glis/gliris, robor, quercus, filia, canis, amnis, leno, nix/nivis*) and apparently gathered together without any evident logic are all discussed in Priscian's (not in Donatus's!) grammar as examples for specific rules. They are not supposed to form a narrative and probably do not refer to episodes of Thiodolt's own life either. They are a mimicry of Thiodolt's poor poetic performances, which requires familiarity with Priscian's text in order to be appreciated. Besides its original satirical purpose, this poem demonstrates that local pupils continued to study Latin on Priscian's grammar after Otfrid's death.

Poem 6 is a short intermezzo written probably by Ercanbert for his teacher, perhaps the Wisiricus mentioned earlier. Given the

---

108 On the remarkable presence of Horace's works at Wissembourg since the first half of the ninth century in a manuscript partly corrected by Walahfrid Strabo and repeatedly annotated (Vatican City, BAV, Reg. lat. 1703) see Stevens, *Rhetoric*, pp. 101–9, and Hennings, *Ostfränkische Sammlungen*, pp. 185–8.

109 Helm, 'Otfrids-Nennungen', 137–8 and Hennings, *Ostfränkische Sammlungen*, p. 194, who refers to the 'obskuren Anspielungen im V. Gedicht, die nicht als Topoi, sondern als Andeutungen für den Eingeweihten verstanden werden müssen'.

similarity of content, it could well be a continuation of poem 3. With these four verses, Ercanbert presents his poems (*carmina*) to his teacher and justifies himself in advance against the possible reproach of having written new texts on his own initiative. By mentioning his *carmina*, perhaps he referred to the very poems we are now dealing with, which he would thus regard as his own collection.

Poem 7 has attracted the attention of modern scholars repeatedly because of the explicit mention of the name Otfrid, which plausibly refers to Otfrid of Wissembourg in his quality of a distinguished former teacher of the local monastic school. The first seven verses had originally been written at the bottom of f. 51v and were then erased. The meaning and the syntax of the extant verses are not always clear, and the prosody is often inaccurate. Perhaps this poem was a work in progress. At any rate, it is certain that the memory of Otfrid and of his excellence is contrasted here with the mediocrity of an unlearned young man, probably a monk, who spent time in the monastic kitchen. He is presented as a poet of poor quality, who annoyed the community with his excessive loquacity. Since this poem is similar in content to number 5 and shares its closing line, modern scholars regard Thiodolt as the object of jest here too.[110]

In poem 8, the author, probably Ercanbert, wishes his beloved teacher Wisiricus good health. Poem 9 is an incomplete attempt to paraphrase the liturgical hymn *Gloria in excelsis deo* in hexameters.

All in all, the nine poems are thematically and stylistically coherent. Except for poem 2, they represent the attempt of a young monk of the Wissembourg community to write verses in which he praised or mocked the people he dealt with in his everyday life. This monk was probably the Ercanbert who features in the title of poem 1 and was praised by his friend Ferdingus in poem 2. In all likelihood, we are dealing with the personal poetical collection of a local pupil. Since these poems are of overall modest quality and, in two cases, are probably unfinished, it seems probable that the author himself wrote them down in his own hand in the final leaves of MS 77 Weiss.[111] He probably used Prudentius's anthology contained in this book for his own study of Latin poetry, revising its text on the basis

---

110 Helm, 'Otfrids-Nennungen', 144.
111 Hennings, *Ostfränkische Sammlungen*, p. 194.

of a further witness of Prudentius's poems and adding a chant with neumes onto f. 1r. Judging from the traits of his hand, he lived and studied within the Wissembourg monastic community around the end of the ninth century.

His poems, imperfect as they certainly are with regard to Latin syntax and prosody, nevertheless deserve more attention than they have earned thus far, and not only because they are funny and full of emotions. They are the actual fruits of a revival of learning which affected Wissembourg around the middle of the ninth century. This cultural flourishing cannot be explained as the implementation of a court-sponsored reform of education imposed on local teachers from a top-down perspective. Other factors played a determinant role, in particular the intellectual network linking Wissembourg scholars, most significantly Otfrid, to Alcuin's legacy. Here, methods and tools were exchanged horizontally through a chain of personal relationships. Moreover, the transmission of knowledge never resulted in passive absorption or slavish reproduction. Otfrid and his colleagues treasured cultural exchange with their peers but felt free to develop new tools and methods responding to the needs of their own audiences and pupils. This speaks against an interpretative model of a 'reform of education' which always expects uniformity and standardised results.

In particular, the manuscripts analysed here show that a new approach to Latin and to Latin poetry can be seen at Wissembourg roughly from the 840s, when Otfrid and his colleagues began to study Priscian's works, here following in Alcuin's and Hrabanus's footsteps.[112] Their glosses provide evidence of their thorough engagement and creative solutions. The later collection of nine poems reveals the same effort and the same type of approach. Ercanbert, the probable author of almost all these poems, was well acquainted with Priscian's grammar, from which he likely drew his distinctive use of Graecisms and transliterated Greek words. Although his engagement with Priscian did not result in flawless verses, he evidently believed knowledge and Latin to be indispensable companions in his own journey to salvation. He did his best to cultivate them and to change for the better by building on his individual talent as well as on the resources and networks he had at his disposal.

---

112 See note 85.

Conclusions

The evidence discussed in this chapter encourages us to challenge the idea that a 'reform' of education ever took place in the Carolingian period. According to the traditional narrative, the Carolingian court acknowledged the value of the learning programme developed by Alcuin and promoted its implementation in every school in the empire. However, several weak points can be spotted in this model. Firstly, we have no proof that Alcuin wrote his pedagogical treatises with the intention of outlining a coherent and modular programme of study applying to every school or learning context. These works are rather to be understood in terms of the needs of particular audiences and petitioners. Secondly, Alcuin's acknowledged authority at court and Charlemagne's attempt to spread his concerns were ultimately less relevant for the dissemination of his vision, methods and works over space and time than the personal networks Alcuin himself created and cultivated in his lifetime. This is demonstrated, thirdly, by the fact that Alcuin's approach was known and implemented at centres of learning like Wissembourg which do not appear to have possessed copies of his didactic treatises. Here the acquaintance with Alcuin's pedagogy was granted by teachers more or less directly connected to him. More relevant than his own books or courtly backing was the bond of esteem, affection and scholarly commitment demonstrated by his pupils and friends in spreading his ideas.

The case of Munich, BSB Clm 6407 copied in Verona around 800 and soon travelling to Freising illustrates the swiftness with which texts could cover long distances as they travelled in the bags of early medieval scholars. The delayed reception of Alcuin's *Opera didascalica* in tenth-century Italy confirms that patterns of transmission can be explained by identifying networks of knowledge between schools, masters and students rather than by assuming an enforced act of royal patronage.[113] As for Wissembourg, the teacher–pupil

---

113 On the circulation of Italian scholars and their books in tenth-century Europe see G. Vocino, 'Migrant masters and their books: Italian scholars and knowledge transfer in post-Carolingian Europe', in S. Greer et al. (eds), *Using and Not Using the Past after the Carolingian Empire* (London: Routledge, 2019), pp. 241–61.

relationships linking Alcuin to Hrabanus and Hrabanus to Otfrid facilitated the spread of Alcuin's didactic methods and, as a consequence, led to an engagement with Priscian's works, which is previously unrecorded in the evidence and lasted, though with results of uneven quality, at least until the end of the ninth century.

Thinking in these terms – networks, communication and local communities with specific features, interests and demands – offers a way out of traditional 'renaissance' or 'reform' paradigms: on the one hand, these interpretative tools dissolve a top-down perspective which has too often been attached to the 'Carolingian reform of education' and, on the other hand, they make visible the channels through which a change did take place in a given community, why and how that happened and to which degree that change was driven and matched the demands, the expectations or the model expressed by the hub from which the 'reform' emanated. Proceeding in such a way prevents clear-cut judgements on the merits of a perceived historical change that we, historians, too easily tend to call a 'reform'. It also discourages thinking in terms of success, failure or limits of reforms by taking the rigid institutional frame out of the limelight and by bringing to the fore the social interactions between men and communities who, after all, never stopped trying to 'correct', 'reform' or even, to use a less historiographically freighted term, simply improve themselves in order to gain eternal salvation.

Appendix

Nine poems from Wissembourg (MS Wolfenbüttel, Herzog August Bibliothek, 77 Weissenburg, fos 50v–52r): an English translation[114]

> 1   *(elegiac couplets)*
> *Verses by Ercanbert the Deacon*
> Now gather, o good cultivator, the tiniest of fruits
> and words I have joined together with a weak metre;
> recognise here at once from many angles a field
> uncultivated and devoid of a fruitful seed.
> Indeed, no learned farmer took care of our plots,

---

114 For the Latin text see Strecker (ed.), *Weissenburg*, pp. 504–7.

after hostile death took away the cultivator.
But in the end God visited us with beneficent mercy
and sent you to help us.
Put an end now to our idleness with [your] pious words
and stand by us for ever as a pious admonisher.
And fill our heart with the seed of your wisdom,
so that you appear in heaven as a shining harvester.

2   *(elegiac couplets)*
Verses by Ferdingus the Subdeacon
Our little verses are approaching you, if you do not reject them from your sight,
joined together with a very modest metre, as I was able to compose them.
O youth, may you now enjoy an even more flourishing youthfulness,
may these sweet words grow in your soul.
O friend, may the Lord, the ruler of heaven, increase your understanding
and keep away scandals, lest they obscure your soul.
Ercanbert, it is now possible for your senses to sail
a wide sea, to catch great-spirited fish.
Now you are able to face the sea on the vessel of wisdom,
which you are able to steer thanks to your learning.

3   *(elegiac couplets)*
O distinguished father, recognise the modest understanding
shining in my body, for I am still young,
and receive first my little verses, put together, of course, as best I could,
as well as my small sentences.
Now, I pray you, Wisiricus, may your wisdom understand
that a desire[115] troubles the spirit of my body.
Another concern fills my oppressed body

---

115 The Latin text reads *invidiam*, which is here translated according to the meaning *studium, voluntas, animus*, provided by the dictionary *Du Cange – Glossarium mediae et infimae Latinitatis*; see http://ducange.enc.sorbonne.fr/invidia (accessed 21 February 2022).

instead of examining the contents of the art of grammar.[116]
May you be mild to me, and Christ's grace mild to you,
farewell, my beautiful hero, and may you be well ever after.

4 (hexameters)
Now a man called Hartwig
has suffered a sudden death in the western region,
in the village of Brumath. He gave himself to heresy from his first years.
He carried a noble family name, but being himself degenerate
by tenacious error adhered to Satan travelling here and there
and disregarded, with a raving mind, our beneficent God
and prefers to serve the vain delights of the transitory world,[117]
and ruined people rightly believing
in Christ, thus gathering a large plunder by the devil's persuasion.
Now he will be deprived of all his wealth and of his life.

5 (elegiac couplets)
by Ercanbert?
O Thiodolt, you boast persistently
of being a good poet, but the teacher stands by you as your [food-]basket.[118]
Now you will always have your merriment through us
and now it behoves you to think of your own discredit.
You recall the dormouse found under an oak-tree,
While your daughter was living, when she was little.
Recall as well the dog, which made you fall

---

116 The Latin text reads *artis grammaticę ingenium*, an expression recurring twice in the prologue of Smaragdus's *Liber in partibus Donati*, as remarked by P. Carmassi, 'Litterae e scrittura nell'insegnamento della grammatica in età altomedievale: premesse teoretiche e aspetti pratici', in P. R. Robinson (ed.), *Teaching Writing, Learning to Write: Proceedings of the XVIth Colloquium of the Comité International de Paléographie Latine* (London: Kings College London, 2010), pp. 37–59, at 44.
117 A contemporary hand wrote the corresponding Latin word *mundi* above the Graecism *cosmi* of the text.
118 Helm, 'Otfrids-Nennungen', 137 interprets this verse differently: 'Er scheint ein Fresser gewesen zu sein: sein Meister ist die *sporta*, d. i. der Speisekorb'. We instead think that Thiodolt is attacked for his lack of creativity and for his vocabulary culled from his grammatical handbooks (see commentary) and not for his voracity.

into the river Lauter when you were a relentless pimp.
At that time you gave the example of snow, when you stayed
on the right path all the way to your tiny cottage.
Now, always reviewing these accomplishments in your heart
stop talking, once and for all, about us.

6   (elegiac couplets)
by Ercanbert?
Understand, o teacher,[119] that the poems you are now seeing
have certainly not been composed out of volition.[120]
But it was the order of our father Babo [?]:[121]
and this affords a little diversion [*ludiculum*] for you as well.

7   (elegiac couplets)
which <a man> called Cormac brought to the excellent
teacher Otfrid, who dwelled rightfully as a *magister*
in the seat of Leucopolis[122] with a pious body.
You, though shining already less brightly with respect to doctrine,
insult the places of the shaved heads[123] with your modest verses.
O harasser of monks with a swelling head,[124]
can indeed no human tongue defeat you in song?
You enter the kitchen, a quarrel begins at once,
and immediately you sit down snatching a three-legged stool,
also turning over the old plants with their stems
and roasting small lumps of dough[125] with short legs

---

119 A contemporary hand wrote the corresponding Latin word *magister* above the Graecism *didascule* of the text.
120 The Latin text reads *invidiam*; see note 101.
121 The Latin text has *Babinis* in the genitive. It is difficult to determine the corresponding nominative, since this name does not occur elsewhere in the sources.
122 This is a further Graecism meaning 'in the monastery of Wissembourg'. See the ninth-century note of possession contained in the MS Wolfenbüttel, HAB, 33 Weiss., f. 78r: 'Liber de monasterio Leucopolitano'.
123 The Latin *calvarum*, probably to be integrated with *testarum*, is an allusion to the tonsured heads of the monks.
124 We interpret the Latin *tumens colla* as referred to *vexator monachorum*. In particular, *colla* would be an accusative of respect (accusative of the part affected) depending from *tumens*.
125 The Latin *massellas* of the text, probably an accusative plural of an otherwise unrecorded word *massella*, could be a diminutive of *massa*, meaning

and always keeping a prolix tongue in your throat.
O unlearned boy, stop talking further.

8   (elegiac couplets)
by Ercanbert?
Wisiricus, dear to me more than all others
stay safe on earth and in heaven as well.
May you always have good fortune for a long time here
and may you always have in heaven a benevolent God.
And may no kind of physical plague hurt you
But rather, my dear, may you be healthy all the time.

9   (hexameters)
by Ercanbert?
Glory to God in the highest
The highest glory be to God in the star-bearing heavens.
And on earth peace to people of good will.
And peace on earth to men, whom a propitious will maintains.
We praise you.
Yet we praise you exulting with the angelic crowd.
We bless you.
And we all bless you and your holy name.
We adore you.
We often beg you on bent knees as well.

'dough' (see *Thesaurus Linguae Latinae* online: see https://publikationen.badw.de/de/thesaurus/lemmata#58083 (accessed 21 February 2022)).

4

Correcting the liturgy and sacred language

Els Rose and Arthur Westwell

Introduction

The language and performance of ritual occupies a central place in the story of Carolingian 'reform'. Classic proof texts, such as the *Admonitio generalis*, show that Carolingian royal and ecclesiastical authorities were preoccupied with correct spelling and pronunciation of sacred language in order to secure the favour of God with prayers in good Latin.[1] The qualified and limited focus of these official calls to improve ritual language does not always cohere with the post-Reformation conception of liturgical 'reform', which emphasised the imposition by a central authority of uniformity in ritual and of authorised and standard liturgical books, as a corrective to the presumed degeneracy of diverse practices and texts.[2] This background understanding of 'reform' has shaped the conception of the Carolingian period as a turning point in liturgical history,

---

1 A. Angenendt, 'Libelli bene correcti: Der "richtige Kult" als ein Motiv der karolingischen Reform', in P. Ganz (ed.), *Das Buch als magisches und als Repräsentationsobjekt* (Wiesbaden: Harrassowitz, 1992), pp. 117–23; M. Mostert, '"…But they pray badly using corrected books": errors in the early Carolingian copies of the *Admonitio generalis*', in R. Meens et al. (eds), *Religious Franks: Religion and Power in the Frankish Kingdom: Studies in Honour of Mayke de Jong* (Manchester: Manchester University Press, 2016), pp. 112–27; E. Rose, '*Emendatio* and *effectus* in Frankish prayer traditions', in Meens et al. (eds), *Religious Franks*, pp. 128–47.
2 C. Vogel, 'La reforme liturgique sous Charlemagne', in W. Braunfels (ed.), *Karl der Grosse Lebenswerk und Nachleben II: Das geistige Leiben* (Düsseldorf: Schwann, 1966), pp. 217–32.

when it was assumed that the Carolingian monarchs imposed (or attempted to impose) by law the uniform performance of ritual on the basis of books imported from Rome. But the manuscript evidence from the ninth century reveals that diversity in liturgical text and practice was fundamental through the entire period, and it does not appear to reflect the centralised imposition of one form of 'correct' liturgy.[3] Rather than a uniform vision of liturgical correctness, such manuscripts reflect many individualised and different initiatives to improve liturgical performance and understanding. What would the 'reform' of a liturgy of such varied character even look like, and under what parameters can we evaluate it to have succeeded or failed?

Additionally, the Carolingian period witnessed an explosion of texts attempting to explain and understand the meaning and function of liturgical texts which, as in other areas, approached this task in all sorts of ways and with all sorts of different techniques, often coming to equally diverse conclusions.[4] As much as the copying and creation of liturgical texts, the creation of these *expositiones* – that is, commentaries on liturgical practice and language – involved authors with diverse backgrounds, although their names often remain hidden from history, and manuscripts of varying sophistication and quality. Indeed, the boundary between the liturgical book itself, used to prepare and celebrate worship, and the study book explaining and contextualising the liturgy is a blurred one, and there are numerous manuscripts that carry both kinds of texts.

---

3 R. McKitterick, 'Unity and diversity in the Carolingian Church', in R. N. Swanson (ed.), *Unity and Diversity in the Church*, Studies in Church History 32 (Oxford: Oxford University Press, 1997) pp. 59–82; Y. Hen, *The Royal Patronage of Liturgy in Frankish Gaul to the Death of Charles the Bald (877)*, HBS Subsidia 3 (London: Boydell & Brewer, 2001); M. Morard, 'Sacramentum immixtum et uniformisation romaine', *Archiv für Liturgiewissenschaft*, 46 (2004), 1–30.

4 A. Wilmart, 'Expositio missae', in F. Cabrol and H. Leclercq (eds), *Dictionnaire d'archéologie chrétienne et de liturgie* (Paris: Letouzey et Ané, 1922), V, cols 1014–27; S. Keefe, *Water and the Word: Baptism and the Education of the Clergy in the Carolingian Empire* (2 vols, Notre Dame, IN: Notre Dame University Press, 2002); C. Jones, 'The book of the liturgy in Anglo-Saxon England', *Speculum*, 73 (1996), 659–702.

Such books present the Carolingian approach as a near-universal collective drive to improve understanding of liturgical text and ritual, without the assumption that there was any one single 'correct' answer. Instead, the manuscripts themselves invite comparison, contrast and synthesis, by placing several or many such *expositiones* of the same ritual side by side.[5] In this spirit, this article discusses two of the most widely represented texts of this nature, each among a host of such *expositiones* addressing the central liturgical event of the mass. Here, we will offer an account of the methodology and manuscript tradition of the anonymous text traditionally entitled *Dominus vobiscum* (after its opening words) and the *expositio missae* contained in Book 3 of Amalarius of Metz's *Liber officialis*, with particular attention paid to their attitudes to liturgical language and to 'correct' Latin in the liturgy.[6]

---

5 Many of the books treated by Keefe, *Water and the Word*, I, offer multiple expositions on baptism; others offer multiple expositions on the mass and other rites too, like St Gall Stiftsbibliothek 446, combining *ordines* and liturgical texts. See M. Andrieu, *Les Ordines Romani du haut Moyen Âge* (reprint, Leuven: Spicilegium Sacrum Lovaniense, 1957), I, pp. 336–43; M. de Heer, '*Expositiones missae* in MS Corbie 230: three commentaries on the mass in a Carolingian pastoral compendium' (unpublished MA thesis, Utrecht University, 2018).

6 *Dominus vobiscum*, ed. J.-M. Hanssens, *Amalarii episcopi opera liturgica omnia*, Studi e Testi 138 (Vatican City: Biblioteca apostolica vaticana, 1948), I, pp. 283–338, where Hanssens compares the text to *Canonis missae interpretatio*, listed among Amalarius's genuine works (p. 49). Hanssens's edition aims at correcting the 'horridam graphiam' in some copies (p. 110). For earlier editions, from the seventeenth century onwards, see C. M. Nason, 'The mass commentary *Dominus vobiscum*: its textual transmission and the question of authorship', *Revue Bénédictine*, 114 (2004), 75–91, at 75–6. See, on the character and manuscript transmission of this treatise, C. van Rhijn, '*Ut missarum preces bene intellegant*. The *Dominus vobiscum*: a Carolingian mass commentary for the education of priests', *Revue Mabillon*, 31 (2020), 7–28. Many thanks to Carine van Rhijn for giving us access to this article before publication. For the second text, see Amalarius of Metz, *Liber officialis*, in J.-M. Hanssens (ed.), *Amalarii episcopi opera liturgica omnia*, Studi e Testi 139 (Vatican City: Biblioteca apostolica vaticana, 1949), II; trans. E. Knibbs, *On the Liturgy* (2 vols, Cambridge, MA: Harvard University Press, 2014).

The *expositiones*: dates, places and manuscripts

Dominus vobiscum

The treatise *Dominus vobiscum* appears in manuscripts from the late eighth or early ninth century onwards and is generally transmitted as an anonymous text written in response to the inclusion of the *canon missae* in Frankish liturgical manuscripts.[7] It is seen in most recent studies as an important link in the chain of the Carolingian reform of liturgy, resulting in the presupposed (but as a concept problematic) 'Romanisation' of the liturgy of mass.[8]

While the treatise is found in the manuscripts mostly as anonymous texts, a few exceptions link it to a known author: Alcuin, whose authorship is strongly defended by Corey Nason; Hrabanus Maurus, who included the work in his *Liber de sacris ordinibus*; and Amalarius of Metz – whence the inclusion by Hanssens in his edition of Amalarius's liturgical oeuvre.[9] Despite these medieval

---

7 The *canon missae* is first found in Frankish sacramentaries of the late seventh and early eighth centuries. It was probably part of the *Missa cotidiana Romensis* in the *Missale Gothicum*, dated to the 690s, where this mass formulary breaks off after the first prayer: MS Vat. Reg. lat. 317, f. 261v; ed. E. Rose, *Missale Gothicum*, CCSL 159D (Turnhout: Brepols, 2005), p. 544; see also E. Rose, *The Gothic Missal*, Corpus Christianorum in Translation 27 (Turnhout: Brepols, 2017), p. 23. The *canon missae* is included in the similar *Missa Romensis* in the Bobbio Missal, MS Paris BnF lat. 13246, f. 10r–19v, ed. E. A. Lowe, *The Bobbio Missal: A Gallican Mass-Book (MS Paris Lat. 13246)* (3 vols, London: Henry Bradshaw Society, 1920), pp. 9–13.
8 Nason, 'Mass commentary', 83–6.
9 It is attributed to Alcuin in Budapest, Széchényi National-Bibliothek cod. lat. 316, f. 45f. The manuscript's provenance is Salzburg, ca. 825, see Nason, 'Mass commentary', 87–9. The text's transmission (indicating a strongly coherent textual tradition in manuscripts related to Tours), rhetoric and style as well as the explanatory character that reminds of a didactic dialogue are important arguments to support Nason's view. Moreover, Nason points to anti-Adoptionist elements in the explanation of the *Pater noster*, which to him provides a *terminus ante quem non* of 781, the beginning of the Adoptionist controversy. See on this C. Chazelle, *The Crucified God in the Carolingian Era: Theology and Art of Christ's Passion* (Cambridge: Cambridge University Press, 2001); J. C. Cavadini, *The Last Christology of the West: Adoptionism in Spain and Gaul, 785–820* (Philadelphia, PA: University of Pennsylvania Press, 1993). The text is attributed to Hrabanus Maurus in MS Merseburg, Chapter

attempts to link the text to an authority in matters liturgical, the question of authorship is yet unsolved.

To know more about the intended audience of the text, the codicological context is relevant. Throughout the Carolingian period and beyond, *Dominus vobiscum* enjoyed striking popularity, as is indicated by the number of manuscripts and early printed sources in which it appears. In his edition, Hanssens listed thirty manuscripts, thirteen of which date to the ninth and tenth centuries.[10] While the list of early copies has grown to date to more than twenty, thanks to the work on baptismal catechesis by Susan Keefe and the tireless and ongoing search by Carine van Rhijn, the relatively large numbers for the post-tenth-century period attest to a continuous transmission in the later medieval and the early modern periods.[11]

The majority of manuscripts in which the text is found concern the instruction of the clergy, from which we may draw the conclusion that the text was intended to teach young clergymen the

---

Library 58. In addition, MS Rome, Biblioteca Nazionale Vittorio Emmanuele lat. 2096 includes DV next to work known to be by Hrabanus; see Nason, 'Mass commentary', 87; Hanssens (ed.), *Amalarii opera*, I, p. 113; see also Hrabanus Maurus, *Liber de sacris ordinibus*, ed. J.-P. Migne, *PL* 112 (Paris: Migne, 1852), cols 1179C–92A. See further the reference to Hrabanus in Rosamond McKitterick, *The Frankish Church and the Carolingian Reforms, 789–895* (London: Royal Historical Society, 1977), pp. 117–18. *Dominus vobiscum* is likewise found in manuscripts containing work by Theodulf of Orléans: *ibid.* and also p. 88. The work is attributed to Amalarius in Paris, BnF lat. 3832; see Hanssens (ed.), *Amalarii opera*, I, pp. 109–10.

10 Hanssens (ed.), *Amalarii opera*, I, pp. 110–14. Hanssens created a synoptic edition based on six manuscripts of the ninth and tenth centuries (St Gallen SB 446 (s. X^{in}); St Gallen SB 40 (s. $IX^{2/3-3/3}$ or c. 840; dated earlier by Nason: s. VIII/IX and qualified by him as the 'earliest dated known manuscript': Nason, 'Mass commentary', 76); Vat. pal. lat. 485 (s. X); Orléans BM 94 (116) (s. IX/X); Paris, BnF lat. 2796 (s. IX, a. 813 according to Hanssens, also Nason, 'Mass commentary', 78); Florence Biblioteca Medicea Laurenziana, Libri 29 (s. IX). Codices Zürich Zentralbibliothek Car. 102 (s. IX/X) and Orléans BM 94 (116) f. 88r–105v are not mentioned in the introduction (p. 114) but still listed in the sigla (p. 283)) and, on the other side, the text taken from Paris BnF lat. 4281 (s. IX) and the *PL*-version of Hrabanus Maurus's version.

11 Keefe, *Water and the Word*, II, pp. 126–7; Nason, 'Mass commentary', 76–80; van Rhijn, 'The *Dominus vobiscum*', 5–6, 10–11; a list of manuscripts is given at 19–21.

detailed meanings of the prayers that accompanied the Eucharistic ritual, more precisely the *canon missae* and the prayers and chants that follow until the completion of mass.[12] This does not mean, however, that the treatise focuses only on ordained clergy in its approach to the performance of mass. In its broader understanding of the community involved in this celebration, the treatise encompasses both clergy and lay people as agents in this ritual.[13] The treatise refers to both groups in the third person singular, thus addressing these categories not as groups but as individuals, while the first person (plural) generally refers to the Christian people as a whole, mostly in the theological sense of the collective subject that undergoes redemption (*quia salutem nobis dedit*), gives thanks to God (*gratias agimus*), or receives and interprets the biblical tradition, such as in the explanation of the Lord's Prayer.[14]

---

12 Nason, 'Mass commentary', 88: 'The tract is intended for the instruction of clergy'. On Carolingian priests' books see S. Patzold and C. van Rhijn (eds), *Men in the Middle: Local Priests in Early Medieval Europe* (Berlin: De Gruyter, 2016); on the place of *Dominus vobiscum* in such priests' manuals, see van Rhijn, 'The *Dominus vobiscum*'. The indication of these series of fixed prayers as 'Roman canon' is problematic since the Roman origin has never been confirmed and the text is often linked to the Milanese rite given the many references to the liturgical treatises attributed to Ambrose; see T. Klauser, 'Der Übergang der römischen Kirche von der griechischen zur lateinischen Liturgiesprache', in *Miscellanea Giovanni Mercati, vol. 1: Bibbia, letteratura cristiana antica* (Vatican City: Biblioteca Apostolica Vaticana, 1946), pp. 467–82, at pp. 480–2; Y. Hen, 'The Liturgy of the Bobbio Missal', in Y. Hen and R. Meens (eds), *The Bobbio Missal. Liturgy and Religious Culture in Merovingian Gaul* (Cambridge: Cambridge University Press, 2004), pp. 140–53, at pp. 150–2.

13 E. Rose, '*Plebs sancta ideo meminere debet*: the role of the people in the early medieval liturgy of mass', in U. Heil (ed.), *Das Christentum im frühen Europa: Diskurse – Tendenzen – Entscheidungen* (Berlin: de Gruyter, 2018), pp. 459–76, esp. pp. 471–2; also E. Rose, *Een gekooide tijger? Over levend Latijn in late Oudheid en (vroege) Middeleeuwen* (Utrecht, inaugural address, 2019), pp. 9–11, https://issuu.com/humanitiesuu/docs/oratie-els-rose_2019?e=11895952/67632473 (accessed 8 April 2020).

14 *Dominus vobiscum*, p. 306: 'Salutaris ideo dicitur, quia salutem nobis dedit, ut si praecepta eius servamus, vitam aeternam capere valeamus'; p. 288: 'per quem nos gratias agimus Patri'; and p. 330: 'Pater noster est ideo, quia nos creavit in tempore, et nos filii sumus sui adoptivi, et hereditatem caelestem

Apart from the one or two instances where the author uses the first-person plural to refer to himself, there are only two or three cases where 'our' (*noster*) is used to refer to the celebrant and an explicit distinction between clergy and faithful is made. The first instance is in the *Hanc igitur* (5), where the sacrifice (*oblationem*) is an offering of both priestly (*seruitutis nostrae*) and lay obedience (*sed et cunctae familiae tuae*).[15] Likewise, in the *Vnde et memores* (6), the use of the first-person plural (*nos*) is linked exclusively to ordained clergy (*sacerdotes*): 'We priests claim to commemorate [Christ's passion]'. In the same phrase, however, the commentator stresses that the faithful likewise participate in this commemoration, for 'Christ did not die only on behalf of the priests but also of the faithful'.[16] If *Dominus vobiscum* makes a difference between clergy and laity by reserving the first-person plural and derivations from *nos* for the clergy, the distinction in Eucharistic agency is not one of including the clergy and excluding the laity, as has long been maintained.[17] Rather, this distinction is employed to emphasise the division of roles and the specific kinds of agency attributed to celebrant and faithful alike: the priest 'who celebrates mass' (*si presbyter missam celebrat*) and the 'male and female' faithful (*circumadstantes*), 'who have come to hear mass' (*masculi et femine qui circumstant* [...] *qui ad audiendam missam uenerunt*) and to bring

---

Patris nostri caelestis possidere debemus, si operibus implemus quae in perceptione fidei spopondimus.'
15 *Dominus vobiscum*, p. 312: 'Hanc igitur oblationem servitutis nostrae sed et cunctae familiae tuae, quaesumus, Domine, ut placatus accipias. Sacerdos oblationem suam atque cunctorum qui Domino famulantur, id est qui Domino serviunt, commendat, ut Domino placeat, et ipse nobis propitius sit.'
16 *Dominus vobiscum*, pp. 316–18: 'Unde et memores sumus, Domine, nos tui servi, sed et plebs tua sancta, Christi Filii tui Domini Dei nostri. Memores nos esse sacerdotes profitemur atque plebem memores esse testamur Christi Filii tui Domini Dei nostri. Ideo sacerdotes fideliter memores esse debent, quia ipsi missam celebrant et sacrificium offerunt Christi exemplo instructi. [...] Plebs sancta ideo meminere debet, quia Christus non solum pro sacerdotibus passus est, sed et pro plebe.'
17 For the historiography of this approach, see Rose, '*Plebs sancta*', pp. 459–61.

their sacrifices (*qui oblaciones suas offerunt*), as is expressed in the *Memento* for the living.[18]

The explanation of the prayer *Nobis quoque* likewise uses the personal pronoun *nos/nobis* as inclusive of clergy and laity, conforming to the way it highlights the distinct roles of clergy and laity in the celebration of mass (*tam a sacerdote quam a populo*).[19] This is even the case in the *Qui pridie* (9), where the phrase 'the sacrifice is completed with our hands' (*per manus nostras*) could refer both literally to the hands of the celebrating priest but also to the hands of the faithful who bring the offerings of bread and wine to church.[20]

Amalarius of Metz (c. 775–c. 850)

Amalarius was indisputably a phenomenon of the Carolingian cultural and intellectual movements which are the subject of this collection. One of the most widely published and influential treatises of the period was his *Liber officialis*, which survives in the three editions the author made over two decades (sixteen manuscripts of the first edition were written in the 820s, ten of the second from 831 and four of the third from 835), as well as many excerpts, quotations and paraphrases in both manuscript collections and in later liturgical scholarship.[21] Book 3 of the *Liber officialis*, which we will focus on in what follows, is a sustained examination of the performance of the mass in the tradition of the *expositiones missae*.

Firstly, the question of why Amalarius wrote the *Liber officialis* must be revisited. Part of the problem of contemporary examination of Amalarius was the attempt to see him as a straightforward

---

18 *Dominus vobiscum*, p. 310. Not all participate in the active bringing in of gifts, e.g. p. 312: 'Ideo offerunt quia vivo et vero Deo omnium fides circumadstantium, offerentium et non offerentium, cognita est nota deuotio.'
19 *Dominus vobiscum*, p. 322: 'Haec omnia sacrificia ideo sunt offerta, tam a sacerdote quam a populo, ut omnipotens Deus peccata nostra non reputat, sed cum sanctis suis nobis portionem tribuat.'
20 *Dominus vobiscum*, p. 316: 'nos docuit quod nos Patrem semper supplicare debemus quod ille tam magnum sacramentum per manus nostras perficere dignetur'. On the contribution of bread and wine by the faithful laity, see Rose, *Gothic Missal*, pp. 71–4 with further references.
21 Hanssens (ed.), *Amalarii episcopi*, I, pp. 120–4.

'reformer' within a more rigid conception of Carolingian liturgical reform, that is the wholesale replacement of a decadent or imperfect liturgy (often used synonymously with one that was diverse) with one that was more correct, i.e. uniform and uniformly understood.[22] At least in part because Amalarius suited this pose so poorly, this has led to the presentation of the work as 'eccentric', as in somehow out of step with the 'proper' liturgical course of the era.[23] The undeniably stimulating use of Amalarius as a mine for incidental historical detail has also contributed to a certain neglect of the coherence in the total system of his work; he is unfavourably compared to contemporaries like Walahfrid Strabo whom Jones, for example, described as 'exceptional' in recognising liturgical diversity, when diversity is in fact axiomatic in Amalarius.[24] The condemnation of the *Liber officialis* at Quierzy in 838 shows how Amalarius could be wilfully misinterpreted even in his time, as we read in Irene van Renswoude's contribution, but the political background to this council was certainly decisive, and it did nothing to check the popularity of his work.[25]

---

22 C. Schnusenberg, *The Mythological Traditions of Liturgical Drama: The Eucharist as Theater* (Mahwah, NJ: Paulist Press, 2010), p. 267: 'Alcuin and later Amalarius were dominant forces in these reforms.'
23 Influentially expressed by Wilmart, 'Expositio missae', cols 1014–27, but prejudice continues to colour assessment: see J.-P. Bouhot, 'Les sources de l'expositio missae de Rémi d'Auxerre', *Revue des études augustiniennes*, 26 (1980), 118–69, 152, who contrasts Amalarius's 'artificial symbolism' unfavourably with the moral and historical readings of the mass in other *expositiones*; see also Y. Hen, 'When liturgy gets out of hand', in E. Screen and C. West (eds), *Writing the Early Medieval West* (Cambridge: Cambridge University Press, 2018), p. 209, 'most eccentric of all, Amalarius'.
24 S. Bobrycki, 'Amalarius' *Liber officialis* and the Mediterranean slave trade', *Haskins Society Journal*, 26 (2014), 47–67; Bobrycki summed up Amalarius's method as a 'pathological need to interpret everything he sees'. See further Jones, 'The book of the liturgy', 671, n. 50: 'Quite exceptional among the Carolingian commentators for his acknowledgment of diversity in the liturgy is Walafrid Strabo, whose *Liber de exordiis et incrementis quarundam in obseruationibus ecclesiasticis rerum* (c. 841) frankly addresses regional and historical variations'.
25 A. Kolping, 'Amalar von Metz und Florus von Lyon: Zeugen eines Wandels im liturgischen Mysterienverständnis in der Karolingerzeit', *Zeitschrift fur katholische Theologie*, 73 (1951), 424–64.

So why did Amalarius write? Amalarius himself introduced the *Liber officialis* and the purpose of his work in his dedication to Emperor Louis the Pious which was present in the book from the first edition:

> I your servant, though least of all, was affected by the desire to know the reason [*ut scirem rationem*] for the order of our mass, which we celebrate according to custom, and even more so from the diversity with which it is done, that is that in one place one epistle is read, in another place, two, and all the other matters, and similarly for the other offices.[26]

The recent translation of Amalarius translates him here as being 'struck' by diversity in the liturgy, but there is no sense in this discussion that Amalarius found diversity in itself surprising or troubling, and the commentary to the translation unfortunately interprets Amalarius largely as operating within a monarchical 'reform' of liturgy.[27] Another matter to note is that the mass is already presented as the object of special attention in Amalarius's preface. When we come to Book 3, the *expositio missae*, its preface reiterates:

> With the prompting of the Lord, and the intercession of the blessed confessor Medard whose feast is celebrated among us today [June 8th], in the joy of the saints, we are prompted in our soul to receive the gift of God, that he may grant to cleanse and pacify the eye, through which we may learn about the office of the mass. We may learn what meaning is contained [*quid rationem in se contineat*] in the diversity with which it is celebrated here and now, when what was done in ancient/the earliest times used to suffice, without cantors and lectors and the rest of what we do here, with only the blessing

---

26 Amalarius, *Liber officialis*, p. 19: 'Servus ego vester, quamvis minimus omnium, afficiebar olim desiderio ut scirem rationem aliquam de ordine nostrae Missae, quam consueto more caelebramus et amplius ex diversitate quae solet fieri in ea – hoc est quod aliquoties una epistola legitur, aliquoties duae, et cetera talia, simulque de ceteris officiis'.

27 Knibbs (trans.), *On the Liturgy*, II, p. 16; e.g. on p. xvi we read that Pippin inaugurated 'centralized efforts to Romanize the Gallican liturgy and his son Charlemagne followed his lead'.

of the bishops and priests for the consecration of the bread, which refreshed the people to the salvation of souls.[28]

Conditioned by the Reformation, we tend to see a return to apostolic purity as the goal of 'liturgical reform', and the closer to the apostles the better, but Amalarius displays a very different attitude here. Of course, plain apostolic practice had everything sufficient unto itself but, at the same time, every development that time had layered upon it to make the mass the complex event he would then describe also had its own *ratio*. Earlier in his career, Amalarius had put this plainly in his letter to Peter of Nonantola:

> I myself consider that there is nothing set down in the church, either among the ancient fathers, or those more recent, which lacks a meaning [*ratio*].[29]

What is important here is not only Amalarius's thirst for *ratio* (ground or reason), but his conviction that all developments in liturgical practice in the true Church from the beginning until the present day had to be rational in the terms Amalarius presented it – that is, they all had some purpose in making known a deeper truth. Within this framework, two diverse or divergent practices might both be rational in their own way and in their own context, provided they were understood with the methods of explanation Amalarius presented. For example, in his own experience of the diversity of liturgical books, he found that some presented a five-week Advent, and some had only four, so he found different meaningful recollections in either number (the ages of the world, and the

---

28 Amalarius, *Liber officialis*, p. 257: 'Domino opitulante, intercedente beato Medardo confessore, cuius festivitate hodie apud nos celebratur, in gaudio sanctorum, prompti sumus animo ad suscipiendum Dei munus, si tamen ipse dignatur purgare et serenare oculum, in quo discamus de officio missa, quid rationis in se contineat diversitas illa quae ibi agitur, cum satis esset, sine cantoribus et lectoribus et ceteris quae ibi aguntur, sola benedictio episcoporum aut presbyterorum ad benedicendum panem et vinum, quo reficeretur populus ad animarum salutem sicut primevis temporibus fiebat'.
29 Amalarius of Metz, *Epistula ad Petrum abbatem Nonatulanum*, in Hanssens (ed.), *Amalarii episcopi*, I, pp. 227–31, here p. 230: 'reputans apud me nihil statutum esse in ecclesia, neque apud anticos patres neque apud recentiores, quod ratione careat'.

types of books prefiguring Christ respectively).[30] That kind of difference, important to liturgical scholars today when tracking developments of liturgical books, was equally obvious to participants in the composite liturgical culture the Carolingian church inherited and continued to develop. The experience of such differences in day-to-day practice would encourage techniques like that of Amalarius to seek the maximal meaning in difference and choice, rather than an insistence that only one way of doing things was valid. Notably, his straightforward presentation and endorsement of diversity in liturgical practice were not raised as one of the criticisms of Amalarius, discussed in Irene van Renswoude's piece. As she noted, Florus of Lyon was, or presented himself to be, dismayed by the lack of solid authoritative grounding in the Bible or the Fathers for some of Amalarius's interpretations. To Amalarius, however, the acceptance by the Church of a liturgical usage necessarily entailed that it had an underlying *ratio* to be discovered, a starting point for his 'reading' of the liturgy with which Florus refused to engage. The similar search for meaning also animated the author of the word-for-word commentary of the mass, *Dominus vobiscum*.

Techniques and purposes

In nostra lingua interpretatur: *a word-for-word explanation of mass*

Dominus vobiscum explains the ritual texts of mass, starting with the dialogue between celebrant and faithful *Dominus vobiscum – et*

---

30 Amalarius, *Liber officialis*, 3.40.1–6, p. 374: 'Auctor lectionarii excitat fidem nostram ad recolendum Domini nostri Iesu Christi venturi in mundum praeconium per quinque aetates mundi; auctor missalis quod vocatur gregorianum et antiphonarii nos tangit, ut recolamus nativitatem Domini caelebratum per tres ordines librorum, scilicet legis, prophetarum et psalmorum et per quartum, id est principium evangelii'. See also Amalarius, *Liber officialis*, 4.30.1, pp. 500–1: 'Scripsimus in superioribus libellis in quinta ebdomada ac quarta ante nativitatem domini inchoari praeparationem adventu domini ... in quinta seu quarta ebdomada, sequendo auctores lectionarii et antiphonarii ac missalis cuius auctorem credimus esse beatum papam Gregorium'.

cum spiritu tuo (The Lord be with you – and with your spirit), and following all prayers of the *canon missae*, the *Pater noster* (the Lord's Prayer), the prayer after Communion and the conclusion of mass and dismissal. The commentary applies an etymological method. In this, the influence of the method chosen by Isidore of Seville (d. 636) in his *Etymologies* is felt even if Isidore himself did not follow this approach in his liturgical commentary *De officiis ecclesiasticis*. Isidore was not, however, the only source of inspiration, since some etymologies are derived from other scholars.

Etymological derivation is applied, first, to words that have their origin in the biblical languages Hebrew and Greek, the latter also providing much liturgical terminology as the sacred language of Rome and the West until well into the fourth century.[31] These etymologies are limited in number. The Hebrew words concerned are *Amen*, *Cherubin*, *Seraphin*, *Sabaoth* and *Osanna*. Of these, *Amen* has the most elaborate, threefold explanation next to a simple translation:

> Amen is (1) the confirmation of the prayer by the people and (2) is to be understood in our language, as if all say that it must be as the priest has prayed. (3) Its own translation is '[said] truly' or 'faithfully'.[32]

This explanation first emphasises the division of roles among those celebrating mass, explaining why the word is used in the liturgy at all and by whom it is performed. Then it explains its meaning, while the third part gives a literal Latin translation. The treatment of the other Hebrew words is more confined and in line with already existing translations and interpretations, e.g. *cherubim*; *seraphim*; *Sabaoth*.[33] The word *osanna* is treated in some detail, as it is seen as

---

31 Klauser, 'Übergang'.
32 *Dominus vobiscum*, p. 284: 'Amen confirmatio orationis est a populo, et in nostra lingua intellegi potest, quasi omnes dicant: Ut ita fiat sicut sacerdos oravit, sed propria eius interpretatio est vere sive fideliter'.
33 The author translates *cherubim* as 'fullness of knowledge': 'cherubim plenitudo scientiae interpretatur'. See Gregory the Great, *Homiliae in Ezechielem*, ed. Marc Adriaen, CCSL 142 (Turnhout: Brepols, 1997), I.6, l. 300. For Seraphim the author gives the meaning 'fire': 'seraphin incendium dicitur'. These translations are found in the work of Gregory the Great, presumably inspired by the work on the celestial hierarchies by Dionysius

a 'corrupt' form for the original *osianna*, to which Jerome refers and in which he is later followed by Bede and Alcuin.[34]

The words with Greek roots explained and translated are pater (*genitor*); Christus (*unctus*), angelus (*nuntius*), archangelus (*excelsi nuntius*), Ihesus (*saluator siue salutaris*), aecclesia (*congregatio*), catholicus (*uniuersalis*), apostolus (*missus*), martyr (*testis*), panis (*omnis*) and diaconus (*minister*). In its reference to the Greek word πᾶν to explain *panis* (bread) with *omnis* (all, each) the treatise follows Isidore, as we will see in more detail in the following.[35]

Much more extensive is the Latin pool of words in need of explanation. Here the author deals with words that were apparently less common or experienced as difficult or obscure. In this category etymological explanation is rare, being given mainly for divine names.

Areopagita: see Gregory the Great, *Homiliae in Ezechielem*, ed. Adriaen, I.8, l. 605. Jerome gives *incendium* as a translation of the Hebrew *seraphim*: Jerome, *Epistulae*, CSEL 54 (Vienna: Verlag der Österreichischen Akademie der Wissenschaften, 1910), p. 81. On the medieval Latin translation of Dionysius, see M. Grabmann, 'Pseudo-Dionysius der Areopagita in lateinischen Übersetzungen des Mittelalters', in A. M. Koeniger (ed.), *Beiträge zur Geschichte des christlichen Altertums und der byzantinischen Liturgie. Festgabe Albert Ehrhard zum 60. Geburtstag dargebracht* (Bonn: Schoeder, 1922), pp. 180–99. To Sabaoth, the author gives the current interpretations: either 'almighty', or 'army': 'sabaoth a multis interpretari solet omnipotens a multis uero exercituum'. See Jerome, *Commentarius in Isaiam*, ed. Marc Adriaen, CCSL 73 (Turnhout: Brepols, 1963), I.1.9, l. 14–17.

34 According to Jerome, *osi* is an 'exclamation by the worshiper' ('interiectio laudantis'), while *anna* means 'save' ('quomodo nunc dicitur corrupte osanna ante dicebatur osianna, osi interiectio est laudantis siue causam magnificantis anna saluifica, uel saluum fac'). Jerome, *Epistulae*, 20.1, p. 104. Alcuin follows this observation in his *Commentary on the Gospel of John*. See Alcuin, *Commentarii in sancti Iohannis Evangelium*, ed. J. P. Migne, PL 100 (Paris: Migne, 1851), cols 733–1007, here col. 909: 'Osanna itaque, salva, obsecro, significat, consumpta littera i vocali, quae verbum prius terminat, cum perfecte dicitur osi, per virtutem litterae vocalis Aleph, a qua verbum sequens incipit anna, quod metrici in versibus scandendis synalepham vocant: quamvis [illi] scriptam litteram scandentes transilient'. Alcuin borrows this passage from Bede, *In Marci euangelii expositio*, in D. Hurst (ed.), *Bedae Operae: Pars II:3 Opera Exegetica*, CCSL 120 (Turnhout: Brepols, 1960), III.xi.10, p. 575. We did not find earlier attestations.

35 Derived from Isidore, *Etymologiae*, ed. W. M. Lindsay (Oxford: Oxford University Press, 1911), XX.2.15 (*De escis*); see further in the following.

Table 4.1 Latin words and their etymological explanation

Dominus	quia dominator est omnium et sub eius dominatione omnia sunt (for he is Lord of all and all things are under his rule)
Deus	Deus a diligendo dicitur quia omnia diligit et gubernat quae creauit. Et aliter, deus a diuinitate dictus est quia diuinus est et omnia scit et omnia diuidit prout uult ('God' is derived from 'loving' [*diligendo*] because he loves all and rules what he has created. Or differently, 'God' is derived from 'divinity' for he is divine and knows everything and separates [cf. Genesis 1, 4] as he wants)
Maiestas	quasi maior est potestas (as if a greater power)
Caelum	a celando dicitur eo quod caelat diuina secreta, aliter caelum a celsitudine dicitur eo quod altior est rebus terrenis ('heaven' [*caelum*] is derived from *celare* 'to hide' because heaven hides the divine secrets. Or else it is derived from height because it is higher than the terrestrial matters)
Terra	a terendo dicitur, eo quod pedibus teritur ('earth' is derived from 'to tread' [*terendo*] because it is trodden by feet)

Notes: For *Dominus*, see further Isidore, *Etymologiae*, VII.1.14; for *Terra*, see further Isidore, *Etymologiae*, XIV.1.1. The derivation of *Deus* was well known in contemporary explanations of the Creed: see *Explanationes symboli aeui Carolini*, ed. Susan Keefe, CCCM 254 (Turnhout: Brepols, 2012), p. 132.

More often, the author gives Latin synonyms to make a word or term more accessible or to explain the (doctrinal) context of a word or phrase. Examples of words that get a full etymological explanation are given in Table 4.2 and include *Dominus*, *deus*, *maiestas*, *caelum* and *terra*.

While the etymological explanations of *dominus* (lord, ruler) – *dominor* (to rule) and *terra* (earth) – *tero* (to rub, to bruise) go back to Isidore, *caelum* (heaven), on the other hand, is not explained along Isidorian lines. Isidore explains *caelum* through *caelare* (to engrave):

> The sky [*caelum*] is so named because, like an engraved [*caelatum*] vessel, it has the light of the stars pressed into it, just like engraved figures; for a vessel which glitters with figures that stand out is called *caelatus*.[36]

---

36 Isidore, *Etymologiae*, XIII.iv.1: 'De caelo. Caelum vocatum eo quod, tamquam caelatum vas, inpressa lumina habet stellarum veluti signa. Nam

Table 4.2 Latin words explained through synonyms

antistes	episcopus (bishop)
supplices	humiles (humbly)
inlibata	i.e. inmaculata et ab omni liuore malitiae aliena (i.e. immaculate and free from all bruise of malice)
puram	hoc est corde puro (i.e. with a pure heart)
saluificare	uel saluum fac (or save)
communicare	hoc est participare (i.e. to participate)
qui domino famulantur	i.e. qui domino seruiant (i.e. who serve the Lord)
in excelsis	i.e. in altis (i.e. on high)
memoriam uenerare	hoc est in memoria honorabiliter tenere (i.e. to keep in memory with reverence)
habere adscriptam	hoc est adsignatam ut sibi placeat (i.e. inscribed so that it may please him)

Dominus vobiscum, however, follows the mid-seventh-century Virgilius Grammaticus, perhaps of insular origin, who explains the word via the verb *celare* (to hide), 'because heaven hides the divine secrets'.[37]

Words that are explained by giving concise Latin synonyms are given in Table 4.3.

---

caelatum dicitur vas quod signis eminentioribus refulget'; trans. S. A. Barney et al., *The Etymologies of Isidore of Seville* (Cambridge: Cambridge University Press, 2006), p. 272.

37 Virgilius Maro Grammaticus, *Epistola de nomine*, ed. B. Löfstedt, *Virgilius Maro Grammaticus opera omnia* (Munich: K. G. Saur, 2003), p. 22: 'celum, quod a celando dicitur'. On Virgilius Grammaticus, see V. Law, *Wisdom, Authority, and Grammar in the Seventh Century: Decoding Virgilius Maro Grammaticus* (Cambridge: Cambridge University Press, 1995), pp. 3–4 giving a brief overview of the status quaestionis of Virgilius's chronological and geographical data. F. Brunhölzl, *Histoire de la littérature latine du Moyen Age. De Cassiodore à la fin de la renaissance carolingienne* (Turnhout: Brepols, 1990), I.1, pp. 146–8, locates him in the seventh century 'somewhere in the South of France', while M. Herren locates him, of continental background, in Ireland around 650: 'Virgil the Grammarian: a Spanish Jew in Ireland?', *Peritia*, 9 (1995), 51–71. For Law, Virgilius's identity and floruit is and remains an 'enigma' (p. 1), leaving us 'with few facts and much speculation' (p. 3). See also Rose, *Gekooide tijger*, p. 13.

Correcting the liturgy and sacred language 157

The list includes words that are in principle well known in classical Latin but receive a specific meaning in the Latin usage of Christian authors. On top of this list are the noun *antistes* (bishop), explained through the Greek loanword *episcopus*, and the verb *famulor* (to serve), which is used primarily in relation to God.[38] In addition, the verb *salvificare* (to save) is a neologism first attested by Christian authors.[39] The verb *communicare* (to communicate/participate in Holy Communion) is common in classical Latin and receives its specific Christian meaning related to participation in the Eucharist.[40]

Finally, explanation through paraphrasis takes place in the cases in Table 4.3. This list includes words with a specific meaning within the context of Christian doctrine, often lexical or semantic neologisms such as the noun *salvator* and the verbs *salvare* and *salutare*. A paraphrase through synonyms is also applied when the character of the Eucharistic offering is explained, as in the prayer *Supplices* where the synonyms *dona*, *munera* and *sacrificia* occur as an asyndetic enumeration (one after the other without any conjunction between them), while the *Memento* for the living adds *vota*.[41] The synonyms explain what the sacrifice tells us about the one bringing it: *dona* are given of one's own free will; *munera* are given in return for something else; *sacrificia* are consecrated with prayers; while *vota* are also linked to free will.[42] The adjectives typifying the sacrifice in the *Supplices* (*ratam* and *rationabilem*) are also paraphrased to explain them further. This rich commentary expresses the importance of the Eucharistic offering, the intention with which

---

38 See Rose, *Missale Gothicum*, p. 130.
39 *Ibid.*, pp. 106–7.
40 A. Blaise, *Le vocabulaire latin des principaux thèmes liturgiques* (Turnhout: Brepols, 1966), p. 407.
41 Qualified as 'abondance solennelle' by B. Botte and C. Mohrmann, *L'ordinaire de la messe* (Paris: Les Editions du Cerf, 1953), p. 38.
42 *Dominus vobiscum*, p. 306: 'Dona sunt quae voluntariae donantur; munera sunt quae pro aliquo munere vel mercede offeruntur ...; sacrificia sunt quae iam cum orationibus consecrantur'. The first part ('dona ... offeruntur') is quoted in what is called the 'Wormser Briefsammlung', a collection of 49 folios transmitted in a ninth/tenth-century palimpsest manuscript (Vat. Pal. lat. 930, f. 45v–46r). See also E. Dümmler (ed.), *MGH Epp.* 3 (Berlin: Weidmann, 1892), pp. 108–9.

158 Rethinking the Carolingian reforms

Table 4.3 Explanation of Latin words through paraphrasis

saluator	eo quod saluat populum suum a peccatis eorum (because he saves his people from their sins)
saluat	ideo saluat a peccatis quia potestatem habet dimittendi peccata, sicut ipse dixit, ut autem sciatis quia filius hominis habet potestatem in terra dimittendi peccata (he saves from sins because he has authority to forgive sins, as he himself said 'so that you may know that the Son of Man has authority on earth to forgive sins' [Luke 5, 24])
salutans	salutans ideo dicitur quia salutem nobis dedit ut si praecepta eius uitam aeternam capere ualeamus ('saving' is said because he gave us salvation so that we may seize eternal life through [following] his precepts)
dona	sunt quae uoluntariae donantur ('gifts' are those things given voluntarily)
munera	sunt quae pro aliquo munere uel mercede offeruntur ('presents' are those things that they offer as a present or reward)
sacrificia	sunt quae iam cum orationibus consecrantur ('offerings' are those things which are consecrated with prayers)
vota	vota dicuntur quae uolenter promittuntur quia uolenter et libenter deo uouere et reddere debemus (promises are called those things which are promised voluntarily, because we must voluntarily and gladly promise and offer to God)
ratam	hoc est iudicatam ut dignam illam iudicet in conspectu suo offerri (which means 'judged', so that he may judge it [the offering, *oblationem*] worthy to be sacrificed in his eyes)
rationabilem	id est iusta ratione plenam facere dignetur quia tunc illi est acceptabilis si recte credentes pro iusta ratione offerimus (i.e. that he may deign to make it [the offering, *oblationem*] full of just reasoning, because it is acceptable to him only if we sacrifice it in the right faith for the right reasons)

(*continued*)

Table 4.3 Continued

quando sacerdos dicit, memento domine famulorum famularumque tuarum et omnium circumadstantium (when the priest says 'O Lord remember your servants male and female and all those standing around here')	deprecat deum patrem ut memorare dignetur omnium ad officium missae siue masculorum siue feminarum aduenientium. Et quod dicit circumadstantium, ipsi sunt masculi et femine qui circumstant (he prays God the father that he may deign to remember all who have come to the service of Mass, both male and female. And he says 'all those standing around here' because it is these men and women that stand around [the holy altar] here)
sancta plebs (the holy people)	ideo dicitur quia fide ac babtismo christi praecepto sanctificata est modo indicat unde meminere debent (they are called thus because the laity are sanctified through Christ's precept in faith and baptism, and he [the priest] now indicates why they must remember)
sine ullius adiutorio (without the help of anyone)	ut intellegitur quod non hominum, nec angelorum nec ullius creaturae ueiculo eum ascendisse in caelum sed a patris maiestate eleuatus est (so that it is clear that he [Christ] ascended to heaven not as a human being, and not with the help of the vehicle of angels or any other creature, but that he was elevated by the majesty of [God] the father)
diuina institutione formati (instructed by divine teaching)	id est formam et exemplum a christo domino nostro accepimus et ausi sumus orare (i.e. we have received the teaching and example by Christ our Lord and dare to pray)
agnus dei (Lamb of God)	dicitur propter innocentiam quia nulli hominum, nec bestiarum nocet, et dum ad uictimam ducitur occidentem se non ledit sed occisorem suum post occisionem suam reficit (he is so called because of his innocence, because he [Christ] hurt no man nor beast, and while he was led to the slaughter he did not show himself hurt, but he restored his slaughterer after the slaughter)

it is sacrificed and the qualities the oblations have to make the ritual legitimate and valid. Paraphrases are further found when the people present at mass are at stake, both male and female: they are indicated with the words *circumadstantes* (*Memento*) and *plebs sancta* (*Vnde et memores*).[43] In the latter section, the indication of the faithful as *sancta plebs* is explained with reference to Baptism. Events in the life of Christ are also explained by paraphrasing, such as his ascent to heaven *sine ullius adiutorio*, the institution of the Eucharist itself during the Last Supper: *diuina institutione formati*, and the application of the lamb symbol to Christ in the context of the *agnus dei*. Finally, explanation by paraphrasing is applied in particular in the commentary on the *Pater noster* and the accompanying interpolation which follows it in the Canon, the Embolism or *Libera Nos*. This part of the treatise *Dominus vobiscum* requires more specific attention elsewhere in order to uncover its links to other, well-known patristic commentaries on the Lord's Prayer.

Now that we have come to know the method and techniques of *Dominus vobiscum*, we may reconsider its character and purpose. Rather than 'reforming' or explicitly correcting liturgical practice, *Dominus vobiscum* aims to create a better understanding of current practice. The character of *Dominus vobiscum* in its relation to those who celebrate the liturgy of mass (clergy and laity together) is closer to exegesis than to reform or *correctio* as such. The treatise must therefore be placed in the long tradition of Christian mystagogical practice (the contemplation of and education in mysteries) that goes back to the earliest centuries.[44] Understanding the *canon missae* was relevant from the moment it occurred in the Frankish

---

43 *Dominus vobiscum*, p. 310: 'Quando sacerdos dicit: Memento, Domine, famulorum famularumque tuarum, deprecatur Deum Patrem, ut memorare dignetur omnium ad officium missae, sive masculorum sive feminarum, advenientium, et quod dicit circumadstantium, ipsi sunt masculi et feminae qui circumstant'.

44 P. van Geest (ed.), *Seeing Through the Eyes of Faith: New Approaches to the Mystagogy of the Church Fathers* (Leuven: Peeters, 2016), in which ch. 2, G. Rouwhorst, 'Mystagogical terminology in liturgical contexts', pp. 23–35. See also N. Ristuccia, *Christianization and Commonwealth in Early Medieval Europe: A Ritual Interpretation* (Oxford: Oxford University Press, 2018), pp. 180–5.

liturgical books around the year 700. Rather than focusing on reform or programmatically searching for a model in Roman liturgical roots, *Dominus vobiscum* sought to interpret and explain in order to understand the rituals and texts of the liturgical celebration, regardless of the origin of these rites.

Amalarius and ratio

As discussed earlier, *ratio* was decisive in Amalarius's own introduction to his goals and methodology, thereby calling into question the attempt to see him as a 'reformer'; he noticeably does not use terms like a 'correct' liturgy. But what did he mean by *ratio*? He significantly used the term in his discussion of the nature of Christ's body and blood:

> LO III.24.8: Here we believe the simple nature of the bread and wine mixed with water to be turned into the true [*rationabilem*] nature, which is to say the body and blood of Christ.[45]

The *naturam simplicem* is the physical matter; the *naturam rationabilem* is the inner truth that is seen by faith (the word *ratio* is also used in the *canon missae*, and thus glossed by *Dominus vobiscum*). This is why Amalarius could even describe in detail what it meant that bells were made of bronze (LO III, 1, 5–6), or argue, in his treatment of the altar, that this is really the city of Jerusalem during the liturgy at LO III, 5, 29 (a point for which he was specifically censured at Quierzy). Both relied on his conception of *ratio* as being an objective inner reality (not a fanciful speculation), something which followed naturally from the idea that the inner, truer reality of the Eucharist was the body and blood of Christ.

Secondly, on the sending of catechumens away from mass before the Gospel, Amalarius uses his own understanding of *ratio* to actually criticise the ancient and, in his time, universal practice of the Frankish church:

---

45 Amalarius, *Liber officialis*, p. 339: 'Hic credimus naturam simplicem panem et vini mixti verti in naturam rationabilem, scilicet corporis et sanguinis Christi'.

> LO III.36.8 Our custom holds that we send the catechumens away before the Gospel. This does not seem to me to accord with reason, for it is without a doubt commissioned to preachers, that they should preach the Gospel to the people.[46]

Ratio was, therefore, more than simply a response to current practice. It might also evaluate and criticise. With current practice he knew well, Amalarius would note the diversity in matters like the number of the signs of the cross, or the time of dipping of the bread into the chalice.[47] He ultimately gave his own opinion in each case (one cross was fine because Christ was crucified once; it seemed right to put the bread in the chalice after the *Pax Domini* because the peace promised by the angels at Christ's birth came about at the resurrection). But the other options were not wrong. For example, if the Roman Church did differently it would clearly have its *mysterium* (the secret of faith).[48]

Ratio could be bent by sufficient power or necessity. Amalarius discusses how he saw Pope Leo III (d. 816) celebrate mass at dawn (this was either in Rome or when Pope Leo was in Francia 799–800).[49] He had devoted a previous chapter to Pope Telesphorus's recommendation (in the *Liber Pontificalis*) that mass should only be at the third or ninth hour, but Pope Leo had done differently in his own sight. Amalarius here preferred Pope Telesphorus, insofar as he had *ratio* for what he prescribed, but Leo's act could not be seen as entirely without *ratio* either. In his revision of the text in Book 4, Amalarius added extra sources he had subsequently found which were relevant to the arguments he made previously, and he returns

---

46 *Ibid.*, p. 371: 'Consuetudo nostra tenet ut catecuminos repellamus ante evangelium. Non mihi hoc videtur ex ratione incumbere, cum procul dubio praedicatoribus gentium praeceptum sit ut Evangelium eis praedicent'.
47 *Ibid.*, III, 24, 6–8, and III.31.1–7.
48 *Ibid.*, III.31.7, p. 363: 'Si hoc ita agitur in Romana ecclesia, ab illis potest addisci quid significat bis positus panis in calicem. Non enim vacat a mysterio quicuid in eo officio agitur iuxta constitutionem patrum'.
49 *Ibid.*, III.42.5, pp. 379–80: 'Namque vidi Leonem apostolicum diluculo intrare ad missam. Nescio utrum causa necessitates intercedente hoc ageret, an sola potestate. Quod legimus in Gestis pontificalibus, hoc scripsimus. Fulget enim potestas ratione decorata. Protulit enim Telesforus memoratus rationem de hora Missae; qua de re sponte incumbimus suae auctoritati'.

Correcting the liturgy and sacred language 163

here to this same question of the timing of the mass, noting that mass could be celebrated at other times on special feast days (night and morning on Christmas, night on Easter, dawn on feasts of John the Evangelist and John the Baptist), but this too was not without *ratio* in each case.[50]

This potential bending of *ratio* also had a pastoral dimension that is key to Amalarius's purpose:

> LO.III.42 Those who by necessity offer sacrifice to God before the third hour, or after the ninth, who are so inspired by divine love that they would not allow a day to pass without their sacrifice, it seems to me that they do not act as if with impudence against the apostolic institution, but they have serious cause, which probably can excuse them.[51]

Amalarius cannot see why we should not excuse those whose intentions were true from a rigid prescription, even one which was rational. Likewise, tradition gave specific days after death for the celebration of masses, but Amalarius suggested that it was certainly alright to stray from these, if, for example, you did not know when the person died:

> LO III.44.17 Yet, it is good at any time to pray for the dead. So if the day of death is not known ... do the solemnities for them nevertheless.[52]

Thus, even where Amalarius does not use the word *ratio* explicitly, he was far more likely to speak in terms of 'order' or 'congruency' or 'harmony' than 'correctness'.[53] Particularly striking is his commentary on the chant:

---

50 *Ibid.*, IV.40.7, p. 530: 'Si enim in ceteris oris ex constituto agitur Missa, ratio quaedam adest qua defendatur eadem hora, veluti est in Nativitate Domini'.
51 *Ibid.*, p. 379: 'Hi qui ante horam tertiam sive post horam nonam necessario offerunt sacrificium Deo, amore divino infecti, ut non praetereat dies sine illorum sacrificum, ut reror, non agunt quasi proterve contra instituta apostolica, sed habeant causam seriam, qua excusari probabiliter se possint'.
52 *Ibid.*, II, p. 386: 'Alioquin omni tempore bonum est orare pro defunctis. Etiam si ne sciatur dies defuncti ... agatur tamen eorum solempnitas'.
53 E.g. *ibid.*, III.8.2, p. 287: 'Non est ordo ut qui Dominus laudare uoluerit, tergum ad eum vertat et pectus ad servos'.

> LO III.3.12 But the saints had their harmonious differences, not dissonant ones, which is to say agreeing together not disagreeing – just as the sweetest song is made from diverse sounds, but not from adversity amongst them.[54]

Understanding this, Amalarius's method and purpose become clearer. It was never his intention to offer a narrative of mass that everyone should follow. His purposes were pastoral and educational and were intended to apply as broadly as conceivably allowed. For example, Amalarius used Augustine to argue that it was equally fine to take communion regularly or rarely, and he knew people who did either.[55]

The pastoral Amalarius, not so often portrayed in scholarship, is tenderly illustrated in his treatment of disability:

> LO III.3.5 Let the cantors here consider the meaning of their symphony. Through it, they urge the people to persist in the unity of the worship of a single God. And even if a deaf person were present, the cantors make the very same point through their arrangement in the well-ordered choir, such that those who cannot grasp the unity with their ears may grasp it with their sight.[56]

It is worth reiterating what this passage is saying. Amalarius appears to envisage that his work might address both the cantors and the clergy more generally.[57] They must remember to present unity, in their *symphonia* (harmony of music) but also in their very position-

---

54 Ibid., p. 269: 'Habebunt enim etiam tunc sancti differentias suas consonantes, non dissonantes, id est consentientes non dissentientes – sicut fit suavissimus cantus ex diversis quidem, sed non adversis inter se'. This is a rather perfect illustration of what is argued in K. Morrison, 'Know thyself: music in the Carolingian Renaissance', *Committenti e produzione aristico-letteriaria nell'alto medioevo occidentale*, Settimane di studio del centro italiano di studio sullo'alto medioevo, 39 (Spoleto: Il Centro, 1992), pp. 369–481.
55 Amalarius, *Liber officialis*, III.34.2, pp. 365–6.
56 Ibid., p. 267: 'Hinc tractent cantores quid significant simphonia eorum; ea ammonent plebem ut in unitate unius Dei cultus perseverent. Etiamsi aliquis surdus affuerit, idipsum statu illorum in choro ordinatissimo insinuant, ut qui auribus capere non possunt unitatem, visa capiant'.
57 Ibid., III.6.3: elsewhere 'an empty vanity' (inanem incantantiam) often accompanies cantors, so the *Kyrie* reminds them to suppress it.

ing, since, by this, they taught the people the unity of God, even those who could not hear song. In this, it becomes much clearer why Amalarius was obsessed with what we might see as minutiae. It was vital to ensure that the clergy, his readers, held a proper understanding of the *ratio* of each custom so that they would take care that their performance transmitted proper theological understanding to the laity at every level of ability and knowledge. Amalarius's sensitivity to lay participation and those less intellectually able is also notable when he suggests they should pray during the blessing of the Gospel:

> LO III.18.9 Meanwhile the people should ask God that the Devil not take the words of God from their hearts and that their hearts not be stony or thorny but good earth, able to receive and bear fruit. He who is not very quick should at least say – I borrow these words from the Gospel 'Glory to you, O Lord'.[58]

It should not be forgotten that Amalarius presents the actors and objects of the mass not only in the type of the Gospel characters, but also, in a more neglected aspect of his thought, as revealing the journey of the soul in repentance, and the proper attitudes and processes that should be taken.[59] The aim to transmit correct moral understanding of the Christian life to the clergy and thereby disseminate it downwards and outwards reflects the broader trends of the Carolingian period exemplified in manuscripts and texts studied elsewhere in this book. The popularity of Amalarius, frustrating to his enemies, makes clear sense. His intention was not that everyone should celebrate the same way, but that the celebrations as they were already done were understood in such a way that the clergy and undoubtedly, by their example and teaching, the laity as well might be able to be taught continually by the constant process of the liturgy to understand the truths of faith and their own role.

---

58 *Ibid.*, p. 309: 'Sed populus interim deprecetur Deum ne diabolus auferat verba Evangelii de corde eius neque petrosa sint corda nec dumosa, sed terra bona, ut fructum possint accipere et fructifare. Dicit saltim qui promptior non est – ut capiam verba Evangelii – Gloria tibi Domini'.
59 *Ibid.*, III 26 13an.

Language and vocabulary

In nostra lingua: *correct(ed) Latin in the manuscript transmission of* Dominus vobiscum

As we have seen, the purpose of *Dominus vobiscum* was to understand the liturgical ritual and to explain its accompanying texts and prayers to those celebrating this ritual. We observed the mixed character of this audience, consisting of clergymen-in-training (probably the main group for which the treatise was composed) but also including the laity, the *plebs sancta*, who take their own part in this celebration.[60] The author of *Dominus vobiscum* expects his audience to be familiar with the Latin language. This is shown by the repeated reference to this language as *nostra lingua*. Three instances of this usage are found.

The first passage where the author explains a loanword *in nostra lingua* is the explanation of the Amen concluding the collect before the dialogue *Sursum corda*, as we have seen earlier. The Hebrew *Amen*, meaning 'verity, truth', is explained *in nostra lingua*, i.e. in Latin. Albert Blaise notes that the word is translated in the Septuagint as γένοιτο, meaning *fiat*, as it is explained here as well.[61] The second example concerns the Greek word *apostolus*, derived from the verb ἀποστέλλω, and translated *in nostra lingua* with the Latin *missus*. The third example concerns the etymology of the word *panis*, bread, derived from Isidore. Our treatise relates

Table 4.4 *Nostra lingua* in *Dominus vobiscum*

Amen ... *in nostra lingua* intellegi potest, quasi omnes dicant ut ita fiat sicut sacerdos orauit (Amen ... can be understood in our language as if all say that it may be so as the priest has prayed)	*Sursum corda*
apostolus dicitur *in nostra lingua* missus (apostle means, in our language, 'sent')	*Communicantes*
panis apud grecos, *in nostra lingua* omnis interpretatur (*panis* [all] in Greek means, in our language, *omnis* [all])	*Pater noster*

60 Rose, '*Plebs sancta*'; see note 13.
61 Blaise, *Vocabulaire*, p. 628.

the word to the Greek πᾶν, meaning 'every, each', in Latin *omnis*. The relationship between *omnis* and *panis* is further explained in the phrase 'that we pray that the *al*mighty [*omnipotens*] God generously may give us *all* [*omnem*] spiritual and physical food at *all* times [*omni tempore*].[62]

In order to see how the words *nostra lingua* should be interpreted in the larger context in which the treatise is written, it helps to consider the occurrences of the expression for the patristic period and the early Middle Ages until the tenth century. The most frequent user is by far Jerome, closely followed by other biblical commentators such as Origen in his Latin translation by Rufinus, and the ninth-century exegetes Hrabanus Maurus and Paschasius Radbertus. Isidore also uses the phrase in his *Etymologies*, primarily to translate Hebrew words into Latin. There are also occurrences of the phrase where *nostra lingua* refers to a Germanic language translating a Latin word or phrase. The use of the phrase in *Dominus vobiscum* relates to the exegetical context represented by the authors mentioned here.

What does the use of *in nostra lingua* tell us about the linguistic context of *Dominus vobiscum*, its users and its intended audience? Must we assume that the author speaks of his own language, i.e. his mother tongue, when he uses the phrase, as Origen and Jerome did? That would imply that the author is a continental person from the area where Latin was experienced as the mother tongue while it gradually developed into the Romance languages in the course of the eighth century.[63] Or must we emphasise the possessive pronoun

---

62 *Dominus vobiscum*, p. 332: 'Panis apud Grecos, in nostra lingua omnis interpretatur, et nos oramus ut omnipotens pater omnem victum spiritalem ac carnalem nobis largire dignetur omni tempore'. See also Isidore, *Etymologiae*, XX.2.15 (*De escis*) and note 35.
63 M. Banniard, 'Language and communication in Carolingian Europe', in R. McKitterick (ed.), *New Cambridge Medieval History* (Cambridge: Cambridge University Press, 1995), II, pp. 695–708; M. Banniard, 'The transition from the Latin to the Romance languages', in M. Maiden et al. (eds), *The Cambridge History of the Romance Languages* (Cambridge: Cambridge University Press, 2013), II, pp. 57–106; R. Wright, 'Evidence and sources', in Maiden et al. (eds), *Romance Languages*, II, pp. 125–42; M. Van Uytfanghe, 'Le latin des hagiographes mérovingiens et la proto-histoire du français. État de la question', *Romanica Gandensia*, 16 (1976), 5–89.

and interpret *nostra lingua* as a way to express identity, referring to the Latin language as reserved for the sacred, biblical and liturgical, tradition transmitted first in Hebrew and Greek, and now transmitted, studied and performed in Latin? If this is the case, the question remains as to who is included in this possessive pronoun. This could be an elite audience or group of users, communicating in a language that they alone had access to and that they proudly claimed as 'ours'. However, this possibility is more or less in contrast with the inclusive use of *noster* throughout the text. As we have seen earlier, the first-person plural and the possessive pronoun connected to it almost always refer to the Christian *ecclesia* as a congregation that, theologically, includes clergy and laity when it comes to the celebration, reception and effectiveness of the sacraments.[64] It seems as if we must extrapolate that this theological perspective likely informed the use of the phrase (*in*) *nostra lingua*.

If Latin is *nostra lingua*, and if its explanation facilitated better participation on the part of all those involved in the ritual of mass, we need to move one step further to see whether this language was marked by a shared practice of usage by which the goal was to make it comprehensible to all. One way to find out this quality of Latin is to seek patterns of correction in the age of presupposed 'reform', with (the Latin) language as one of its main objects.[65] The Carolingian rulers are well known for their concern with linguistic correctness, particularly in a ritual context, and their sharp condemnation of their predecessors' sloppy usage of Latin: *maiorum nostrorum desidia*.[66] In the address to monks *Epistola de litteris colendis*, issued in Charlemagne's name, correct Latin usage is

---

64 Rose, *Gekooide tijger*, pp. 9–11.
65 See also Chapter 3 for the contribution by Cinzia Grifoni and Giorgia Vocino to this volume.
66 A. Boretius (ed.), *MGH Capit.* 1 (Hanover: Hahn, 1883), no. 30, p. 80: 'Igitur, quia curae nobis est, ut nostrarum ecclesiarum ad meliora semper proficiat status, oblitteratam pene maiorum nostrorum desidia reparare vigilanti studio litterarum satagimus officinam, et ad pernoscenda studia liberalium artium nostro etiam quos possumus invitamus exemplo. Inter quae iam pridem universos veteris ac novi instrumenti (testamenti) libros, librariorum imperitia depravatos, Deo nos in omnibus adiuvante, examussim correximus'.

Correcting the liturgy and sacred language 169

thought to exemplify moral correctness. Just as monks are required to obey the monastic rule for their correct behaviour, they are asked to obey the grammatical rule for a correct expression which is supposed to mirror correct thinking.[67] Since monks were the guardians of the ecclesiastical ritual, they were held especially responsible for correct usage and, if needed, restoration of the Latin language.[68]

The earliest manuscripts transmitting *Dominus vobiscum* give us insight into tendencies of correction and correctness of Latin. Most of all, they teach us that to a certain extent the same variation in Latin was still common in the period 'after Alcuin', who was traditionally seen as marking a watershed between Latin as a living language and its medieval variant as a restored and essentially learned language.[69] The reality of handwritten transmission teaches us, however, that Carolingian manuscripts after Alcuin display similar tendencies as their predecessors from the seventh and eighth. In this volume, the contribution of Cinzia Grifoni and Giorgia Vocino likewise undermines the notion that Alcuin inaugurated any such coherent educational programme, which could have resulted in the uniform usage of Latin.

One manuscript of this text may serve as an example: the codex St. Gall SB 40, selected by Corey Nason as the 'earliest dated known manuscript' (although several early copies compete with each other

---

67 *Epistula de litteris collendis*, in E. Stengel (ed.), *Urkundenbuch des Klosters Fulda* (Marburg: N. G. Elwert Verlag, 1956), pp. 246–54, at p. 251: 'qualiter, sicut regularis norma honestatem morum, ita quoque docendi et discendi instantia ordinet et ornet seriem verborum, ut, qui Deo placere appetunt recte vivendo, ei etiam placere non negligant recte loquendo'. See also H. H. Kortüm, 'Le style – c'est l'époque? Urteile über das "Merowingerlatein" in Vergangenheit und Gegenwart', *Archiv für Diplomatik Schriftgeschichte Siegel- und Wappenkunde*, 51 (2005), 30–48.

68 M. de Jong, 'Carolingian monasticism: the power of prayer', in McKitterick (ed.), *New Cambridge Medieval History*, II, pp. 622–53, at p. 630.

69 See for a historiographic overview J. Ziolkowski, 'Towards a history of medieval Latin literature', in F. A. C. Mantello and A. G. Rigg (eds), *Medieval Latin: An Introduction and Bibliographical Guide* (Washington, DC: Catholic University of America Press, 1996), pp. 505–36; see, for a modification of the notion of (grammatical) normativity, R. McKitterick, 'Latin and Romance: an historian's perspective', in R. Wright (ed.) *Latin and the Romance Languages in the Early Middle Ages* (London: Routledge, 1991), pp. 130–45, at pp. 132–3.

for this title[70]) and dated by him in the late eighth or early ninth century.[71] As with many St. Gall codices, the text shows a rich practice of correction in several layers. A brief overview of the grammatical and orthographic characteristics occurring in the text display the tendency to take pronunciation into account. First, a number of deviations from classical grammar can be attributed partly to the influence of spoken language on written accounts, and partly also to modifications in the application of the complex inflectional system of the Latin verb and noun – two processes that were mutually interdependent and influenced the transitional Latin of the postclassical period.[72]

The influence of spoken Latin is found, first, in the spelling of vowels and consonants, often caused by the fading or entire absence of phonetic distinction, such as the rendition of the diphthongs [ae] or [oe] by the single (monopthong) [e] or the addition or lack of word-initial [h]. Very few of these deviations in spelling are corrected, either by the scribe in writing or by later users or correctors. Some of the elements that are corrected can be interpreted as scribal errors, not prompted by changes in language or pronunciation, e.g. *supplacacio* corrected into *supplicacio* (p. 309) (Figure 4.1).

Figure 4.1 Correction of a scribal error in St. Gall SB 40, p. 309 (detail).

70 Van Rhijn, 'The *Dominus vobiscum*'.
71 Nason, 'Mass commentary', 76. Later in the same article Nason chooses Paris BnF 2796 as the earliest copy: *ibid.*, 80. The manuscript was produced in St. Gall; see www.e-codices.unifr.ch/en/searchresult/list/one/csg/0040 (accessed 11 April 2018). Paris BnF 9490 is identified by Hanssens as a copy of SB 446, see Nason, 'Mass commentary', 76. All this is in favour, in Hanssens's view, of a St. Gall origin of the text.
72 J. Herman, *Vulgar Latin*, trans. R. Wright (University Park, PA: Penn State University Press, 2000), especially pp. 52–3.

Correcting the liturgy and sacred language

Some corrections, however, can be traced back to the correction of a first layer where the spelling is influenced by pronunciation, e.g.:

epiccopo → *episcopo* (the *c* is in many cases pronounced and perceived as a sibilant) (p. 312) (see Figure 4.2)

adsumpsisti → *adsumsisti* (the bilabial plosive [p] is hardly perceived in pronunciation and often omitted in writing) (p. 316)

cottidianum → *cotidianum*: both spellings occur, also in classical orthography (p. 319)

But most of the orthographic variants that might confuse us, as modern readers used to a fixed grammatical norm learned in a school situation, apparently did not hinder the medieval users of this copy of *Dominus vobiscum*.

As for morphological characteristics, this is slightly different. Although cases of exchanges in spelling far outnumber the variants in all other grammatical categories, deviations from the classical norms of morphology are often more informative of language change. They concern cases after certain prepositions or verbs; deviation in the chosen gender or incongruency (e.g. *in nostro lingua*); the choice of a second declension ending linked to a third-declension noun, e.g. *societatum* for *societatem* (p. 317); incongruency in the number of verbs as related to the subject and the choice for an indicative where a subjunctive would be expected. In this domain, contemporary correctors intervene more often. Morphological corrections are the largest category in contemporary corrections, and they are concerned with all categories given above: gender and case in nouns; verbal inflection; and the level of a whole sentence or phrase. Given the abundant instances of correcting these morphological elements, the lack of correction in similar or also substantially more problematic phenomena in the

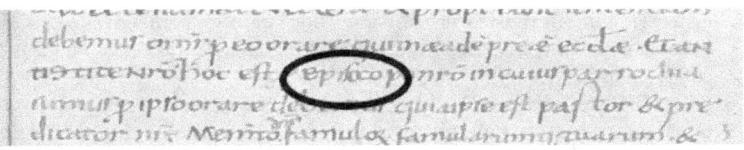

Figure 4.2 Correction of Latin orthography in St. Gall SB 40, p. 312 (detail).

same text leaves us with the question of why these cases, complicating the comprehension of the text, remain uncorrected.[73]

The work presented here asks for a more systematic approach to a larger set of data than dealt with here in this preliminary exploration of methodology. The St. Gall text of *Dominus vobiscum*, with its layered correction, shows us that Latin, *nostra lingua*, was a language that allowed for variation, and very often escaped a single norm of correctness and uniformity, even in texts dealing with the most sacred rituals of the Christian liturgy.

Language in Amalarius

While most attention has focused on his discussion of material matters, Amalarius does devote significant time to the language of the mass too. At several points, he even parses each word of the prayers offering his own explanations for each one in turn, a methodology similar to that used by *Dominus vobiscum*.[74] Also like that text, Amalarius explains the meaning of liturgical words in Greek, like *basilica* (LO III, 2.1) or *organo*.[75] What is said in the liturgy also directs people to the correct state of mind as they witness and take part in the liturgical acts, and, notably, the responses of the laypeople are essential in order to fully enact this true meaning.[76] At the same time, the words are also the words of the Gospel stories:

---

[73] Corrected: p. 309 *confessionem* (corrected to *confiteris*; corrected in writing?); p. 316 *perpercit* (corrected to *pepercit*); p. 318 *ueuniae* (corrected to *ueniae*); p. 321 *uictimam* (incompletely corrected to *huctimam*); p. 321 *semeipsum* (completed to *semetipsum*). Uncorrected: p. 314 *ngneris* (for *digneris*); p. 315 *dilex* (for *dilexit*); p. 315 *ponitati* (for *bonitati*); p. 319 *utiam* (for *ut etiam*); p. 321 *Christus est nostra* (for *Christus est pax nostra*).

[74] Amalarius, *Liber officialis*, III.24.3, III.26.18.

[75] Ibid., III.3.10, p. 269: 'Nam cum organum vocabulum Grecum sit, ut dixi, generale omnibus musicis instrumentis, hoc cui folles adhibentur, alio Greci nomine appellant; ut autem organum dicitur, magis Latina et ea vulgaris est consuetudo'.

[76] Ibid., III.19.32–3, p. 321: 'Ideo et sacerdos, ante orationem praefatione praemissa, parat fratrum mentes dicendo: "Sursum corda", ut dum respondet plebs: "Habemus ad dominum", admoneatur nihil aliud se quam Deum cogitare debere. Claudatur contra adversarium pectus et soli Deo pateat, nec ad se hostem Dei tempora orationis adire patiatur'.

Correcting the liturgy and sacred language 173

Dominus vobiscum is seen as a greeting that Amalarius imagined Christ said to the people who met him on Palm Sunday.[77] By saying *Sursum Corda*, the priest and his listeners ascend to the Upper Room in Jerusalem where the Last Supper took place and the first Eucharist was celebrated:

> LO III.21.4 The priest follows this order. With his listeners, he ascends in the Upper Room when he says: Sursum corda.[78]

During the *Te Igitur*, the priest says three prayers 'in the role of Christ' in the Garden of Gethsemene.[79]

The correspondence Amalarius attached to the end of Book 3 of the *Liber officialis* reveals both his concern and expertise in linguistic matters. For Bishop Rantgar of Noyon, he discussed the words: *Hic est calix sanguinis mei, Novi et aeterni Testamenti mysterium fidei*.[80] Amalarius wrote on the gender of the words seraphim and cherubim to Hatto, likely the abbot of Reichenau, and here he invoked the *canon missae* itself as 'an authority in the custom of the Church'. It, along with Jerome, stood for a neuter gender of seraphim.[81] The Canon was, then, disclosive and authoritative, a deposit of useful meaning handed down to the present, in the same way as Jerome or the other Fathers. Amalarius's letter to Jeremiah of Sens (818–27) is particularly interesting, since it suggests that there was an observable change in the pronunciation of the name of Jesus among Frankish clergy since the year 800:

> Before the lord Charles entered Rome for the last time, I heard the priests of Gaul singing 'Gisus' which agreed neither with the

---

77 *Ibid.*, III.19.11, p. 314: 'Non est dubium quin salutaret eam secundum morem bonum antiquae traditionis quem etiam nostra, non solum perita ecclesia, sed etiam vulgaris tenet'.
78 *Ibid.*, pp. 324–5: 'Hunc ordinem sequitur sacerdos. Cum suis auditoribus ascendit in cenaculum quando dicit: "Sursum Corda"'.
79 *Ibid.*, III.23.13, p. 333: 'Primo vice Christi sacerdos tres orationes exercet, sicut Dominus fecit postquam exivit in Montem Oliveti'.
80 *Ibid.*, p. 389.
81 *Ibid.*, p. 392: 'Habemus et non minimam auctoritatem ex consuetudine ecclesiae, quae solet cotidie in oratione quae fit super mensam, proferre "Beata seraphin"'. The reference is to the prayer 'Per quem tuam maiestatem laudant angeli ... beata seraphin' in the *canon missae*.

Hebrews nor with the Greeks. Since that time, I hear 'Iesus', which I think agrees with the Hebrews, the name of whose leader we read was Jesus.[82]

Does Amalarius here witness a small but significant shift in Frankish linguistic practice, in the pronunciation of liturgical formulae like the *canon missae*? If so, we cannot doubt that the educational programme of clerical instruction in which he and the anonymous exposition *Dominus vobiscum* played such a role probably helped to enable it.

Conclusions

The two expositional texts we have discussed differ in the sophistication and breadth of their analysis, but, once compared, they offer the same basic picture of Carolingian liturgical culture as a fundamentally collaborative exercise in deeper understanding. 'Reform', in the sense of correction to a single standard form of liturgical practice, does not appear here. Actors within this culture like Amalarius and the anonymous author of *Dominus vobiscum* shared the conviction that there was a 'reason' for the words and actions of the daily celebration of the mass. But there is no sense in any of these texts that only one understanding of liturgy was possible or acceptable. This is even clearer when we consider the manuscript context in which the texts are found among varied works of liturgical commentary with different methods and different conclusions. This would encourage readers to see such texts not as the final word on the liturgy's true meaning, but as the invitation to even deeper contemplation and, potentially, the uncovering of further moral and spiritual truth in the liturgy for themselves. In a society suffused with the exegetical analysis of the Bible, the texts trained their readers to subject the liturgy to the same forms of analysis, which would give rise to a similar multiplicity of truths

---

82 *Ibid.*, pp. 386–7: 'Ante quam pergeret domnus Karolus Romam novissime audivi sacerdotes Galliae nostrae sonare "Gisus" quod neque cum Ebreis neque cum Grecis conveniebat. Ab illo tempore audio "Iesus" ut opinor, quod convenit cum Ebreis quorum ducis nomen legimus Iesus'.

and lessons as biblical exegesis did. Given the likely audience of the texts were clergy, who were liturgical actors themselves, the deeper thinking encouraged by the authors might have countenanced certain practical consequences in the way liturgy was then performed. Among the potential lessons for clergymen was the importance of the responses of the laity, who are also plainly acknowledged as agents in the performance of the Eucharist.

5

Error assessment: how to distinguish between true and false?

Irene van Renswoude

In the present age of fake news and crisis of trust in authorities, the question of how to determine what is true or reliable knowledge and what is not seems more pressing than ever. Yet it was no less important to assess which statements were valid and which were dangerous and misleading to those who were involved in controversies and debates in the early middle ages. The (re)introduction of classical texts in the late eighth and ninth centuries not only affected the curriculum of knowledge but also had a profound impact on traditional modes of assessment and interpretation.[1] Although the texts that were added to the programme of studies were for the most part already known, and their content did not substantially alter what people thought they knew about the world, the intensified study of these texts did challenge hitherto accepted interpretations and practices of assessment.

This chapter focuses on two instances of controversy over new interpretations that arose in the ninth century and explores what methods were developed to detect errors of analysis and distinguish true from false knowledge. What was at stake during these debates was not new knowledge as such, but rather new interpretations of a shared body of foundational texts and agreed-upon practices. I shall not only deal with methods of distinction, but also with the social aspects of error assessment, and address the question of how communities in dealt with new and divergent readings. How were errant thinkers 'corrected' and brought back in line with the established

---

1 For a reassessment of the label 'Carolingian renaissance', see Carine van Rhijn's Introduction to this volume.

interpretations of the group to which they belonged? As Carine van Rhijn pointed out in the introduction to this volume, the term *correctio* (correction) was not as central to Carolingian discourse as has long been assumed. Yet, as we shall see, we do encounter the term *correctio* and its semantic correlates occasionally in a rhetoric of rectification and reintegration of individuals who were perceived to have erred.[2]

Communities of interpretation – the danger within

Early medieval literate communities have often been studied as 'textual communities', a term coined by Brian Stock to denote social groups whose sense of identity is organised around a common understanding of authoritative texts. In Stock's model, the members of a textual community develop rules, moral aims and rituals based on a shared evaluation and interpretation of key texts. Stock originally introduced this concept in a study of reform movements in the eleventh and twelfth centuries.[3] In the early middle ages, comparable textual communities can be found, which consisted mainly of the literate male, sometimes female, elite, who lived together in institutional settings, such as monasteries and cathedral chapters. A shared reading of foundational texts was part of the daily routine of their communal life. But we can also think of networks of scholars as examples of textual communities, such as the group of scholars

---

2 See also Chapter 6 of this volume for Kristina Mitelaitė's discussion of a semantic field of *correctio* that encompassed individual spiritual perfection.
3 B. Stock, *The Implications of Literacy: Written Language and Models of Interpretation in the Eleventh and Twelfth Centuries* (Princeton, NJ: Princeton University Press, 1983). See also the discussion in J. Heath, '"Textual communities": Brian Stock's concept and recent scholarship on antiquity', in F. Wilk (ed.), *Scriptural Interpretation at the Interface between Education and Religion* (Leiden: Brill, 2018), pp. 5–35. For an application of the concept 'textual communities' to early medieval communities, see A. Merrills, 'Texts and early medieval rulers. The Moorish kingdoms and the written word: three "textual communities" in fifth- and sixth-century Mauretania', in E. Screen and C. West (eds), *Writing the Early Medieval West: Studies in Honour of Rosamond McKitterick* (Cambridge: Cambridge University Press, 2018), pp. 185–202.

Charlemagne, Louis and Charles the Bald assembled at their courts, who drew on the same body of religious and secular texts to demonstrate their learning and develop a shared set of methods to assess new texts and interpretations.

Since most early medieval literate communities regarded the same texts as foundational for the identity of their community, modes of interpretation are perhaps a more distinguishing feature to identify such communities in this context than the key texts themselves. 'Communities of interpretation' may be a more accurate descriptive label for the processes of social formation described by Stock, since he considered interpretation and evaluation as central to his model and ascribed a prominent position to 'the interpreter' within the social fabric of the group. As recent research has shown, the concept 'communities of interpretation' offers a useful analytical tool to study differences between literate communities.[4] It may also help to understand why the introduction of new interpretations and new methods of determining truth disrupted the balance within a given community.

From the days of the early church, individuals who held interpretations that were at variance with the established opinion of their community have been labelled heretics. Propagators of divergent readings were to be set straight and reintegrated, or, if corrective treatment failed, excluded from the community to which they belonged. Such patterns of social inclusion and exclusion are not specific to Christianity, nor are they reserved to religious groups for that matter. In a seminal article published in 1983, the sociologist George Zito mapped the development and structure of heresy as a social phenomenon, rather than as a historical event or religious problem. He observed that the label 'heretic' is generally applied to members of one's own group. Alternative interpretations and

---

4 See, for example, the studies that have recently appeared in the series *New Communities of Interpretation. Contexts of Religious Transformation in Late Medieval and Early Modern Europe*: S. Folkerts (ed.), *Religious Connectivity in Urban Communities (1400–1550): Reading, Worshipping, and Connecting through the Continuum of Sacred and Secular* (Turnhout: Brepols, 2021); I. Johnson and A. M. Rodrigues (eds), *Religious Practices and Everyday Life in the Long Fifteenth Century (1350–1570): Interpreting Changes and Changes of Interpretation* (Turnhout: Brepols, 2021).

different schools of thought that exist outside a community, Zito argued, are generally not perceived to pose an immediate threat. Divergent thinkers who emerge from *within* the group, however, are considered much more dangerous, since they employ the exact same language and retain the same values as the other members of the community. They challenge the shared interpretation of the community and introduce difference into what is so far an unquestioned, undifferentiated practice of determining truth.[5] Zito's analysis may offer an explanation as to why divergent modes of interpretation emerging from within a given community in the Carolingian period, when new texts were added to a foundational body of knowledge, were met with resistance.

In this chapter, I shall discuss two instances of controversy that arose in response to a danger arising from within a community. The first is the case of the liturgist Amalarius (d. c. 850), temporary bishop of Lyon, who shook the community of Lyon cathedral by presenting a novel interpretation of the meaning and purpose of the liturgy. The second is the case of the scholar John Scotus (d. 877) who (re-)introduced a method of distinguishing true from false statements, thereby causing a ripple among the group of scholars to which he belonged. I shall analyse the methods and means by which the errors of these two individuals were detected and assessed, and address the question of whether or not attempts were made to rectify their divergent interpretations and bring the offenders in line with the consensus of the group. As I intend to show, appointed or self-appointed experts of assessment made an effort to ease the disturbance within their communities by presenting the divergent interpreters as outsiders. In the analysis of the two cases, I shall pay special attention to the occurrence or absence of terms that have long been considered key to the Carolingian vocabulary of reform, such as *correctio* (correction) and *emendatio* (emendation), and their verbal forms, and explore their relation to a discourse of rectification and reintegration.

---

5 G. V. Zito, 'Toward a sociology of heresy', *Sociological Analysis*, 44:2 (1983), 123–30, at 125.

The liturgist Amalarius: a shocking new interpretation

Amalarius, commonly known as Amalarius of Metz (d. c. 850), devoted his scholarly career to studying the meaning of the liturgy of the mass and the offices.[6] He started to compose a commentary on the mass during a diplomatic mission to Constantinople in 813; upon his return, he embarked upon an investigation of the meaning of the offices. It is not difficult to imagine how a new interpretation of the mass or of the liturgical hours, that is, the public service of worship and praise, might risk incurring criticism, since liturgical practices were equally formative for the identity of communities as a shared reading of foundational texts. In the preface to the first edition of his major work on the liturgy, *Liber officialis*, completed around 822 and dedicated to Emperor Louis the Pious, Amalarius expressed a fear that his interpretation of the liturgical hours would be harshly criticised. Although professions of fear of a bad reception were a commonly invoked *topos* that we find in many prefaces, Amalarius's defence against anticipated criticism deserves some attention. In the preface to the *Liber officialis*, Amalarius takes refuge in Augustine's treatise on Christian teaching, *De doctrina christiana*. Here, he found a forgiving stance towards interpreters who, with the best intentions, proposed an interpretation that was not in accordance with the intended meaning of the author of the text. In Augustine's view, Amalarius says, an interpreter cannot go seriously wrong, as long as his intentions are good and he is willing to be corrected when he is found to have made a mistake. Amalarius quotes Augustine, saying:

> whoever proposes a scriptural interpretation that reinforces love, although it is obviously something other than the author intended, has not made a pernicious mistake, and is not at all guilty of lying, for in the liar is the wish to say false things. […] If his interpretation errs in a manner that reinforces love, which is the purpose of the commandment, he is wrong in this way: He is like someone who wanders from the road through a field, but reaches the same destination as the road. But he should be corrected (*corrigendus est*) and

---

6 On Amalarius and his study of the liturgy, see also Els Rose and Arthur Westwell's contribution of Chapter 4 in this volume.

shown how much more useful it is not to wander from the road, so that he does not develop the habit of wandering sideways or in the wrong direction.[7]

Amalarius uses Augustine's understanding stance towards those who err unintentionally as a shield of defence against imagined critics wishing to catch him out, as if he had 'written dangerously'.[8] Evidently it was not his intention to propose dangerous interpretations. He had thoroughly studied all authors who had first established the offices and fully acknowledged the authoritative interpretations of the fathers as superior to his own. To show his deference, he added the sign of the cross by way of a citation marker at the end of each quotation from the fathers, to clearly indicate where their words ended and his own words began, so 'I cannot be accused of secretly weaving my own words with theirs'.[9] The sign of the cross symbolised Amalarius's respect for authorities and highlighted the orthodoxy of patristic statements. It served as a safety

---

[7] Amalarius of Metz, *Liber officialis*, preface, ed. and trans. E. Knibbs, *Amalar of Metz, On the Liturgy*, Dumbarton Oaks Medieval Library 35, 36 (2 vols, Cambridge, MA: Harvard University Press, 2014), I, preface, pp. 20–3: 'Quisquis vero talem inde sententiam dixerit, ut huic aedificandae caritati sit utilis, nec tamen hoc dixerit quod ille quem legit eo loco sensisse probabitur, non perniciose fallitur, nec omnino mentitur. Inest quippe in mentiente voluntas falsa dicendi [...] si ea sententia fallitur qua aedificet caritatem, quae finis praecepti est, ita fallitur ac si quisquam errore deserens viam, eo tamen per agrum pergat, quo etiam via illa perducit. Corrigendus est tamen, et quam sit utilius viam non deserere demonstrandum est, ne consuetudine deviandi etiam in transversum aut perversum ire cogatur'. Cf. Augustine, *De doctrina Christiana*, ed. and trans. R. P. H. Green (Oxford: Oxford University Press, 1995), I, 36, p. 28.

[8] Amalarius, *Liber officialis*, pp. 20–1: 'Let me be defended by Augustine's treatise *On Christian Doctrine* from those who may wish to catch me out, as if I had written dangerously' ('Ex libro Agustini De doctrina Christiana defender ab illis qui me voluerint capere, *quasi periculose scripsissem*' (emphasis added)).

[9] Ibid., pp. 22–3: 'Note also that I have added the sign of the cross where the words of the fathers end and my own words begin, so that I cannot be accused of secretly weaving my own words with theirs' ('Notandum est etiam, *ne videretur parvitas mea quasi furtim interpolare meis verbis sanctorum dicta patrum*, interposui in fine eorum et principium meorum signum crucis' (emphasis added)).

measure against critics who might accuse him of following his own interpretations or misleadingly presenting his own views as those of the church fathers. But the cross also served as an interpretative aid, a tool to produce verifiable knowledge. The visual marker offered readers the opportunity to assess content, identify the sources of arguments for themselves and check the working methods of the author.

Amalarius's fear of a negative reception was not unfounded. His *Liber officialis* would indeed become the object of fierce criticism, but not immediately after he issued the first edition in 822. Initially, the work was well-received and enjoyed widespread circulation.[10] It would take more than a decade before Amalarius's interpretation of the liturgy met with opposition, within one particular community. Between 829 and 830 Amalarius expanded his *On the Liturgy* with a fourth book on the Divine Office, and in 831 he revised and updated the work for the third time. In that same year, he composed his own antiphonary, in which he combined antiphons from Metz with features of Roman usage.[11] In his antiphonary (of which only the prologue has survived), Amalarius also employed a system of signs as an interpretative aid to help readers identify his sources. This time the signs were not graphic symbols, but rather letters of the alphabet which had no intrinsic value comparable to the sign of

---

10 On Amalarius and the popularity of his *Liber officialis* both before and after the condemnation of his teaching in 838, see S. van Daalen, 'The reception of Amalarius of Metz's Liber officialis in medieval manuscripts' (MA thesis, Amsterdam 2021) and Els Rose and Arthur Westwell's contribution in Chapter 4 of this volume. Yet we only have the word of Amalarius's opponent, Florus of Lyon, that Amalarius's interpretation of the liturgy enjoyed widespread popularity soon after it was first issued. No manuscripts have been preserved that can be dated before its condemnation in 838. In a treatise composed for the occasion, Florus stated that Amalarius's teaching was 'known almost everywhere through the very many books he has brought forth'; see Florus, *Opera polemica*, ed. K. Zechiel-Eckes, CCCM 260 (Turnhout: Brepols, 2014), *Relatio synodalis*, pp. 83–90, at p. 87: 'utpote quae in libris quamplurimis ab ipso editis fere ubique uulgata sit'. Florus may well have exaggerated the case to suit his argument that Amalarius's teaching formed a danger to the entire realm. The later popularity of Amalarius's *Liber officialis*, however, is attested by a substantial number of manuscripts and is beyond doubt.

11 See here Knibb's introduction to Amalarius, *Liber officialis*, pp. x–xi.

the cross. Material of Roman origin was marked with an 'R', material of Metz with an 'M' and material that he introduced himself with an 'I', for *ingenium* ('invention', 'clever thought') and 'indulgence', or a 'C', for *caritas* (love).[12] The reference to love is reminiscent of the defence strategy Amalarius propounded in the first preface to the *Liber officialis* where he presented love as a safety net that prevented interpretations from going too far off the mark. Where Amalarius obtained the material he marked with an 'I' or a 'C' is not clear, but apparently he did not hesitate to allow himself some freedom to insert a few 'clever thoughts'. Amalarius's habit of introducing material and opinions of his own eventually got him into trouble, or perhaps it was rather the fact that he was open about his working methods. In a proem added to the third edition of the *Liber officialis*, Amalarius wrote: 'In all that I write I am supported by the judgement [*iudicio*] of the true, holy and pious fathers', to which he added: 'Meanwhile I say what I judge [to be true] [*sentio*]'.[13] It was acceptable practice for someone in a position of authority to add their own assessments and interpretations to the judgements of the fathers. Archbishop Hrabanus Maurus of Mainz (d. 865), for one, did not shy away from marking his own interpretations with the letter M and putting them side by side with

---

12 *Ibid.*, p. xi; Amalarius of Metz, *Opera liturgica omnia*, ed. J.-M. Hanssens (3 vols, Vatican City: Biblioteca Apostolica Vaticana, 1948–50), I, *Prologus antiphonarii*, 8, p. 362: 'Ubi ordinabilius visum est mihi scriptum haberi in antiphonario romano quam in nostro, ibi scripsi in margine R, propter nomen urbis Romae; et ubi in nostro, M, propter Metensem civitatem; ubi nostrum ingenium cogitavit aliquid posse rationabilius illis ordinare I C, propter indulgentiam et caritatem'. On the prologue to the antiphonary, see G. Ward, 'The order of history: liturgical time and the rhythms of the past in Amalarius of Metz's *De ordine antiphonarii*', in Screen and West (eds), *Writing the Early Medieval West*, pp. 98–112.

13 Amalarius, *Liber officialis*, I, Proem, p. 4: 'In omnibus quae scribo, suspendor verorum, sanctorumque, ac piorum patrum iudicio; interim dico quae sentio'. Eric Knibbs, whose translation I largely follow, translates 'interim dico quae sentio' as 'I also say what I feel'. 'To feel' or 'to experience' is indeed one of the meanings of 'sentire', but since Amalarius juxtaposes *sentio* to *iudicio*, judgement, of the fathers in the first part of the sentence, I consider 'to deem', 'to judge' or 'to opine' a more accurate translation.

patristic commentaries.[14] It could nonetheless become a dangerous enterprise as soon as critics started to question the authority or expertise of the interpreter.

Between 822 and 835, Amalarius's interpretations of the liturgy went unchallenged; that is to say, we have no evidence that his commentaries provoked discussions or debate. Only in 835, when he became interim bishop in Lyon, was his work met with severe criticism. The criticism was local and was in all likelihood related to his appointment to the see of Lyon. At the council of Thionville of 835 Amalarius was selected to replace Archbishop Agobard (d. 840), who had been deposed because of his part in the rebellion against Emperor Louis the Pious. Agobard, although in exile, still had loyal supporters in Lyon who did not welcome a replacement. One of these supporters was Florus, deacon of Lyon (d. after 855), Agobard's close co-operator of many years. As Warren Pezé has pointed out, Florus's concerted efforts to harm Amalarius's reputation and criticise his scholarly work can be seen in the light of a deliberate campaign to ensure the deposition of the unwanted interim bishop and the reinstatement of Agobard.[15] This is not to

---

14 See M. de Jong, 'The empire as *ecclesia*: Hrabanus Maurus and biblical *historia* for rulers', in Y. Hen and M. Innes (eds), *The Uses of the Past in the Early Middle Ages* (Cambridge: Cambridge University Press, 2000), pp. 191–226, at p. 202. Hrabanus said he marked his own commentaries with an 'M' to distinguish them from the commentaries of the church fathers, but this implies he placed his own interpretations perhaps not on a par, but at least alongside, patristic exegesis.

15 W. Pezé, 'Florus, Agobard et le concile de Quierzy de 838', in Marie-Céline Isaia, François Bougard and Alexis Charansonnet (eds), *Lyon dans l'Europe carolingienne: autour d'Agobard (816–840)*, Collection Haut Moyen Âge 36 (Turnhout: Brepols, 2019), pp. 175–90. On the circumstances of Amalarius's contested appointment to the see of Lyon and Florus's subsequent campaign to have Amalarius removed, see further K. Zechiel-Eckes, 'Florus von Lyon, Amalarius von Metz und der Traktat über die Bischofswahl. Mit einer kritischen Edition des sog. "Liber de electionibus episcoporum"', *Revue Bénédictine*, 106 (1996), 109–33; K. Zechiel-Eckes, *Florus von Lyon als Kirchenpolitiker und Publizist. Studien zur Persönlichkeit eines karolingischen 'Intellektuellen' am Beispiel der Auseinandersetzung mit Amalarius (835–838) und des Prädestinationsstreits (851–855)*, Quellen und Forschungen zum Recht im Mittelalter 8 (Stuttgart: Thorbecke, 1999), pp. 21–89; W. Pezé, 'Amalaire et la communauté Juive de Lyon. À propos de

say that Florus's criticism did not spring from genuine concern for the stability of his community of interpretation – for how are we to judge that? – but rather that political motives were part of his crusade against the 'intruder' Amalarius.

While in Lyon, Amalarius produced the final layer of text to complete his magnum opus on the liturgy. He issued an addition, called the *Embolis* (meaning 'insertion' or 'interpolation'), which constituted a final statement of his liturgical theories.[16] Florus took issue with Amalarius's allegorical interpretations of the liturgy that, to his mind, were unfounded and far-fetched, but also with the way the bishop tried to force his own understanding of the meaning of the liturgy upon the community. According to Florus, Amalarius ordered the cathedral scribes to copy the work and had them learn the content by heart.[17] Moreover, he persuaded the bishops of the council of Thionville, who had appointed him to replace Agobard, to subscribe his book with their own hands.[18] Such a procedure of subscription, if it indeed took place, may have been intended to increase the authority and validity of Amalarius's *Liber officialis* and may have provided leverage to press the community of Lyon cathedral to accept the commentary.[19]

---

l'antijudaïsme lyonnais à l'époque carolingienne', *Francia*, 40 (2013), 1–25; I. van Renswoude, 'Crass insults: *ad hominem* attacks and rhetorical conventions', in U. Heil (ed.), *Das Christentum im frühen Europa* (Berlin: de Gruyter, 2019), pp. 171–94.

16 C. A. Jones, *A Lost Work by Amalarius of Metz: Interpolations in Salisbury, Cathedral Library, MS. 154*, Henry Bradshaw Society: Subsidia 2 (Woodbridge: Boydell and Brewer, 2001), p. 19; see also Knibb's introduction to Amalarius, *Liber officialis*, p. ix; Amalarius, *Opera liturgica omnia*, I, pp. 117–19.

17 Amalarius, *Opera liturgica omnia*, I, p. 383; Zechiel-Eckes, *Florus von Lyon*, p. 41, n. 132; Jones, *A Lost Work*, p. 19.

18 Florus writes to the bishops of Thionville that he cannot believe they really subscribed Amalarius's books, but his expression of unbelief seems a rhetorical strategy to rub it in that they were fools for having agreed to this in the first place, yet without accusing them directly. Florus, *Opera polemica*, *Epistola ad synodum Teodonis*, 3,14–16, p. 3: 'ut omnes manu propria suis ineptissimis libris subscribere et sic unanimiter sentire atque observare velletis'.

19 According to Florus, this is what Amalarius claimed had happened, which he found hard to believe (see the previous note).

Emotional assessment and source criticism

Florus composed several polemical treatises and speeches against Amalarius's *On the Liturgy* and his antiphonary to publicise his disagreement with his liturgical theories, some of which he considered to be highly unorthodox. His fight against Amalarius was mainly fought with rhetorical means. Although Florus was well acquainted with Aristotelian logic, as he showed some years later in a refutation of the teaching of the scholar John Scotus, he did not employ dialectical heuristic methods in his treatises and speeches against Amalarius to distinguish whether Amalarius's interpretations were true or false, acceptable or unacceptable. Florus's assessment of Amalarius's teaching was mainly emotional. I do not mean to say that Florus was overcome by anger or frustration, but rather that he used emotional words to express his assessment of Amalarius's statements.

In Florus's judgement, Amalarius's conclusions were ridiculous: he was telling lies and was a raving madman.[20] By attacking Amalarius's ethos and showing him to be an unreliable person, he disqualified his views without so much as addressing their content. To modern readers, this does not seem to be a very rational or convincing rebuttal, but in rhetorical theory emotions, and in particular, the emotion of indignation, were considered viable tools to assess veracity. If a statement aroused anger and indignation in the audience, it was a sure indication that something was amiss.[21]

Florus's main critique, apart from emotional assessment, was that Amalarius did not build his teaching on solid authoritative proof, but followed his own train of thought.[22] Amalarius took his

---

20 For an extensive list of abusive epithets in Florus's pamphlets against Amalarius, see H. de Lubac, *Corpus Mysticum. L'eucharistie et l'église au moyen âge. Étude historique* (2nd ed., Paris: Aubier, 1949), p. 297.
21 van Renswoude, 'Crass insults', p. 14; R. Dürr, 'Regulating dangerous knowledge: John Lockman's (1698–1771) Enlightened Readings of Jesuit Letters', in F. Jan Dijksterhuis (ed.), *Regulating Knowledge in an Entangled World*, Knowledge Societies in History 4 (London: Routledge, forthcoming).
22 Florus, *Opera polemica*, *Epistola ad rectores ecclesiae*, p. 50: 'cui talia ex suo sensu inseruit, ut pro eius impudenti audacia frons legentis pudore ac rubore feriatur'; see also Florus, *Opera polemica*, *Relatio synodalis*, pp. 87–9, discussed in the following.

interpretations from within himself. When he did use arguments from authority, Florus said, he misquoted or misinterpreted biblical and patristic texts. We see this pattern of refutation also in manuscript Paris, BnF, NAL 329, produced in Lyon in the late ninth century or early tenth century, in a set of annotations to Amalarius's *Liber officialis*.[23] The annotations were originally made by an anonymous Lyon scribe at the time of the conflict, but they were copied into Paris, BnF, NAL 329, a manuscript that ended up in Cluny.[24] It is not known when the manuscript was brought to Cluny, but it would appear that Lyon scribes 'exported' their negative interpretation of *Liber officialis* to another community long after the conflict ended. Let us pass over the abusive language and sarcastic comments of the marginal annotations, which have been discussed sufficiently elsewhere, and turn to some more detailed and substantial refutations.[25] The annotator objected to Amalarius's free interpretation of the statements of patristic authors and, like Florus, ridiculed his habit of quoting the fathers incorrectly. When Amalarius, for example, mistakenly attributed a saying of Hrabanus Maurus to church father Ambrose, the annotator wrote: 'You are following the wrong Ambrose' and 'You treat Ambrose poorly, accusing him and asserting that he said what he did not say'.[26] Elsewhere he added the snide comment: 'Blessed Augustine wrote well about the sanctification of the seventh day, but he did not speak about

---

23 For the dating and provenance of the manuscript, see the online catalogue of the Bibliothèque nationale de France, Archives et manuscrits, https://archivesetmanuscrits.bnf.fr/ark:/12148/cc71056g (accessed 21 February 2022). The information of the catalogue is taken from L. Delisle, *Inventaire du manuscrits de la Bibliothèque nationale: Fonds de Cluny* (Paris: H. Champion, 1884), p. 6.

24 André Wilmart suggests the manuscripts may have arrived in Cluny during the abbacy of Odo (927–42): see A. Wilmart, 'Un lecteur ennemi d'Amalaire', *Revue Bénédictine*, 36 (1924), 317–29, at 318.

25 For discussions of the abusive language in the marginal annotations, see Wilmart, 'Un lecteur ennemi d'Amalaire'; Zechiel-Eckes, *Florus von Lyon*, pp. 72–6; Pezé, 'Amalaire et la communauté Juive de Lyon'; van Renswoude, 'Crass insults'.

26 Amalarius, *Liber officialis*, I, p. 534: 'Male agis adversum Ambrosium, accusans eum et affirmans eum dixisse quod non dixit'.

ordination, as you falsely maintain'.[27] The annotator also accused Amalarius of letting his interpretations wander too far from the intended meaning of the texts and authors he drew upon: 'Truly you depart from the meaning of the Gospel and Augustine as much as darkness differs from light'.[28] Barbed comments such as these, added in the narrow space of the margin, which did not allow for elaborate, well-structured refutations, were effective in spite of their brevity. They cast doubt on Amalarius's expertise, undermined his authority and emphasised the inherent foreignness of his interpretations. Amalarius's critics presented him as an outsider, who was not familiar with their liturgical traditions and certainly no match for their high scholarly standards. Agobard, writing from exile, reminded the cantors of the church of Lyon, 'his beloved brothers', of how they used to sit together and discuss the liturgy. They completely agreed with one another, Agobard said, that 'levity should be avoided and solemnity should be followed in celebrating divine praises' – a barely veiled criticism of Amalarius's 'frivolous' liturgical innovations.[29] Thus Agobard subtly placed their traditional liturgical customs squarely opposite Amalarius's new-fangled ideas.

Techniques of interpretation

Florus's objections to Amalarius's interpretation of the liturgy went beyond criticism of his careless use of authoritative sources. He also challenged the methodology of his interpretation. Amalarius

---

27 *Ibid.*, I, p. 523: 'Bene beatus Augustinus de sanctificatione diei septimi, sed ille non dixit de consecratione, ut tu mentiris'. For other examples of accusations of misquotation or deviation from the teachings of the church fathers, see *ibid.*, I, p. 523: 'The blessed Augustine did not teach you this', and *ibid.*, I, p. 528: 'You are not in accord with him (Gregory Nazianzen), but rather radically disagree'.
28 *Ibid.*, I, p. 529: 'Dic, rogo, in qua regione, in qua ecclesia, fuit Christus ostiarius? Vere tantum distas a sensu Evangelii vel Augustini, quantum differunt tenebrae a luce'.
29 Agobard of Lyon, *De antiphonario*, ed. L. Van Acker, *Agobardi Lugdunensis, Opera omnia*, CCCM 52 (Turnhout: Brepols, 1981), I, p. 337: 'In divinis laudibus celebrandis quanto studio fugienda sit levitas, gravitasque sectanda, frequenter dilectioni vestrae in mutual conloquutione suggesimus'.

applied techniques of interpretation that were originally developed for the exegesis of texts to explain the purpose and meaning of liturgical ritual.[30] Liturgy was not a text; it was a performative act. To Florus's mind, one could not simply apply the rules of textual exegesis to 'read' liturgical acts. Furthermore, Florus objected to Amalarius's claim that his insights into the meaning of the liturgy had been inspired by the holy spirit. The type of knowledge Amalarius claimed he had access to was essentially prophetic. In Florus's view, this was pseudo-knowledge (*pseudoscientia*) and mere fantasy.[31] Amalarius's claim to divine inspiration complicated Florus's assessment of his interpretations, for how should one assess the content or verify the source of prophetic statements? Perhaps this is why Florus took recourse to emotional assessment and polemical rhetoric as the most effective way to combat pseudo-knowledge.

There was one particular section in Amalarius's *Liber officialis* that provided Florus with more solid ground to refute his opponent's interpretations. In the third book, Amalarius explained the meaning of the liturgical rite of breaking the Eucharist host. According to Amalarius, the breaking of the host into three parts revealed the three-form body of Christ (*corpus triforme*). Florus latched onto this explanation because it provided him with an angle to bring Amalarius's teaching to the terrain of Christology, his own area of expertise, where he was sure-footed. It is highly unlikely that Amalarius intended to make a doctrinal statement about the nature of Christ when he spoke of the three-form body of Christ. As Enrico Mazza pointed out, Amalarius's allegorical mode of interpretation, which allowed several meanings to be given to the same liturgical rite, hardly amounted to formulating a doctrine.[32] Moreover, his interpretation was not radical and can already be found in earlier commentaries on the Office.[33] But the expression *corpus triforme*

---

30 See the explanation of Jones, *A Lost Work*, p. 156.
31 Florus, *Opera polemica, Relatio synodalis*, p. 89: 'Cum ergo istiusmodi pseudoscientia et profana vocum novitas fidei excidium et naufragium faciat'.
32 E. Mazza, *The Celebration of the Eucharist: The Origin of the Rite and the Development of Its Interpretation*, trans. M. J. O'Connell (Collegeville, MN: The Liturgical Press, 1999), p. 169.
33 Jones points out that Amalarius's teaching was already present in embryonic form in earlier commentaries on the office: see Jones, *A Lost Work*,

gave Florus sufficient cause to attack what he could now safely call Amalarius's 'dogma'.[34] Florus stated that Amalarius's expression *corpus triforme* denied the integrity and unity of Christ. Did he really want to see Christ broken into three parts? According to Klaus Zechiel-Eckes, Florus deliberately misinterpreted Amalarius, but it is possible that Florus was simply more versed in addressing and refuting Christological issues and was genuinely disturbed by Amalarius's mixing of categories, what with the shadow of the most recent Christological controversy, the debate on adoptionism, still hanging over Lyon.[35]

Reading in the spirit

In 838, the exiled bishop Agobard managed to persuade Emperor Louis to put the case of Amalarius on the agenda of the Council of Quierzy and to have the assembly examine his writings. At the meeting, Florus delivered a speech to the assembled bishops in which he expounded the errors of Amalarius's teaching, focusing on his interpretation of the three-form body of Christ. If we are to go by the report that Florus drew up of the proceedings, the bishops asked Amalarius if 'this was really his teaching', and 'where he had read such things'. According to Florus, Amalarius was caught off guard and could not find the right words to explain himself:

> He responded that he had read in his spirit [*in suo spiritu se legisse*] the material that was neither derived from sacred scriptures, nor taken from the doctrine of the catholic fathers, nor even presumed by the heretics themselves – for he had absolutely nothing else to say.

---

pp. 158–9.
34 Florus, *Opera polemica, Relatio synodalis*, pp. 87, 89.
35 Jones suggests that the adoptionist controversy, and the fact that Felix of Urgell was kept in custody in Lyon, causing a stir even after his death, may explain Florus's vehement response to Christological claims he thought he recognised in Amalarius's writings: see Jones, *A Lost Work*, p. 157. On Florus deliberately misinterpreting Amalarius, see Zechiel-Eckes, *Florus von Lyon*, pp. 71, 226, 227.

Then the venerable synod, in contempt of such a proud and absurd response, said: 'That was truly the spirit of error'.[36]

Florus pictured Amalarius as a confused person, who was at a loss for words. He was unable to defend himself against the accusation that his liturgical theories were not sufficiently based on patristic or scriptural authority. His reply that he read unaccounted-for material 'in his spirit' may have been the worst thing he could have said in his defence. The choice of words, however, is interesting. Although the contested interpretations were, as Amalarius is said to have admitted, not based on reading and interpreting written sources, the process of developing ideas is nonetheless described as an act of reading. But we only have Florus's word for it that this was indeed Amalarius's response. There are no other sources to confirm Florus's account. Apparently when Amalarius had nothing further to say and remained silent, the council decided to condemn his teaching, because his doctrine diverged from the true faith and was 'alien' (*peregrinam*) to the church.[37] It is, however, unclear whether all of Amalarius's writings were condemned, or only those parts where he discussed the controversial three-form body of Christ. Neither is it made explicit in Florus's report of the council whether the bishops formally deposed Amalarius.[38] All that is certain is that

---

36 Florus, *Opera polemica*, *Relatio synodalis*, p. 86: 'Tunc ille [...] quae neque de scripturis sumpta est neque de catholicorum patrum dogmatibus tracta, sed nec ab ipsius etiam hereticis praesumpta – quia aliud, quod diceret, penitus non habebat – in suo spiritu se legisse respondit. Sed mox tam suberbam et fatuam responsionem veneranda synodus execrans dixit: "Vere ille fuit spiritus erroris"'; trans. Knibbs, *Amalar of Metz, On the Liturgy* 1, Introduction, p. xxv.
37 Florus, *Opera polemica*, *Relatio synodalis*, p. 86: 'Cumque illo reticente ac de mendaciorum suorum depraehensis fallaciis confuso veneranda synodus plurima loqueretur, deliberatum est doctrinam hanc esse omnino damnabilem et ab omnibus catholicae fidei cultoribus funditus respuendam [...] diversam esse istam doctrinam a sinceritate verae fidei et omnino ab ecclesia peregrinam'.
38 One might expect that a condemnation of a bishop's teaching automatically implied his removal from office, but the case of Felix of Urgell, whose teaching was condemned on more than one occasion at the end of the eighth century, shows that this was not necessarily the case. Felix was prepared to recant his error and was allowed to return to his see and resume his office.

within a year Agobard was recalled from exile and reinstated as bishop.

Amalarius corrected?

None of Amalarius's critics in Lyon appears to have seen it as their task to *correct* Amalarius and give him the opportunity to rectify his views. Amalarius was not encouraged to rewrite his commentaries on the liturgy in such a way that his interpretations would become acceptable to the community of Lyon cathedral, compatible with their own views and liturgical practices. As we have seen, Amalarius issued no less than three editions of *Liber officialis* before 834, but, as far as we know, he did not issue a fourth one in response to the criticism he received in Lyon.[39] The main goal of Florus's campaign against Amalarius was to have him removed from the city of Lyon and see his writings burned so that no one else would get infected by reading his errors.[40] He succeeded in the first aim but not in

---

   Only the third condemnation resulted in custody. Zechiel-Eckes, however, speaks of a 'Absetzungssentenz' and argues that there is no doubt that the condemnation pronounced by the council came down to Amalarius's removal from office: see Zechiel-Eckes, *Florus von Lyon*, p. 59.
39 A twelfth-century manuscript contains a version of Amalarius's *On the Liturgy*, which Jean-Michel Hanssens has dubbed a *retractatio*, but this text constitutes a compendium of highlights, not a *retractatio* in the sense of a revision of a text to meet (received or anticipated) criticism; see Van Daalen, 'The reception', pp. 12–13.
40 Florus issued a strong call to burn Amalarius's books in the *Sermo synodalis*: see Florus, *Opera polemica, Sermo synodalis*, pp. 77–8. On the risk of readers getting infected and corrupted by reading Amalarius's books, followed by another call to burn the books, see Florus, *Opera polemica, Liber de tribus epistolis*, pp. 401–2: 'Amalarium [...] qui et verbis et libris suis mendaciis et erroribus et fantasticis atque hereticis disputationibus plenis omnes paene apud Franciam ecclesias et nonnullas etiam aliarum regionum, quantum in se fuit, infecit atque corrupit, ut non tam ipse de fide interrogari quam omnia scripta eius saltim post mortem ipsius debuerint ignem consummi, ne simpliciores quique, qui eos multum diligere, et legendo frequentare dicuntur, eorum lectione et inaniter occuparentur et perniciose fallerentur et deciperentur'. Florus employs a virus metaphor here to denote the risk of an 'infection' with error spreading throughout the community. This metaphor is often used in the discourse on heresy and doctrinal errors,

the second. Amalarius's writings were not burned or otherwise suppressed, as Florus had insisted. Although his antiphonary has not survived, apart from the introduction, his *On the Liturgy* spread far and wide and enjoyed a favourable reception.[41] As Sebastiaan van Daalen discovered, quite a number of manuscripts of the *Liber officialis* contain notes and symbols of readers' appreciation in the margins. A manuscript produced in the Bodensee area in the second half of the ninth century (Fulda, Hochschul- und Landesbibliothek, Aa 20), contains more than two hundred chi-rho symbols in the margin.[42] This symbol, also known as the chresimon, was used as an attention sign to express appreciation of the content and mark sections as orthodox.[43] The annotator who added these chi-rho symbols apparently did not consider these sections error-ridden or shocking at all. There are no indications that this particular reader was in any way disturbed by Amalarius's interpretations of the liturgy. On the contrary, with the chi-rho symbols, they demonstrated they not only appreciated many sections they read in the *Liber officialis*, but also considered them highly orthodox.[44]

Hardly anywhere in the extensive polemical dossier of Florus and his fellow critics do we encounter *correctio*, *emendatio* or a rhetoric of reintegration. Only in a letter to Bishop Drogo, the chair

---

see W. Pezé, *Le virus de l'erreur. La controverse carolingienne sur la double predestination. Essai d'histoire sociale*, Haut Moyen Âge 26 (Turnhout: Brepols, 2017). See also the contribution of Cinzia Grifoni and Giorgia Vocino in Chapter 3 of this volume.

41 See the contribution of Els Rose and Arthur Westwell in Chapter 4 of this volume, and Van Daalen, 'The reception'.
42 See Van Daalen's discussion of Ms. Fulda, Hochschul- und Landesbibliothek, Aa 20 in 'The reception', pp. 51–4. For the date and place of origin of the manuscript, see R. Hausmann, *Die theologischen Handschriften der Hessischen Landesbibliothek Fulda bis zum Jahr 1600* (Wiesbaden: Harrassowitz, 1992), pp. 57–8.
43 I. van Renswoude and E. Steinová, 'The annotated Gottschalk: symbolic annotation and control of heterodoxy in the Carolingian age', in P. Chambert Protat et al. (eds), *La controverse carolingienne sur la prédestination: histoire, textes, manuscrits*, Haut Moyen Âge 32 (Turnhout: Brepols, 2019), pp. 249–78; E. Steinová, *Notam superponere studui. The Use of Annotation Symbols in the Early Middle Ages*, Bibliologia 52 (Turnhout: Brepols, 2019), pp. 119, 207–8.
44 Van Daalen, 'The reception', pp. 51–2.

of the council of Quierzy, and other bishops did Florus acknowledge the possibility that Amalarius would humbly acknowledge his *error* (singular), and he even expressed the hope that he would not stubbornly adhere to his insane fabrications. Nevertheless, in the same breath, Florus called on the bishops to do what they had to do if Amalarius remained firm in his beliefs. His report of the council concludes ominously with a quotation from Paul's letter to Titus: 'Reject a man who is a heretic after the first and the second censure [*correptio*], knowing that he who is subverted and sins is condemned by his own judgement'.[45]

In the ensuing controversy over the teaching of John Scotus, whom Florus attacked no less severely than he did Amalarius, he is somewhat more open to the possibility that John might be willing to correct his opinions and his work and avoid condemnation. About John, Florus writes disparagingly: 'He is so full of fanciful inventions and errors that he should be pitied as deluded or condemned as a heretic, with all his books worthy of derision and contempt', but he concludes on a slightly more positive note: 'unless he hastens to correct and emend' ('nisi corrigere et emendare festinet').[46] When it came to John, Florus was willing to envision a road to redemption and re-integration into the community of orthodox interpretation by revising his work. In his campaign against Amalarius he never even mentioned that option.

The condemnation at Quierzy did not spell the end of Amalarius's scholarly career. During the predestination controversy, discussed in the following, he was one of the four experts who were invited to give their expert opinion on the issue of whether God had predestined some people to salvation and others to damnation. Amalarius's report has not survived, so we do not know what his opinion on the

---

45 Florus, *Opera polemica*, *Relatio synodalis*, p. 90: 'Hereticum hominem post unam et secundam correptionem devita, sciens, quia subversus est eiusmodi et peccat proprio iudicio condemnatus'. Cf. Titus 3: 10–11.
46 Florus, *Opera polemica*, *Adversus Johannem Scotum*, p. 402: 'ita quibusdam phantasticis adinventionibus et erroribus plenus est, ut [...] cum ipsis omni inrisione et dispectione dignis scriptis suis, *nisi corrigere et emendare festinet*, vel sicut demens sit miserandus vel sicut hereticus anathematizandus' (emphasis added).

matter was.⁴⁷ It is, however, interesting to note that the condemnation of his teaching in 838 did not disqualify him, in the eyes of contemporary authorities, from being able to judge the teaching of others and to distinguish between valid and invalid statements.

John Scotus: a controversial method of distinction

In the 840s and 850s, a new controversy shook the Frankish realm, sparked by the divergent teaching of the monk Gottschalk of Orbais (d. 868). Gottschalk maintained that God predestined some people to salvation and others to damnation. His doctrine was condemned at the council of Mainz in 848 and again in Quierzy 849, but Gottschalk was unwilling to recant and let himself be corrected. He was, however, prepared to undergo an 'examination' (*examen*) involving boiling water, oil, lard and pitch, to prove the truth of his assertions, but no one took him up on his challenge.⁴⁸ Four experts were invited to give their opinion, but their reports did not sufficiently clarify the matter.⁴⁹ In fact, two of them, Lupus of Ferrières and Prudentius of Troyes, held positions that were very similar to Gottschalk's views, which was not the outcome Archbishop Hincmar (d. 882), a fierce opponent of Gottschalk, had in mind.⁵⁰ Hincmar decided to ask a scholar, instead of a member of the ecclesiastical elite, and invited the Irish scholar John Scotus (d. 877) to write an expert report on Gottschalk's teaching.

John jumped at the opportunity to refute Gottschalk and used the occasion to demonstrate how the liberal arts provided the perfect means to acquire true knowledge about God and his creation.

---

47 Zechiel-Eckes, *Florus von Lyon*, p. 82. On the experts who were invited to give their opinion, see note 48.
48 M. Gillis, *Heresy and Dissent in the Carolingian Empire: The Case of Gottschalk of Orbais* (Oxford: Oxford University Press, 2017), p. 129.
49 These four experts were Archbishop Hrabanus Maurus, Abbot Lupus of Ferrières, Bishop Prudentius of Troyes and (former bishop) Amalarius. In a second round of reviews, when Hincmar invited John Scotus, Charles the Bald invited Ratramnus of Corbie to give his opinion.
50 For an in-depth study of the predestination controversy, see Pezé, *Le virus de l'erreur*.

Dialectic (logic) was in his opinion excellently suited to distinguish true from false assertions and to arm oneself against 'advocates of falsehoods'.[51] To his mind, ignorance of the liberal arts and of Greek writings had led to errors in thinking on predestination.[52] John argued for the logical necessity of single predestination and, while he was at it, posited that God did not punish sinners in any case. From a logical point of view, he maintained, the traditional vision of hell made no sense. For that reason alone, it was impossible that God had predestined sinners to be punished with hell fire. By applying Aristotelian categorical logic, John formulated a vision of hell in which sinners were left to deal with the consequences of their own poor life choices. As a result of their wickedness, he argued, they were deprived of knowledge itself and suffered 'the darkness of eternal ignorance'.[53] Archbishop Wenilo of Sens (d. 865) suspected that John's report and his spiritual interpretation of hell were rather unorthodox, to put it mildly. He made excerpts of the work and sent them to his suffragan bishop Prudentius of Troyes (d. 861) to test the validity of John's statements.

Prudentius was one of the expert theologians who had been invited to assess Gottschalk's teaching. Now he was asked to review the assessment of a fellow expert in a third round of examination. Prudentius was not satisfied with assessing excerpts from John's refutation, which he had received from Wenilo and which were already based on his archbishop's pre-examination and rejection of the treatise. He managed to obtain a manuscript of the entire text of John's *De divina predestinatione* (*On Divine Predestination*) and set to work. Within a year after receiving Wenilo's request, he finished

---

51 John Scotus Eriugena, *De divina praedestinatione liber*, ed. G. Madec, CCCM 50 (Turnhout: Brepols, 1978), c. 1, LLA 695, l. 45: 'Ne igitur defensores ueritatis inermes cum assertoribus falsitatis confligere uideamur, non incongrue regulis disputatoriae artis utemur'.
52 See especially *ibid.*, c. 18.
53 *Ibid.*, p. 102: 'et eo carcere iniquitatis propriae, in quo hic se ipsum incluserat, *tenebras aeternae ignorantiae* inextricabiliter poenaliter non evitet' (emphasis added). This passage is discussed in J. Marenbon, 'John Scottus and Carolingian theology: from the *De Praedestinatione*, its background and its critics, to the *Periphyseon*', in M. T. Gibson and J. L. Nelson (eds), *Charles the Bald: Court and Kingdom* (2nd ed., Aldershot: Variorum, 1990), pp. 303–26, at p. 310.

his report *De predestinatione contra Joannem* (*On Predestination against John*). Prudentius objected not only to John's statements but also to the procedure through which he had arrived at his conclusions. He took issue with the fact that John's arguments were for a large part based on logic, instead of on a solid body of proof consisting of quotations from patristic and scriptural sources.

John's dialectical method of distinguishing true from false statements was not new in itself.[54] In the late eighth and early ninth centuries, interest in dialectical modes of reasoning increased with the (re)introduction of logical texts and commentaries, and scholars started to experiment with applying the rules of logic to theological matters.[55] Both Theodulf of Orleans (d. 821) and Alcuin of York (d. 804) had employed dialectical modes of assessment in religious controversies some 60 years before John, but they had not brought their method to the fore as *the* road to truth as emphatically as John did. Prudentius's main issue with John's treatise was not logic as such (for Prudentius applied logic himself in his refutation), but the balance between authoritative and logical proof.[56] Although John did offer quite a number of quotations from scripture and patristic writings in his *Liber de divina praedestinatione*, to Prudentius's mind his mix of logic and authoritative proof was uneven. Where was the scriptural or patristic evidence to support John's shockingly new and outrageous interpretation of hell? As far as Prudentius was concerned, there was no need for sophisticated logic to help clarify the meaning of ambiguous passages in scripture because scripture made abundantly clear that the bodies and souls of sinners would most certainly be tortured in eternity.[57]

---

54 See for example Isidore, *Etymologiae*, ed. W. M. Lindsay, 2 vols (Oxford: Oxford University Press, 1911), II.22: 'Docet enim in pluribus generibus quaestionum quemadmodum disputando vera et falsa diiudicentur'.
55 I. van Renswoude, 'The art of disputation: dialogue, dialectic and debate', *Early Medieval Europe*, 25:1 (2017), 38–53.
56 Marenbon, 'John Scottus and Carolingian theology'.
57 Prudentius, *De predestinatione contra Erigenam*, ed. J.-P. Migne, *PL* 115 (Paris: Migne, 1852), cols 1009C–1366A, at col. 1364: 'Dicere Scripturam: Ubi nullus ordo et sempiternus horror inhabitat [...] Eos et animarum et corporum aeternos cruciatus'.

Layout as a visual argument

Prudentius submitted his report to Wenilo in 852. The excerpts with selections of John's controversial statements, which Prudentius had received from Wenilo, were also sent to Florus of Lyon for a second opinion. It is possible that Prudentius forwarded the excerpts to Florus himself after he had obtained a copy of the complete manuscript.[58] Florus also finished his report within a year. In 853, at the council of Valence, John's views were formally condemned. Prudentius continued to revise the report of his refutation until his death in 861. Paris, Bibliothèque nationale de France, lat. 2445 (Troyes, ninth century) is the working copy of his treatise against John. The manuscript shows how Prudentius found new arguments from patristic authorities to bolster his case against John, which he added in the margin or wrote on slips of parchment, bound in with the codex.[59] What is particularly striking about this autograph manuscript is its layout. Jared Wielfaert rightly remarked that the layout of the text in the manuscript is a visual argument.[60] Prudentius rubricated the names of the authors he quoted, and he marked the statements of John, which he integrated into his own work, with the sign of the theta, the mark of rejection, written in red ink. Quotations from patristic authorities, including his own arguments, he annotated with the chi-rho sign, the mark of approval.[61] This was

---

58 Zechiel-Eckes, *Florus von Lyon*, pp. 84–5.
59 For a discussion of this manuscript, see P. Petitmengin, 'D'Augustin à Prudence de Troyes: les citations augustiniennes dans un manuscrit d'auteur', in L. Holtz et al. (eds), *De Tertullien aux Mozarabes: mélanges offerts à Jacques Fontaine, à l'occasion de son 70e anniversaire, par ses élèves, amis et collègues*, Série Moyen-Âge et Temps Moderne 26 (2 vols, Turnhout: Brepols, 1992), II, pp. 229–51.
60 J. Wielfaert, 'Prudentius of Troyes (861) and the reception of the patristic tradition in the Carolingian era' (PhD thesis, University of Toronto, 2015), p. 200.
61 Prudentius, *De predestinatione*, preface, col. 1012: 'Verba quoque eiusdem Iohannis ut ab eo digesta sunt pluribus locis inserui, praeposito etiam nomine ipsius cum praecedente illud nota quae grece dicitur theta quam sententiis capitalibus damnandorum antiqui praescribere solebant. [...] Ubicunque autem mei sermonis interpositio necessarium locum expetit, ne quid michi tribuerem, si quid boni superna gratia per meae linguae organum loqueretur, notam superponere studui, quae ab Artigraphis crisimon

a rather bold move, as the sign implied that Prudentius's own arguments should be credited with the same authority as those of the fathers. As Prudentius explained in his introduction, he took these signs from the 'ancient grammarians' – a reference to Alexandrian scholars who used these graphic symbols as tools of textual criticism.[62] Prudentius, however, interpreted the signs differently: he took the chi-rho sign to be a monogram of Christ and interpreted the theta, which originally stood for athetesis, 'setting aside as spurious', as the mark of condemnation. This symbol, Prudentius said, 'the men of old used to attach to the decrees of capital punishment of men to be executed'.[63] With the theta he marked the statements of John as invalid and obsolete, condemning them, as it were, to death by execution. Although Prudentius interpreted the old signs of textual criticism differently, he used them in a comparable manner as the Alexandrian text critics had done, except that he did not use them to judge the form of the text, but its content.

According to Klaus Zechiel-Eckes, Prudentius's refutation follows the classical scheme of *definitio* and *correctio*; that is, definition and rebuttal.[64] If one consults the edition of the treatise in the *Patrologia Latina*, the most recent edition of the text to date, the term *correctio* indeed appears to be central to Prudentius's refutation and a structuring principle of the treatise. Each time Prudentius rebuts a statement of John, his refutation receives the heading '*correctio*', thus dividing the treatise into alternating sections of propositions and corrections. The '*correctio*' headings are, however, an intervention of the editor. We do not find them in Prudentius's working copy (Paris, BnF, lat. 2445, Troyes, ninth century), which is the only surviving manuscript of his treatise. Although the correction of John was central to the aim of Prudentius's refutation, as we shall see in the following, the term *correctio* is not used as an

---

nuncupatur, quoniam velut monogramma nominis Christi effigiare quodam modo cernitur'. Prudentius's annotation with graphic signs is discussed more fully in Van Renswoude and Steinová, 'The annotated Gottschalk'.

62 'ab artigraphis': see note 60.
63 Prudentius, *De predestinatione*, col. 1012: 'nota quae grece dicitur theta quam sententiis capitalibus damnandorum antiqui praescribere solebant'.
64 Zechiel-Eckes, *Florus von Lyon*, p. 98: 'Eine Auflistung inhaltlicher Schwerpunkte nach dem Schema Definitio – Correctio'.

organising principle of the text, nor was it part of the visual argument of the page.

At the end of Prudentius's treatise is a list with numbered items, 77 in all, to which the heading 'Recapitulatio totius operis; Summary of the main points of the entire work' is added, written in red uncial script.[65] In this case, the heading is not an intervention of the editor but rather part of the manuscript. Since the scribe who copied the manuscript worked under the author's supervision, we can be fairly certain that Prudentius supplied this heading.[66] At first sight, this numbered list of items could be easily mistaken for a table of contents, but it is in fact a list of errors. At the end of his refutation, Prudentius collected the statements of John that he rejected and went over the main points again (*recapitulatio*). The list is structured as if it is a dialogue between Prudentius and John. Each statement of John in this list is introduced by 'you say' (*dicis*), followed by Prudentius's refutation which is each time introduced by 'we respond' (*respondemus*), in red capitals. Significantly, Prudentius is 'we', because he considers himself to be a representative of the community of orthodox interpretation, backed by the authority of the church fathers, while John, the errant individual, is an individual 'you'.

In the final paragraph of the treatise proper, when Prudentius introduces the list and explains its purpose, he addresses John directly as 'brother Joannes' (*frater Joannes*). Instead of speaking about him as an opponent, an enemy of truth, he now speaks to him as a brother and a member, albeit an errant member, of the same community. He drew up this list, Prudentius says, for John's correction (*tuae quoque correctionis, frater Joannes*).[67] He refuted his statements one by one, briefly and concisely, so that those 'who

---

65 Paris, BnF, lat. 2445, ff. 129r–132v; Prudentius, *De predestinatione*, cols 1351–66.
66 The annotations in the margin of Paris, BnF, lat. 2445 are in Prudentius's hand, but the main text was written by a scribe; see Petitmengin, 'D'Augustin à Prudence de Troyes'.
67 Prudentius, *De predestinatione*, col. 1352: 'tuae quoque correctionis, frater Joannes [...] valeat commendare'.

read or hear it can commit them more easily to memory'.[68] The tone of the list is staccato; there are no terms of abuse, no emotional language as in the rest of the treatise, but short and cool refutations.[69] In the edition of the text in the *Patrologia Latina*, John's statements are also marked with the sign of the theta, but it is important to note that this is not the case in the manuscript. As soon as Prudentius shifts perspective and addresses John as his brother, instead of his opponent, and offers him correction, he no longer marks his statements with the mark of damnation. There was a difference between correcting statements in a text and offering correction to a person. The latter required dialogue, not condemnation.

Although Prudentius's treatise only survived in one manuscript, his summary of John's errors and their refutation was also transmitted independently of the treatise. It is preserved in the Vatican, Biblioteca Apostolica Vaticana, Reg. lat. 91 (ninth c.), where it is curiously attributed to Florus. The heading to the list, written in red rustic capitals, runs: 'Florus contra ioannem recapitulatio totius operis' ('Florus against John, summary of the main points of the entire work').[70] After Prudentius's death, the working copy of his treatise against John ended up in Rheims, where it received a negative assessment. On a slip of parchment attached in front of the codex, a Rheims annotator wrote: 'The composer of this book, Prudentius, does not hold catholic opinions on certain ecclesiastical dogmas, as his other writings testify'.[71] Thus the censor himself got

---

68 *Ibid.*, 'libet quam breviter quamque succincte capitulatim singula adnotare, quo legentis audientisve intentio lecta vel audita memoriae tenacius valeat commendare'.
69 For example, the issue of eternal punishment, discussed in full in the treatise, is summarised as follows, in *ibid.*: 'You say: except for the blessing of which they shall be deprived, there is no punishment. We respond: Their bodies and minds suffer torture to the full in eternity' ('Dicis: Excepta beatudine qua privabuntur, nullam habere poenam. Respondemus [in red capitals, alternating uncial script and rustic capitals]: Eos et animarum et corporum aeternos perpeti cruciatus').
70 Vatican, Biblioteca Apostolica Vaticana, Reg. lat. 91 (9th c.), f. 84v. The 'recapitulatio' runs to f. 87v where it breaks off mid-sentence in item (or statement) 71.
71 Paris, Bibliothèque nationale de France, lat. 2445, f. 1bis: 'Iste liber qui quasi ad defensionem fidei contra infidelitatem loquitur et testimonia

censured. The ultimate assessor, however, according to the annotator, is the reader, who is encouraged to be careful when reading this work and to follow apostolic advice 'to test all things and hold fast to what is good'.[72]

When the council of Valence in 853 condemned John's *Liber de divina praedestinatione*, or, to be more precise, 19 *capitula* (chapters or statements) from this treatise, the bishops did not base their sentence on their own examination of his work, but on the expert reports of Prudentius and Florus.[73] In the verdict of the council, John was presented as an outsider. Prudentius had called John 'brother', a member of the same community, and addressed him by his name. In the acts of the council of Valence, he was labelled 'that Irishman', while his teaching was put down as 'Irish porridge'.[74] Thus the verdict of the council echoed the judgement of church father Jerome, who had used the expression 'Irish porridge' to reject and denigrate the teaching of Pelagius, another outsider who was expelled from the community of orthodox interpretation. John, however, was not 'excommunicated' in a strict sense after the council of Valence. Apparently, he was prepared to recant and accept correction, which was the litmus test that distinguished an errant individual from an obstinate heretic.[75] John did not revise his treatise on predestina-

---

scripturarum atque catholicorum nomina profert caute legendus est et in eius lectione apostoli est sequenda sententia qua dicit omnia probate, quod bonum est tenete. Nam compositor eius *Prudentius de quibusdam ecclesiasticis dogmatibus non sensit catholice sicut alia eius scripta demonstrant*' (emphasis added). Prudentius, *De predestinatione*, col. 1009.

72 *Ibid.*: 'caute legendus est et in eius lectione apostoli est sequenda sententia qua dicit omnia probate, quod bonum est tenete'. The last part of the sentence is a quotation from I Thess 5:21. See the full text the annotator added on a slip of parchment in the preceding note.
73 Zechiel-Eckes, *Florus von Lyon*, pp. 167–74.
74 W. Hartmann (ed.), *MGH Conc.* 3 (Hanover: Hahn, 1984), no. 33, pp. 347–65, at c. 6, p. 356: 'Scottorum pultes'.
75 By way of comparison, Gottschalk, whose teaching on predestination was condemned just four years earlier, refused to recant and was sentenced to eternal silence. According to the canons collected in Gratian's *Decretum*, a person who has erred but is open to correction is not a heretic. The *Decretum* was composed much later, around 1149, but the canons on heresy were taken from and/or attributed to Augustine, Jerome, Pope Leo the Great and the letters of Paul. The canons assert that only those who resist correction

tion, but in his next work, the *Periphyseon*, he did take Prudentius's and Florus's criticisms on board.[76] Like Amalarius, John's scholarly career does not seem to have been much affected by his condemnation, except that he was never invited to act as an expert assessor again.[77]

Conclusion

As Carine van Rhijn pointed out in the introduction to this volume, the term *correctio* was not as central to Carolingian discourse as has

---

obstinately and arrogantly and refuse to emend their views can be called heretics. Keywords are *pertinacia* and *contumacia* (sometimes *praesumptio*) ('qui suum errorem defendit pertinaciter'; 'Qui in ecclesia Christi morbidum aliquid pravumque sapiant, *si correcti (var: correpti) resistunt contumaciter* suaque pestifera et mortifera dogmata *emendare nolunt*, sed defensare persistunt, heretici sunt' (emphasis added). See Gratian, *Decretum*, ed. A. L. Richter and E. Friedburg, Corpus iuris canonici 1 (Leipzig: Tauschnitz 1879), c. 30.

76 Marenbon, 'John Scottus and Carolingian theology'. John's *Liber de praedestinatione* has survived in only one copy (Paris, BnF, lat. 13386, ninth c., provenance Corbie, ff. 103r–58v), but this was not unusual for treatises composed for the occasion of a debate. A low survival rate does not neccesarily indicate a campaign of suppression. The treatise of his opponent Prudentius did not fare much better. Paris, BnF, lat. 13386 bears polemical annotations, critical of John's teaching, but also attention signs that indicate interest on the part of the annotator. The fact that condemnation does not neccesarily lead to suppression is exemplified by John's *Periphyseon*. Although condemned in 1225, it has survived in a substantial number of manuscripts.

77 The one other indication we do have that his reputation was affected by the condemnation is a letter by Pope Nicholas I to Charles the Bald about John's translation of pseudo-Dionysius, reminding Charles that it was customary to send a work to the pope first and submit it to his judgement, especially in the case of an author of so much learning, about whom 'constant rumours' were said to circulate (*frequenti rumore diceretur*). E. Perels (ed.), *MGH Epp.* 6 (Berlin: Weidmann, 1925), p. 130. Posthumously John's name became associated with suspicious learning. The treatise *De corpore et sanguine Christi*, written by Ratramnus of Corbie, was erroneously attributed to John at the time of its condemnation in 1050, and in 1225 the council of Paris condemned John's *Periphyseon*.

long been assumed; it was rarely, if at all, used to refer to the reform of society or of entire institutions. Yet as I hope to have shown, the notion was relevant to a rhetoric of rectification and rehabilitation of the individual.[78] Although references are not consistent, we encounter *correctio* and its semantic correlates in reference to attempts to bring errant individuals back in line with the shared interpretation of the community, into which they had introduced difference.[79] The aim was not only to protect a community from infection with error but also to reintegrate those who had erred, at least in theory. Excommunicating a person and eliminating their writings to prevent others from falling into error was a drastic solution that was rarely chosen at the time. Apart from being ineffective, this strategy did little to restore the balance within a given community, shaken by a new interpretation or method of interpretation. The exceptional case of the condemnation of Gottschalk, who was sentenced to eternal silence and forced to burn the writings he had brought to the council, must have demonstrated to all involved that this was not the most effective way to regain order and consensus within a community.

Correctio was also an important term for those who stood corrected and wished (or were pressed) to acknowledge their error.[80]

---

78 On *correctio* as an instrument of moral improvement and a mutual obligation, see M. de Jong, *The Penitential State: Authority and Atonement in the Age of Louis the Pious, 814–840* (Cambridge: Cambridge University Press, 2009), especially pp. 112–47; on *correctio* as a rhetorical figure, related to free speech and moral improvement, see H. Lausberg, *Handbook of Literary Rhetoric: A Foundation for Literary Study* (Leiden: Brill, 1998), par. 786, 4.
79 See Florus's and Prudentius's use of the term *correctio* and its correlates in the quotations in notes 45 and 66. Another example is offered by Alcuin, who expresses the wish to correct the errant Bishop Felix of Urgell: 'Scripsi epistolam pridem Felici episcopo charitatis calamo, non contentionis stimulo, fraternae salutis desiderio, non mordacis reprehensionis stylo; *cupiens eum corrigere* in Christi dilectione, quem in cuiusdam nominis novitate de Christo ac catholicae pacis unitate recedere notum habetur' (emphasis added). See Alcuin, *Adversus Felicem*, ed. J.-P. Migne, *PL* 101 (Paris: Migne, 1851), cols 127–230, here col. 127D.
80 For example, the scholar Candidus Wizo, Alcuin's student, writes: 'I am a man and can make mistakes; but I love truth and therefore love to be corrected'; see E. Dümmler (ed.), *MGH Epp.* 4 (Berlin: Weidmann, 1895), no. 39, p. 560, lines 13–18: 'homo sum et falli possum; et veritatem tamen amo,

Writing a formal *confessio* in which one publicly admitted to having erred was a means to bring controversy to a close and to be readmitted into the community of orthodox interpretation.[81] In that respect, it is striking that we do not have *confessiones* from Amalarius or John or an indication from other sources that they publicly admitted to error. It would appear that they were allowed to pursue their scholarly (but not ecclesiastical) careers without much ado. Procedures and methods to assess error and distinguish true from false, which would become more fixed and formalised in the later middle ages, especially in university circles from the thirteenth century onwards, were in flux throughout this period.[82] We see experiments with critical signs and visual arguments, dialectical modes of assessment and textual means to enable reintegration into the community. Some of these experiments found wide acceptance and formed the basis of formal procedures of censorship in later ages, while others disappeared. Perhaps it is hardly surprising that in this period of experiment and change, partly induced by the

---

ideoque et corrigi'. This text is discussed in C. A. Jones, 'Candidus Wizo, Arn of Salzburg and the treatise *De sole et luna*', *Early Medieval Europe*, 27 (2019), 546–66.

81 For example, when Bishop Felix of Urgell was defeated by the scholar Alcuin in a public debate, he drew up a profession of faith (*confessio*) in which he owned his mistakes and promised to 'correct and restrain' the error which he himself had spread. A. Werminghoff (ed.), *MGH Conc.* 2.1 (Hanover: Hahn, 1906), no. 25, pp. 220–5, at p. 222: 'si scandalum seu error in fide, qui per me usque nunc inter utrasque partes duravit, per me iterum omnino correcta atque sedata fuerint adque omnia ecclesiae membra in unitate fidei et concordia caritatis velud in unum corpus conpaginata'. Gottschalk also wrote a profession of faith (*confessio*) after his teaching was condemned, but did not acknowledge any error.

82 On censorship procedures and methods of error assessment, developed at universities from the thirteenth century onwards, see J. Miethke, 'Mittelalterliche Theologenprozesse (9. bis 15. Jahrhundert), *Zeitschrift der Savigny-Stiftung für Rechtsgeschichte: Kanonistische Abteilung*, 131 (2014), 261–311; J. M. M. H. Thijssen, *Censure and Heresy at the University of Paris, 1200–1400* (Philadelphia, PA: University of Pennsylvania Press, 1998); J. Koch, 'Philosophische und theologische Irrtumslisten von 1270–1329: Ein Beitrag zur Entwicklung der theologische Zensuren', in J. Koch (ed.), *Kleine Schriften* 2, Storia e letteratura. Raccolta di studi e testi 127 (Rome: Edizione di Storia e Letteratura, 1973), pp. 423–50.

introduction of new texts and methods, there was no consistent attitude towards error assessment and rectification, both of texts and of individuals, or a homogeneous set of ideas on what one hoped to achieve by it.

I would like to conclude this chapter by quoting an anonymous ninth-century author who expressed, like Amalarius, his fear of committing an error and incurring criticism. 'I am stayed', he wrote, 'by the familiar and dangerous criticism of certain persons who, whenever we begin to say anything, immediately and unanimously assert that, for the sake of avoiding error, one should be silent on a topic rather than say anything about it'.[83] The author pointed out that it was important to acknowledge error as soon as it is demonstrated, but he also maintained that avoiding error at all costs could be an impediment to discovering the truth. Against those who asserted that it was better not to say anything and stay clear of error, he wrote:

> I know for certain that no one can err too badly, so long as he is prepared to assent to truth once it has been demonstrated. I would also call myself fortunate, even if I could not be responsible for truth's discovery, if I were at least the cause of it being sought.[84]

---

83 Text II in A. Borst (ed.), *Schriften zur Komputistik im Frankenreich von 721 bis 818*, *MGH* Quellen zur Geistesgeschichte des Mittelalter 21.1–3 (3 vols, Hanover, Hahn: 2006), II, pp. 855–6: 'Sed prohibet me quorundam nota et cavenda cavillatio, qui, cum aliquid dicere coeperimus, statim, quasi cavendi erroris gratia, de hoc tacendum magis quam aliquid dicendum pari consensus proclamant'; trans. Jones, 'Candidus Wizo', 555–6.

84 *Ibid.*, 'Videmus aliquantos in tantum fugisse errores, ut iam pene totum quod sciunt, ipsius error sit […] Ego certe scio nullum posse male errare, quamdiu veritati ostensae paratus est consentire. Et bene mecum agi dicerem, si forte non possim inveniendae veritatis, fuissem saltim causa quaerendae'.

6

Reformatio and *correctio* in Carolingian theology and orthodoxy: reformation or *aggiornamento*?

Kristina Mitalaité

When Pope John XXIII decided to organise Vatican II in 1959, he intentionally avoided the term 'reform' due to its association with the Protestant Reformation. Instead, he described the council's aims with the term *aggiornamento*, or 'update' – that is to say, the council should strive to 'update' the Catholic church to contemporary realities. Nevertheless, the term 'reform' was still employed by one of his successors, albeit in the Greek form. At the opening of the Consistory of 1994, Pope John Paul II declared: 'As she faces this great jubilee, the church needs *metanoia* [conversion/reform], that is, the discernment of her children's historical shortcomings and negligence with regard to the demands of the Gospel'.[1] According to Giuseppe Alberigo, this pontifical announcement was met with astonishment by the cardinals. John Paul II here conceived *metanoia* as a repentance to be undertaken not only by every individual Christian, but also by the church as a whole.[2]

First, a brief point on terminology. As Gerhard Ladner noted in his seminal study on reformation ideas, there are two essential

---

* I wish to thank Ingrid Rembold and Arthur Westwell for helping to improve the English of my chapter.

1 *Extraordinary Consistory, 13 June 1994*, in *Il Regno-Att.*, 39 (1994), p. 388, quoted in G. Alberigo, *Chiesa Santa e Peccatrice: Conversione della Chiesa?* (Monastero di Bose: Edizioni Qiqajon, 1997), p. 12: 'Di fronte a questo grande giubileo la Chiesa ha bisogno della *metanoia*, cioè del discernimento delle mancanze storiche e delle negligenze dei suoi figli nei confronti delle esigenze del vangelio'.
2 Alberigo, *Chiesa Santa*, p. 12.

stages in becoming Christian: *metanoia* (conversion/reform) and *epistrophe* (renewal). The important point is that no Christian culture or society excludes *metanoia*, for it represents the impulse for self-perfection which is integral to all Christian and religious ethics. Even though the two terms are often used synonymously in the New Testament, *metanoia* can designate baptism (Acts 2:38) and the forgiveness of sins, while *epistrophe* denotes a return to God (Acts 3:19). While in early Christianity, baptism was taken to imply repentance, over time more emphasis began to be placed upon the so-called second penance, here corresponding to *epistrophe* and denoting the ongoing work of spiritual perfection – the *reformatio* (reformation) and *correctio* (correction) of individual actions.[3] While Carolingian authors did not use the terms *metanoia* and *epistrophe*, they clearly imply these two stages in their discussions of 'reforming' individuals.

The first part of this chapter will analyse Carolingian theological semantics of individual *reformatio* using these concepts of *metanoia* and *epistrophe* through an examination of one of the

3 G. Ladner, *The Idea of Reform, Its Impact on Christian Thought and Action in the Age of the Fathers* (Cambridge, MA: Harvard University Press, 1959), p. 49. On this study, see also the Introduction by Carine van Rhijn. On the semantic shifts of *metanoia* and *epistrophe*, see G. Stroumsa, 'From repentance to penance in early Christianity: Tertullian's *De Paenitentia* in Context', in J. Assmann and G. Stroumsa (eds), *Transformations of the Inner Self in Ancient Religions* (Leiden: Brill, 1999), pp. 167–78. See also other articles in these two collections. For a recent discussion of these two terms, see T. Nagy, 'Conversion vs. initiation: recovering the initial Christian experience in a Catholic context', *Pneuma*, 40 (2018), 192–211, here 201–3. Nagy argues that *epistrophe* was used for a Platonic understanding of conversion, while *metanoia* was considered to be a Christian conversion, but still argues for the relevance of both terms to Christianity, for example 203: '*Metanoia* describes the initial Christian experience. It is a part of the process, *epistrophe*, and it is the catalyst process'. The distinction between philosophical conversion defined as *epistrophe* and Christian conversion described as *metanoia* was established by the French historian of philosophy Pierre Hadot: see P. Hadot, '*Epistrophè* et *metanoia* dans l'histoire de la philosophie', in *Proceedings of the XIth International Congress of Philosophy 12: History of Philosophy: Methodology – Antiquity and Middle Ages* (Amsterdam: North-Holland Publishing Company, 1953), pp. 31–6.

most popular genres of Carolingian theology, exegetical commentaries. I will focus in particular on commentaries on Genesis 1:26 and on a cluster of core verses in Pauline Epistles describing *reformatio* or *renovatio* (renewal): Romans 6:4–6 and 12:2, Ephesians 4:23 and II Corinthians 3:18.[4] Most of these Pauline verses are hortatory instructions for renewal. For example, in the Epistle to the Romans 12, the apostle entreats the community to the unity that signifies, for him, a new 'age' (12:2: 'Do not conform yourselves to this present world, but be transformed by a renewal of your whole way of thinking so that you may discern what is God's will, what is good, what is acceptable to him and perfect'). For Paul, 'renewal of the mind' pertains to reason (*nous*), i.e. internal and not external changes; this is made possible by the Holy Spirit, who 'leads' Christian renewal or metamorphosis through faith and baptism.[5] In his Epistle to the Corinthians, Paul speaks about being 'transformed by a renewal' and about a transformation that occurs 'day by day', while in the Epistle to the Ephesians he conveys the idea of 'becoming new' (Ephesians 2:15) and clearly points to 'becoming entirely new' (4:23–4: 'And be renewed in the spirit of your mind. And that ye put on the new man, which after God is created in righteousness and true holiness'). The sacrificial act of Christ restores corrupted creation, but it also reveals itself as a new act of creation. Paul's *renovatio* thus foregrounds the divine image in man, corrupted by the original sin, and for this reason, I will also deal with Genesis 1:26.

The second part of this chapter, meanwhile, will explore the discourse of *correctio* in the context of heterodox teaching within the institutional church.[6] Here, I will examine treatises on theological controversies from the reign of Charlemagne which allow for a

---

4 J. Barrow, 'Ideas and application of reform', in T. F. X. Noble and Julia M. H. Smith (eds), *The Cambridge History of Christianity III: Early Medieval Christianities, c. 600–c. 1100* (Cambridge: Cambridge University Press, 2008), pp. 345–62, here p. 346.
5 J. A. Fitzmeyer, *Romans: A New Translation with Introduction and Commentary* (New York: The Anchor Bible, 1992), pp. 640–1.
6 On *correctio* see also the Introduction to this volume by Carine van Rhijn; on the other aspects of 'correcting' see Chapter 5 for Irene van Renswoude's contribution to this volume.

more precise reconstruction of *correctio* within a doctrinal context. Put simply, doctrinal refutation necessarily implied *correctio*. Thus, while the first part of this chapter deals with Carolingian theological conceptions of the *reformatio* of individuals, the second part turns to the official, institutional, meaning of *correctio*.

Exegesis on Genesis

Commentaries on Genesis were extremely popular in the Carolingian period, and the verse Genesis 1:26–7 was widely quoted by exegetes. Alcuin of York and Wicbod wrote important commentaries on Genesis which were built upon by later generations of scholars, including Claudius of Turin (780–827), Hrabanus Maurus (c. 780–856) and Angelomus of Luxeuil (d. 855).

Alcuin, Wicbod and Theodulf of Orléans

Alcuin's *Interrogationes et responsiones in Genesim* were widely copied in the Carolingian period.[7] Alcuin emphasised Augustine's trinitarian interpretation of the divine image and endorsed Augustine's idea that this image truly concerns only beings endowed with reason, i.e. human beings; he did not, however, incorporate any Pauline discussion on the *renovatio* of the divine image.[8]

Wicbod wrote an impressive exegetical Carolingian treatise on the Octateuch, dated between 775 and 800. This commentary was requested by Charlemagne for his personal reading, and, in the

---

7 On this commentary, see M. Fox, 'Alcuin the exegete: the evidence of the *Quaestiones in Genesim*', in C. Chazelle and B. v. N. Edwards (eds), *The Study of the Bible in the Carolingian Era* (Turnhout: Brepols, 2003), pp. 39–60. Alcuin's treatise survives in fifty-two manuscripts, see p. 43; for a description of the ninth-century manuscripts, see pp. 52–60.
8 Here, Alcuin turns to Augustine to argue that the plural subject (men) of the verb *faciamus* implies that soul is the image of the Trinity: Alcuin, *Interrogationes et responsiones in Genesin*, ed. J.-P. Migne, *PL* 100 (Paris: Migne, 1851), cols 515–69, here cc. 81, 146, cols 525A, 533A–B; for Alcuin's discussion of the divine image reflecting Augustinian roots, see c. 36, col. 520B.

same way as Alcuin, Wicbod structured his treatise as a dialogue.[9] Even though Wicbod's commentary is a catena, i.e. an 'anthology' or 'collection' of extracts from Patristic authors on particular biblical verses, he nevertheless expressed his own theological ideas by actively selecting and excerpting the biblical passages he copied. Wicbod proposed the first Carolingian metaphysical view on the world's creation that evolves as a dialogue between a pupil and a teacher, thus preceding Eriugena's metaphysics of the *Periphyseon*. Here, the pupil is presumably Charlemagne himself, who could take its lessons about God's creation and its foundations and apply them to his own rule.[10] Wicbod was strongly influenced by the Augustinian idea of man's supremacy over other non-rational creatures. Only man is destined for *reformatio* after the incarnation. Here Wicbod, following Augustine, argues that the mind or spirit (*mens*) is deformed by primordial sin and then is reformed and renewed in God's image through man's search for inner conversion.[11] It is worth noting, however, that Wicbod omitted the particular passage of Augustine's commentary on the *reformatio* of the divine image.[12] There are also some political overtones in Wicbod's reading of this verse, for he stated that the divine image in man can

---

9 Wigbod, *Liber quaestionum super liber Genesis*, ed. J.-P. Migne, *PL* 96 (Paris: Migne, 1851), cols 1105–1204, here cols 1132A–333C. On this commentary, see M. Gorman, 'The encyclopedic commentary on Genesis prepared for Charlemagne by Wigbod', *Recherches Augustiniennes et patristiques*, 17 (1982), 173–201; M. Gorman, 'Wigbod and biblical studies under Charlemagne', *Revue Bénédictine*, 118 (2008), 5–45; L. J. Dorfbauer, 'Wigbod und der pseudoaugustinische Dialogus quaestionum LXV', *Studi Medievali*, 51 (2010), 893–919. Please note that Wigbod is an alternative spelling of Wicbod.
10 On this question, see K. Mitalaité, 'La puissance révélatrice de la parole et sa mise en voix dans la spiritualité et la politique carolingiennes', *The Journal of Medieval Latin*, 26 (2016), 263–89 at 269–71.
11 Wigbod, *Liber quaestionum super liber Genesis*, col. 1132; Augustine, *De Genesi ad litteram*, ed. I. Zycha, *Sancti Aureli Augustini*, CSEL 28 (Prague: F. Tempsky, 1894), III:19–20, pp. 85–7. For the identification of these sources, cf. Gorman, 'The encyclopedic commentary', 181.
12 Augustine's Pauline exegesis of *renovatio* comes right after his commentary on the supremacy of rational animals which Wicbod includes in his commentary. Augustine, *De Genesi ad litteram*, III:20, p. 86: 'Unde et apostolus dicit: renovamini in spiritu mentis uestrae et induite … [Ephesians

be read in two ways: having his mind created to the image of God, man is destined to live a rational life; that means the contemplation of the truth and 'the governance of the temporal affairs'.[13]

Wicbod further introduced a Pauline theme of *renovatio* with clear eschatological significance: namely, that if *renovatio* entails the remaking of man's spirit according to God's image, it must necessarily involve man's corporeal body.[14] Here, Wicbod endorsed Augustine's theory concerning the corporeal body of Adam, which was based on I Corinthians 15:44 ('It is sown a natural body; it is raised a spiritual body. If there is a natural body, there is also a spiritual body'). According to this interpretation, Christ's incarnation inaugurated our progressive *renovatio*, which promises us a better body than the one lost by our sinful father; this new, spiritual body will be gained as a reward in the Last Judgement. Here, Wicbod's theological thinking is Pauline. This *renovatio* describes the renewal that leads us not backwards to the old state before sin, but forward to the better one. The eschatological context of Pauline ideas determined that *reformatio* or *renovatio* was approached in Wicbod's commentary as an atemporal eschatological plan whose full accomplishment is only to come after the resurrection.

Another of Wicbod's contemporaries, Theodulf (c. 750–821), included an extended commentary on this same verse of Genesis in his discussion of the question of the divine image in his *Opus Caroli regis*, a treatise against the cult of icons. In a similar vein to Wicbod and Alcuin, Theodulf was fascinated by the trinitarian structure of the divine image in the soul of man. He was equally interested in the interpretation which perceives only the human soul as the divine image. Inspired by the Pauline anthropological ideas, i.e. concerning

---

4:23–4 and Colossians 3:10] ... satis ostendens, ubi sit homo creatus ad imaginem, etc'.

13 Wigbod, *Liber quaestionum super librum Genesis*, col. 1133A: 'rerum temporalium administratio'. Wicbod's source is Augustine, *De Genesi ad litteram*, III:22, pp. 88–9; identification by Gorman, 'The encyclopedic commentary', 181.

14 Wigbod, *Liber quaestionum super librum Genesis*, cols 1135A–B. Wigbod's source is Bede, *De sex dierum creatione*, ed. J.-P. Migne, PL 93 (Paris: Migne, 1850), cols 207–34; identification by Gorman, 'The encyclopedic commentary', 182.

human existence, he includes long passages from Augustine's commentary on II Corinthians 4:16 ('Though our outer self is wasting away, our inner self is being renewed day by day').[15] Theodulf's conception of *reformatio* – and thus of *epistrophe* – highlights the differences between the old man and the new man from an eschatological perspective. The eschatological theme of the renewal is discussed in relation to the corruption of the old exterior man, the one of vices, and the cultivation of the new, interior man, the one of justice. Paralleling Wicbod's commentary, Theodulf describes how the dissolution of the corporal man fertilises the spiritual body to be given in the times of resurrection, a theme which recurs in the second book of his treatise (II Corinthians 4:16: 'but though our outward man perishes, yet the inward man is renewed day by day').[16] The eschatological culmination of *renovatio* is as clearly stated as in Wicbod's commentary: the everyday *reformatio* (based on II Corinthians 3:18) is oriented accordingly. Both theologians conceptualise *reformatio* as related to the extemporal level of resurrection, as opposed to the temporal matters of the church.

Claudius of Turin, Hrabanus Maurus and Angelomus of Luxeuil

We are afforded a unique window onto Claudius of Turin, who authored a dense commentary on Genesis: one of the manuscripts where this commentary is preserved, Paris BnF lat. 9575, was probably prepared by Claudius himself.[17] For his explanation of

---

15 Theodulf of Orleans, *Opus Caroli regis contra synodum*, ed. A. Freeman and P. Meyvaert, *MGH Conc.* 2, Supplementum 1 (Hanover: Hahn, 1998), I:7, pp. 140–4.
16 Theodulf of Orleans, *Opus Caroli regis contra synodum*, II:28, p. 298: 'quanto exterior homo corrumpatur tanto interior renovatur de die in diem'.
17 M. Gorman, 'The commentary on Genesis of Claudius of Turin and biblical studies under Louis the Pious', *Speculum*, 72:2 (1997), 279–329; L. J. Dorfbauer, 'Der Genesiskommentar des Claudius von Turin, der Pseudoaugustinische *Dialogus quaestionum* und das wisigotische *Intexuimus*', *Revue d'histoire des textes*, 8 (2013), 269–305. B. Bischoff believed ('Manuscripts in the Age of Charlemagne', in *Manuscripts and Libraries in the age of Charlemagne*, trans. M. Gorman (Cambridge:

Genesis 1:26, Claudius relies upon an earlier anonymous work, the so-called *Intexuimus* commentary.[18] As well as touching on some of the trinitarian ideas covered earlier, Claudius explored the ethical idea of *reformatio* based on the distinction between 'likeness' and 'image' in Genesis 1:26–7. Here, Claudius advanced a conception of grace that foreshadows the later debate over predestination: 'image' corresponds to general human nature, while 'likeness' designates the grace conferred by God to the few.[19] This idea of grace was adapted to show the supremacy of human creation: the spirit/mind (*mens*) and image (*imago*) refer to the excellence of human nature, while likeness was defined as the Creator's more glorious gift, which allows man to attain the likeness of angels.[20] Claudius did not develop the eschatological idea of the glorious body as it was employed by Wicbod; rather, he followed the commentary *Intexuimus*, in which the image involved only man's soul, not his body.[21] Here, he echoed *Intexuimus* in drawing upon the Pauline idea of *renovatio* as becoming a new man, stated in Ephesians. This idea is expanded by the citation of Colossians 3:9–10 ('ye have put off the old man with his deeds, and have put on the new man') and Paul's idea that the *renovatio* is accomplished in the divine image.

Hrabanus Maurus's extended explanation of this particular verse is largely dependent on Bede's commentary on Genesis.[22] Following

---

Cambridge University Press, 2007), p. 33) that this text was corrected by Claudius himself, while Gorman (295–7) argues that this copy was prepared by Claudius for his own use or as a presentation copy to be offered to Dructeramnus: see here Dorfbauer, 'Der Genesiskommentar', 295–6.

18 *Intexuimus*, ed. M. Gorman, 'The Visigothic commentary on Genesis in Autun 27 (S. 29)', *Recherches Augustiniennes*, 30 (1997), 167–269.

19 This can be found under the name of John Cassian, *Commentarii in Genesim*, ed. J.-P. Migne, *PL* 50 (Paris: Migne, 1846), cols 893–1047, here lib. I, col. 900 D: 'Et imago dei est omnium, similitudo uero paucorum, quia illa anima creata est per naturam, haec dabitur consummatae per gratiam'. *Intexuimus*, ed. Gorman, p. 249.

20 For Claudius's sources, cf. Gorman, 'The Visigothic commentary', 313, and especially Dorfbauer, 'Der Genesiskommentar', 297–306.

21 Cassian, *Commentarii in Genesim*, lib. I, col. 901A; Paris, BnF, lat. 9575, fols 12–13v. Claudius inserted source marks into his manuscript, but not in this particular section.

22 S. Cantelli Berarducci, *Hrabani Mauri opera exegetica: repertorium fontium* (3 vols, Turnhout: Brepols, 2006), I, pp. 263–7; for these sources'

Bede, the abbot of Fulda presented a trinitarian analysis: the unity and consubstantiality of the three persons are described through their equal share of power in their common action as divine persons. Hrabanus paid particular attention to the Christological reading of this verse, which diverges completely from Wicbod's interpretation. The Pauline call for *renovatio* (Ephesians 4:23–4) was developed by Bede and, subsequently, by Hrabanus into an extended theology of *reformatio*. Here, Bede drew on the Pauline theology of two Adams: Christ as a second Adam is free from all the failures of the original Adam, therefore Christ's example and gifts are active agents that 'restore' (*restaurare*) our image and likeness. Hrabanus designated Christ's gifts as tools of what I have defined earlier as *epistrophe*. Hrabanus's commentary concludes with a telling addition to Bede's original work, his source text. According to the abbot of Fulda, the *reformatio* of the divine image is accomplished individually, according to everyone's ability – an insertion which can be readily connected to Hrabanus's own position in the predestination controversy.[23]

Angelomus of Luxeuil's anthropological ideas in his commentary on Genesis are close to those of Claudius, but, unlike Claudius, he was not attracted to the Christological ideas of *reformatio*.[24] He underscored the divine 'likeness' of Genesis 1:26 as *epistrophe*. If 'image' defines the common human condition (as every human is created according to the divine image), 'likeness' characterises individual moral achievement. He quoted equally the popular idea of

---

identification, see II, pp. 452–80. See also C. Tristano, 'Un nuovo testimone dei Commentaria in Genesim di Rabano Mauro', *Studi Medievali*, 51 (2010), 839–91; Hrabanus Maurus, *Commentariorum in Genesim*, ed. J.-P. Migne, PL 107 (Paris: Migne, 1851), cols 439–669, here lib. I, cols 459A–61A; Bede, *Libri quatuor in principium Genesis*, ed. C. W. Jones, CCSL 118A (Turnhout: Brepols, 1967), pp. 24–6.

23 Hrabanus Maurus, *Commentariorum in Genesim*, col. 4601B: 'Reformemus ergo in nobis in novo homine, pro captu nostro, imaginem Dei, quam in veteri perdidimus homine, id est in quantum possumus, exempla ejus sequamur: adhaereamus donis, obtemperemus mandatis'.

24 M. Gorman, 'The commentary on Genesis of Angelomus of Luxeuil and biblical studies under Lothar', *Studi Medievali*, 40 (1999), 559–631. Angelomus wrote two recensions of this commentary, the second of which includes excerpts from Isidore's commentary: Gorman, 'Angelomus', 578.

'the likeness is to be discerned in the habits'.[25] Angelomus upheld the eschatological focus of 'likeness' used here in the sense of a supporting structure for the predestination of those chosen for salvation (*electi*): the perfection and achievement of likeness in Genesis 1:26 is reinforced by the eschatological message of I John 3:2 ('Beloved, now are we the sons of God, and it doth not yet appear what we shall be: but we know that, when he shall appear, we shall be like him; for we shall see him as he is').[26]

The commentaries on the Pauline epistles

Theodulf's *Opus Caroli regis* developed a coherent view on *reformatio* grounded in Pauline theology, connecting this term with both the divine image and baptism. From the very first chapter of his first book, Theodulf described baptism with a reference to Romans 6:4 ('We were buried therefore with him by baptism into death, in order that, just as Christ was raised from the dead by the glory of the Father, we too might walk in newness of life'). Dying 'together' with Christ in baptism entailed leaving behind the old world of sin and becoming the new man in spiritual resurrection. Here, Theodulf drew on Ambrosiaster, a source often invoked by Carolingian exegetes to explain the Pauline epistles. Being born again with Christ in baptism defines the new life.[27]

---

25 'Similitudo in moribus cernenda est'. This appears as a very common formula in Carolingian exegetical and moral texts: the famous *Dicta Albini de Imagine* describes the *similitudo* which encapsulates all the virtues (charity, kindness, etc.). The possession of these reveals man's proximity to God, while their absence implies man's likeness to ferocious animals. See *Dicta Albini de Imagine*, ed. J. Marenbon, *From the Circle of Alcuin to the School of Auxerre: Logic, Theology and Philosophy in the Early Middle Ages* (Cambridge: Cambridge University Press, 1981), p. 160.
26 Angelomus, *Commentarius in Genesin*, ed. J.-P. Migne, PL 115 (Paris: Migne, 1852), cols 107–243, here col. 122: 'Sed si imago Dei est ipsa ratio animae, similitudo vero ipsius est aeternae vita, quam daturus est omnibus electis, quando erit illud quod Joannes ait: Similes ei erimus [I John 3:2]'.
27 Theodulf of Orleans, *Opus Caroli regis contra synodum*, ed. Freeman, I:1, pp. 111–12. For Theodulf's pronounced emphasis on baptismal *reformatio*, see II:16, pp. 266–7.

The bishop of Orléans further reflected on the Pauline *reformatio* in his biblical *vademecum*, preserved in Paris, BnF, lat. 15679. Here, quoting Pelagius, he put forward an interpretation of *epistrophe* (Ephesians 4:23–4) as leading from the 'old' to the 'new man', here paralleling his emphasis in the *Opus Caroli regis*. According to Theodulf, conversion affects the spirit or mind, not the body. Finally, the conversion to the new man was grounded on the Christian anthropological principle of being created according to the image and likeness of God. His use of *epistrophe* thus invoked virtues to be cultivated: one should be upright, saintly and truthful.[28] The same anthropological idea of *renovatio* as self-improvement was expounded by Theodulf in his explanation of Romans 12:2. The initial source was Jerome's commentary on the same verse. Once again, *reformatio* concerns the mind (*sensus*), which should reign over the body and its parts. According to Theodulf, the 'new mind' (*novus sensus*), in subduing all the parts of the body, can discern the will of God.[29]

Claudius of Turin

Claudius also wrote one of the most important commentaries on the Pauline epistles in the Carolingian period.[30] In his commentary

---

28 Paris, BnF, lat. 15679, fol. 464; Pelagius, *Expositio in Ephesios*, ed. A. Souter, *Pelagius's Expositions of Thirteen Epistles of St Paul* (Cambridge: Cambridge University Press, 1922), pp. 368–9.

29 Paris, BnF, lat. 15679, fol. 429; Jerome, *Commentarius in epistolam ad Romanos*, ed. J.-P. Migne, *PL* 30 (Paris: Migne, 1846), cols 645–717, here c. 12, col. 700D.

30 On the exegesis of Pauline epistles in the Carolingian period, with particular attention paid to Claudius's commentary, see a series of important articles written by P. Boucaud: P. Boucaud, 'Commentaires pauliniens inédits du haut Moyen Âge dans un manuscrit du Mont-Cassin', *Revue d'histoire des textes*, 7 (2012), 159–219; P. Boucaud, '*Corpus Paulinum*: l'exégèse grecque et latine des "Épîtres" au premier millénaire', *Revue de l'histoire des religions*, 230:3 (2013), 299–332; P. Boucaud, 'Claude de Turin († ca. 828) et Haymon d'Auxerre (fl. 850): deux commentateurs d'I Corinthiens', in S. Shimahara (ed.), *Études d'exégèse carolingienne: autour d'Haymon d'Auxerre: Atelier de recherches, Centre d'études médiévales d'Auxerre, 25–26 avril 2005* (Turnhout: Brepols, 2007), pp. 187–236. Claudius's

on Romans, Claudius elucidated Romans 6:4–6 extensively, and he identified baptism here as the mystical death of all of man's sins through a comparison to the likeness of crucifixion, in which men were transformed from the sons of perdition into the sons of adoption.[31] Claudius described at length the symbolism of 'old' and 'new' men. The 'newness' (*novitas*) is glorified in our conversion by putting away the old man and putting on the new (Ephesians 4:22, 24).[32] Claudius thus grasped baptism as a real Christian *metanoia*, which signifies dying with Christ entirely and completely. Turning to Romans 12:2, he gave a clear definition of *reformatio* of the mind which draws on Origen. *Renovatio* is here a process which begins with the cultivation of wisdom through meditation on the spiritual meaning of the word of God.[33] Only once illuminated by divine

---

commentaries on Romans and Corinthians can be found in Paris, BnF, lat. 12289 and BnF, lat. 2392. Claudius's authorship of the commentaries on Thessalonians and Timothy, found in Codex 48 of Monte Casino, remains a subject of contention: cf. Boucaud, 'Commentaires pauliniens', 159–212. The attribution to Claudius nevertheless seems highly plausible. The commentaries on Ephesians and Philippians were edited by Cristina Ricci: Claudius of Turin, *Tractatus in Epistolas ad Ephesios*, *Tractatus ad Philippenses*, ed. C. Ricci, CCCM, 263 (Turnhout: Brepols, 2014).

31 Paris, BnF, lat. 2392, fols 26v–7v.

32 *Ibid.*, 27r: 'quomodo glorificatur pater per resurrectionem filii ita est per conversationis nostrae novitatem glorificatur. Novitas autem vitae est ubi veterem hominem cum actibus suis deposuimus et induimus novum quis deus creatus est'. In his commentary on Ephesians, Claudius paid particular attention to the explanation of this verse where he endorsed Augustine's point of view: see *Tractatus in Epistolas ad Ephesios*, IV:23–4, pp. 69–70. He starts by quoting Marius Victorinus (in Eph. 4:23–4), who defined the ongoing *renovatio* (*renovabitur*) as a process of becoming better than Adam's original state; the extensive quotation from Augustine's *De Trinitate* (XIV, 16, 22), in which Augustine considers Ephesians 4:23–4 alongside I Corinthians 15:35, leads Claudius to consider ongoing *reformatio* and *renovatio* as centred around the mind. Claudius concludes as follow: 'That is why it is said "according to the image of God", for this *renovatio* should be understood as occurring there where the image of God is found, that is in the mind. To be sure, this *renovatio* did not occur at the moment of the conversion, as it occurred at baptism with the *renovatio* by the remission of all the sins'. Claudius thus clearly distinguishes between two *reformationes*, defined here as *metanoia* and *epistrophe*.

33 Paris, BnF, lat. 2392, fol. 51r.

wisdom and grace in our mind can man discern his real will (II Corinthians 3:18).[34]

In his commentary on II Corinthians 3:18, Claudius took up the idea of freedom and grace as it was expounded by Ambrosiaster.[35] Claudius explained that we are transformed by the grace of Christ into the image of our hope. The fulfilment of the eschatological expectation was adduced here from the passage of I John 3:2 ('when he shall appear, we shall be like him'). The accomplishment of the *renovatio* of the divine image will be the beatific vision which man will behold when he achieves the likeness of God and sees him face to face.[36] Once again, *renovatio* appeared here as an eschatological project.

Paris, BnF lat. 11574

An impressive exegetical treatise on the Pauline epistles preserved in Paris, BnF lat. 11574, is attributed by Bernard Bischoff to Louis the Pious's chancellor Helisachar (d. 835). Some scholars have followed this attribution, notably Michel Huglo and Paul-Irenée Fransen, with Michael Gorman sounding a dissenting note.[37] There is no doubt that the author was a highly educated man and had access to

---

34 Ibid., fol. 51r; see also Origen, *In epistulam Pauli ad Romanos explicationum liber IX*, ed. C. P. Hammond Bammel, *Der Römerbriefkommentar des Orgines: Kritische Ausgabe der Übersetzung Rufins, Buch 7–10* (Freiburg: Verlag Herder, 1998), IX:1 p. 717.
35 Paris, BnF, lat. 12289, 165r; Vatican, vat. lat. 5775, f. 111r.
36 II Corinthians 3:18; Ambrosiaster, *Commentarius in epistulas Paulinas*, ed. H. K. Vogels, CESL 81 (Prague: Tempsky, 1968), p. 219. Hrabanus Maurus takes up the same gloss: Hrabanus Maurus, *Expositio in epistolam II ad Corinthios*, ed. J.-P. Migne, *PL* 112 (Paris: Migne, 1852), cols 159–246, here cols 177B–8C.
37 M. Huglo, 'D'Hélisachar à Abbon de Fleury', *Revue Bénédictine*, 104:1–2 (1994), 204–30; P.-I. Fransen, 'Le dossier patristique d'Hélisachar: le manuscrit Paris, BnF lat. 11574 et l'une de ses sources', *Revue Bénédictine*, 111:3–4 (2001), 464–82; M. Gorman, 'Paris lat. 12124 (Origen on Romans) and the Carolingian Commentary on Romans in Paris lat. 11574', *Revue Bénédictine*, 117:1 (2007), 64–128. Questioning B. Bishoff's hypothesis, Gorman doubts that the author of Paris BnF, lat. 11574 consulted Paris, BnF, lat. 12124 (the Commentary of Origen on the Romans).

a rich library: around 840 patristic extracts were woven together in this treatise.[38] His commentary on Romans brings together excerpts from Origen, Ambrosiaster and Pelagius, to name just a few. Fransen also noticed that his technique in cutting and editing his sources was particularly meticulous. It seems that the author was interested in the question of predestination: he had in his possession the *Hypomnesticon* attributed to Augustine, which included *Contra Pelagianos: Contra adamantem* and *Ex libro de praedestinatione*.[39] Shari Boodts, who is preparing an edition of the Paris lat. 11547 commentary, examined the possible involvement of its author in the Carolingian controversy over predestination, specifically by analysing the exegesis of Romans 8:28–30.[40] Her conclusion was that the author was not involved in the debate and that the Augustinian material collected in the commentary does not correspond to the positions defined there.

Nevertheless, the treatise's author had a cohesive, theological vision. In his discussion of Romans 6:4, the author approached baptism in terms of *metanoia* and as a mystery, in a similar manner to Theodulf and Claudius: to die or die together with Christ is to renounce man's previous life of crime and sin. Quoting Pelagius (identified as John), the author described conversion as a new life, in stark contrast to the life of the old man.[41] Turning to Romans 12:2, the author excerpted from Origen to advance the same popular idea of self-perfection as a precondition for understanding the divine word in Scripture. Here he echoed Claudius's statement that moral perfection fulfils the divine will; the author later elaborated on the same idea of *reformatio* as self-sacrifice and the fulfilment of the divine will with the inclusion of an excerpt from Augustine's

---

38 Huglo, 'D'Hélisachar', 464.
39 Fransen, 'Le dossier', 465.
40 S. Boodts, 'The reception of Augustine in the ninth-century Commentary on Romans (Paris, BnF, lat. 11574) with the analysis of its position in relation to the Carolingian debate on predestination', in G. Guldentops, C. Laes and G. Partoens (eds), *Felici curiositate: Studies in Latin Literature and Textual Criticism from Antiquity to the Twentieth Century in Honour of Rita Beyers* (Turnhout: Brepols, 2017), pp. 437–57.
41 Paris, BnF, lat. 11574, fol. 31v.

De civitate dei (X, 6).⁴² Drawing further on Augustine's corpus (*De perfectione iustitiae hominis*, 11) the author stated that the main actor of our *reformatio* is the Holy Spirit and not ourselves, an idea that clearly reinforced a position on predestination. The *reformatio* of the divine image was put forward clearly by the author but with different theological resonances than those found in Theodulf's interpretation: man can deform the divine image, but he cannot reform it by himself; rather, *reformatio* must be accomplished by God, who originally formed the image (*De Trinitate*, XIV, 16, 22). Even if the author was not interested in the minutiae of the particular debate on predestination, he clearly belonged to the later generation of theologians who viewed man's salvation as dependent on God.

The edition and combination of excerpts found in Paris, BnF lat. 11574 is not haphazard. It has a clear theological line on the *reformatio* of the divine image: described in terms of *epistrophe*, the *reformatio* of man's image signifies man's obedience to the divine will through the perfection of virtues, while the main agent of *reformatio* is identified as the Holy Spirit.

Haimo of Auxerre

Haimo of Auxerre, whose commentaries on Romans and Hebrews were very popular during the Middle Ages, wrote commentaries on the Pauline corpus in the period between 850 and 856. If Claudius was known for his sharp and sometimes combative language, Haimo adopts a more pedagogical style.⁴³ His commentaries nevertheless convey contemporary ideas and theological themes: debates on the soul, the question of Mary's virginal maternity, etc.⁴⁴

---

42 *Ibid.*, fols 46r–v. We find Origen's interpretation in Sedulius's Scottus commentary on Romans: Sedulius Scottus, *In epistolam ad Romanos, In epistolam ad Corinthios usque ad Hebraeos*, ed. H. J. Frede and H. Stanjek, *Collectaneum in Apostolum* (2 vols, Freiburg: Herder, 1996–7), I, pp. 264–5.
43 J. Heil, 'Haimo's commentary on Paul: sources, methods and theology', in Shimahara (ed.), *Études d'exégèse carolingienne*, pp. 103–21.
44 Cf. Boucaud, 'Claude de Turin', pp. 206–11.

Haimo's commentary also tackled current ecclesiastical affairs.[45] Commenting on Romans 6:4 ('we should walk in newness of life'), Haimo explains 'newness' in terms of life after baptism, suggesting the absence of sins and crimes. The relevance of this to the predestination controversy is clear: Haimo implied that only the 'elect' can be renewed, that is: perfect themselves through the cultivation of virtue.[46] Haimo's position on this question is made even more obvious when he explains Romans 6:6 ('our old man is crucified with him'): the old man signifies the devil or the head of all the condemned, while Christ is the head of the elect and the saints, defined here as one body.[47] When commenting on Romans 12:2 ('but be ye transformed by the renewing of your mind'), his explanation drew in part on that of Claudius: according to Haimo, *reformatio* here refers to the reading of the Sacred Scripture, for the law should be understood in the spiritual sense.[48] Haimo continued to pursue this reading of the Pauline *renovatio* as spiritual in his commentary on Ephesians 4:23 ('And be renewed in the spirit of your mind'); spirit and mind are represented here as identical entities. Interestingly, he put forward a double sense of *renovatio*: the first *renovatio*, baptism, is 'sudden' (*subitanea*) and results in the cleansing of man's sins and crimes, while the second *renovatio* extends over time and pertains to man's pursuit of moral perfection, which he delineated as consisting of one's assiduous reading of the Scripture and giving oneself up to good works. Haimo thus expounded *renovatio* in terms of *metanoia* and *epistrophe*. Haimo remained consistent in his use of terminology throughout: everyday virtuous life and the intelligence of God renew man.[49]

---

45 Cf. Heil, 'Haimo's commentary', p. 108.
46 Haimo of Auxerre, *In Divi Pauli Epistolas Expositio*, ed. J.-P. Migne, PL 117 (Paris: Migne, 1852) cols 361–936, here col. 412 C. For some other examples, see Heil, 'Haimo's commentary', pp. 111–12.
47 Haimo of Auxerre, *In Divi Pauli Epistolas Expositio*, col. 414 A.
48 Romans 12:2: 'sed reformamini in novitate sensus vestrum'; Haimo of Auxerre, *In Divi Pauli Epistolas Expositio*, cols 470 B–C: 'amissis tenebris carnalis intelligentiae ad fructum transsit spiritalis allegoriae'.
49 Haimo of Auxerre, *In Divi Pauli Epistolas Expositio*, cols 721 C–D.

Renovatio *as penance: commentaries on Hebrews*

Alcuin applied the Pauline concept of *reformatio* to the theology of penance in his commentary on the Epistle to the Hebrews, the first ever written on this Pauline text.[50] Here, Alcuin put forward the importance of *reformatio* as penance, particularly when explaining Hebrews 6:4–6 ('if they shall fall away, to renew them again unto repentance; seeing they crucify to themselves the Son of God afresh').[51] Here, Alcuin excerpted and expanded upon a section of John Chrysostom's *Homily on Hebrews* (as translated by Mutianus Scholasticus).[52] First, Alcuin stated that *renovari* means becoming new (*hoc est novum fieri*). The 'strength' (*virtus*) of the birth received in the ritual of baptism by the new man is closely linked to man's imitation of the death of Christ (Romans 6:5) in which the old man is crucified with Christ. Alcuin condensed Chrysostom's long argument against rebaptism into the assertion that there is no possibility of a new baptism; the perfection or cleansing of sins after baptism comes from the tears of penance. The theologian marked penance as the main form of spiritual *reformatio*. This formulation proved extremely popular: Claudius of Turin borrowed verbatim from Alcuin's exegesis on this verse in his commentary, as did Hrabanus Maurus and Sedulius Scottus.[53] Haimo of Auxerre likewise drew on

---

50 On this commentary, cf. R. Savigni, 'Le commentaire d'Alcuin sur l'épître aux Hébreux et le theme du sacrifice', in P. Depreux and B. Judic (eds), *Alcuin de York à Tours: Écriture, pouvoir et réseaux dans l'Europe du Haut Moyen Âge*, Annales de Bretagne et des Pays de l'Ouest, 111:3 (2004), 245–67; M. Fox, 'Alcuin's *Expositio in epistolam ad Hebraeos*', *The Journal of Medieval Latin*, 18 (2008), 326–45. On penance in the work of Alcuin, cf. M. S. Driscoll, *Alcuin, et la pénitence à l'époque carolingienne* (Münster: Aschendorff, 1999).

51 Alcuin, *Tractus super tres sancti Pauli ad Titum, ad Philemonem et ad Hebraeos Epistolas*, ed. J.-P. Migne, PL 100 (Paris: Migne, 1851), cols 1007–83, here cols 1057–8.

52 On Alcuin's use of Mutianus, see Fox, 'Alcuin's *Expositio*', 332; on the reworking of Mutianus, 334. *Mutiani Scholastici interpretatio homiliarum Joannis Chrysostomi homiliae in epistolam Hebreos*, ed. J.-P. Migne, PG 63 (Paris: Migne, 1862), cols 297–304, here cols 299–302.

53 For Claudius of Turin (in a text the edition erroneously attributes to Atto), see Atto of Vercelli, *Expositio in epistolas sancti Pauli*, ed. J.-P. Migne, PL 134 (Paris: Migne, 1853), cols 125–833, here cols 758C–9C; Hrabanus

Alcuin's commentary, though he took greater pains to distinguish between the first penance undertaken before baptism and penance undertaken thereafter, which cleanses the crimes and sins in everyday Christian life.[54] Alcuin thus clearly formulated baptism as *metanoia*, while *epistrophe* revitalised the first sense of *metanoia* as a second repentance or penance.

A connection between penance and Pauline *renovatio* was drawn in *Expositiones breves in Epistulas Pauli, Ad Romanos et Galatos et Commentatio brevis in quasdam sancti Pauli apostoli sententias*, preserved in Vienna, Österreichische Nationalbibliothek Cod. 795 (fols 148v–50v) and Munich, Bayerische Staatsbibliothek, Clm 14500 (fols 92v–4v).[55] It is interesting that penance was one of the main theological issues discussed in the catena, which precedes the commentary in both manuscripts.[56] In this commentary, which contains a doubtful attribution to Alcuin in Cod. 795, penitential ideas are connected to the themes of resurrection, for example in the hortatory verse of Ephesians 5:14 ('Wherefore he saith, Awake thou that sleepest, and arise from the dead, and Christ shall give thee

---

Maurus, *Expositio in epistolam ad Hebraeos*, ed. J.-P. Migne, *PL* 112 (Paris: Migne, 1852), cols 711–833, here lib. 27, cols 749–50; Sedulius Scottus, *In epistolam ad Romanos, In epistolam ad Corinthios usque ad Hebraeos*, II, In Hbr 6,5, p. 739.

54 Haimo of Auxerre, *In Divi Pauli Epistolas Expositio*, cols 859D–60.
55 The Vienna manuscript is of great interest as it transmits important Carolingian material from the time of Charlemagne, notably Wizo's *Dicta Candidi*, ed. Marenbon, *From the Circle of Alcuin to the School of Auxerre*, pp. 161–3. It contains a florilegium with extracts from Augustine's *De vera religione* which were subsequently used in the Augustinian florilegium prepared in Lyon for use in the debate over the cult of images. Part of this manuscript was published in an appendix to Alcuin's commentary on Hebrews: Alcuin, *Commentatio brevis in quasdam sancti Pauli sententias*, ed. J.-P. Migne, *PL* 100 (Paris: Migne, 1851), cols 1083–6. While this commentary is attributed to Alcuin in the Vienna manuscript, the Munich manuscript omits the first paragraph beginning with 'Alcuinus de hoc quod dicit apostolus'. I am not persuaded that this is one of Alcuin's genuine works.
56 According to this anonymous author, the main point of Romans 11:29 ('For the gifts and calling of God are without repentance') is that the Lord did not repent; rather, he liberated the whole world from sin: Munich, Bayerische Staatsbibliothek, Clm 14500, fols 91v; Österreichische Nationalbibliothek Cod 795, fol. 147v.

light'). The author, Paul, here speaking with the voice of the Holy Spirit, urges those 'cast in the darkness of sins' to rise up through penance and be in the presence of the divine light of grace.[57] The exegete of the commentary of Clm 14500 stumbled over the meaning of Hebrews 6:4–6, a verse easily interpreted by Alcuin; he complained that '[this portion] of text is covered up with important obscurities'.[58] The author of the commentary, more precisely its initial source, defended the idea of one baptism, i.e. that it cannot be repeated or 'renovated' as a means to cleanse the sin of infidelity. He argued that if Christ only died once for the Salvation of everybody, then likewise *renovatio* through baptism is only possible once, whereas penance can be repeated.[59]

Even though Carolingian exegetes mostly resorted to the same patristic sources, their commentaries still show their uniqueness due to the authors' particular theological positions. The process of compiling and developing these commentaries also relied on a shared base of theological concepts and these exegetical treatises reveal a coherent theological conception of Pauline *reformatio*. Carolingian authors clearly privileged the idea of *reformatio* as self-perfection, the action that I have defined as *epistrophe*. This was delineated as a personal, individual process for all Christians and placed within an eschatological perspective of one's individual salvation. This emphasis on personal *reformatio* was brought even more to the fore in the controversy on predestination.

Controversies

Carolingian theology and its methods evolved in large part through controversies. The second part of this chapter will examine several doctrinal confrontations with external opponents, namely the

---

57 Clm 14500, fol. 92v: 'His etiam dicitur qui in tenebris peccatorum iacunt immo et moriuntur qui se per penitentiam surgunt mox sibi divinae gratiae lumen adesse sentiunt'. Öster. National. Cod 795, fol. 149r.
58 Öster. National. Cod 795, fol. 150r: '[hic locus] magnis obscuritatibus obvolutus est'.
59 Clm 14500, fol. 94 r°. Öster. National. Cod 975, fol. 150r.

Spanish and Greek Churches, from three different angles.[60] First, what did the *correctio* of those deemed to be deviant constitute in practice? Second, what role did papal authority play in setting out and defending orthodoxy? Given that Rome was the main religious model for the renewal of Christian religion in the Carolingian world, we can assume that Carolingian authors would have necessarily considered Roman doctrinal authority.[61] But did *correctio* and 'the preoccupation with authority' go hand-in-hand with such 'compliance with Rome'?[62] How unified was theological argumentation in these debates, and can we detect and perceive unity among the theologians in their theological argumentation fighting for orthodoxy? Finally, can we discern any degree of consistency in the employment of patristic sources in Carolingian controversies?

Correcting heresies

Jerome's Latin translation of the Old Testament created a semantic field of *correctio* that encompassed individual spiritual perfection – a range of meaning that has been lost in modern translations of the Bible.[63] Among the church fathers, Ambrose proposed an interesting distinction between the verbs 'to correct' (*corrigere*) and

---

60 As Rosamond McKitterick remarked, '[t]he most dramatic statements of Frankish orthodox belief, however, were collective reactions to developments elsewhere': see R. McKitterick, *Charlemagne: The Formation of a European Identity* (Cambridge: Cambridge University Press, 2009), p. 311.
61 Cf. D. A. Bullough, 'Roman books and Carolingian *renovatio*', *Studies in Church History*, 14 (1977), 23–50.
62 Y. Hen, 'The Romanization of the Frankish liturgy: ideal, reality and the rhetoric of reform', in C. Bolgia et al. (eds), *Rome Across Time and Space: Cultural Transmission and the Exchange of Ideas c. 500–1400* (Cambridge: Cambridge University Press, 2011), pp. 111–23, here p. 120.
63 The terms *correctio* or *corrigere* do not appear in the Vulgate translation of the New Testament. This terminology appears most frequently in the Wisdom books. Surprisingly, the term disappears in the King James Bible translation and in the French *Bible de Jérusalem*. Take, for example, Ps 119 (118):9: 'In quo *corrigit* adolescentior viam suam? in custodiendo sermones tuos'. The King James Bible gives the following translation: 'BETH. Wherewithal shall a young man *cleanse* his way? by taking heed thereto according to thy word', while the French translation (by l'École biblique

'to emend' (*emendare*). As he argued, only God does not sin, only wise men can emend, but everyone can correct themselves through penance.[64] But it is in Augustine's extensive corpus that *correctio* occurs most frequently: according to Augustine, *conversio* ('baptism') is followed by *epistrophe* or the ongoing act of becoming Christian.[65] The dispute over free will refined Augustine's position on individual responsibility: God requires human cooperation, i.e. self-correction, for individual salvation.[66] Correspondingly – and somewhat surprisingly – the church and its bishops could admonish or excommunicate, but *correctio* remained a personal issue. The verb *corrigere* also appears in Augustine's controversies with the Donatists, Manicheans and Pelagians. Notably, Augustine does not employ *corrigere* to describe the active role of a *corrector*: it is not applied to those who correct heretics. Rather, it is used self-reflexively: Augustine invites his readers to correct themselves: 'it would be better if they correct themselves than to subvert the holy gospels'.[67]

When talking about controversies as reforming and correcting deviant beliefs we should ask if, in the case of Christian doctrine, *reformatio* and *correctio* can be undertaken and what exactly can be reformed and corrected. In his *Commonitorium*, a guide against heresies, Vincent of Lerins explains how the core of Christian doctrine should be preserved, although Christian observances would

---

de Jérusalem) is as follows: 'Comment, jeune, *garder pur* son chemin? A observer ta parole'.

64 For his discussion of corrupted human nature, see *Epistula et acta*, ed. O. Faller, *Sancti Ambrosii Opera*, CSEL 82 (Vienna: Hoelder-Pichler-Tempsky, 1968), I, Livre 1, ep. 3, 4, pp. 20, 32. *Emendare* is used the same way by Hilarius of Poitiers as well: Hilarius of Poitiers, *De trinitate*, ed. P. Smulders, CCSL 62A (Turnhout: Brepols, 1980), 10, p. 65: 'Non intellegentes docemus et nescientes arguimus et dicta Dei homines emendamus et non dignamur secundum apostolum ita credere: Quis criminabitur electos Dei?' For the terms *emendare* and *corrigere*, cf. also Barrow, 'Ideas', p. 354.

65 T. J. Van Bavel, 'Correctio, corrigere', *Augustinus-Lexikon*, I, fasc. 5/6 (Bâle: Schwabe, 1992), cols 22–7.

66 For example, see *ibid.*, col. 25.

67 *Contra donatistas*, 14, quoted in Van Bavel, 'Correctio', col. 24: 'Melius se ipsos corrigent quam evangelia sancta peruertunt'.

of course develop following the laws of progress.[68] This question appears in some Carolingian controversies. The rule of faith (*regula fidei*), as identified in Carolingian theological writing, defines the heart of Christian teaching, that is to say, it delineates what is irrefutable and cannot be changed, for it expresses the truth itself.[69] It encapsulates the most authentic teaching of apostles received from Christ, transmitted in scripture; notably, it preceded any heretical teaching. The rule of faith thus transmits scripture, catechetical teaching and creed. For Carolingian authors, the creeds encapsulated the rule of faith perfectly and therefore expressed the core of orthodoxy. Accordingly, Theodulf denounced and corrected the Greek creeds pronounced during the iconophile Second Council of Nicea in the name of Charlemagne.[70]

A distinction should be drawn between the 'rule of faith' and local customs of cultic observance.[71] Ladner pointed out the example of Tertullian, who contrasted 'custom' and 'progress'.[72] As Tertullian wrote, the rule of faith cannot be reformed, but ecclesiastical discipline and ways of life admit the 'novelties of *correctio*'.[73]

---

68 Vincent, *Commonitorium*, ed. R. Demeulenaere, CCSL 64 (Turnhout: Brepols, 1985), XXIII:8, p. 178; trans. C. A. Heurtley, *Select Library of Nicene and Post-Nicene Fathers of the Christian Church*, Second series 11 (Oxford: James Parker, 1894), p. 148: 'it behoves Christian doctrine to follow the same laws of progress, so as to be consolidated by years, enlarged by time, refined by age, and yet, withal, to continue uncorrupt and unadulterate, complete and perfect in all measurement of its parts, and, so to speak, in all its proper members and senses, admitting no change, no waste of its distinctive property, no variation in its limits'.
69 D. Van Eyden, *Les norms de l'enseignement chrétien dans la littérature patristique des trois premiers siècles* (Paris: Gabalda & Fils, 1933), p. 312; R. Braun, *Deus christianorum: Recherches sur le vocabulaire doctrinal de Tertullien* (Paris: Presses universitaires de France, 1962), pp. 447–8; Y. M. Congar, *Tradition and Traditions: An Historical and a Theological Essay*, trans. by M. Naseby (London: Burns & Oats, 1963), pp. 26–30.
70 Cf. the first eight chapters of book three: Theodulf of Orleans, *Opus Caroli regis contra synodum*, ed. Freeman, III:1–8, pp. 336–71.
71 Congar, *Tradition*, pp. 28–9.
72 Ladner, *The Idea of Reform*, pp. 137–8.
73 Tertullian, *De virginibus velandis*, ed. E. Dekkers, *Tertullianus: Opera II, Opera Monastica*, CCSL 2 (Turnhout: Brepols, 1954), I:3–7, p. 1209, quoted in Ladner, *The Idea of Reform*, p. 137: 'novitas correctionis'.

This distinction is clearly stated by Hadrian I in his letter that was read at the Council of Frankfurt in 794. According to the pope, Charlemagne's action against Spanish teaching betrayed his eagerness to renew his royal or his canonical custom: 'it seemed right to him to renew royal or canonical regulation'.[74] In his refutation of Elipandus read at the same council, Alcuin draws on Hadrian's idea of *renovatio*, albeit with different phrasing: as he writes, Charlemagne summoned the council in order to 'renew the condition' of the peaceful and harmonious church and to preach the truth of the orthodox faith, which in itself does not allow any enlargement or diminishment and should stay one for all Christians: 'there is nothing to be increased or diminished in it which should be one for all Christians'.[75]

While customs can undergo *renovatio*, no novelties may be introduced to the faith.[76] Novelty is one of the main charges brought against accused heretics and deviants. The *Opus Caroli regis* denounces the decisions of the Second Nicaean Council as new regulations imposed on the Church. They are no more and no less than schism, a spot on the bride of Christ.[77] It is important to remember that this treatise was written in the name of Charlemagne and that the Frankish king was eager to correct what he considered to deviate from the orthodox faith. Yet Theodulf did not urge the Greeks, whom he criticised very harshly, to correct themselves; he did not exhort them to reform their society, which was, in his view, tangled up in dubious, hardly Christian habits concerning material images. Somewhat strangely, the vocabulary of emendation (*emendatio*) features here in a negative light: the patriarch Tarasios

---

74 A. Werminghoff (ed.), *MGH Conc.* 2.1 (Hanover: Hahn, 1906), no. 19, p. 122: 'regiam scilicet vel canonicam placuit ei consuetudinem renovare'. The same idea of 'correcting of customs' is found in the 615 Council of Paris and in the Fourth Council of Toledo (633) quoted by Barrow, 'Ideas', p. 355.

75 *MGH Conc.* 2.1, no. 19, p. 143: 'ad renovandum statum'; 'cui nihil augeri potest vel minui, quae una decet esse omnium Christianorum'.

76 See also Barrow, 'Ideas', p. 347.

77 Theodulf of Orleans, *Opus Caroli regis contra synodum*, ed. Freeman, *praefatio*, p. 101: 'novas et insolitas ecclesiae nituntur inferre constitutiones, quibus ei maculam potius quam decorem adscribant'.

emends (*emendare*) the forbidden custom by introducing another proscribed one.[78]

Alcuin likewise condemned the introduction of new titles for Christ. In his letter read at the council, Charlemagne questioned new Spanish additions, never heard before in the ancient times of the universal church.[79] In the anti-adoptionist controversy with Felix of Urgel, Alcuin frequently reproached his opponent for bringing novelties and innovations into the Catholic church.[80]

An important question is, quite simply, who was correcting whom? Carolingians, with one exception which I will return to shortly, often used *correctio* in the Augustinian sense: a deviant and/or heretic was invited to correct himself.[81] In the Council of Frankfurt, Charlemagne employed *correctio* as a hope: 'Your *correctio* is our joy; for we hope you would join us as the allies in the Christian faith and co-workers in preaching the truth'.[82] Alcuin, by contrast, assumed the role of the one who corrects: in his treatise *Adversus Felicem libri VII*, he clearly stated his wish to correct Felix in the name of the Christian charity.[83] Nevertheless, in the same

---

78 *Ibid.*, III:1, pp. 341–2: 'qui [Tarasius] per rem penitus interdictam et nullatenus proficientem nititur emendare rem penitus interdictam et prorsus officientem'. The same remark concerns the only appearance of *correctio* in III:31, p. 483: 'nihil in eo correctionis exhibuit, sed ei deteriorem peccandi viam ostendit'. For Theodulf, *corrigere* is a matter of individual will, as in I:9, p. 154: 'errorem suum corrigere nolunt'.
79 *MGH Conc.* 2.1, no. 19, p. 159: 'novae adsertiones'.
80 Alcuin, *Adversus Felicem*, ed. J.-P. Migne, *PL* 101 (Paris: Migne, 1851), cols 126–230, here cols 131A; 133B: 'non nova fingentes nomina', 'Nolite novas versare questiunculas'; lib. II, col. 152B: 'novi doctores'. See also *MGH Conc.* 2.1, no. 19, p. 156.
81 This conception of *correctio* is endorsed by the Council of Paris (829), in which priests are exhorted to encourage the others to correct themselves (*se corrigere*) and to convert and to turn their hearts to God (chapter V). *Correctio* is thus understood to constitute spiritual, inward and personal movement. See A. Werminghoff (ed.), *MGH Conc.* 2.2 (Hanover: Hahn, 1908), no. 50, c. 5, p. 612: 'De periculo, quod sacerdotibus imminent, et quod unusquisque in suis parroechiis suis populis specialiter denuntient, ut se corrigant et ad Deum ex toto corde convertant'.
82 *MGH Conc.* 2.1, no. 19, p. 159.
83 Alcuin, *Adversus Felicem*, col. 127D: 'Scripsi epistolam pridem Felici … cupiens eum corrigere in Christi dilectione'.

treatise, he used also *correctio* as an invitation to Felix to correct himself. He summoned him to correct his erroneous sentence and to 'convert' himself to the unity of the Apostolic doctrine.[84] In this case, it seems that *correctio* acquired the meaning of *metanoia*.[85]

Correctio *and the question of authority and orthodoxy*

During Charlemagne's reign, Carolingians only rarely appealed to papal authority in doctrinal controversies. The exceptions relate to particular political expediencies: sometimes Carolingian authors were compelled to invoke papal authority, while at other points popes were criticised for their failure to correct deviant teaching; sometimes the controversy confronted the pope himself, for example in the debate over images or over *filioque*.[86] In the *Colloquium* or Synod of Paris (825) the bishops bitterly criticised Hadrian I who, according to them, failed to exercise his highest authority insofar as he did not correct the decisions of the Second Council of Nicaea which established the cult of images: 'he who is provided with the highest authority should correct those who took a wrong turn'.[87] According to the bishops, the failure of the pope opened up an opportunity for Louis the Pious to become a key agent in restoring the orthodox faith and the unity of the Church.[88]

---

84 *Ibid.*, II:3, col. 148C.
85 *Correctio* was equated to *conversio* in similar terms in the Council of Reisbach, Freiburg and Salzburg. *MGH Conc.* 2.1, no. 24, p. 209: 'Ut, si quis sacerdotum contra statuta decretalia praesumptiose agit et *converti nolens*, ab officio suo moveatur' (emphasis added).
86 Theodulf was forced to insert a chapter on Roman authority after the Carolingians failed to convince the pope on the question of images. Alcuin, meanwhile, asserted the superiority of the Roman Church over other sees (Alcuin, *Adversus Felicem*, col. 133A), but this reference most likely relates to the pope's recent condemnation of Felix's teaching: see J. J. Cavadini, *The Last Christology of the West* (Philadelphia, PA: University of Pennsylvania Press: 1993), pp. 89–90. Nevertheless, and perhaps surprisingly, Alcuin does not give any priority to the papal theological argumentation.
87 *MGH Conc.* 2.2, no. 44, p. 482: 'qui summa auctoritate praediti deuiantes quosque debuerant corrigere'. I am currently in the process of preparing a new edition and study of the proceedings of this council.
88 *Ibid.*

During Charlemagne's reign, the apostolic faith was regarded as the most authentic Christian teaching. In his letter read during the Council of Frankfurt, Alcuin established the chain of tradition as follows: patriarchs, prophets, apostles and finally their holy interpreters.[89] Apostles thus acquired a special authority, and Alcuin referred to them often: he regarded apostolic teaching as the nucleus of the faith, while the church fathers acted as its faithful interpreters.[90] Alcuin included particularly extensive quotations from the Pauline epistles as 'apostolic testimony' in his letter to the Frankish bishops.[91]

Alcuin appears to have held a somewhat ambiguous attitude towards papal authority: for example, he depicts Gregory the Great as a 'pontiff of the Holy See', but also as 'the most glorious doctor in the whole world', suggesting that Gregory's authority rested not on his position as pope, but rather on his status as a 'doctor of the church'.[92] Hadrian's letter to Elipandus, which was clearly read aloud during the proceedings at Frankfurt, was never referred to as an authoritative text by any Carolingian author – not even by Alcuin, who drew heavily on its theological argumentation. In his letter to Spanish bishops, Hadrian had used quotations from Matthew 3:13, 16–17, 19; these were marshalled to support the authority of Peter, the 'first shepherd of the Church', to buttress papal authority, and to argue that Rome constituted the foundation of the faith.[93] Alcuin, meanwhile, stripped the verses of their papal connotation and included them in a cluster of quotations from the Gospel; he presented his arguments in terms of apostolic, not papal, authority.[94]

---

89 *MGH Conc.* 2.1, no. 19, p. 154.
90 *Ibid.*, no. 19, p. 154: 'iuxta praecedentia apostolorum testimonia et sanctorum doctorum dogmata'.
91 Colossians 1, 12–19, see also *MGH Conc.* 2.1, no. 19, p. 146. Hebrews 1, 1–6; see also *MGH Conc.* 2.1, no. 19, p. 148.
92 *MGH Conc.* 2.1, no. 19, p. 148: 'pontifex Romanae sedis'; 'clarissimus doctor toto orbe doctor'.
93 *Ibid.*, no. 19, p. 124.
94 *Ibid.*, no. 19, p. 155; Alcuin, *Adversus Felicem*, lib. I, cols 138 and 143.

Alcuin's letter to the Council of Frankfurt and his treatise against Felix, produced for the Council of Friuli, bear constructive comparison to the writings of Paulinus of Aquilea. While Paulinus was exclusively interested in the theological aspects of the dispute, Alcuin, by contrast, emphasised its ideological resonances. By distancing himself from papal authority, he affirmed the apostolic church and its faith as the most authentic tradition, sufficient in and of itself to resist all heresies. Alcuin thus rejected any submission to Rome as a doctrinal authority and affirmed the Frankish church as an independent and equal member of the Christian ecumenical church. In his *Adversus Felicem libri VII*, the highest authority remains the apostles. At the end of his treatise, Alcuin unexpectedly claimed that he followed Roman and not Spanish authority; he even singled out the Roman popes as a potential source of opposition to the Spanish church.[95] Nevertheless, Alcuin is only making a comparative point here: Roman authority is to be preferred over Spanish authority. Overall, and in stark contrast to the view from Rome, Alcuin places these disputes in the context of the universal church; his counterarguments are scattered with references to authorities from different Christian Sees such as Alexandria, Constantinople, etc.[96] Alcuin thus affirmed the authority of the universal church as a whole; Rome was simply a part of it.

Filioque *and divergent discourses on the universal church*

The *filioque* controversy marked a transitional period in Carolingian ideas of the universal church. According to Harald Willjung, the editor of the treatises and proceedings of the Council of Aachen, Arn of Salzburg's treatise, transmitted in Laon, BM, man. 122bis,

---

95 Alcuin, *Adversus Felicem libri VII*, lib. 7, XIII, 226C and XIV, 227C.
96 Alcuin, *Adversus Felicem libri VII*, mentions Eastern councils ('Legimus namque Orientales synodos', lib. 1, V, 131B) as well as Western councils ('Simel et occidentales synodos', lib. 1, V, 131B); he cites Proclus, bishop of Constantinople (lib. II, 6, col. 151B); 'Cyrillus episcopus Alexandriae' (lib. IV, 3, col. 175A); and 'Petrus quoque Ravennensis episcopus' (lib. 2, IV, col. 177A).

served as a prototype for the proceedings of the Council of Aachen (809) which defended the famous *filioque* clause.[97] Arn's work, the *Testimonia ex sacris volumnibus collecta*, was a highly sophisticated treatise. Its title announced its two main theological themes: first, the Holy Spirit was sent and proceeded from two divine persons, and second, it is called the spirit of the Father and of the Son.[98] Arn dedicated his treatise to Charlemagne, and its preface was written as praise of the emperor: Charlemagne is depicted here spreading the Christian cult and condemning heresies, and is further acclaimed as one of the greatest admonishers (*admonitores*) of the Universal Church.[99] Yet Arn does not press this point: notably, the emperor does not appear as a main actor in the universal church or as a reformer of ecclesiastical customs. As far as the treatise is concerned, Arn wrote an original systematic theological treatise on the doctrine of the Holy Spirit: he invented his own highly sophisticated method of using authority.[100]

Arn was reaching for what I might term ecumenical language, a means of expressing the unity of the Church. His attempt was founded on his own original use of 'authorities' (*auctoritates*): he identified the evangelists as authorities and justified his designation of Church Fathers as authorities by quoting the list provided in the Council of Constantinople: 'We are following in every matter [of the faith] the Holy Fathers and Doctors of the Holy Church of God, i.e. Athanasius, Hilary of Poitiers, Basil, Gregory the Theologian and Gregory of Nazianzus, Ambrose, Theophilius, etc.'.[101] He further invoked Pope Gelasius, i.e. Pseudo-Gelasius, and his list 'On the Books that should not be accepted in the Church' (*libris qui non*

---

97 H. Willjung (ed.), *MGH Conc.* 2, Supplementum 2 (Hanover: Hahn, 1998), pp. 43–7. On this controversy, cf. P. Gemeinhardt, *Die Filioque-Kontroverse zwischen Ost- und Westkirche im Frühmittelalter* (Berlin, New York: Walter de Gruyter, 2002), pp. 140–64.
98 *MGH Conc.* 2, Supplementum 2, p. 254.
99 *Ibid.*, pp. 253–4.
100 I will deal with this question in a separate article.
101 *MGH Conc.* 2, Supplementum 2, VIII.24, p. 267: 'Sequimur autem in omnibus sanctos patres et doctores sanctae dei ecclesiae, id est Athanasium, Hilarium, Basilium, Gregorium theologum et Gregorium Nazanzenum, Ambrosium, Theophilum'.

sunt in ecclesia recipiendi).[102] Through his explicit reference to the authority of the Council of Constantinople, Arn not only sought to underscore the relevance of the controversy to the universal church, but also to convince his Greek adversaries that the authorities which they accepted in Constantinople supported the use of the *filioque* clause. But why, then, did he include 'Pope Gelasius'? One could argue that he sought to promote papal authority, but I would propose an alternative explanation – namely, that Arn included Gelasius in anticipation of the Carolingians' eventual confrontation with Pope Leo III and his anti-*filioque* position.[103] Arn's deployment of 'Pope Gelasius' as one of his 'canonical authors' (*probati auctores*) thus attempted to forestall Leo III's assertion of his own papal authority.

Arn's treatise was used as a draft for writing the decretal of the Council of Aachen. He is unlikely to have participated in the final preparation and editing of this official document, as many of his arguments were entirely transformed.[104] The chapter claiming the authority of Gelasius disappeared; Gennadius and Boethius and their respective works are no longer claimed as authorities. The final decretal preserves the original subdivision of the chapters as conceived by Arn: its writer followed the chronological order and logic of the councils. Arn's emphasis on ecumenical Christianity, by contrast, was lost.

Theodulf also wrote a treatise on the *filioque*, the *Libellus de processione spiritus sancti*.[105] In contrast to Arn's approach, Theodulf's strategy was purely theological: he notably did not try to defend *filioque* within the framework of the universal church. Unlike Arn, Theodulf did not construct his arguments around biblical quotations, and Gelasius was not mentioned in this treatise, despite the fact that Theodulf had previously appealed to 'Pope Gelasius's'

---

102 *Ibid.*, VIII.25, pp. 267–8.
103 Arn constructed his treatise's arguments with reference to canon law, here notably the other canon collections in the manuscript of Laon.
104 Willjung believed that the Aachen decretal was edited during the council: *MGH Conc.* 2, Supplementum 2, p. 90.
105 For a different interpretation of Theodulf's treatise, cf. Gemeinhardt, *Die Filioque-Kontroverse*, pp. 153–7.

authority in his *Opus Caroli regis*.¹⁰⁶ Instead, Theodulf constructed a systematic theological treatise on the Holy Spirit. In his theological compendium, his arguments followed the historical development of the orthodox faith and not the hierarchy of authorities. Theodulf started clearly with the highest authority, i.e. the credo of Athanasius and Cyrillus, and then moved to Hilary of Poitiers, Ambrose, Didymus, etc. The authority order is thus chronological and the popes were no exception: he quoted from Popes Hormisdas, Leo I and Gregory I, i.e. he ranked them only in the eighth, ninth and tenth positions. His quotations are lengthy, and his theological thought is both intricate and sophisticated.

Significantly, Theodulf's use of some of these patristic excerpts finds a parallel in the writings of Adalwin and Smaragdus. It would be difficult, nevertheless, to prove that either Adalwin or Smaragdus were directly influenced by the bishop of Orléans in their ecclesiological and theological thinking; in fact, they make substantially different use of the excerpts. For example, while Theodulf and Adalwin both quoted the Pseudo-Augustinian *Altercatio cum Pascentio Ariano*, Theodulf was interested in the concept of *homousion* and the unity of the substance in the Trinity, while Adalwin used the excerpt to prove the common activity of the three Persons of the Trinity that proves their consubstantiality and gave a biblical example from Genesis 1:18.¹⁰⁷

What do these controversial writings on the Holy Spirit have in common and do they reveal any trace of *reformatio* as such? It appears that there was no attempt to establish a theological unity, and hence to reform, improve or correct Carolingian theological thought: the method of 'chaining together' quotations shows the surprising originality of Carolingian authors' theological reasoning of every author, even in the cases where they made use of the same patristic excerpts. Carolingian authors' defence of orthodoxy was overwhelmingly *dis*unified.

---

106 Theodulf of Orleans, *Opus Caroli regis contra synodum*, ed. Freeman, I:6, II:13, and IV:10, pp. 132, 261 and 511.
107 Theodulf of Orleans, *Libellus de processione spiritus sancti*, ed. H. Willjung, *MGH Conc.* 2 Supplementum 2 (Hanover: Hahn, 1998), pp. 315–82, c. 30, p. 354; *MGH Conc.* 2, Supplementum 2, c. 12, p. 402.

Willjung assumed that the preparation leading up to the Council of Aachen involved some level of cooperation between theologians: it is highly probable that some level of prior consultation was set up in order to establish the main ecclesiastical arguments. For example, both Arn and Theodulf, and afterwards other theologians, employed Cyril of Alexandria's letter to Nestorius, which was quoted in the Council of Ephesus.[108] Yet they used different translations of the proceedings of the council, different practices of excerption, and – perhaps unsurprisingly – reached radically different conclusions. There was no attempt to use one approved or 'correct' Latin translation of the ecumenical council and, as a result, participants used different doctrinal terminology (e.g. *substantia* versus *subsistentia*) at various important points in the debate.[109]

Aggiornamento of the ecclesiological discourse

There was no one definitively established and uncontested ecclesiological discourse. In his treatise, Arn followed a unitarian ecclesiology along the lines set forth by Theodulf in his *Opus Caroli regis* (the unity of the faith means the purity of the divine cult that precludes idolatry). This discussion of unity in these tracts overlaps with the ideological discourse of empire and the conversion of the pagans by the emperor. Arn's concept of universality was marshalled to support his orthodoxy in spite of the ongoing disagreement with the pope – here paralleling Alcuin's earlier line of argumentation.

---

108 *MGH Conc.* 2, Supplementum 2, VII:16, p. 262; compare to *MGH Conc.* 2, Supplementum 2, cc. 4, 10, pp. 238, 241. Chapter 10 quotes Cyril, *Epistola*, ed. E. Schwartz, *Concilium universale Ephesenum* (Berlin: de Gruyter, 1925–26), I.2, p. 50; Theodulf of Orleans, *Libellus de processione*, 8, p. 335 (quoting the same letter but translated by Dionysius Exiguus, in Schwarz (ed.), *Concilium universale Ephesenum*, pp. 241–2).

109 Theodulf's version does include *substantia* (p. 335), as does that of Smaragdus of St Mihiel (*Epistula de processione spiritus sancti*, 22, in *MGH Conc.* 2, Supplementum 2, p. 310), who drew on Theodulf; Arn, meanwhile, uses *subsistentia* (*MGH Conc.* 2, Supplementum 2, p. 262), the same form that occurs in the 809 conciliar decretal, in *MGH Conc.* 2 Supplementum 2, pp. 237–49.

Arn's conception of the universal Church soon fell out of favour. When the issue was raised again in the anti-Photian controversy in 861, Carolingian ecclesiastical discourse was radically different.[110] Ratramnus of Corbie, who probably read Arn's treatise, chose to entirely exclude emperors from discussions of dogma in order to argue against the involvement of the Byzantine Emperor Michael III.[111] Here, Ratramnus turned to the biblical example of the king Uzziah who burned incense on the altar in the Temple of the Lord and was punished with leprosy (II Chronicles 26). Ratramnus asserted that the Eastern church and the Western church remained in the same faith according to apostolic teaching: 'one faith, one baptism'.[112] He compared the heresies which erupt on the body of the Church to the malevolent fish that damaged the fisherman's net, while the shirt of Christ remained untouched. Ratramnus likewise placed weight upon Ephesians 4:5. According to him, the unity of the church means the orthodox faith is summarised by the apostolic creed and thus the creed itself cannot be changed; by contrast, diverse religious customs were already present in apostolic times in the first community established in Jerusalem.[113] Ratramnus was one of the first Carolingian theologians who defended different customs and habits practised in the Christian ecumenical church.[114] In the fourth book of his treatise, he included examples of different rites concerning fasting, baptism and the celebration of Easter. According to Ratramnus, these differences in religious customs were approved by the apostles and recorded in church histories by Eusebius and Socrates. He thus sought to refute all the accusations levied by his Greek opponents – for instance, regarding the custom of wearing a beard – by distinguishing between 'the authority of its own church'

---

110 Cf. Gemeinhardt, *Die Filioque-Kontroverse*, p. 168ff.
111 Ratramnus of Corbie, *Contra Graecorum opposite libri quatuor*, ed. J.-P. Migne, *PL* 121 (Paris: Migne, 1852), cols 223–346, here col. 228A: 'De sacris dogmatibus, de ecclesiastico ritu, non imperatorum, sed episcoporum fuerat disputare'.
112 *Ibid.*, 'una fides, unum baptisma'.
113 *Ibid.*, IV:1, col. 303C–305A.
114 Cf. Els Rose and Arthur Westwell's contribution to this volume in Chapter 4, which discusses Amalarius's defence of different rituals and liturgical customs.

and 'the authority of the divine law'.[115] Ratramnus's argumentation may be characterised as one of 'diversity within unity' insofar as he defended local church customs.

Never stopping *correctio*

Ecclesia semper reformanda est ('The church always must be reformed'), a famous adage among theologians, can be applied to the Carolingians as well.[116] The Carolingian discourse of reform was usually invoked when the unity of the church was a matter of pressing concern. Over the course of the Carolingian period, we can observe the clear evolution of their interpretation of one faith (*una fides*): from the unity that is conceived within the framework of the Christian ecumenical church to the consciousness of protecting the unity of the church, which meant, in the case of Ratramanus, defending the Latin church, of which the Roman church was an integral part. The theology of unitarian ecclesiological discourse thus shifted radically and quickly: it was more an aggiornamento to the political agenda and issues than a *reformatio*.

Some cases of the treatises of controversy reveal to us a peculiar phenomenon which entailed the *correctio* of the correctors. To put it another way, the correctors of the deviant faith were themselves corrected. This was the case with both Theodulf's *Opus Caroli regis* and Arn's pneumatological treatise, both of which were corrected by anonymous readers and censors who represented the highest

---

115 Ratramnus of Corbie, *Contra Graecorum opposite libri quatuor*, IV, 7, col. 332A–B: 'ecclesiae suae auctoritas'; 'divinae legis auctoritas'.
116 In his *Homily*, pronounced on 28 November 2020 in the Consistory for the creation of new cardinals, Pope Francis once again evoked the idea of 'conversion'. In contrast to Pope John Paul II, Francis did not use the term of *metanoia*, but the idea of 'reforming' or 'changing' was clearly implied: 'We too, Pope and Cardinals, must always see ourselves reflected in this word of truth. It is a sharpened sword; it cuts, it proves painful, but it also heals, liberates and converts us. For conversion means precisely this: that we pass from being *off the road* to journeying *on God's road*' (emphasis added).

authority of the court.[117] Unfortunately, these 'correctors of correctors' were less versed theologians than Theodulf and Arn, and their corrections correspondingly fail to grasp the original character of these treatises.

The theology of *reformatio* was deeply rooted in Carolingian conceptions of human nature. The exegesis on Genesis and on the Pauline Letters reveals constant and coherent views – the same ideas were expressed over and over again creating a preponderant religious ethics – on conversion to the Christian religion and becoming Christian defined as *reformatio* and *renovatio*. On the other side, there was no regularity or coherence in using the ideas of *correctio*, especially in the treatises of controversy or on an institutional level; on the contrary, it revealed a perfect diversity. The discourse of *correctio* was flexible, quickly changing and adaptable to the ecclesiastical circumstances, and in this way can be constructively compared to what John XXIII called *aggiornamento* of the church.

---

117 The second book of this treatise underwent substantial changes to the point that we can no longer reconstruct Theodulf's thought. On this point, see also Chapter 5 for Irene van Renswoude's contribution to this volume.

Bibliography

Manuscripts

Berlin, Staatsbibliothek zu Berlin Preussischer Kulturbesitz, Diez B Santen 66
Bern, Burgerbibliothek AA.90.11
Bern, Burgerbibliothek 289
Budapest, Széchényi National-Bibliothek cod. lat. 316
Erfurt, Forschungsbibliothek Gotha, Memb. I 84
Florence, Biblioteca Medicea Laurenziana Libri 29
Leiden, Bibliotheek der Rijksuniversiteit, BPL 81
Leiden, Bibliotheek der Rijksuniversiteit, Voss. Lat. F. 94
Köln, Erzbischöfliche Diözesan- und Dombibliothek Cod. 200
Merseburg, Bibliothek des Domstifts 58
Munich, Bayersche Staatsbibliothek, Clm 6407
Munich, Bayerische Staatsbibliothek Clm 13084
Munich, Bayerische Staatsbibliothek Clm 13984
Munich, Bayersche Staatsbibliothek, Clm 14500
Munich, Bayerische Staatsbibliothek Clm 14727
Naples, Biblioteca Nazionale IV.A.34
Orléans, Bibliothèque Municipale 94
Oxford, Bodleian Library Junius 25
Paris, Bibliothèque Nationale de France lat. 2392
Paris, Bibliothèque Nationale de France lat. 2445
Paris, Bibliothèque Nationale de France lat. 2796
Paris, Bibliothèque Nationale de France lat. 3832
Paris, Bibliothèque Nationale de France lat. 4281
Paris, Bibliothèque Nationale de France lat. 7530
Paris, Bibliothèque Nationale de France lat. 9490
Paris, Bibliothèque Nationale de France lat. 9575
Paris, Bibliothèque Nationale de France lat. 11574

Paris, Bibliothèque Nationale de France lat. 12124
Paris, Bibliothèque Nationale de France lat. 12289
Paris, Bibliothèque Nationale de France lat. 13246
Paris, Bibliothèque Nationale de France lat. 13377
Paris, Bibliothèque Nationale de France lat. 13386
Paris, Bibliothèque Nationale de France lat. 15679
Paris, Bibliothèque Nationale de France NAL 329
Rome, Biblioteca Nazionala Vittorio Emmanuele lat. 2096
Sankt Gallen, Stiftsbibliothek 40
Sankt Gallen, Stiftsbibliothek 249
Sankt Gallen, Stiftsbibliothek 268
Sankt Gallen, Stiftsbibliothek 446
Sankt Gallen, Stiftsbibliothek 878
Sankt Gallen, Stiftsbibliothek 903
Valenciennes, Bibliothèque Municipale 404
Vatican, Biblioteca Apostolica Vaticana Pagès 1
Vatican, Biblioteca Apostolica Vaticana pal. lat. 555
Vatican, Biblioteca Apostolica Vaticana pal. lat. 930
Vatican, Biblioteca Apostolica Vaticana reg. lat. 91
Vatican, Biblioteca Apostolica Vaticana reg. lat. 317
Vatican, Biblioteca Apostolica Vaticana reg. lat. 423
Vatican, Biblioteca Apostolica Vaticana reg. lat. 1209
Vatican, Biblioteca Apostolica Vaticana reg. lat. 1703
Vatican, Biblioteca Apostolica Vaticana vat.lat. 3850
Vatican, Biblioteca Apostolica Vaticana vat.lat. 5775
Vatican, Biblioteca Apostolica Vaticana vat.lat. 11506
Verona, Biblioteca Capitolare LXXXII.
Vienna, Österreichische Nationalbibliothek 795
Wolfenbüttel, Herzog August Bibliothek, 35 Weissenburg
Wolfenbüttel, Herzog August Bibliothek, 45 Weissenburg
Wolfenbüttel, Herzog August Bibliothek, 50 Weissenburg
Wolfenbüttel, Herzog August Bibliothek, 60 Weissenburg
Wolfenbüttel, Herzog August Bibliothek, 62 Weissenburg
Wolfenbüttel, Herzog August Bibliothek, 77 Weissenburg
Zürich, Zentralbibliothek Car. C. 102

Primary sources

Admonitio Generalis, ed. and trans. H. Mordek et al., *Die Admonitio Generalis Karls des Grossen*, MGH Fontes iuris 16 (Hanover: Hahn, 2012).

Bibliography 243

Ado, *Chronicon*, ed. G. Pertz, *MGH SS* 2 (Hanover: Hahn, 1829).
Agobard of Lyon, *De antiphonario*, ed. L. Van Acker, *Agobardi Lugdunensis, Opera omnia*, CCCM 52 (Turnhout: Brepols, 1981).
Alcuin, *Adversus Felicem*, ed. J.-P. Migne, *PL* 101 (Paris: Migne, 1851), cols 127–230.
Alcuin, *Commentarii in sancti Iohannis Evangelium*, ed. J.-P. Migne, *PL* 100 (Paris: Migne, 1851), cols 733–1007.
Alcuin, *Commentatio brevis in quasdam sancti Pauli sententias*, ed. J.-P. Migne, *PL* 100 (Paris: Migne, 1851) cols 1083–6.
Alcuin, *De orthographia*, ed. S. Bruni (Florence: Sismel, 1997).
Alcuin, *De rhetorica*, ed. A. Costrino, 'Alcuin's *Disputatio de rhetorica*. A critical edition with studies of aspects of the text, the stemma codicum, the didactic diagrams and a reinterpretation of sources for the problem of the duality of the dialogue' (unpublished PhD dissertation, University of York, 2016).
Alcuin, *Epistolae*, ed. E. Dümmler, *MGH Epp.* 4 (Berlin: Weidmann, 1895).
Alcuin, *Excerptiones super Priscianum*, ed. L. Holtz and A. Grondeux, CCCM 304 (Turnhout: Brepols, 2020).
Alcuin, *Interrogationes et responsiones in Genesin*, ed. J.-P. Migne, *PL* 100 (Paris: Migne, 1851), cols 515–69.
Alcuin, *Opera didascalica*, ed. J.-P. Migne, *PL* 101 (Paris: Migne, 1851), cols 847–1002; excerpts trans. R. Copeland, and I. Sluiter, *Medieval Grammar and Rhetoric: Language, Arts and Literary Theory, AD 300–1475* (Oxford: Oxford University Press, 2012), pp. 272–98.
Alcuin, *Tractus super tres sancti Pauli ad Titum, ad Philemonem et ad Hebraeos Epistolas*, ed. J.-P. Migne, PL 100 (Paris: Migne, 1851), cols 1007–83.
Amalarius of Metz, *Opera liturgica omnia*, ed. J.-M. Hanssens (3 vols, Vatican City: Biblioteca Apostolica Vaticana, 1948–50).
Amalarius of Metz, *Epistula ad Petrum abbatem Nonatulanum*, ed. J.-M. Hanssens, *Amalarii episcopi opera liturgica omnia*, Studi e Testi 138 (Vatican City: Biblioteca apostolica vaticana, 1948) I, pp. 227–31.
Amalarius of Metz, *Liber officialis*, ed. J.-M. Hanssens, *Amalarii episcopi opera liturgica omnia*, vol. II, Studi e Testi 139 (Vatican City: Biblioteca apostolica vaticana, 1949); ed. and trans. E. Knibbs (2 vols, Cambridge, MA: Harvard University Press, 2014).
Ambrose of Milan, *Epistula et acta*, ed. O. Faller *Sancti Ambrosii Opera CSEL*, 82, 1 Vatican City: Hoelder-Pichler-Tempsky, 1968).
Ambrosiaster, *Commentarius in epistulas Paulinas*, ed. H. K. Vogels, *CSEL* 81 (Prague: Hölder-Pichler-Tempsky, 1968).
Angelomus, *Commentarius in Genesin*, ed. J.-P. Migne, *PL* 115 (Paris: Migne, 1852), cols 107–243.

Annales Laureshamenses, ed. G. H. Pertz, *MGH SS* 1 (Hanover: Hahn, 1826), pp. 22–39.

Annales regni Francorum, ed. F. Kurze, *MGH SRG* 6 (Hanover: Hahn, 1895); trans. B. Scholz, *Carolingian Chronicles* (Ann Arbor, MI: University of Michigan Press, 1970), pp. 35–127.

Ardo, *Vita Benedicti Anianensis*, ed. W. Kettemann, 'Subsidia Anianensia: Überlieferungs- und textgeschichtliche Untersuchungen zur Geschichte Witiza-Benedikts, seines Klosters Aniane und zur sogenannten "anianischen Reform"' (unpublished PhD dissertation, Gerhard-Mercator-Universität – Gesamthochschule Duisburg, 2000), pp. 139–223; trans. A. Cabaniss, *The Emperor's Monk: Contemporary Life of Benedict of Aniane by Ardo* (Ilfracombe: A. H. Stockwell, 1979).

Attone di Vercelli, Polipticum quod appellatur Perpendiculum. Edizione critica, traduzione e commento, ed. G. Vignodelli (Florence: Sismel, 2019).

Augustine, *De doctrina Christiana*, ed. and trans. R. P. H. Green (Oxford: Oxford University Press, 1995).

Augustine, *De Genesi ad litteram*, ed. I. Zycha, *Sancti Aureli Augustini*, CSEL 28 (Prague: Tempsky, 1894).

Barney, S. A. et al. (eds), *The Etymologies of Isidore of Seville* (Cambridge: Cambridge University Press, 2006).

Bauer, J. (ed.), 'Die Schrift "De pressuris ecclesiasticis" des Bischofs Atto von Vercelli. Untersuchung und Edition' (unpublished PhD dissertation, Tübingen, 1975).

Bede, *De sex dierum creatione*, ed. J.-P. Migne, *PL* 93 (Paris: Migne, 1853) cols 207–34.

Bede, *In Marci euangelii expositio*, in D. Hurst (ed.), *Bedae Operae: Pars II:3 Opera Exegetica*, CCSL 120 (Turnhout: Brepols, 1960).

Bede, *Libri quatuor in principium Genesis*, ed. C. W. Jones, CCSL 118A (Turnhout: Brepols, 1967).

Bertram, J. (ed. and trans.), *The Chrodegang Rules: The Rules for the Common Life of the Secular Clergy from the Eighth and Ninth Centuries: Critical Texts with Translations and Commentary* (Aldershot: Ashgate, 2005) pp. 27–84.

Boniface, *Epistolae*, ed. E. Dümmler, *MGH Epp.* 3 (Berlin: Weidmann, 1892); trans. E. Emerson, *Letters of Saint Boniface* (New York: Columbia University Press, 1940).

Boretius, A. (ed.), *MGH Capit.* 1 (Hanover: Hahn, 1883).

Boretius, A., and Krause, V. (eds), *MGH Capit.* 2 (Hanover: Hahn, 1897).

Borst, A. (ed.), *Schriften zur Komputistik im Frankenreich von 721 bis 818*, *MGH* Quellen zur Geistesgeschichte des Mittelalter 21.1–3 (3 vols, Hanover: Hahn, 2006).

Brommer, P. (ed.), *MGH Capit. episc.* 1 (Hanover: Hahn, 1984).

Wormser Briefsammlung, MGH Briefe der deutschen Kaiserzeit 3 (Hanover: Hahn, 1949) pp. 13–118.

Candidus, *Vita Aegil*, ed. G. Becht-Jördens, *Vita Aegil Abbatis Fuldensis a Candido ad Modestum edita prosa et versibus: Ein Opus geminum des IX. Jahrhunderts* (Marburg: Selbstverlag G. Becht-Jördens, 1994).

Cantelli Berarducci, S., *Hrabani Mauri opera exgetica: repertorium fontium*, Instrumenta Patristica et Mediaevalia 38 (3 vols, Turnhout: Brepols, 2006).

Capitula tractanda cum combitibus, episcopis et abbatibus, ed. A. Boretius, *MGH Capit.* 1 (Hanover: Hahn, 1883), no. 71, pp. 161–2; trans. J. L. Nelson, 'The voice of Charlemagne', in R. Gameson and H. Leyser (eds), *Belief and Culture in the Middle Ages: Studies Presented to Henry Mayr-Harting* (Oxford: Oxford University Press, 2001), pp. 85–6.

Claudius of Turin, *Commentarii in Genesim*, ed. J.-P. Migne, *PL* 50 (Paris: Migne, 1846), cols 893–1047.

Claudius of Turin, *Expositio in epistolas sancti Pauli*, ed. J.-P. Migne, *PL* 134 (Paris: Migne, 1853), cols 125–833.

Claudius of Turin, *Tractatus in Epistolas ad Ephesios, Tractatus ad Philippenses*, ed. C. Ricci, CCCM, 263 (Turnhout: Brepols, 2014).

Codex Carolinus, ed. W. Gundlach, *MGH Epp.* 3 (Berlin: Weidmann, 1892), pp. 476–657; trans. R. McKitterick and D. Espello, *Codex Epistolaris Carolinus: Letters from the Popes to the Frankish Rulers, 739–791* (Liverpool: Liverpool University Press, 2021).

Concilium Antiochensum: Canones, ed. C. H. Turner, *Ecclesiae Occidentalis: Monumenta Iuris Antiquissima* (Oxford: Clarendon, 1913), II:2, pp. 232–311.

d'Herbomez, A. (ed.), *Cartulaire de l'abbaye Gorze*, Mettensia 2 (Paris: C. Klincksleck, 1902).

Dolbeau, F., 'Le *Liber XXI sententiarum* (CPL 373): Édition d'un texte de travail', *Recherches Augustiniennes et Patristiques*, 30 (1997), 113–65.

Dominus vobiscum, ed. J.-M. Hanssens, *Amalarii episcopi opera liturgica omnia*, Studi e Testi 138 (Vatican City: Biblioteca apostolica vaticana, 1948), I, pp. 283–338.

Dümmler, E. (ed.), *MGH Epp.* 3 (Berlin: Weidmann, 1892).

Dümmler, E. (ed.), *MGH Epp.* 4 (Berlin: Weidmann, 1895).

Dümmler, E. (ed.), 'Weissenburger Gedichte', *Zeitschrift für deutsches Altertum und deutsche Literatur*, 19 (1876), 115–17.

Dutton, P. E. (ed. and trans.), *Carolingian Civilization: A Reader* (Peterborough, Ont.: Broadview Press, 1993).

Emerton, E. (trans.), *Letters of Saint Boniface* (New York: Columbia University Press, 1940).

Epistola de litteris colendis, ed. E. E. Stengel, *Urkundenbuch des Klosters Fulda, Band 1.2: Die Zeit des Abtes Baugulf*, Veröffentlichungen der

Historischen Kommission für Hessen und Waldeck 10. 1.2 (Marburg: N. G. Elwer, 1956), no. 166, pp. 246–54.

Explanationes symboli aeui Carolini, ed. S. Keefe, CCCM 254 (Turnhout: Brepols, 2012).

Extraordinary Consistory, 13 June 1994, in Il Regno-Att., 39 (1994). www.vatican.va/content/john-paul-ii/en/speeches/1994/june.index.html (accessed 15 August 2022).

Fitzmeyer, J. A., *Romans: A New Translation with Introduction and Commentary* (New York: The Anchor Bible, 1992).

Flodoard, *Historia Remensis ecclesiae*, ed. G. Waitz and J. Heller, *MGH SS* 13 (Hanover: Hahn, 1881).

Florus, *Opera polemica*, ed. K. Zechiel-Eckes, *CCCM* 260 (Turnhout: Brepols, 2014).

Godman, P. (trans.), *Poetry of the Carolingian Renaissance* (London: Duckworth, 1985).

Gratian, *Decretum*, ed. A. L. Richter and E. Friedburg, Corpus iuris canonici 1 (Leipzig: Tauschnitz, 1879).

Gregory the Great, *Homiliae in Ezechielem*, ed. Marc Adriaen, *CCSL* 142 (Turnhout: Brepols, 1971).

Grigoras, I., 'Breuiarium artis grammaticae Alcuini: edition and study', *The Journal of Medieval Latin*, 30 (2020), 183–226.

Grondeux, A., and Cinato, F. (eds), *Liber glossarum digital* (Paris, 2016), available online at http://liber-glossarum.huma-num.fr/index.html (accessed 15 August 2022).

Guise, Jacques de, *Annales historiae illustrium principum Hanoniae*, ed. A. Sackur, *MGH SS* 30.1 (Hanover: Hahn, 1896).

Haimo of Auxerre, *In divi Pauli epistolas expositio*, ed. J.-P. Migne, *PL* 117 (Paris: Migne, 1852), cols 361–936.

Hartmann, W. (ed.), *MGH Conc.* 3 (Hanover: Hahn, 1984).

Häse, A., *Mittelalterliche Bücherverzeichnisse aus Kloster Lorsch. Einleitung, Edition und Kommentar* (Wiesbaden: Harrassowitz, 2002).

Helm, K., 'Otfrid-Nennungen?', *Beiträge zur Geschichte der deutschen Sprache und Literatur*, 66 (1942), 134–45.

Hilarius of Poitiers, *De trinitate*, ed. P. Smulders, *CCSL* 62A (Turnhout: Brepols, 1980).

Hilduin of Saint-Denis, *The Passio S. Dionysii in Prose and Verse*, ed. M. Lapidge (Leiden: Brill, 2017).

Hincmar, *Epistolae*, ed. E. Perels, *MGH Epp.* 8:1 (Hanover: Hahn, 1985).

Hrabanus Maurus, *Commentariorum in Genesim*, ed. J.-P. Migne, *PL* 107 (Paris: Migne, 1851), cols 439–669.

Hrabanus Maurus, *Excerptio de arte grammatica Prisciani*, ed. J.-P. Migne, *PL* 111 (Paris: Migne, 1852), cols 613–78.

Hrabanus Maurus, *Expositio in epistolam ad Hebraeos*, ed. J.-P. Migne, *PL* 112 (Paris: Migne, 1852), cols 711–833.
Hrabanus Maurus, *Expositio in epistolam II ad Corinthios*, ed. J.-P. Migne, *PL* 112 (Paris: Migne, 1852), cols 159–246.
Hrabanus Maurus, *Liber de sacris ordinibus*, ed. J.-P. Migne, *PL* 112 (Paris: Migne, 1852), cols 1179C–1192A.
Hrabanus Maurus, *Opera exegetica: repertorium fontium*, ed. S. Cantelli Berarducci, Instrumenta Patristica et Mediaevalia 38 (3 vols, Turnhout: Brepols, 2006).
Intexuimus, ed. M. Gorman, 'The Visigothic commentary on Genesis in Autun 27 (S. 29)', *Recherches Augustiniennes*, 30 (1997), 167–269.
Isidore, *Etymologiae*, ed. W. M. Lindsay, 2 vols (Oxford: Oxford University Press, 1911); trans. S. A. Barney et al., *The Etymologies of Isidore of Seville* (Cambridge: Cambridge University Press, 2006).
Jaffé, P., *Regesta pontificum Romanorum* (Leipzig: Veit, 1885).
Jerome, *Commentariorum in evangelium Matthaei libri IV*, ed. D. Hurst and M. Adriaen, *CCSL* 77 (Turnhout: Brepols, 1969).
Jerome, *Commentarius in epistolam ad Romanos*, ed. J.-P. Migne, *PL* 30 (Paris: Migne, 1846) cols 645–717.
Jerome, *Commentarius in Isaiam*, ed. Marc Adriaen, *CCSL* 73 (Turnhout: Brepols, 1963).
Jerome, *Epistulae*, ed. Hilberg, I., *CSEL* 54 (Vienna: Verlag der Österreichischen Akademie der Wissenschaften, 1910).
John Scotus Eriugena, *De divina praedestinatione liber*, ed. G. Madec, *CCCM* 50 (Turnhout: Brepols, 1978).
Jullien, M.-H., and Perelman, F. (eds), *Clavis scriptorum latinorum medii aevi. Auctores Galliae 735–987* (Turnhout: Brepols, 1999).
Keefe, S. (ed.), *Water and the Word, Volume II. Baptism and the Education of the Clergy in the Carolingian Empire: Editions of Texts* (Notre Dame, IN: Notre Dame University Press, 2002).
King, P. D., *Charlemagne: Translated Sources* (Kendal: 1987).
Kölzer, T. (ed.), *MGH DD LdF* (3 vols, Wiesbaden: Harrassowitz, 2016).
Laudes Veronensis civitatis, ed. E. Dümmler, *MGH Poetae* 1 (Berlin: Weidmann, 1881), pp. 118–22.
Levillain, M. L. (ed.), *Recueil des actes de Pépin Ier et de Pépin II, rois d'Aquitaine (814–48)*, Chartes et diplômes relatifs à l'histoire de France 8 (Paris: Imprimerie nationale, 1926).
Liber de Episcopis Mettensibus, ed. and trans. D. Kempf, *Paul the Deacon, Liber de Episcopis Mettensibus: Edition, Translation, and Introduction* (Leuven: Peeters, 2013).
Liber pontificalis, ed. L. Duchesne, *Le liber pontificalis: texte, introduction et commentaire* (Paris: E. Thorin, 1886), I; trans. R. Davis, *The Lives of the Eighth Century Popes* (Liverpool: Liverpool University Press, 1992).

Lowe, E. A, *The Bobbio Missal: a Gallican Mass-Book (MS Paris Lat. 13246)* (3 vols, London: Henry Bradshaw Society, 1920).
Loyn, H. R., and Percival, J. (trans.), *The Reign of Charlemagne* (London: Edward Arnold, 1975).
Marenbon, J., 'Candidus [Hwita, Wizo]', *Oxford Dictionary of National Biography* (Oxford: Oxford University Press, 2004).
Marenbon, J. (ed.), *From the Circle of Alcuin to the School of Auxerre: Logic, Theology and Philosophy in the Early Middle Ages* (Cambridge: Cambridge University Press, 1981).
Meersseman, G. G., and Pacini, G. P., *Ordo Fraternitatis: confraternite e pietà dei laici nel Medioevo* (Rome: Herder, 1977).
Missale Gothicum, ed. E. Rose, CCSL 159D (Turnhout: Brepols, 2005); trans. E. Rose, *The Gothic Missal*, Corpus Christianorum in Translation 27 (Turnhout: Brepols, 2017).
Mühlbacher, E. (ed.), *MGH DD Karol.* 1 (Hanover: Hahn, 1906).
Mutiani Scholastici interpretatio homiliarum Joannis Chrysostomi homiliae in epistolam ad Haebreos, Homilia IX, ed. J.-P. Migne, *PG* 63 (Paris: Migne, 1862), cols 297–304.
Neufville, J. (ed.), 'Règle des IV pères et seconde règle des pères: texte critique', *Revue Bénédictine*, 77 (1967), 47–106; trans. T. G. Kardong, 'The rule of the four fathers: a new English translation and commentary', *American Benedictine Review*, 54:2 (2003), 142–80.
Origen, *In epistulam Pauli ad Romanos explicationum liber IX*, ed. C. P. Hammond Bammel, *Der Römerbriefkommentar des Origines: Kritische Ausgabe der Übersetzung Rufins, 7–10* (Freiburg: Verlag Herder, 1998).
Otfrid von Weißenburg, *Evangelienbuch*, ed. W. Kleiber and E. Hellgardt (2 vols, Tübingen:, Max Niemayer, 2004–7).
Pelagius, *Expositio in Ephesios*, ed. A. Souter, *Pelagius's Expositions of Thirteen Epistles of St Paul* (Cambridge: Cambridge University Press, 1922).
Perels, E. (ed.), *MGH Epp.* 6 (Berlin: Weidmann, 1925).
Pokorney, R. (ed.), *MGH Capit. episc.* 3 (Hanover: Hahn, 1995).
Pokorny, R. (ed.), *MGH Capit. episc.* 4 (Hanover: Hahn, 2005).
Priscian, *Institutiones grammaticae*, ed. M. Hertz, in H. Keil (ed.), *Grammatici Latini* II (Leipzig: Teubner, 1855).
Prudentius, *De predestinatione contra Erigenam*, ed. J.-P. Migne, *PL* 115 (Paris: Migne, 1852), cols 1009C–1366A.
Ratramnus of Corbie, *Contra Graecorum opposite libri quatuor*, ed. J.-P. Migne, *PL* 121 (Paris: Migne, 1852), cols 223–346.
Regesta Alsatiae aevi merovingi et karolini, 490–918, ed. A. Bruckner (Strasbourg: P. H. Heitz, 1949).

Schwartz, E., *Concilium universale Ephesenum* (Berlin: de Gruyter, 1925–26).
Sedulius Scottus, *In epistolam ad Romanos, In epistolam ad Corinthios usque ad Hebraeos*, ed. H. J. Frede and H. Stanjek, *Collectaneum in Apostolum* (Freiburg: Herder, 1996–7), I–II.
Semmler, J. (ed.), *Legislatio Aquisgranensis*, ed. K. Hallinger, *Corpus consuetudinem monasticarum I: Initia consuetudinis Benedictinae, consuetudines saeculi octavi et noni* (Sieburg: Schmitt, 1963), pp. 423–582.
Solinus, G. I., *Collectanea rerum memorabilium*, ed. T. Mommsen (Berlin: Weidmann, 1895).
Stewart, C., 'The literature of early western monasticism', in B. M. Kaczynski (ed.), *The Oxford Handbook of Christian Monasticism* (Oxford: Oxford University Press, 2020), pp. 85–100.
Strecker, K. ed., *Versus Scottorum I. Problemata arithmetica*, MGH Poetae 4,2.3 (Berlin: Weidmann, 1923), pp. 1117–20.
Strecker, K. ed., *Weissenburg*, MGH Poetae 5,1.2 (Leipzig: Hiersemann, 1937), pp. 504–7.
Tardif, J. (ed.), *Monuments Historiques* (Paris: J. Claye, 1866).
Tertullian, *De virginibus velandis*, ed. E. Dekkers, *Tertullianus: opera II, opera monastica*, CCSL 2 (Turnhout: Brepols, 1954).
Theodulf of Orleans, *Libellus de processione spiritus sancti*, ed. H. Willjung, MGH Conc. 2 Supplementum 2 (Hanover: Hahn, 1998), pp. 315–82.
Theodulf of Orleans, *Opus Caroli regis contra synodum*, ed. A. Freeman and P. Meyvaert, MGH Conc. 2, Supplementum 1 (Hanover: Hahn, 1998).
Veyrard-Cosme, C. ed., *La vita beati Alcuini (IXe s.). Les inflexions d'un discours de sainteté. Introduction, edition et traduction annotée du texte d'après Reims, BM 1395 (K 784)* (Paris: Institut d'études augustiniennes, 2017).
Vincent, *Commonitorium*, ed. R. Demeulenaere, CCSL 64 (Turnhout: Brepols, 1985); trans. C. A. Heurtley, *Select Library of Nicene and Post-Nicene Fathers of the Christian Church*, Second series 11 (Oxford: James Parker, 1894).
Virgilius Maro Grammaticus, *Epistola de nomine*, ed. B. Löfstedt, *Virgilius Maro Grammaticus opera omnia* (Munich: K. G. Saur, 2003).
Vita sanctae Balthildis, ed. B. Krusch, MGH SSRM 2 (Hanover: Hahn, 1888), pp. 475–508.
Vitae Willibaldi et Wynnebaldi auctore sanctimoniali Heidenheimensi, ed. O. Holder-Egger, MGH SS 15:1 (Hanover: Hahn, 1887), pp. 80–117; trans. C. H. Talbot, in T. F. X. Noble and T. Head (eds), *Soldiers of Christ:*

Saints and Saints' Lives from Late Antiquity and the Early Middle Ages (Pennsylvania, PA: Penn State University Press, 1995), pp. 141–65.
Weiland, L. (ed.), *MGH Constitutiones et acta publica imperatorum et regum* 1 (Hanover: Hahn, 1893).
Werminghoff, A. (ed.), *MGH Conc.* 2.1 (Hanover: Hahn, 1906).
Werminghoff, A. (ed.), *MGH Conc.* 2.2 (Hanover: Hahn, 1908).
Wiegand, W. (ed.), *Urkunden und Akten der Stadt Strassburg* (Strasbourg: K. J. Trübner, 1879).
Wigbod, *Liber quaestionum super librum Genesis*, ed. J.-P. Migne, PL 96 (Paris: Migne, 1851), cols 1105–1204.
Willjung, H. (ed.), *MGH Conc.* 2, Supplementum 2 (Hanover: Hahn, 1998).
Wizo, *Dicta Candidi*, ed. J. Marenbon, *From the Circle of Alcuin to the School of Auxerre: Logic, Theology and Philosophy in the Early Middle Ages* (Cambridge: Cambridge University Press, 1981), pp. 161–3.
Woestijne, P. van de (ed.), *La Périégèse de Priscien* (Brugge: De Tempel, 1953).

Secondary sources

Airlie, S., 'Private bodies and the body politic in the divorce case of Lothar II', *Past & Present*, 161 (1998), 3–38.
Alberi, M., '"The better paths of wisdom": Alcuin's monastic "true philosophy" and the worldly court', *Speculum*, 74:4 (2001), 896–910.
Alberigo, G., *Chiesa Santa e Peccatrice: Conversione della Chiesa?* (Monastero di Bose: Edizioni Qiqajon, 1997).
Ampère, J. J., *Histoire littéraire de la France avant le douzième siècle*, 3 vols (Paris: Le Hachette, 1839).
Andrieu, M. 'L'Ordo *romanus antiquus* et le *Liber de divinis officiis* du Pseudo-Alcuin', *Revue des sciences religieuses*, 5 (1925), 642–50.
Andrieu, M., *Les Ordines Romani du haut Moyen Âge* (reprint, Leuven: Spicilegium Sacrum Lovaniense, 1957), I.
Angenendt, A., 'Libelli bene correcti: der "richtige Kult" als ein Motiv der karolingischen Reform', in P. Ganz (ed.), *Das Buch als magisches und als Repräsentationsobjekt* (Wieshahuser: O. Harrassowitz, 1992), pp. 117–23.
Antonini, A., 'Archéologie du site abbatial (des origines au Xe siècle)', in B. Andenmatten and L. Ripart (eds), *L'abbaye de Saint-Maurice d'Agaune, Vol. 1: historie et archéologie* (Gollion: Infolio éditions, 2015), pp. 59–109.
Antonini, A., 'The monastery of Saint Maurice of Agaune (Switzerland) in the First Millenium', in C. Bielmann and B. Thomas (eds), *Debating*

Religious Space & Place in the Early Medieval World (c. AD 300–1000) (Leiden: Sidestone, 2018), pp. 143–58, here p. 155.

Banniard, M., 'Language and communication in Carolingian Europe', in Rosamond McKitterick (ed.), *New Cambridge Medieval History* (Cambridge: Cambridge University Press, 1995), II, pp. 695–708.

Banniard, M., 'The transition from the Latin to the Romance languages', in M. Maiden et al. (eds), *The Cambridge History of the Romance Languages*, vol. 2 (Cambridge: Cambridge University Press, 2013), pp. 57–106.

Barrow, J., 'Developing definitions of reform in the church in the ninth and tenth centuries', in R. Balzaretti et al. (eds), *Italy and Early Medieval Europe: Papers for Chris Wickham* (Oxford: Oxford University Press, 2018), pp. 501–11.

Barrow, J., 'Ideas and applications of reform', in T. F. X. Noble and J. Smith (eds), *The Cambridge History of Christianity* (Cambridge: Cambridge University Press, 2008), pp. 345–62.

Barrow, J., 'Review article: Chrodegang, his rule and its successors', *Early Medieval Europe* 14:2 (2006), 201–12.

Becker, G., *Catalogi Bibliothecarum Antiqui* (Bonn: M. Cohen, 1885).

Beckonhofer, R. F., *Day of Reckoning: Power and Accountability in Medieval France* (Philadelphia, PA: University of Pennsylvania Press, 2004).

Bischoff, B., 'Wer ist die Nonne von Heidenheim?', *Studien und Mitteilungen zur Geschichte des Benediktinerordens und seiner Zweige*, 49 (1931), 387–97.

Bischoff, B., *Katalog der festländischen Handschriften des neunten Jahrhunderts (mit Ausnahme der wisigotischen)* (3 vols, Wiesbaden: Harrassowitz, 1998–2017).

Bishop, E., 'The liturgical reforms of Charlemagne: their meanings and value', *The Downside Review*, 38 (1919), 1–16.

Blaise, A., *Le vocabulaire latin des principaux thèmes liturgiques* (Turnhout: Brepols, 1966).

Bobrycki, S., 'Amalarius' *Liber officialis* and the Mediterranean slave trade', *Haskins Society Journal*, 26 (2014), 47–67.

Bodarwé, K., 'Eine Männerregel für Frauen. Die Adaption der Benediktsregel im 9. und 10. Jahrhundert', in G. Melville and A. Müller (eds), *Female vita religiosa between Late Antiquity and the High Middle Ages: Structures, Developments and Spatial Contexts*, Vita regularis 47 (Zürich: Lit Verlag, 2011), pp. 235–72.

Boodts, S., 'The reception of Augustine in the ninth-century Commentary on Romans (Paris, Bn Flat. 11574) with the analysis of its position in relation to the Carolingian debate on predestination', in G. Guldentops, C. Laes and G. Partoens (eds), *Felici curiositate: Studies in Latin Literature and Textual Criticism from Antiquity to the Twentieth Century in Honour of Rita Beyers* (Turnhout: Brepols, 2017), pp. 437–57.

Borst, A., *Die karolingische Kalenderreform*, MGH Schriften 46 (Hanover: Hahn, 1998).

Boswell, J., *Christianity, Social Tolerance, and Homosexuality: Gay People in Western Europe from the Beginning of the Christian Era to the Fourteenth Century* (Chicago, IL: University of Chicago Press, 1981).

Botte, B., and Mohrmann, C., *L'ordinaire de la messe* (Paris: Les Editions du Cerf, 1953).

Boucaud, P., 'Claude de Turin († ca. 828) et Haymon d'Auxerre (fl. 850): deux commentateurs d'I Corinthiens', in S. Shimahara (ed.), *Études d'exégèse carolingienne: autour d'Haymon d'Auxerre: Atelier de recherches, Centre d'études médiévales d'Auxerre, 25–26 avril 2005* (Turnhout: Brepols, 2007), pp. 187–236.

Boucaud, P., 'Commentaires pauliniens inédits du haut Moyen Âge dans un manuscrit du Mont-Cassin', *Revue d'histoire des textes*, 7 (2012), 159–219.

Boucaud, P., '*Corpus Paulinum*: l'exégèse grecque et latine des "Épîtres" au premier millénaire', *Revue de l'histoire des religions*, 230:3 (2013), 299–332.

Bougard, F., 'Was there a Carolingian Italy? Politics, institutions and book culture', in C. Gantner and W. Pohl (eds), *After Charlemagne: Carolingian Italy and its Rulers* (Cambridge: Cambridge University Press, 2019), pp. 54–81.

Bouhot, J.-P., 'Les sources de l'expositio missae de Remi d'Auxerre', *Revue d'Etudes Augustiniennes et Patristiques*, 26:1–2 (1980), 118–69.

Braun, R., *Deus christianorum: Recherches sur le vocabulaire doctrinal de Tertullien* (Paris: Presses universitaires de France, 1962).

Brooks, N., 'Was cathedral reform at Christ Church Canterbury in the early ninth century of continental inspiration?', in H. Sauer and J. Story (eds), *Anglo-Saxon England and the Continent* (Tempe, AZ: Arizona Centre for Medieval and Renaissance Studies, 2011), pp. 303–22.

Brown, G., 'Introduction: the Carolingian Renaissance', in R. McKitterick (ed.), *Carolingian Culture: Emulation and Innovation* (Cambridge: Cambridge University Press, 1994), pp. 1–52.

Brunhölzl, F., *Histoire de la littérature latine du Moyen Age: De Cassiodore à la fin de la renaissance carolingienne* (Turnhout: Brepols, 1990), I.1.

Buck, T. M., *Admonitio und Praedicatio. Zur religiös-pastoralen Dimension von Kapitularien und kapitulariennahen Texten (507–814)*, Freiburger Beiträge zur mittelalterlichen Geschichte 9 (Frankfurt: Peter Lang, 1997).

Bullough, D., 'The dating of the Codex Carolinus nos. 95, 96, 97, Wilchar, and the beginnings of the archbishopric of Sens', *Deutsches Archiv für Erforschung des Mittelalters*, 18 (1962), 227–30.

Bullough, D. A., *Alcuin: Achievement and Reputation* (Leiden: Brill, 2004).

Bullough, D. A., 'Roman books and Carolingian *renovatio*', *Studies in Church History*, 14 (1977), 23–50.

Burckhardt, J., *Die Cultur der Renaissance in Italien: ein Versuch* (Basel: Schweighauser, 1860).

Burdach, K., 'Sinn und Ursprung der Worte Renaissance und Reformation', *Sitzungsberichte der Königliche Preussischen Akademie der Wissenschaften*, 13 (1910), 594–646.

Büren, V. von, 'Une édition critique de Solin au IXe siècle', *Scriptorium*, 50:1 (1996), 22–87.

Butzmann, H. *Die Weissenburger Handschriften*, Kataloge der Herzog-August-Bibliothek Wolfenbüttel: Die neue Reihe 10 (Frankfurt: Vittorio Klostermann, 1964).

Cantelli, S., Berarducci, 'L'esegesi della Rinascita Carolingia', in G. Cremascoli and C. Leonardi (eds), *La Bibbia nel Medio Evo* (Bologna: Edizioni Dehoniane Bologna, 1996), pp. 167–98.

Carmassi, P., 'Litterae e scrittura nell'insegnamento della grammatica in età altomedievale: premesse teoretiche e aspetti pratici', in P. R. Robinson (ed.), *Teaching Writing, Learning to Write. Proceedings of the XVIth Colloquium of the Comité International de Paléographie Latine* (London: Kings College London, 2010), pp. 37–59.

Cavadini, J. C., *The Last Christology of the West* (Philadelphia, PA: University of Pennsylvania Press: 1993).

Chazelle, C., *The Crucified God in the Carolingian Era: Theology and Art of Christ's Passion* (Cambridge: Cambridge University Press, 2001).

Choy, R., *Intercessory Prayer and the Monastic Ideal in the Time of the Carolingian Reforms* (Oxford: Oxford University Press, 2016).

Cinato, F., *Priscien glosé. L'Ars grammatica de Priscien vue à travers les gloses carolingiennes*, Studia Artistarum 41 (Turnhout: Brepols, 2015).

Claussen, M. A., 'Practical exegesis: the Acts of the Apostles, Chrodegang's *Regula canonicorum* and early Carolingian reform', in D. Blanks et al. (eds), *Medieval Monks and Their World: Ideas and Realities* (Leiden: Brill, 2006), pp. 119–47.

Claussen, M. A., *Reform of the Frankish Church: Chrodegang of Metz and the Regula Canonicorum in the Eighth Century* (Cambridge: Cambridge University Press, 2005).

Congar, Y. M., *Tradition and Traditions: An Historical and a Theological Essay*, trans. M. Naseby (London: Burns & Oats, 1963).

Constable, G., 'Carolingian monasticism as seen in the Plan of St Gall', in W. Fałkowski and Y. Sassier (eds), *Le monde carolingien: bilan, perspectives, champs de recherches: actes du colloque international de Poitiers, Centre d'études supérieures de civilization médiévale, 18–20 novembre 2004* (Turnhout: Brepols, 2009), pp. 199–217.

Contreni, J. J., 'The Carolingian Renaissance: education and literary culture', in R. McKitterick (ed.), *The New Cambridge Medieval History* II, ca. 700–ca. 900 (Cambridge: Cambridge University Press, 1995), pp. 721–55.

Contreni, J. J., 'Learning for God: education in the Carolingian age', *The Journal of Medieval Latin*, 24 (2014), 89–129.

Contreni, J. J., 'Let schools be established ... for what? The meaning of *Admonitio generalis*, chapter 70 (*olim* 72)', in G. Boone (ed.), *Music in the Carolingian World: Witnesses to a Metadiscipline* (Columbus, OH: Ohio State University Press, in press).

Contreni, J. J., 'The pursuit of knowledge in Carolingian Europe', in R. E. Sullivan (ed.), *The Gentle Voices of Teachers. Aspects of Learning in the Carolingian Age* (Columbus, OH: Ohio State University Press, 1995), pp. 106–41.

Corbeill, A., *Sexing the World: Grammatical Gender and Biological Sex in Ancient Rome* (Princeton, NJ: Princeton University Press, 2015).

Corradini, R., 'ZeitNetzWerk. Karolingische Gelehrsamkeit und Zeitforschung im Kompendium des Walahfrid Strabo' (unpublished Habilitation, University of Vienna, 2014).

Costambeys, M., Innes, M., and MacLean, S., *The Carolingian World* (Cambridge: Cambridge University Press, 2011).

Cubitt, C., 'The clergy in early Anglo-Saxon England', *Historical Research*, 78:201 (2005), 273–87.

Daalen, S. van, 'The reception of Amalarius of Metz's Liber officialis in medieval manuscripts' (MA thesis, Amsterdam, 2021).

Davis, J. R., *Charlemagne's Practice of Empire* (Cambridge: Cambridge University Press, 2015).

Delisle, L., *Inventaire du manuscrits de la Bibliothèque nationale: Fonds de Cluny* (Paris: H. Champion, 1884).

De Paolis, P., 'L'insegnamento dell'ortografia latina fra Tardoantico e alto Medioevo: teorie e manuali', in L. Del Corso and O. Pecere (eds), *Libri di scuola e pratiche didattiche. Dall'Antichità al Rinascimento* (Cassino: Università di Cassino, 2010), vol. 1, pp. 229–91.

Depreux, P., 'Ambitions et limites des réformes culturelles à l'époque carolingienne', *Revue Historique*, 623 (2002/3), 721–53.

Diem, A., 'The Carolingians and the *Regula Benedicti*', in R. Meens et al. (eds), *Religious Franks Religion and power in the Frankish Kingdoms:*

Studies in Honour of Mayke de Jong (Manchester: Manchester University Press, 2016), pp. 243–61.

Diem, A., 'Choreography and confession: the *Memoriale qualiter* and Carolingian monasticism', in R. Kramer et al. (eds), *Monastic Communities and Canonical Clergy in the Carolingian World (780–840): Categorizing the Church* (Turnhout: Brepols, 2022), pp. 59–98.

Diem, A., 'The gender of the religious: women and the invention of monasticism', in J. Bennet and R. Karras (eds), *The Oxford Handbook of Women and Gender in Medieval Europe* (Oxford: Oxford University Press, 2013), pp. 432–46.

Diesenberger, M., and Wolfram, H., 'Arn und Alkuin 790 bis 804: zwei Freunde und ihre Schriften', in M. Niederkorn-Bruck and A. Scharer (eds), *Erzbischof Arn von Salzburg* (Vienna: Oldenbourg, 2004), pp. 81–106.

Dorfbauer, L., 'Wigbod und der pseudoaugustinische Dialogus quaestionum LXV', *Studi Medievali*, 51 (2010), 893–919.

Dorfbauer, L. J., 'Der Genesiskommentar des Claudius von Turin, der Pseudoaugustinische *Dialogus quaestionum* und das wisigotische *Intexuimus*', *Revue d'histoire des textes*, 8 (2013), 269–305.

Driscoll, M. S., *Alcuin, et la pénitence à l'époque carolingienne* (Münster: Aschendorff, 1999).

Dubreucq, A., 'Les relations entre Condat et Agaune', in N. Brocard et al. (eds), *Autour de Saint Maurice* (Besançon: Fondation des archives historiques de l'Abbaye de Saint-Maurice, 2012), pp. 133–46.

Dunn, M., *The Emergence of Monasticism: From the Desert Fathers to the Early Middle Ages* (Oxford: Blackwell, 2000).

Duplessis, F., 'Les sources des gloses des *Gesta Berengarii* et la culture du poète anonyme', *Aevum*, 89:2 (2015), 205–63.

Dürr, R., 'Regulating dangerous knowledge: John Lockman's (1698–1771) Enlightened Readings of Jesuit Letters', in Fokko Jan Dijksterhuis (ed.), *Regulating Knowledge in an Entangled World*, Knowledge Societies in History 4 (London: Routledge, forthcoming).

Eber, M., 'Loose canonesses? (Non-)gendered aspects of the Aachen *Institutiones*', in R. Kramer et al. (eds), *Monastic Communities and Canonical Clergy in the Carolingian World (780–840): Categorizing the Church* (Turnhout: Brepols, 2022), pp. 217–39.

Emerick, J. J., 'Building *more Romano* in Francia during the third quarter of the eighth century: the abbey church of Saint-Denis and its model', in C. Bolgia et al. (eds), *Rome Across Time and Space: Cultural Transmission and the Exchange of Ideas, c.500–1400* (Cambridge: Cambridge University Press, 2011), pp. 127–50.

Englisch, B., 'Alkuin und das Quadrivium in der Karolingerzeit', *Annales de Bretagne et des Pays de l'Ouest*, 111:3 (2004), 163–74.

Ewig, E., 'Saint Chrodegang et la réforme de l'église franque', in *Saint Chrodegang. Communications présentées au colloque tenu à l'occasion du douzième centenaire de sa mort* (Metz: Editions le Lorrain, 1967), pp. 25–53.

Felten, Franz J., *Vita religiosa sanctimonialium: Norm und Praxis des weiblichen religiösen Lebens vom 6. Bis 13. Jahrhundert*, Studien und Texte zur Geistes- und Sozialgeschichte des Mittelalters 4 (Korb: Didymos-Verlag, 2011).

Ferrari, M. C., 'Pangite celi, reboemus odas', *Zeitschrift für schweizerische Kirchengeschichte*, 83 (1989), 155–76.

Fleckenstein, J., *Die Bildungsreform Karls des Grossen als Verwirklichung der Norma Rectitudinis* (Bigge-Ruhr: Josefs, 1953).

Folkerts, S. (ed.), *Religious Connectivity in Urban Communities (1400–1550): Reading, Worshipping, and Connecting through the Continuum of Sacred and Secular* (Turnhout: Brepols, 2021).

Foot, F., 'Reading Anglo-Saxon charters: memory, record, or story?', in E. M. Tyler and R. Balzaretti (eds), *Narrative and History in the Early Medieval West* (Turnhout: Brepols, 2006), pp. 39–67.

Fox, M., 'Alcuin the exegete: the evidence of the *Quaestiones in Genesim*', in C. Chazelle and B. V. N. Edwards (eds), *The Study of the Bible in the Carolingian Era* (Turnhout: Brepols, 2003), pp. 39–60.

Fox, M., 'Alcuin's *Expositio in epistolam ad Hebraeos*', *The Journal of Medieval Latin*, 18 (2008), 326–45.

Fransen, P.-I., 'Le dossier patristique d'Hélisachar: le manuscrit Paris, BNF lat. 11574 et l'une de ses sources', *Revue Bénédictine*, 111:3–4 (2001), 464–82.

Ganz, D., 'Does the Copenhagen Solinus contain the autograph of Walahfrid Strabo?', in N. Golob (ed.), *Medieval Autograph Manuscripts* (Turnhout: Brepols, 2013), pp. 79–86.

Ganz, D., 'Handschriften der Werke Alkuins aus dem 9. Jahrhundert', in K. Schmuki and E. Tremp (eds), *Alkuin von York und die geistige Grundlegung Europas* (St. Gallen: Verlag am Klosterhof, 2010), pp. 185–94.

Garrison, M., 'Les reseaux d'Alcuin et la formation d'une culture européenne', *Annales de Bretagne et des Pays de l'Ouest*, 111:3 (2004), 319–31.

Garver, V., *Women and Aristocratic Culture in the Carolingian World* (Ithaca, NY: Cornell University Press, 2009).

Gavinelli, S., 'Early Carolingian Italy', in F. T. Coulson and R. G. Babcock (eds), *The Oxford Handbook of Latin Palaeography* (Oxford: Oxford University Press, 2020), pp. 262–77.

Geest, P. van (ed.), *Seeing Through the Eyes of Faith: New Approaches to the Mystagogy of the Church Fathers* (Leuven: Peeters, 2016).

Gemeinhardt, P., *Die Filioque-Kontroverse zwischen Ost- und Westkirche im Frühmittelalter* (Berlin, New York: Walter de Gruyter, 2002).

Gibson, M., 'Milestones in the study of Priscian, circa 800 – circa 1200', *Viator*, 23 (1992), 17–33.

Gillis, M., *Heresy and Dissent in the Carolingian Empire: The Case of Gottschalk of Orbais* (Oxford: Oxford University Press, 2017).

Glauche, G., *Katalog der lateinischen Handschriften der Bayerischen Staatsbibliothek München. Die Pergamenthandschriften aus dem Domkapitel Freising*, II (Wiesbaden: Harrassowitz, 2011).

Goldberg, E. J., *Struggle for Empire: Kingship and Conflict under Louis the German, 817–876* (Ithaca, NY: Cornell University Press, 2006).

Goody, J., *Renaissances: The One or the Many?* (Cambridge: Cambridge University Press, 2010).

Gorman, M., 'The commentary on Genesis of Angelomus of Luxeuil and biblical studies under Lothar', *Studi Medievali*, 40 (1999), 559–631.

Gorman, M., 'The commentary on Genesis of Claudius of Turin and biblical studies under Louis the Pious', *Speculum*, 72:2 (1997), 279–329.

Gorman, M., 'The encyclopedic commentary on Genesis prepared for Charlemagne by Wigbod', *Recherches Augustiniennes et patristiques*, 17 (1982), 173–201.

Gorman, M., 'Paris lat. 12124 (Origen on Romans) and the Carolingian commentary on Romans in Paris lat. 11574', *Revue Bénédictine*, 117:1 (2007), 64–128.

Gorman, M., 'Wigbod and biblical studies under Charlemagne', *Revue Bénédictine*, 118 (2008), 5–45.

Grabmann, M., 'Pseudo-Dyonisius der Areopagita in lateinischen Übersetzungen des Mittelalters', in A. M. Koeniger (ed.), *Beiträge zur Geschichte des christlichen Altertums und der byzantinischen Liturgie. Festgabe Albert Ehrhard zum 60. Geburtstag dargebracht* (Bonn: Schoeder, 1922).

Grifoni, C., 'Reading the Catholic epistles: glossing practices in early medieval Wissembourg', in M. Teeuwen and I. van Renswoude (eds), *The Annotated Book in the Early Middle Ages: Practices of Reading and Writing* (Turnhout: Brepols, 2017), pp. 705–42.

Grifoni, C., 'Un giovane promettente: la rappresentazione alcuiniana di Pipino d'Italia nella *Disputatio Pippini cum Albino* (con traduzione italiana del testo)', in G. Albertoni and F. Borri (eds), *Spes Italiae*.

Pippins Königreich, die Karolinger und Italien (781–810) (Turnhout: Brepols, forthcoming).

Guglielmetti, R., 'Un'esegesi incontentabile', in I. Pagani and F. Santi (eds), *Il secolo di Carlo Magno. Istituzioni, letterature e cultura del tempo carolingio* (Florence: Sismel, 2016), pp. 177–200.

Hack, A. T., *Codex Carolinus: Päpstliche Epistolographie Im 8. Jahrhundert.* Vol. 1 (Stuttgart: A. Hiersemann, 2006).

Hadot, P., '*Epistrophè* et *metanoia* dans l'histoire de la philosophie', in *Proceedings of the XIth International Congress of Philosophy 12: History of Philosophy: Methodology – Antiquity and Middle Ages* (Amsterdam: North-Holland Publishing Company, 1953), pp. 31–6.

Halfond, G. I., *The Archaeology of Frankish Church Councils, AD 511–768* (Leiden: Brill, 2010).

Hartmann, W., 'Alkuin und die Gesetzgebung Karls des Grossen', in K. Schmuki and E. Tremp (eds), *Alkuin von York und die geistige Grundlegung Europas* (St Gallen: Verlag am Klosterhof, 2010), pp. 33–48.

Hartmann, W., *Die Synoden der Karolingerzeit im Frankenreich und Italien* (Paderborn: Schöningh, 1989).

Hartrich, E., 'Charters and inter-urban networks: England, 1439–1449', *English Historical Review*, 132:555 (2017), 219–49.

Haubrichs, W. 'Eine prosopographische Skizze zu Otfrid von Weißenburg', in W. Kleiber (ed.), *Otfrid von Weißenburg* (Darmstadt: Wissenschaftliche Buchgesellschaft, 1978), pp. 397–413.

Haubrichs, W., 'Nekrologische Notizen zu Otfrid von Weißenburg', in H. Wenzel (ed.), *Adelsherrschaft und Literatur* (Bern: Lang, 1980), pp. 7–113.

Hausmann, R., *Die theologischen Handschriften der Hessischen Landesbibliothek Fulda bis zum Jahr 1600* (Wiesbaden: Harrassowitz, 1992).

Heath, J., '"Textual communities": Brian Stock's concept and recent scholarship on antiquity', in Florian Wilk (ed.), *Scriptural Interpretation at the Interface between Education and Religion* (Leiden: Brill, 2018), pp. 5–35.

Heer, M. de, '*Expositiones missae* in MS Corbie 230: three commentaries on the mass in a Carolingian pastoral compendium' (unpublished MA thesis, Utrecht University, 2018).

Heil, J., 'Haimo's commentary on Paul: sources, methods and theology', in S. Shimahara (ed.), *Études d'exégèse carolingienne: autour d'Haymon d'Auxerre* (Turnhout: Brepols, 2007), pp. 103–21.

Hellgardt, E., *Die exegetischen Quellen von Otfrids Evangelienbuch* (Tübingen: Niemeyer, 1981).

Helvétius, A., 'L'abbaye d'Agaune de la fondation de Sigismond au règne de Charlemagne (515–814)', in B. Andenmatten and L. Ripart (eds), *L'abbaye de Saint-Maurice d'Agaune, Vol. 1: historie et archéologie* (Gollion: Infolio éditions, 2015), pp. 111–33.

Hen, Y., 'The liturgy of the Bobbio Missal', in Y. Hen and R. Meens (eds), *The Bobbio Missal: Liturgy and Religious Culture in Merovingian Gaul* (Cambridge: Cambridge University Press, 2004), pp. 140–53.

Hen, Y., 'The Romanization of the Frankish liturgy: ideal, reality and the rhetoric of reform', in C. Bolgia, R. McKitterick and J. Osborne (eds), *Rome across Time and Space: Cultural Transmission and the Exchange of Ideas c. 500–1400* (Cambridge: Cambridge University Press, 2011), pp. 111–23.

Hen, Y., *The Royal Patronage of Liturgy in Frankish Gaul to the Death of Charles the Bald (877)*, HBS Subsidia 3 (London: Boydell & Brewer, 2001).

Hen, Y., 'When liturgy gets out of hand', in Elina Screen and Charles West (eds), *Writing the Early Medieval West* (Cambridge: Cambridge University Press, 2018).

Hennings, T., *Ostfränkische Sammlungen von Dichtung im 9. Jahrhundert*, Nova Mediaevalia 19 (Göttingen: Vandenhoeck & Ruprecht, 2021).

Herman, J., *Vulgar Latin*, trans. R. Wright (University Park, PA: Penn State University Press, 2000).

Herren, M., 'Virgil the Grammarian: a Spanish Jew in Ireland?' *Peritia*, 9 (1995), 51–71.

Hoffmann, H., *Schreibschulen des 10. und des 11. Jahrhunderts im Südwesten des Deutschen Reichs*, 2 vols (Hanover: Hahn, 2004).

Holtz, L., 'Alcuin et la renaissance des arts libéraux', in P. L. Butzer, M. Kerner and W. Oberschelp (eds), *Karl der Grosse und sein Nachwirken. 1200 Jahre Kultur und Wissenschaft in Europa* (2 vols, Turnhout: Brepols, 1997), I, pp. 45–60.

Holtz, L., 'Raban Maur et l.' *Excerptio de arte grammatica Prisciani*', in P. Depreux et al. (eds), *Raban Maur et son temps*, Collection Haut Moyen Âge 9 (Turnhout: Brepols, 2010), pp. 203–18.

Holtz, L., 'L'œuvre grammaticale d'Alcuin dans le contexte de son temps', in K. Schmuki and E. Tremp (eds), *Alkuin von York und die geistige Grundlegung Europas* (St Gallen: Verlag am Klosterhof, 2010), pp. 129–49.

Howlett, D., 'Two mathematical poets', *Peritia*, 21 (2010), 151–7.

Huglo, M., 'D'Hélisachar à Abbon de Fleury', *Revue Bénédictine*, 104:1–2 (1994), 204–30.

Innes, M., *State and Society in the Early Middle Ages: The Middle Rhine Valley, 400–1000* (Cambridge: Cambridge University Press, 2000).

Iogna-Prat, D. (ed.), *L'école carolingienne d'Auxerre, de Muretach à Remi, 830–908* (Paris: Beauchesne, 1991).
Irvine, M., *The Making of Textual Culture: 'Grammatica' and Literary Theory, 350–1100* (Cambridge: Cambridge University Press, 1994).
Jarnut, J., 'Bonifatius und die fränkischen Reformkonzilien (743–748)', *Zeitschift der Savigny-Stiftung für Rechtsgeschichte, Kanonisctische Abteilung*, 66 (1979), 1–26.
Jayatilaka, R., 'The Old English Benedictine Rule: writing for women and men', *Anglo-Saxon England*, 32 (2003), 147–87.
Johnson, I., and Rodrigues, A. M. (eds), *Religious Practices and Everyday Life in the Long Fifteenth Century (1350–1570): Interpreting Changes and Changes of Interpretation* (Turnhout: Brepols, 2021).
Jones, C. A., 'The book of the liturgy in Anglo-Saxon England', *Speculum*, 73 (1996), 659–702.
Jones, C. A., 'Candidus Wizo, Arn of Salzburg and the treatise *De sole et luna*', *Early Medieval Europe*, 27 (2019), 546–66.
Jones, C. A., *A Lost Work by Amalarius of Metz: Interpolations in Salisbury, Cathedral Library, MS. 154*, Henry Bradshaw Society: Subsidia 2 (Woodbridge: Boydell and Brewer, 2001).
Jones, C. A., 'The sermons attributed to Candidus Wizo', in K. O'Brien et al. (ed.), *Latin Learning and English Lore: Studies in Anglo-Saxon Literature for Michael Lapidge* (2 vols, Toronto: University of Toronto Press, 2005), I, pp. 260–83.
Jong, M. de, 'Carolingian monasticism: the power of prayer', in Rosamond McKitterick (ed.), *New Cambridge Medieval History*, vol. 2 (Cambridge: Cambridge University Press, 1995), pp. 622–53.
Jong, M. de, 'Charlemagne's church', in J. Story (ed.), *Charlemagne: Empire and Society* (Manchester: Manchester University Press, 2005), pp. 103–35.
Jong, M. de, 'The empire as *ecclesia*: Hrabanus Maurus and biblical *historia* for rulers', in Yitzhak Hen and Matthew Innes (eds), *The Uses of the Past in the Early Middle Ages* (Cambridge: Cambridge University Press, 2000), pp. 191–226.
Jong, M. de, *The Penitential State: Authority and Atonement in the Age of Louis the Pious, 814–840* (Cambridge: Cambridge University Press, 2009).
Kardong, T. G., 'The rule of the four fathers: a new English translation and commentary', *American Benedictine Review*, 54:2 (2003), 142–180.
Kasten, B., *Adalhard von Corbie. Die Biographie eines karolingischen Politikers und Klostervorstehers* (Düsseldorf: Droste, 1986).
Keefe, S., *A Catalogue of Works Pertaining to the Explanation of the Creed in Carolingian Manuscripts*, Instrumenta Patristica et Mediaevalia (Turnhout: Brepols, 2012).

Keefe, S., *Water and the Word: Baptism and the Education of the Clergy in the Carolingian Empire* (2 vols, Notre Dame, IN: University of Notre Dame Press, 2002).

Kelly-Gadol, J., 'Did women have a Renaissance?', in R. Bridenthai and C. Koonz (eds), *Becoming Visible: Women in European History* (Boston, MA: Houghton Mifflin, 1977), pp. 139–64.

Kempshall, M. S., 'The virtues of rhetoric: Alcuin's *Disputatio de rhetorica et de virtutibus*', *Anglo-Saxon England*, 37 (2008), 7–30.

Klauser, T., 'Der Übergang der römischen Kirche von der griechischen zur lateinischen Liturgiesprache', in *Miscellanea Giovanni Mercati, vol. 1: Bibbia, letteratura cristiana antica* (Vatican City: Biblioteca Apostolica Vaticana, 1946), pp. 467–82.

Kleiber, W., 'Otfrid von Weißenburg als Priscian-Glossator. Eine sprachhistorische Skizze', in R. Bergmann and S. Stricker (eds), *Die althochdeutsche und altsächsische Glossographie. Ein Handbuch* (Berlin: De Gruyter, 2009), II, pp. 1601–10.

Kleiber, W., *Otfrid von Weißenburg. Untersuchungen zur handschriftlichen Überlieferung und Studien zum Aufbau des Evangelienbuches* (Bern: Niemeyer, 1971).

Kleiber, W., 'Zur Sprache der althochdeutschen Glossen Otfrids in Cod. Guelf, 50 Weiss.', in R. Bergmann et al. (eds), *Althochdeutsch, Band 1: Grammatik. Glossen und Texte* (Heidelberg: Carl Winter Universitätsverlag, 1987), pp. 532–44.

Knibbs, E., *Ansgar, Rimbert and the Forged Foundations of Hamburg-Bremen* (Farnham: Ashgate, 2011).

Koch, J., 'Philosophische und theologische Irrtumslisten von 1270–1329: Ein Beitrag zur Entwicklung der theologische Zensuren', in J. Koch (ed.), *Kleine Schriften 2*, Storia e letteratura. Raccolta di studi e testi 127 (Rome: Edizione di Storia e Letteratura, 1973), pp. 423–50.

Kolping, A., 'Amalar von Metz und Florus von Lyon: Zeugen eines Wandels im liturgischen Mysterienverständnis in der Karolingerzeit', *Zeitschrift fur katholische Theologie*, 73 (1951), 424–64.

Kortüm, H.H., 'Le style – c'est l'époque? Urteile über das "Merowingerlatein" in Vergangenheit und Gegenwart', *Archiv für Diplomatik Schriftgeschichte Siegel- und Wappenkunde*, 51 (2005), 30–48.

Kramer, R., et al. (eds), *Monastic Communities and Canonical Clergy in the Carolingian World (780–840): Categorizing the Church* (Turnhout: Brepols, 2022).

Kramer, R., 'Monasticism, reform and authority in the Carolingian era', in A. I. Beach and I. Cochelin (eds), *The Cambridge History of Medieval Monasticism in the Latin West* (Cambridge: Cambridge University Press, 2020), pp. 432–49.

Krämer, S., *Handschriftenerbe des deutschen Mittelalters. Teil 2: Köln-Zyfflich*, Mittelalterliche Bibliothekskataloge Deutschlands und der Schweiz. Ergänzungsband 1 (Munich: Beck, 1989).

Kramer, R., 'Order in the church: understanding councils and performing *ordines* in the Carolingian world', *Early Medieval Europe*, 25:1 (2017), 54–69.

Kramer, R., *Rethinking Authority in the Carolingian Empire: Ideals and Expectations during the Reign of Louis the Pious* (Amsterdam: Amsterdam University Press, 2019).

Kramer, R., 'Teaching emperors: transcending the boundaries of Carolingian monastic communities', in E. Hovden et al. (eds), *Meaning of Community across Medieval Eurasia* (Leiden: Brill, 2016), pp. 309–37.

Krautheimer, R., 'The Carolingian revival of early Christian architecture', *The Art Bulletin*, 24 (1942), 1–38.

Ladner, G., *The Idea of Reform, Its Impact on Christian Thought and Action in the Age of the Fathers* (Cambridge, MA: Harvard University Press, 1959).

Langefeld, B., *The Old English Version of the Enlarged Rule of Chrodegang* (Frankfurt: Lang, 2003).

Lapidge, M., 'Beda Venerabilis', in P. Chiesa and L. Castaldi (eds), *La trasmissione dei testi latini del Medioevo* (Florence: Sismel, 2008), III, pp. 44–140.

Lapidge, M. 'The hermeneutic style in tenth-century Anglo-Latin literature', *Anglo-Saxon England*, 4 (1975), 67–111.

Lausberg, H., *Handbook of Literary Rhetoric: A Foundation for Literary Study* (Leiden: Brill, 1998).

Law, L., *Wisdom, Authority, and Grammar in the Seventh Century: Decoding Virgilius Maro Grammaticus* (Cambridge: Cambridge University Press, 1995).

Law, V., and Carley, J. P., 'Grammar and arithmetic in two thirteenth-century English monastic collections: Cambridge, Sidney Sussex College, MS 75 and Oxford, Bodleian Library, MS Bodley 186 (S. C. 2088)', *The Journal of Mediaeval Latin*, 1 (1991), 140–67.

Law, V., 'Grammars and language change: an eighth-century case', in V. Law, *Grammar and Grammarians in the Early Middle Ages* (London: Longman, 1997), pp. 188–99.

Lendinara, P., 'A poem for all seasons: Alcuin's "O vos, est aetas"', in G. Dinkova-Bruun and T. Major (eds), *Teaching and Learning in Medieval Europe: Essays in Honour of Gernot R. Wieland* (Turnhout: Brepols, 2017), pp. 123–46.

Leyser, C., 'Review article: church reform – full of sound and fury, signifying nothing', *Early Medieval Europe*, 24 (2016), 478–99.

Lifshitz, F., *Religious Women in Early Carolingian Francia: A Study of Manuscript Transmission and Monastic Culture* (New York: Fordham University Press, 2014).

Limor, O., 'Pilgrims and authors: Adomnàn's *De Locis Sanctis* and Hugeburc's *Hodoeporicon Sancti Willibaldi*', *Revue Bénédictine*, 114:2 (2004), 253–75.

Ling, S., 'The cloister and beyond: regulating the life of the canonical clergy in Francia, from Pippin III to Louis the Pious' (unpublished PhD thesis, Leicester, 2015).

Ling, S., 'Interactions between the clerical enclosure and the extra-claustral clergy: a sacred space with porous walls', in C. Bielmann and B. Thomas (eds), *Debating Religious Space and Place in the Early Medieval World* (Leiden: Sidestone Press, 2018), pp. 127–39.

Ling, S., '"Superior to canons, and remaining inferior to monks": monks, canons and Alcuin's third order', in R. Kramer et al. (eds), *Monastic Communities and Canonical Clergy in the Carolingian World (780–840): Categorizing the Church* (Turnhout: Brepols, 2022), pp. 241–66.

Lobrichon, G., 'Le texte des bibles alcuiniennes', *Annales de Bretagne et des Pays de l'Ouest*, 111:3 (2004), 209–19.

Lubac, H. de, *Corpus Mysticum. L'eucharistie et l'église au moyen âge. Étude historique* (2nd ed., Paris: Aubier, 1949).

Marenbon, J., 'Alcuin, the Council of Frankfurt and the beginnings of medieval philosophy', in R. Berndt (ed.), *Das Frankfurter Konzil von 794* (2 vols, Mainz: Selbstverl. der Ges. für Mittelrheinische Kirchengeschichte, 1997), II, pp. 603–15.

Marenbon, J., *From the Circle of Alcuin to the School of Auxerre: Logic, Theology and Philosophy in the Early Middle Ages* (Cambridge: Cambridge University Press, 1981).

Marenbon, J., 'John Scottus and Carolingian theology: from the *De Praedestinatione*, its background and its critics, to the *Periphyseon*', in M. T. Gibson and J. L. Nelson (eds), *Charles the Bald: Court and Kingdom* (2nd ed., Aldershot: Variorum, 1990), pp. 303–26.

Masai, F., 'La Vita *patrum Iurensium* et les debuts du monachisme à Saint-Maurice d'Agaune', in J. Autenrieth and F. Brunhölzl (eds), *Festschrift Bernhard Bischoff* (Stuttgart: A. Hiersemann, 1971), pp. 52–3.

Mazza, E., *The Celebration of the Eucharist: The Origin of the Rite and the Development of Its Interpretation*, trans. Matthew J. O'Connell (Collegeville, MN: The Liturgical Press, 1999).

McKitterick, R., 'The Carolingian renaissance of culture and learning', in J. Story (ed.), *Charlemagne: Empire and Society* (Manchester: Manchester University Press, 2005), pp. 151–66.

McKitterick, R., *Charlemagne: The Formation of a European Identity* (Cambridge: Cambridge University Press, 2009).

McKitterick, R., *The Frankish Church and the Carolingian Reforms, 789–895* (London: Royal Historical Society, 1977).

McKitterick, R., *The Frankish Kingdoms under the Carolingians, 751–987* (London: Routledge, 1983).

McKitterick, R., *History and Memory in the Carolingian World* (Cambridge: Cambridge University Press, 2004).

McKitterick, R., 'Latin and Romance: an historian's perspective', in R. Wright (ed.), *Latin and the Romance Languages in the Early Middle Ages* (London: Routledge, 1991), pp. 130–45.

McKitterick, R., 'Unity and diversity in the Carolingian church', in R. N. Swanson (ed.), *Unity and Diversity in the Church*, Studies in Church History 32 (Oxford: Oxford University Press, 1997), pp. 59–82.

McLaughlin, M., *Consorting with Saints: Prayer for the Dead in Early Medieval France* (Ithaca, NY: Cornell University Press, 2018).

McNamara, J. A., *Sisters in Arms: Catholic Nuns through Two Millennia* (Cambridge, MA: Harvard University Press, 1998).

Meeder, S., *The Irish Scholarly Presence at St. Gall: Networks of Knowledge in the Early Middle Ages* (London: Bloomsbury, 2018).

Merrills, A., 'Texts and early medieval rulers. The Moorish kingdoms and the written word: three "textual communities" in fifth- and sixth-century Mauretania', in E. Screen and C. West (eds), *Writing the Early Medieval West: Studies in Honour of Rosamond McKitterick* (Cambridge: Cambridge University Press, 2018), pp. 185–202.

Mersiowsky, M., *Die Urkunde in der Karolingerzeit: Originale, Urkundenpraxis und politische Kommunikation*, Schriften der Monumenta Germaniae Historica, 60 (Wiesbaden: Harrasowitz, 2015).

Michelet, J., *Histoire de la France* 6 vols (Paris: L. Hachette, 1833–44).

Miethke, J., 'Mittelalterliche Theologenprozesse (9. Bis 15. Jahrhundert)', *Zeitschrift der Savigny-Stiftung für Rechtsgeschichte: Kanonistische Abteilung*, 131 (2014), 261–311.

Miskimin, A., 'Two reforms of Charlemagne? Weights and measures in the middle ages', *The Economic History Review*, 20 (1967), 35–52.

Mitalaité, K., 'La puissance révélatrice de la parole et sa mise en voix dans la spiritualité et la politique carolingiennes', *The Journal of Medieval Latin*, 26 (2016), 263–89.

Morard, M., 'Sacramentum immixtum et uniformization romaine', *Archiv für Liturgiewissenschaft*, 46 (2004), 1–30.

Mordek, H., *Bibliotheca capitularium regum Francorum manuscripta: Überlieferung und Traditionszusammenhang der fränkischen Herrschererlasse* (Munich: Monumenta Germaniae Historica, 1995).

Morhain, E., 'Origine et histoire de la *Regula canonicorum* de Saint Chrodegang', *Miscellanea Pio Paschini, Studi di Storia Eccelesiastica*, vol. 1 *Lateranum*, N.S. XIV (1948), 173–85.

Morrison, K., 'Know thyself: music in the Carolingian Renaissance', *Committenti e produzione aristico-letteriaria nell'alto medioevo occidentale*, Settimane di studio del centro italiano di studio sullo'alto medioevo, 39 (Spoleto: Il Centro, 1992), pp. 369–481.

Mostert, M., '"…But they pray badly using corrected books": errors in the early Carolingian copies of the *Admonitio generalis*', in R. Meens et al. (eds), *Religious Franks: Religion and Power in the Frankish Kingdom: Studies in Honour of Mayke de Jong* (Manchester: Manchester University Press, 2016), pp. 112–27.

Moyse, G., 'Les origines du monachisme dans le diocèse de Besançon (Ve–Xe Siècles)', *Bibliothèque de l'Ecole des Chartes*, 131:1 (1973), 21–104.

Munier, C., 'Le premier millénaire', in F. Rapp (ed.), *Le diocèse de Strasbourg* (Paris: Beauchesne, 1982), pp. 10–32.

Munzi, L., *Multiplex Latinitas. Testi grammaticali latini dell'Alto Medioevo* (Naples: Istituto universitario orientale, 2004).

Nagy, T., 'Conversion vs. initiation: recovering the initial Christian experience in a Catholic context', *Pneuma*, 40 (2018), 192–211.

Nason, C. M., 'The mass commentary *Dominus vobiscum*: its textual transmission and the question of authorship', *Revue Bénédictine*, 114 (2004), 75–91.

Nelson, J. L., 'Alcuin's letters sent from Francia to Anglo-Saxon and Frankish women religious', in A. J. Langlands and R. Lavelle (eds), *The Land of the English Kin: Studies in Wessex and Anglo-Saxon England in Honour of Professor Barbara Yorke*, Brill's Series on the Early Middle Ages, 26 (Leiden: Brill, 2020), pp. 355–72.

Nelson, J. L., *King and Emperor: A New Life of Charlemagne* (London: Allen Lane, 2019).

Nelson, J. L., 'Revisiting the Carolingian Renaissance', in J. Kreiner and H. Reimitz (eds), *Motions of Late Antiquity: Essays on Religion, Politics, and Society in Honour of Peter Brown*, Cultural Encounters in Late Antiquity and the Middle Ages 20 (Turnhout: Brepols, 2016), pp. 331–46.

Nelson, J. L., 'The voice of Charlemagne', in R. Gameson and H. Leyser (eds), *Belief and Culture in the Middle Ages: Studies Presented to Henry Mayr-Harting* (Oxford: Oxford University Press, 2001), pp. 77–88.

Oexle, O. G., 'Conjuratio et ghilde dans l'Antiqué et dans le Haut Moyen Âge: Remarques sur la continuité des formes de la vie sociale', *Franica*, 10 (1982), 151–214.

O'Sullivan, S., *Early Medieval Glosses on Prudentius' Psychomachia: the Weitz tradition* (Leiden, Boston, MA: Brill, 2004).

O'Sullivan, S., 'Text, gloss, and tradition in the early medieval West: expanding into a world of learning', in G. Dinkova-Bruun and T. Major (eds), *Teaching and Learning in Medieval Europe* (Turnhout: Brepols, 2017), pp. 3–24.

Palmer, J., *Anglo-Saxons in a Frankish World, 690–900* (Turnhout: Brepols, 2009).

Palmer, J., 'The "vigorous rule" of Bishop Lull: between the Bonifatian mission and Carolingian church control', *Early Medieval Europe*, 13:3 (2005), 249–76.

Parsons, D., 'Some churches of the Anglo-Saxon missionaries in southern Germany: a review of the evidence', *Early Medieval Europe*, 8:1 (Mar., 1999), 31–40.

Patzelt, E., *Die Karolingische Renaissance: Beiträge zur Geschichte der Kultur des frühen Mittelalters* (Vienna: Österreichischer Schulbücherverlag, 1923, reprinted Graz: Akademische Druck- und Verlagsanstalt, 1965).

Patzold, S., and van Rhijn, C. (eds), *Men in the Middle: Local Priests in Early Medieval Europe* (Berlin: De Gruyter, 2016).

Petitmengin, P., 'D'Augustin à Prudence de Troyes: les citations augustiniennes dans un manuscrit d'auteur', in L. Holtz et al. (eds), *De Tertullien aux Mozarabes: mélanges offerts à Jacques Fontaine, à l'occasion de son 70e anniversaire, par ses élèves, amis et collègues*, Série Moyen-Âge et Temps Moderne 26 (2 vols, Turnhout: Brepols, 1992), II, pp. 229–51.

Pezé, W., 'Amalaire et la communauté Juive de Lyon. À propos de l'antijudaïsme lyonnais à l'époque carolingienne', *Francia*, 40 (2013), 1–25.

Pezé, W., 'Florus, Agobard et le concile de Quierzy de 838', in M.-C. Isaia, F. Bougard and A. Charansonnet (eds), *Lyon dans l'Europe carolingienne: autour d'Agobard (816–840)*, Collection Haut Moyen Âge 36 (Turnhout: Brepols, 2019), pp. 175–90.

Pezé, W., *Le virus de l'erreur. La controverse carolingienne sur la double predestination. Essai d'histoire sociale*, Haut Moyen Âge 26 (Turnhout: Brepols, 2017).

Phelan, O. M., *The Formation of Christian Europe: The Carolingians, Baptism and the* Imperium Christianum (Oxford: Oxford University Press, 2014).

Raaijmakers, J., *The Making of the Monastic Community of Fulda c. 744–c. 900* (Cambridge: Cambridge University Press, 2012).

Radiciotti, P., '*Romania* e *Germania* a confronto: un codice di Leidrat e le origini medievali della minuscola carolina', *Scripta*, 1 (2008), 121–44.

Rädler-Bohn, E. M. E., 'Re-dating Alcuin's *De dialectica*: or, did Alcuin teach at Lorsch?', *Anglo-Saxon England*, 45 (2016), 71–104.

Ramsey, S., 'A reevaluation of Alcuin's *Disputatio de rhetorica et de virtutibus* as consular persuasion: the context of the late eighth century revisited', *Advances in the History of Rhetoric*, 19:3 (2016), 324–43.

Réal, I., 'Nuns and monks at work: equality or distinction between the sexes? A study of Frankish monasteries from the sixth to the tenth century', in A. I. Beach and I. Cochelin (eds), *The Cambridge History of Medieval Monasticism in the Latin West* (Cambridge: Cambridge University Press, 2020), pp. 258–77.

Rembold, I., 'The "apostates" of Saint-Denis: reform, dissent, and Carolingian monasticism', in R. Kramer et al. (eds), *Monastic Communities and Canonical Clergy in the Carolingian World (780–840): Categorizing the Church* (Turnhout: Brepols, 2022), pp. 301–22.

Rennie, K. R., *Freedom and Protection: Monastic Exemption in From, c. 590–1100* (Manchester: Manchester University Press, 2018).

Renswoude, I. van, 'The art of disputation: dialogue, dialectic and debate around 800', *Early Medieval Europe*, 25:1 (2017), 38–53.

Renswoude, I. van, 'Crass insults: *ad hominem* attacks and rhetorical conventions', in U. Heil (ed.), *Das Christentum im frühen Europa* (Berlin: de Gruyter, 2019), pp. 171–94.

Renswoude, I. van, and Steinová, E., 'The annotated Gottschalk: symbolic annotation and control of heterodoxy in the Carolingian age', in P. Chambert Protat et al. (eds), *La controverse carolingienne sur la prédestination: histoire, textes, manuscrits*, Haut Moyen Âge 32 (Turnhout: Brepols, 2019), pp. 249–78.

Reuter, T., '"Kirchenreform" und "Kirchenpolitik" im Zeitalter Karl Martells: Begriffe und Wirklichkeit', in J. Jarnut et al. (eds), *Karl Martell in seiner Zeit* (Sigmaringen: Thorbecke, 1994), pp. 35–59.

Reymond, M., 'La charte de Sigismond pour Saint-Maurice d'Agaune 515', *Zeitschrift für Schhweizerische Geschichte*, 6 (1926), 1–60.

Rhijn, C. van, '"Et hoc considerat episcopus, ut ipsi presbyteri non sint idiothae": Carolingian local *correctio* and an unknown priests' exam from the early ninth century', in R. Meens et al. (eds), *Religious Franks: Religion and Power in the Frankish Kingdoms: Studies in Honour of Mayke de Jong* (Manchester: Manchester University Press, 2016), pp. 162–80.

Rhijn, C. van, 'Ut missarum preces bene intellegant. The Dominus vobiscum: a Carolingian mass commentary for the education of priests', Revue Mabillon, 31 (2020), 7–28.

Ripart, L., 'Les temps séculiers (IXe–Xe siècle)', in B. Andenmatten and L. Ripart (eds), L'abbaye de Saint-Maurice d'Agaune, Vol. 1: Historie et Archéologie (Gollion: Infolio éditions, 2015), pp. 134–49.

Ristuccia, N., Christianization and Commonwealth in Early Medieval Europe: A Ritual Interpretation (Oxford: Oxford University Press, 2018).

Rose, E., Een gekooide tijger? Over levend Latijn in late Oudheid en (vroege) Middeleeuwen (Utrecht, inaugural address, 2019).

Rose, E., 'Emendatio and effectus in Frankish prayer traditions', in R. Meens et al. (eds), Religious Franks: Religion and Power in the Frankish Kingdom: Studies in Honour of Mayke de Jong (Manchester: Manchester University Press, 2016), pp. 128–47.

Rose, E., 'Plebs sancta ideo meminere debet: the role of the people in the early medieval liturgy of mass', in Uta Heil (ed.), Das Christentum im frühen Europa: Diskurse – Tendenzen – Entscheidungen (Berlin: De Gruyter, 2018).

Rosenwein, B., Negotiating Space: Power, Restraint and Privileges of Immunity in Early Medieval Europe (Ithaca, NY: Cornell University Press, 1999).

Rosenwein, B., 'One site, many meanings: Saint-Maurice d'Agaune as a place of power in the early middle ages', in M. de Jong et al. (eds), Topographies of Power in the Early Middle Ages (Leiden: Brill, 2001), pp. 283–4.

Rosenwein, B., 'Perennial prayer at Agaune', in S. Farmer and B. Rosenwein (eds), Monks and Nuns, Saints and Outcasts: Religion in Medieval Society (Ithaca, NY: Cornell University Press, 2000), pp. 37–57.

Rouwhorst, G., 'Mystagogical terminology in liturgical contexts', in P. van Geest (ed.), Seeing Through the Eyes of Faith: New Approaches to the Mystagogy of the Church Fathers (Leuven: Peeters, 2016), pp. 180–5.

Rudolf, W., 'A tenth-century booklist in the Biblioteca Capitolare of Vercelli', Manuscripta, 62:2 (2018), 249–77.

Ruysschaert, J., Bibliothecae Apostolicae Vaticanae codices manu scripti recensiti. Codices vaticani latini. Codices 11414–11709 (Vatican City: Biblioteca Apostolica Vaticana, 1959).

Savigni, R., 'Le commentaire d'Alcuin sur l'épître aux Hébreux et le theme du sacrifice', in P. Depreux and B. Judic (eds), Alcuin de York à Tours: Écriture, pouvoir et réseaux dans l'Europe du Haut Moyen Âge (Annales de Bretagne et des Pays de l'Ouest), 111:3 (2004), 245–67.

Scheibe, F.-C., 'Alcuin und die *Admonitio generalis*', *Deutsches Archiv für Erforschung des Mittelalters*, 14 (1958), 221–9.
Schilp, T., *Norm und Wirklichkeit religiöser Frauengemeinschaften im Frühmittelalter* (Göttingen: Vandenhoeck & Ruprecht, 1998).
Schnusenberg, C., *The Mythological Traditions of Liturgical Drama: The Eucharist as Theater* (Mahwah, NJ: Paulist Press, 2010).
Schramm, P. E., 'Karl der Grosse: Denkart und Grundauffassungen – Die von ihm bewirkte "correctio" ("Renaissance")', *Historische Zeitschrift*, 198 (1964), 306–45.
Schröder, W., and Hartmann, H., 'Otfrid von Weißenburg', in R. Bergmann (ed.), *Althochdeutsche und altsächsische Literatur* (Berlin: De Gruyter, 2013), pp. 322–45.
Schulenburg, J. T., *Forgetful of Their Sex: Female Sanctity and Society, ca. 500–1100* (Chicago, IL: University of Chicago Press, 1998).
Schulenburg, J. T., 'Strict active enclosure and its effects on the female monastic experience (500–1100)', in J. A. Nichols and L. T. Shank (eds), *Medieval Religious Women I: Distant Echoes* (Kalamazoo, MI: Cistercian Publications, 1984), pp. 51–86.
Semmler, J., 'Benedictus II: una regula – una consuetudo', in W. Lourdaux and D. Verhelst (eds), *Benedictine Culture, 750–1050* (Leuven: Leuven University Press, 1983) pp. 1–49.
Semmler, J., 'Chrodegang, Bischof von Metz', in F. Knöpp (ed.), *Die Reichsabtei Lorsch: Festschrift zum Gedenken an ihre Stiftung 764* (Darmstadt: Hess. Histor. Komm., 1973), pp. 229–45.
Semmler, J., 'Iussit ... princeps renovare ... praecepta: Zur verfassungsrechtlichen Einordnung der Hochstifte und Abteien in der karolingischen Reichskirche', in J. F. Angerer and J. Lenzenweger (eds), *Consuetudines monasticae: eine Festgabe für Kassius Hallinger aus Anlass seines 70. Geburtstages*, Studia Anselmiana 85 (Rome: Pontificio Ateneos S. Anselmo, 1982), pp. 97–124.
Semmler, J., 'Mönche und Kanoniker im Frankenreich Pippins III. und Karls des Großen', in Max-Planck-Institut für Geschichte (ed.), *Untersuchungen zu Kloster und Stift* (Göttingen: Vandenhoeck & Ruprecht, 1980), pp. 78–111.
Semmler, J., 'Reichsidee und kirchliche Gesetzgebung bei Ludwig dem Frommen', *Zeitschrift für Kirchengeschichte*, 71 (1960), 37–65.
Semmler, J., 'Traditio und Königsschutz', *Zeitschrift der Savigny-Stiftung für Rechtsgeschichte: Kanonistische Abteilung*, 45 (1959), 1–33.
Smith, J., 'Did women have a transformation of the Roman world?', *Gender & History*, 12:3 (2000), 552–71.
Smith, J., 'The problem of female sanctity in Carolingian Europe, c. 780–920', *Past & Present*, 146 (1995), 3–37.

Smith, J. M. H., '"Emending evil ways and praising God's omnipotence": Einhard and the uses of Roman martyrs', in K. Mills and A. Grafton (eds), *Conversion in Late Antiquity and the Early Middle Ages: Seeing and Believing* (Rochester, NY: University of Rochester Press, 2003), pp. 189–223.

Springsfeld, K., *Alkuins Einfluß auf die Komputistik zur Zeit Karls des Großen* (Stuttgart: Franz Steiner, 2002).

Steckel, S., *Kulturen des Lehrens im Früh- und Hochmittelalter. Autorität, Wissenskonzepte und Netzwerke von Gelehrten* (Cologne: Böhlau, 2011).

Steinová, E., *Notam superponere studui. The Use of Annotation Symbols in the Early Middle Ages*, Bibliologia 52 (Turnhout: Brepols, 2019).

Stevens, W. M., *Rhetoric and Reckoning in the Ninth Century: The 'Vademecum' of Walahfrid Strabo* (Turnhout: Brepols, 2018).

Stock, B., *The Implications of Literacy: Written Language and Models of Interpretation in the Eleventh and Twelfth Centuries* (Princeton, NJ: Princeton University Press, 1983).

Stoclet, A. J, 'Fulrad de Saint-Denis (710–784), abbé et archprêtre de monastères "exempts"', *Le Moyen Âge*, 88 (1982), 210–35.

Stoffella, M., 'Staying Lombard while becoming Carolingian? Italy under King Pippin', in C. Gantner and W. Pohl (eds), *After Charlemagne: Carolingian Italy and Its Rulers* (Cambridge: Cambridge University Press, 2020), pp. 135–47.

Stone, R., 'Introduction: Hincmar's world', in R. Stone and C. West (eds), *Hincmar of Rheims: Life and Work* (Manchester: Manchester University Press, 2015), pp. 1–43.

Story, J., *Carolingian Connections: Anglo-Saxon England and Carolingian Francia, c. 750–870* (Aldershot: Ashgate, 2003).

Story, J., 'Cathwulf, kingship, and the royal abbey of Saint-Denis', *Speculum*, 74:1 (1999), 1–21.

Story, J. (ed.), *Charlemagne: Empire and Society* (Manchester: Manchester University Press, 2005).

Stricker, S., 'Die Prudentiusglossierung', in R. Bergmann and S. Stricker (eds), *Glossenstudien. Ergebnisse der neuen Forschung* (Heidelberg: Universitätsverlag Winter, 2020), pp. 313–22.

Stroumsa, G., 'From repentance to penance in early Christianity: Tertullian's *De Paenitentia* in context', in J. Assmann and G. Stroumsa (eds), *Transformations of the Inner Self in Ancient Religions* (Leiden: Brill, 1999), pp. 167–78.

Sullivan, R. E. (ed.), *'The Gentle Voices of Teachers': Aspects of Learning in the Carolingian Age* (Columbus, OH: Ohio State University Press, 1995).

Sullivan, R. E., 'Introduction: factors shaping Carolingian studies' in R. E. Sullivan (ed.), *'The Gentle Voices of Teachers': Aspects of Learning in the Carolingian Age* (Columbus, OH: Ohio State University Press, 1995), pp. 1–50.

Sullivan, R. E., 'The context of cultural activity in the Carolingian age', in R. E. Sullivan (ed.), *'The Gentle Voices of Teachers': Aspects of Learning in the Carolingian Age* (Columbus, OH: Ohio State University Press, 1995), pp. 51–105.

Tellenbach, G., *Die westliche Kirche vom 10. bis zum frühen 12. Jahrhundert* (Göttingen: Vandenhoeck & Ruprecht, 1988).

Thacker, A., 'Popes, emperors and clergy at Old St. Peter's from the 4th to the 8th Century', in R. McKitterick et al. (eds), *Old St. Peter's, Rome* (Cambridge, Cambridge University Press, 2013), pp. 137–57.

Theurillat, J., *L'abbaye de Saint-Maurice: des origines à la réforme canoniale* (Sitten: Extrait de Vallesia, 1954).

Thijssen, J. M. M. H., *Censure and Heresy at the University of Paris, 1200–1400* (Philadelphia, PA: University of Pennsylvania Press, 1998).

Thorndike, L., 'Renaissance or Prenaissance?', *Journal of the History of Ideas*, 4 (1943), 65–74.

Treadgold, W. (ed.), *Renaissances before the Renaissance. Cultural Revivals of Late Antiquity and the Middle Ages* (Stanford, CA: Stanford University Press, 1984).

Tristano, C., 'Un nuovo testimone dei Commentaria in Genesim di Rabano Mauro', *Studi Medievali*, 51 (2010), 839–91.

Troncarelli, F., 'Il diavolo nello specchio. I disegni di Alcuino nel *codex pagesianus*', *Litterae Caelestes*, 8 (2017), 75–112.

Tsuda, T., 'On the so called Capitulary of Frankfurt and communication between Charlemagne and Bavaria at the end of the eighth century', *Spicilegium*, 3 (2019), available online at www.spicilegium.net/03_tsuda.html (accessed 21 February 2022).

Ullmann, W., *The Carolingian Renaissance and the Idea of Kingship: The Birkbeck Lectures 1968–9* (London: Methuen, 1969).

Uytfanghe, M. van, 'Le latin des hagiographes mérovingiens et la protohistoire du français. État de la question', *Romanica Gandensia*, 16 (1976), 5–89.

Van Bavel, T. J., 'Correctio, corrigere', *Augustinus-Lexikon*, I, fasc. 5/6 (Bâle: Schwabe, 1992), col. 22–7.

Van Eyden, D., *Les norms de l'enseignement chrétien dans la littérature patristique des trois premiers siècles* (Paris: Gabalda & Fils, 1933).

Vanderputten, S., *Dark Age Nunneries: The Ambiguous Identity of Female Monasticism, 850–1050* (Ithaca, NY: Cornell University Press, 2018).

Vignodelli, G., 'The making of a tenth-century self-commentary: the glosses to Atto of Vercelli's *Perpendiculum* and their sources', in M. Teeuwen and I. van Renswoude (eds), *The Annotated Book in the Early Middle Ages. Practices of Reading and Writing* (Turnhout: Brepols, 2017), pp. 157–96.

Vocino, G., 'Between the palace, the school and the forum: rhetoric and court culture in late Lombard and Carolingian Italy', in C. Gantner and W. Pohl (eds), *After Charlemagne: Carolingian Italy and Its Rulers* (Cambridge: Cambridge University Press, 2020) pp. 250–74.

Vocino, G., 'Migrant masters and their books: Italian scholars and knowledge transfer in post-Carolingian Europe', in S. Greer, A. Hicklin and S. Esders (eds), *Using and Not Using the Past after the Carolingian Empire* (London: Routledge, 2019), pp. 241–61.

Vogel, C., 'La réforme liturgique sous Charlemagne', in W. Braunfels (ed.), *Karl der Grosse Lebenswerk und Nachleben II: Das geistige Leiben* (Düsseldorf: Schwann, 1966), pp. 217–32.

Von Padberg, L. E., *Bonifatius: Missionar und Reformer* (Munich: Beck, 2003).

Wallace-Hadrill, J. M., *The Frankish Church* (Oxford: Clarendon, 1983).

Wallace-Hadrill, J. M., 'History in the mind of Archbishop Hincmar', in R. H. C. Davis and J. M. Wallace-Hadrill (eds), *The Writing of History in the Middle Ages: Essays Presented to Richard W. Southern* (Oxford: Oxford University Press, 1981), pp. 43–70.

Wallach, L., 'Charlemagne's *De litteris colendis* and Alcuin: A diplomatic-historical study', *Speculum*, 26:2 (1951), 288–305.

Ward, G., 'The order of history: liturgical time and the rhythms of the past in Amalarius of Metz's *De ordine antiphonarii*', in E. Screen and C. West (eds), *Writing the Early Medieval West* (Cambridge: Cambridge University Press, 2018), pp. 98–112.

Wemple, S. F., *Women in Frankish Society: Marriage and the Cloister, 500 to 900* (Philadelphia, PA: University of Pennsylvania Press, 1981).

Wentzcke, P., *Regesten der Bischöfe von Straßburg bis zum Jahre 1202* (Innsbruck: Wagner, 1908).

Werminghoff, A., 'Die Beschlüsse des Aachener Conzils im Jahre 816', *Neues Archiv der Gesellschaft für ältere Deutsche Geschichtskunde zur Beförderung einer Gesamtausgabe der Quellenschriften deutscher Geschichten des Mittelalters*, 27:3 (1901), 605–76.

Wickham, C., *Medieval Europe* (New Haven, CT: Yale University Press, 2007).

Wickham, C., *The Inheritance of Rome: A History of Europe from 400 to 1000* (London: Penguin, 2009).

Wielfaert, J., 'Prudentius of Troyes (861) and the reception of the patristic tradition in the Carolingian era' (PhD thesis, University of Toronto, 2015).

Wilmart, A., 'Expositio missae', in F. Cabrol and H. Leclercq (eds), *Dictionnaire d'archéologie chrétienne et de liturgie*, vol. 5 (Paris: Letouzey et Ané, 1922), col. 1014–27.

Wilmart, A., 'Un lecteur ennemi d'Amalaire', *Revue Bénédictine*, 36 (1924), 317–29.

Wood, I., 'A prelude to Columbanus: the monastic achievement in the Burgundian territories', in H. B. Clarke and M. Brennan (eds), *Columbanus and Merovingian Monasticism* (Oxford: B. A. R, 1981), pp. 3–32.

Wood, I., *The Missionary Life: Saints and the Evangelisation of Europe, 400–1050* (London: Routledge, 2001).

Wood, I., 'Reform and the Merovingian church', in R. Meens et al. (eds), *Religious Franks: Religion and Power in the Frankish Kingdoms. Studies in Honour of Mayke de Jong* (Manchester: Manchester University Press, 2016), pp. 95–111.

Wormald, P., 'Bede and Benedict Biscop', in G. Bonner (ed.), *Famulus Christi: Essays in Commemoration of the Thirteenth Centenary of the Birth of the Venerable Bede* (London: SPCK, 1976), pp. 141–69.

Wright, R., 'Alcuin's *De Orthographia* and the Council of Tours (A.D. 813)', in R. Wright (ed.), *A Sociophilological Study of Late Latin* (Turnhout: Brepols, 2002) pp. 127–46.

Wright, R., 'Evidence and sources', in M. Maiden et al. (eds), *The Cambridge History of The Romance Languages* (Cambridge: Cambridge University Press, 2013), II, pp. 125–42.

Wright, R., 'How Latin came to be a foreign language for all', in R. Wright (ed.), *A Sociophilological Study of Late Latin* (Turnhout: Brepols, 2002), pp. 3–17.

Wright, R., 'Viva voce', in R. Wright (ed.), *A Sociophilological Study of Late Latin* (Turnhout: Brepols, 2002) pp. 49–68.

Zamboni, A., *Alle origini dell'italiano. Dinamiche e tipologie della transizione dal latino* (Rome: Carocci, 2000).

Zechiel-Eckes, K., 'Florus von Lyon, Amalarius von Metz und der Traktat über die Bischofswahl. Mit einer kritischen Edition des sog. "Liber de electionibus episcoporum"', *Revue Bénédictine*, 106 (1996), 109–33.

Zechiel-Eckes, K., *Florus von Lyon als Kirchenpolitiker und Publizist. Studien zur Persönlichkeit eines karolingischen 'Intellektuellen' am Beispiel der Auseinandersetzung mit Amalarius (835–838) und des Prädestinationsstreits (851–855)*, Quellen und Forschungen zum Recht im Mittelalter 8 (Stuttgart: Thorbecke, 1999).

Ziolkowski, J., 'Towards a history of medieval Latin literature', in F. A. C. Mantello and A. G. Rigg (eds), *Medieval Latin: An Introduction and Bibliographical Guide* (Washington, DC: Catholic University of America Press, 1996), pp. 505–36.

Zito, G. V., 'Toward a sociology of heresy', *Sociological Analysis*, 44:2 (1983), 123–30.

Internet sources

http://archives.esf.org/coordinating-research/research-networking-programmes/humanities-hum/completed-rnp-programmes-in-humanities/the-transformation-of-the-roman-world.html (accessed 21 February 2022).

http://blogs.bl.uk/digitisedmanuscripts/2017/03/insular-manuscripts-ad-650-850-networks-of-knowledge.html (accessed 21 February 2022).

http://cantusindex.org/id/g00596.Tp1 (accessed 21 February 2022).

http://diglib.hab.de/?db=mss&list=ms&id=50-weiss (accessed 21 February 2022).

http://diglib.hab.de/?db=mss&list=ms&id=77-weiss (accessed 21 February 2022).

http://ducange.enc.sorbonne.fr/invidia (accessed 21 February 2022).

http://liber-glossarum.huma-num.fr/index.html (accessed 21 February 2022).

https://archivesetmanuscrits.bnf.fr/ark:/12148/cc71056g (accessed 21 February 2022).

https://brill.com/view/serial/TRW (accessed 21 February 2022).

https://daten.digitale-sammlungen.de/~db/0003/bsb00036088/images/ (accessed 21 February 2022).

https://daten.digitale-sammlungen.de/~db/0004/bsb00042784/images/ (accessed 21 February 2022).

https://digital.bodleian.ox.ac.uk/inquire/p/b779d6c3-28e0-456a-b9b6-8effab18dd8b (accessed 21 February 2022).

https://digital.dombibliothek-koeln.de/hs/content/zoom/290998 (accessed 21 February 2022).

https://digital.onb.ac.at/RepViewer/viewer.faces?doc=DTL_3112149&order=1&view=SINGLE (accessed 21 February 2022).

https://digi.vatlib.it/view/bav_vat_lat_11506 (accessed 21 February 2022).

https://digi.vatlib.it/view/MSS_Pages.1 (accessed 21 February 2022).

https://digi.vatlib.it/view/MSS_Reg.lat.1209 (accessed 21 February 2022).

https://digi.vatlib.it/view/MSS_Vat.lat.3850 (accessed on 21 February 2022).

https://gallica.bnf.fr/ark:/12148/btv1b8452582n (accessed 21 February 2022).
https://gallica.bnf.fr/ark:/12148/btv1b90667074 (accessed 21 February 2022).
https://nbn-resolving.org/urn:nbn:de:urmel-f72988ea-e48d-4855-b3f4-12e08774fc810 (accessed 31 March 2022).
https://publikationen.badw.de/de/thesaurus/lemmata#58083 (accessed 21 February 2022).
www.earlymedievalmonasticism.org/manuscripts/Bern-289.html (accessed 21 February 2022).
www.e-codices.unifr.ch/en/list/one/csg/0249 (accessed 21 February 2022).
www.e-codices.unifr.ch/en/list/one/csg/0268 (accessed 21 February 2022).
www.e-codices.unifr.ch/fr/list/one/csg/0878 (accessed 21 February 2022).
www.oeaw.ac.at/en/imafo/research/historical-identity-research/projects/margins-at-the-centre (accessed 21 February 2022).

Index

Note: 'n.' after a page reference indicates the number of a footnote on that page.

Aachen 54
  802 council 51–2
  809 council 233–5, 237
  816–817 councils 43–8
  836 council 40–1, 44
Adalhard of Corbie 106
Admonitio generalis 5, 19–22, 96, 141
Agobard of Lyon 184–5, 188, 190, 192
Alcuin of York 84, 96–117, 120, 135–6, 144, 154, 169, 197, 204n.79, 205n.81, 210, 223–5, 229–33
  see also Opera didascalia
Amalarius of Metz 110, 144, 148–52, 161–5, 172–4, 179–95
  see also Liber officialis
Ambrose of Milan 146n.12, 187, 226–7, 234, 236
Ambrosiaster 216, 219, 220
Angelomus of Luxeuil 210, 215–16
Angilbert of Saint-Riquer 105, 106
Angilramn of Metz 74n.26, 79, 93–4
Aniane 55, 57–8
Argenteuil 60, 61
Arn of Salzburg 104, 107, 233–5, 237, 239–40
  see also Testimonia ex sacris volumnibus collecta
Arnulfsau-Schwarzach 76

Attigny
  762 council 74
  Totenbund of 66–8, 81
Atto of Vercelli 114–15
Augustine of Hippo 100, 164, 180–1, 187–8, 210, 211, 213, 220–1, 227, 230
Auxerre 114–16

Bede 102, 112, 154, 212n.14, 214–15
Benedictine Rule *see Regula Benedicti*
Benedict of Aniane 44, 54, 59
Bildungsreform 14–15, 17, 20
Bobbio 111–12
Bobbio, Missal of 144n.7
Boniface 14, 34, 68–9, 75, 80
Bonmoutier 60

Candidus 58, 107–8, 204–5n.80
canon missae 144, 146, 153, 160–1, 173
capitularies 19, 21, 33, 38–43, 48–53
  see also Admonitio generalis; *Epistola de litteris collendis*
Carloman 93
Cassiodorus 100, 102
Chalon-sur-Saône, 813 council 42
Charlemagne 5, 9, 14, 18–20, 22, 26, 35, 57, 66, 84–5, 88, 93,

95, 104, 106, 120, 168, 178, 210–11, 228–30, 234
Charles Martel 68, 86, 93
Charles the Bald 178, 195n.49, 203n.77
Chrodegang of Metz 65–95
  see also *Regula canonicorum*
Claudius of Turin 213–14, 217–20, 222, 223
Codex Carolinus 68–74
Compiègne, 757 council 74–5
Corbény, 771 council 86–7
Corbie 55, 103, 109
correctio
  contemporary usage 19–23, 31, 63–4, 176–7, 179, 193, 199–201, 203–5, 208–10, 226–8, 230–1, 239–40
  historiographical usage 6–9, 16–18, 160
corrigere 8, 17n.37, 18–20, 22–3, 63, 194, 226–7, 230n.78
Corvey 55

Dominus vobiscum 144–8, 152–61, 166–72
Donatus 112, 123, 132

Echternach 103, 104
Eichstätt 80–3
Eigil 58
Elipandus of Toledo 229, 232
emendare 17n.37, 18–20, 63, 194, 226–7, 229–30
emendatio 19, 63–4, 179, 193, 229–30
enclosure 46–7, 49–51, 53
Epistola de litteris collendis 19, 96, 120, 168–9
epistrophe 208–9, 213, 215, 217, 221, 222, 224, 225, 227
Ercanbert 130–4, 136–40
Erfurt 80
Eriugena *see* John Scotus
Ettenheim 77

Felix of Urgell 190n.35, 191n.38, 204n.79, 205n.81, 230–1, 233

Ferdingus 130–1, 133, 137
filioque 233–7
Florus of Lyon 152, 182n.10, 184–95, 198, 201, 202, 204n.79
Frankfurt, 794 council 41–2, 79, 97n.2, 229, 230, 232–3
Fulda 4, 50, 58, 105, 109, 119, 128
Fulrad of Saint-Denis 83–4, 86, 88, 91–4

Gorze 75–7
Gottschalk of Orbais 195, 196, 204, 205n.81
Greek 131, 134, 153–4n.33, 157, 166–7, 172, 174, 228
Gregory I, pope 79, 153–4n.33, 232, 236

Hadrian I, pope 92, 229, 231, 232
Haimo of Auxerre 221–4
Hebrew 153–4, 166, 167, 174
Heddo of Strasbourg 76–7
Helisachar 219
heresy, definitions of 178–9, 226–31
Hilduin of Saint-Denis 119
Hincmar of Rheims 195
Hirmingard 61
Hodoeporicon 81–3
Hohenburg 60
Hrabanus Maurus 105, 108, 119–20, 123–4, 136, 144, 167, 183–4, 187, 195n.49, 210, 214–15, 219n.36, 223
Huneberc of Heidenheim 81–3
  see also *Hodoeporicon*

immunity 56–60, 84, 87, 91, 93–4
Inden 54–5
Institutio canonicorum 43–4, 46, 66
Institutio sanctimonialium 43–4, 46, 63
Isidore of Seville 125, 153–6, 166–7, 197n.54, 215n.24

Jerome 79, 122–3, 154, 167, 173, 202, 217, 226

Index

John Scotus 179, 186, 194–203, 211
Judith 62

Leidrad of Lyon 104–5
Leo III, pope 162, 235
Libellus de processione spiritus sancti 235–6
Liber officialis 148–52, 161–5, 172–4, 180–5, 187–90, 192–3
Lorsch 4, 65–6n.2, 103, 108
Lothar I 56n.73, 61–2
Louis the German 118
Louis the Pious 52–4, 56–60, 62, 66, 150, 178, 180, 184, 190, 231
Lull of Mainz 67, 75–6
Lupus of Ferrières 195
Luxeuil 103
Lyon 103, 104, 108, 179, 184, 187, 192

Mainz 75–6
  813 council 40
  848 council 195
metanoia 207–9, 218, 220, 222, 224, 231
Metz 76, 79, 93–4, 182–3
Monte Cassino 81–2, 95
Moyenmoutier 50

networks 27–8, 35–6, 51–63, 102–9, 114–20, 134, 136, 177–8
Nicholas I, pope 203n.77

Opera didascalia 99–116, 135
Opus Caroli regis 212–13, 216–17, 229–30, 235–6, 239–40
Origen 167, 218–21
Otfrid of Wissembourg 118–24, 126–8, 133, 134, 136, 139

Paris, 825 synod 231
Paschasius Radbertus 167
Paulinus of Aquileia 108, 233
Pelagius 202, 217, 220
Pippin I of Aquitaine 62

Pippin II of Aquitaine 58
Pippin III 60, 68, 84, 92, 93, 150n.27
Pippin of Italy 106–7
Priscian 112, 119–26, 132, 134, 136
Prudentius of Troyes 195–203, 204n.79

Quadam nocte 127–9
Quierzy
  838 council 149, 161, 190–2, 194
  849 council 195

Ratramnus of Corbie 195n.49, 203n.77, 238–9
reform 6–9, 12–16, 36, 63–4, 96–7, 109, 111–13, 134–6, 141–2, 148–9, 151, 160, 174, 207, 239
reformare 12–13, 17n.37, 18–20
reformatio 12–13, 31, 63–4, 208–25, 236, 239–40
Regula Benedicti 33–5, 38, 42–8, 51–2, 57–60, 72, 81–2, 90
Regula canonicorum 65–7, 71–9
Reichenau 55
Remigius of Auxerre 110, 114
Remi of Strasbourg 77–9, 94
Remiremont 54
renaissance 6–12, 23–4
renovare 18, 20
renovatio 31, 209–25, 229, 240
restaurare 17n.37, 215
restituere 18
revocare 20
Rheims 201
  813 council 19–20
Rome 107, 142, 162, 182–3, 232–3
  769 council 86

Saint-Amand 103
Saint-Denis 50, 83–5, 91–4, 119
Sainte-Croixe 62
St. Gall 4, 55, 103, 169–72
Saint-Julien, Auxerre 60
St. Leodegar, Schönenwerd 77–8

Saint-Martin, Tours 84, 102–3, 105
Saint-Maurice d'Agaune 83–91
Salonnes 93–4
Salzburg 103, 107, 109
San Salvatore, Brescia 54, 60–1
Santa Maria Theodata, Pavia 60–1
Sedulius Scottus 221n.42, 223
Smaragdus 138n.116, 236
Solignac 58
Stephen II, pope 74, 84, 88
Strasbourg 76–9

Testimonia ex sacris volumnibus collecta 233–5
Theodulf of Orléans 4, 17, 108, 197, 212–13, 216–17, 228–30, 231n.86, 235–7, 239–40
see also *Admonitio generalis*; *Libellus de processione spiritus sancti*; *Opus Caroli regis*
Thionville, 835 council 184, 185

Valence, 853 council 198, 202–3
Ver, 755 council 70–2
Vercelli 113–15
Verona 103, 106–9, 112n.48, 135
Vincent of Lerins 227–8

Walahfrid Strabo 105, 132n.108, 149
Wenilo of Sens 196
Wicbod 210–15
Wilicar of Sens 83–8
Willibald of Eichstätt 80–3
Wissembourg 109, 116–40
Wizo *see* Candidus

Zacharias, pope 68–76, 80, 84, 91, 94

EU authorised representative for GPSR:
Easy Access System Europe, Mustamäe tee 50,
10621 Tallinn, Estonia
gpsr.requests@easproject.com